Women, Power and Policy

Pergamon Titles of Related Interest

Kramarae THE VOICES AND WORDS OF WOMEN AND MEN
Spender MEN'S STUDIES MODIFIED: The Impact of Feminism
on the Academic Disciplines
Stewart THE WOMEN'S MOVEMENT IN COMMUNITY POLITICS
IN THE U.S.: The Role of Local Commissions on the Status
of Women

Related Journals*

HISTORY OF EUROPEAN IDEAS
INTERNATIONAL JOURNAL OF INTERCULTURAL RELATIONS
TECHNOLOGY IN SOCIETY
WOMEN'S STUDIES INTERNATIONAL FORUM
WORLD DEVELOPMENT

*Free specimen copies available upon request.

Women, Power and Policy

Edited by
Ellen Boneparth

WITHDRAWN

PERGAMON PRESS
New York   Oxford   Toronto   Sydney   Paris   Frankfurt

Burg.
HQ
1426
.W645
1982
copy 1

Pergamon Press Offices:

U.S.A.   Pergamon Press Inc., Maxwell House. Fairview Park.
                    Elmsford, New York 10523. U.S.A.

U.K.   Pergamon Press Ltd., Headington Hill Hall.
                    Oxford OX3 0BW. England

CANADA   Pergamon Press Canada Ltd., Suite 104, 150 Consumers Road.
                    Willowdale, Ontario M2J 1P9. Canada

AUSTRALIA   Pergamon Press (Aust.) Pty. Ltd., P.O. Box 544.
                    Potts Point, NSW 2011. Australia

FRANCE   Pergamon Press SARL. 24 rue des Ecoles.
                    75240 Paris. Cedex 05. France

FEDERAL REPUBLIC   Pergamon Press GmbH. Hammerweg 6
OF GERMANY   6242 Kronberg/Taunus. Federal Republic of Germany

Copyright © 1982 Pergamon Press Inc.

Library of Congress Cataloging in Publication Data
Main entry under title:

Women, power, and policy

    Includes bibliographical references and
index.
    1. Feminism--United States--Political
aspects--Address, essays, lectures.
I. Boneparth, Ellen, 1945-
HQ1426.W645   1982   305.4′2′0973   81-13825
ISBN 0-08-028048-X   AACR2
ISBN 0-08-028047-1 (pbk.)

*All Rights reserved. No part of this publication may be reproduced,
stored in a retrieval system or transmitted in any form or by any means:
electronic, electrostatic, magnetic tape, mechanical, photocopying,
recording or otherwise, without permission in writing from the
publishers.*

Printed in the United States of America

cym 84-09-28   RSH 400749

To Josephine

Contents

Foreword

Ever since the Nineteenth Amendment was adopted in 1920, giving women the right to vote, there has been an expectation—a hope to some and a foreboding to others—that women would vote differently than men. That they would vote more Democratic or more Republican, vote for women candidates, even a women's party.

There were inklings at first that women might indeed tend to vote for women. In Michigan's first state election the League of Women Voters turned out 70 percent of eligible female voters and elected women to many posts. In Sherman, Michigan, after the men refused to nominate any women, the women ran their own slate and won. When Al Smith ran for governor of New York in 1920, he asked the Democrats to nominate a female running-mate. Both the Democratic and Republican parties installed women as co-chairs and adopted the League of Women Voters planks in their 1920 platforms.

Fresh from their suffrage victory, 10 organizations representing 10 million women formed the Women's Joint Congressional Committee, which was soon to become the most powerful lobby in Washington. By 1926, 22 organizations belonged.

As its first major project, the women's lobby advocated an infancy and maternal health care bill previously introduced in Congress by the first woman member, Jeanette Rankin (D-Montana). They pointed out that more mothers died during World War I in childbirth than doughboys died in the war, and that Congress spent more money to fight hog cholera and the boll weevil than it did on women's health problems. The 1920s version of the new right, which included the American Medical Association and the National Association Opposed to Women Suffrage, trotted out the familiar argument: the proposal was a socialist plot that would lead to federal control over the family. But the WJCC lobbied hard, and even President Harding, fearing retaliation at the polls, endorsed the bill. It was signed into law in 1921 as the Sheppard-Towner Act.

Next, the WJCC took on yet another Rankin bill, which granted citizenship rights to women independent of their husbands. Under laws in effect at that time, if an American woman married an alien in the U.S., she lost her citizenship. The bill finally passed in 1922 as the Cable Act.

A constitutional amendment to ban child labor was the next women's crusade. The horrors of child labor in the field, factory, and mill, were well chronicled. The amendment sprinted through the House and Senate amidst great rejoicing. This only served to catalyze the opposition. A great hoot and cry went up among the reactionaries that the amendment would suffer parents to bureaucratic inquisitions and deprive children of the joys of work at home— even washing dishes after dinner would be outlawed. The Massachusetts legislature rejected the child labor amendment, saying it was a Bolshevik plot financed with Russian gold.

A torrent of slander drenched the country. By January 1925, 13 states had rejected the amendment and it was dead. (It was not until 1941 that the Supreme Court reversed a long string of cases and held that Congress could restrict child labor.) The surprising, swift rejection of the amendment was in part a reaction against the reform movement's success with prohibition and women's suffrage. The "Red Scare" of the 1920s fanned the reactionary flames.

The WJCC never again mounted a serious lobby; male legislators ceased to fear female retribution at the polls, and by 1930 most observers believed that female suffrage had had no impact on voting patterns, except to increase the total number of voters.

The women's movement did not get a second wind until the 1960s, when it became part of a national political reform effervescence that included the civil rights, environmental, and anti-war movements. *Women, Power and Policy* takes a look at how this latter day women's movement, which is certainly here to stay, has affected public policy. The study is comprehensive and long overdue. It should find a prominent place on the shelves of America's policy makers.

The Honorable Patricia Schroeder
House of Representatives
Washington, DC

Preface

This book is written from a feminist perspective. By this, I do not simply mean that the contributors are feminists, although they are. Nor do I mean to suggest that there is a single feminist perspective on any or all of the issues raised here. Like any political grouping, feminists have their share of differences and debates over policy goals, priorities for different policies, and the appropriate strategies for achieving them. The feminist perspective that runs through the chapters in this volume argues that changes in the status of women are necessary and can be effected through public policy.

Reference is made throughout this volume to "women's issues." This term is used as short-hand to identify issues which explicitly concern the status of women in American society, issues which, in most cases, have been raised by the contemporary women's movement. Three important points must be made, however, with respect to the use of this term. First, the issues considered in this volume do not represent an exclusive set of women's concerns. Many women's issues, both longstanding and newly emerging, are not treated here either because of limitations of space or because they have been aired fully elsewhere.

Second, the contemporary women's movement recognizes that women have a stake in all political issues confronting American society. As Congresswoman Barbara Mikulski so eloquently stated in a speech on the steps of the Capitol on Women's Rights Day, 1981:

> Every issue is a women's issue. We have too long been identified with single issues.
> A budget that gets balanced by cutting food stamps is a budget balanced on the
> backs of women. As long as military aid is sent to El Salvador and used to kill and
> mutilate women, foreign aid is a women's issue.[1]

While focusing on issues which explicitly affect the status of women, this volume also emphasizes the necessity for women to be able to influence policy decisions on everything from the nuclear family to the nuclear age.

Last, women's issues are to be understood as issues which have significant consequences for the lives of men as well as women. In fact, it is difficult to conceive of any policies which carry direct benefits for women which do not also carry indirect benefits for men. Moreover, it is an obvious political reality that policy change cannot occur without the involvement and support of men either at the grass roots or in policy-making positions. This volume is therefore intended for an audience of men as well as women. Its goal is to engender discussion in women's groups, men's groups, living rooms, classrooms, and hearing rooms. If discussion leads to action, individual or collective, its goal will have been realized.

It goes without saying that this volume represents a collaborative effort. The fine work of the contributors, the time and insights provided by people I have interviewed, the cooperation of *The Western Political Quarterly* and *The Journal of Politics,* and the editorial and secretarial support I have received have all made this undertaking professionally rewarding. The encouragement of friends and family have made it personally rewarding as well.

Note

1. Quotation from *Spokeswoman 11,* 3 (March, 1981): inside cover.

Part I
Introduction

Chapter 1
A Framework for Policy Analysis
Ellen Boneparth

The greatest challenge facing the contemporary women's movement is the translation of its goals and objectives into public policy. The rebirth of feminism in the United States in the mid-1960s was accompanied by a drive to extend equal opportunity in employment to women. As the women's movement expanded in the late 1960s, however, its main thrust became raising women's consciousness of the impact of sexism on *all* aspects of their individual lives and collective roles in society.

Consciousness raising is a necessary stage in the evolution of any social movement. Through consciousness raising individuals begin to see their personal concerns as group concerns and to identify as members of a group. Consciousness raising has enabled women in the United States to see that male domination takes many forms—discrimination, sex-role stereotyping, sexual abuse, violence—and that the struggle to end male domination is not only an individual challenge but also, necessarily, a group struggle.

By the beginning of the 1970s, feminists came to realize that many of their goals could best be achieved by improving the status of women through public policy. While governmental programs do not provide the solutions to all problems, they do carry with them authority and resources to change behavior, if not attitudes. Appreciating the power of government to effect social change, the women's movement in the past decade has focused more and more of its attention on the policy-making process.

The women's movement has met with varying degrees of success in the public arena. Significant new legislation has been passed, only to be weakened by ineffectual enforcement or unfavorable administrative regulations. Victories in the courts have been won, only to be superseded by judicial or legislative actions which reversed initial decisions. New policy proposals have received verbal endorsements only to founder at the first attempts to develop concrete programs. The new conservatism of the 1980s promises to make women's struggles for policy changes more difficult than ever.

If women are to become more effective in influencing public policy, they must understand the obstacles they face and develop strategies to overcome them. Such an understanding can come in part from an analysis of past attempts to influence the policy-making process. Case studies of public policy constitute an important element of such an analysis, as they allow an in-depth examination of a particular issue. The case studies in this volume shed light on women's issues which have already become public policy, as well as issues which have yet to appear on the policy agenda.

Another important element of the analysis is a framework for understanding why some efforts at influencing policy are more successful than others. Policy analysis involves examining a wide range of variables including environmental, systemic, and political variables, and policy characteristics, in order to assess the prospects for policy change. In this introductory chapter, we will chart the course of various women's policies which have appeared on the national agenda over the last decade in order to lay out a framework for analysis in the years to come.

ENVIRONMENTAL VARIABLES

Social Climate

In the broadest sense, the social climate affects prospects for policy change. No one can deny that the years of the 1960s and early 1970s brought a new climate to the American scene, a climate characterized by a concern for the oppressed, changing lifestyles, new political activism, and demands for governmental responses to social problems.

The contemporary women's movement was born in this climate of social change, benefiting in particular from the civil rights movement of the 1960s. Women achieved notable policy successes in the very areas where the civil rights movement had made its greatest strides—employment, education, legal equality. The passage of the Equal Pay Act of 1963, Title VII of the 1964 Civil Rights Act, the signing of Executive Order 11375 extending affirmative action to women in 1967, the passage of Title IX of the Education Amendments in 1972 and the passage by Congress of the Equal Rights Amendment in 1972 may, in part, be attributed to a social climate in which women became recognized as an oppressed group whose needs were a legitimate concern of the policy-making process.[1] The most striking change of the period, however, did not involve legal or economic issues, but, rather, a uniquely women's issue—reproductive rights.

The reform of abortion laws by numerous states in the late 1960s, culminating with the landmark Supreme Court decision of *Roe* v. *Wade* in 1973, which declared abortion a constitutional right, held out the hope that women could press their policy demands beyond issues of economic and legal equality to issues of social justice.

The social climate has changed dramatically since the early 1970s. The disruptions of war, political corruption, domestic violence, and a faltering economy have all contributed to an increasing distrust of social change which has eroded widespread support for governmental solutions to social problems. While the women's movement has grown in this period, pressing a whole new set of policy demands, the popular mood has been to turn away from social movements and revert to politics as usual.

Economic Climate

The economic climate also helps to set the stage for policy making. In an expanding economy, new programs, especially programs involving substantial government expense, get a more favorable reception than in an economy beset by recession and/or inflation. Just as the general social climate of the 1960s supported new policy initiatives, so did the economic climate, with its generally healthy economic indicators. While fiscal conservatives always oppose government spending on social programs, economic arguments were not a powerful deterrent in the late 1960s and early 1970s to the passage of new programs. Even so, the policy achievements of the women's movement in this period were primarily in the realm of antidiscrimination policies which are far less costly than programs providing economic benefits.

By the end of the 1970s, the economic situation in the United States had worsened to the point that the economy was suffering the effects of "stagflation," simultaneous inflation and recession. The prevailing mood of both the executive and the Congress was one of economic conservatism. Whereas economic concerns were a significant but not determining source of opposition to women's policy demands in the early 1970s, by the end of the decade economic arguments against new programs became paramount for many policy makers.

A good example is the issue of child care. Although government-subsidized day care was recognized as expensive in the early 1970s, liberals and moderates in Congress weighed the social advantage of child-care programs against the costs and passed a substantial child-care package in 1971, only to have it vetoed by President Nixon. In contrast, by the end of the 1970s, child-care programs failed even to move out of congressional committees as supporters concluded that it would be impossible to obtain a national child-care program in a climate of extreme fiscal restraint.

Political Climate

The political climate is perhaps the hardest to assess as a variable. With respect to policy change, it identifies the extent to which a social movement's goals are recognized as legitimate and deserving of a political response. The challenge for a social movement in this regard is to raise issues which may never have been part of the national political agenda and to establish them as subjects for serious political debate.

In contrast to a worsening social and economic climate in the 1970s, the political climate may in some ways have improved for the women's movement. In the years since its rebirth, the feminist movement evolved from a movement primarily concerned with equal rights to a movement whose policy demands ranged over a wide set of issues including economics, reproduction, family relations, and sexuality. The women's movement took "private" concerns and turned them into public issues—a process called "politicizing the personal."[2] By the end of the 1970s, issues previously relegated to the private sphere, such as sex stereotyping, pregnancy, child care, displaced homemakers, rape, pornography, and domestic violence, were not only matters of public discussion but also matters meriting at least some governmental attention.

A second important aspect of the political climate of the 1970s was the rise of organized opposition to the women's movement. In the 1960s, one of the movement's greatest problems involved being taken seriously. More detrimental in some ways than political opposition was the ridicule heaped on the movement by opinion leaders in government, in the arts, in universities, and most significantly, in the media. Women's issues were noted mostly for their entertainment value and, when not ignored entirely, were trivialized.

One way of demonstrating that the women's movement has reached political maturity is to measure the strength of its opposition. Initially, opposition took the form of personal diatribes by men and women as well as the promotion of femininity as the alternative to feminism; today, opposition to the movement is firmly established in a wide variety of organizations with considerable financial backing and grass-roots support. While the rallying call of these groups vary (antiabortion, anti-ERA, morality, and preservation of the family), they have a common rationale, namely, to keep women in their traditional roles of wife, mother, and homemaker. The support for these organizations comes from religious groups such as the Catholic, Mormon, and fundamentalist Christian churches, from the political organizations of the far right, and from segments economic losses, of social change.

While the women's movement may once have enjoyed the luxury of diffuse opposition, today it faces highly organized opposition which has the resources to challenge any and all efforts to alter the status of women. The political climate of the 1980s will be characterized not only by the recognition that the women's movement has serious public policy claims which it intends to pursue but also by the reality that these claims are highly antagonistic to the goals of other organized groups and will be disputed in every conceivable political arena.

SYSTEMIC VARIABLES

Decentralized Government

One of the major obstacles to rapid social change is a decentralized political system. Decentralized policy making has brought the women's movement great despair in the last decade, as policy successes in one governmental arena foundered or collapsed in others.

The most glaring examples of this phenomenon are the issues of the ERA and abortion. The passage in 1972 of the ERA, 50 years after its first introduction, by two-thirds majorities of Congress, seemed to herald a new era of legal equality for women. The legislative proponents of the ERA were so confident of its ratification by the states that they wrote a ratification deadline into the amendment's language. Yet the seven-year deadline came and passed with ratification efforts stalled at 35 states, three states short of the three-fourths constitutional requirement. Even with an extended deadline, which involved a lengthy congressional battle in 1979, ratification by the new deadline, June 30, 1982, is questionable.

The failure to ratify the ERA illustrates the rise of organized opposition to the women's movement. It is crucial to understand, however, that this opposition is regionally based. Of the 15 states which have failed to ratify the ERA, all but two are in or border on the south or southwest. A decentralized political system has thus far enabled a minority, intense though it may be, to block the will of the popular majority.

The decentralized process of constitutional amendment necessarily slows the pace of political change and has caused great frustration for the women's movement in the battle for the ERA. Ironically, on another key women's issue, abortion, the complexities of the constitutional amending process have thus far prevented the passage of a proposed constitutional amendment to ban abortion. While there is support for such an amendment, as evidenced by the 19 states where there have been calls for a constitutional convention on abortion, pro-choice forces in Congress were able to forestall any such move in the 1970s. With a more conservative Congress in the 1980s, a Human Life Bill or Amendment might pass.

Yet, proponents of abortion have encountered the frustrations of divided government in other arenas. While the Supreme Court gave abortion proponents a great victory in 1973 in its *Roe* v. *Wade* decision, which held that abortion in the first six months of pregnancy was protected by the right of privacy, opponents of abortion have used the legislative process to undermine this right. When in 1976 Congress passed the Hyde Amendment, eliminating federal funding under Medicaid for abortion except in very limited circumstances, it began the process of denying access to abortion for most low-income women. The assault on abortion did not stop with the Hyde Amendment; abortion opponents in Congress have obstructed the policy-making process with amendments to numerous appropriation bills to restrict abortions in the military, in the District of Columbia, and under health insurance plans for federal employees. A constitutional challenge to the Hyde Amendment based on the equal protection clause failed in 1980 when the Supreme Court upheld, 5–4, in *McRae* v. *Harris,* the power of Congress to deny Medicaid funding for abortions. While a very few states have continued to pay for abortions for low-income women with state funds, the *McRae* decision leaves the states free to impose new restrictions on abortion funding. Like the ERA, the abortion issue has foundered on the rocks of a system of divided government in which the minority may prevail when it wields control over a crucial part of the policy-making process.

Incremental Policy Making

A second systemic variable, related to the first, which inhibits rapid social change is a policy-making process characterized by incrementalism. In a system of divided government it is easier to obtain agreement to move in new policy directions in increments than to fashion major policy out of whole cloth. Thus, initiatives which expand the coverage of existing policies, which take the form of amendments to existing legislation, or which are introduced as "pilot" programs, are more likely to succeed than initiatives which are presented as highly visible, large-scale new programs, moving in directions different from existing policy.

The major governmental responses to the demands of the women's movement over the past 20 years have occurred through incremental policy making. Progress in equal employment opportunity has been made by extending to women the same protections afforded racial minorities. In fact, antidiscrimination policy generally, while once representing a major new policy thrust, today fits with accepted notions, at least for liberals and moderates, of the proper exercise of governmental power. Thus, the policies of the 1960s and 1970s prohibiting discrimination based on sex in employment, education, and credit may be seen as products of incremental policy making.

In contrast, women have been less successful in achieving policy goals in areas which have no history of governmental involvement. For example, the new issues of aid to displaced homemakers, violence against women, and rape prevention have received government support in terms of small pilot programs but have not yet been recognized as widespread social needs deserving of major funding. Even child care, which is a policy demand with a long history, has never been recognized as a fundamental right for working women, but rather has been provided as a temporary solution to other problems such as labor shortages or welfare. Therefore, the style of incremental policy making, while perhaps assisting social change in established policy areas, inhibits the process of change when the demand is for policy in new realms.

POLITICAL VARIABLES

Lobbying

While environmental and systemic variables set the broader stage for policy making, political variables determine the immediate prospects for effective policy change. In the past 15 years, the women's movement has evolved from a diffuse social movement to an increasingly organized political interest. New women's groups such as the National Organization for Women (NOW), the National Women's Political Caucus (NWPC), and the Women's Equity Action League (WEAL) have established themselves as general lobbying organizations. Many other lobbies have been established in specialized issue areas such as employment, health, education, reproductive rights, and violence against women.

The success of a lobbying organization depends on many factors. Financial resources are critical to support the functions of information gathering, communicating with group members and the general public, making political contacts, and establishing a presence in the many institutional arenas where policy making occurs. All these functions require personnel who have substantive expertise and who are highly knowledgeable about the intricacies of the policy-making process. While the women's movement has had since its inception some leaders with extensive political experience, lobbying efforts have rarely kept pace with the growth of new issues, in part because of insufficient financial resources and in part because of a dearth of experienced personnel.

Today, the list of organized interest groups in Washington dealing with women's concerns is impressive. Moreover, women's organizations are learning the techniques of fund raising, utilizing direct mail solicitations, tax-exempt legal and defense funds, and appeals to large financial interests such as corporations and foundations which have not traditionally supported women's programs. While scarce resources will remain a problem for women, the principal concern for women's lobbies today is less one of organizational survival and more one of channeling resources into areas where their efforts will yield the most tangible results.

Political Coalitions

Rarely is an organized interest so influential that it can achieve its policy goals without the help of allies. In the case of the women's movement, political allies have been difficult to find either because likely allies such as other oppressed groups are competing for their own share of government benefits or because potential allies such as labor unions, liberal religious groups, and civil rights groups, while professing a progressive ideology, are also defending themselves against challenges by women for more power.

A good example of the competition between likely allies is the struggle between women and minorities in the field of equal employment opportunity. Women's groups argue that enforcers of equal opportunity legislation put racial minorities before women; blacks and hispanics argue that affirmative action goals are met by the hiring of white women rather than minority women and men. While there is a certain amount of justification for both these positions, the tensions between women and minorities have made them antagonists in many situations where they could be allies.

The child-care issue illustrates the difficulties of forming alliances with organizations which may be on the liberal end of the political spectrum but which espouse traditional responses to social problems. When child care was a live issue in the early 1970s, both women's groups and labor unions strongly agreed that child-care centers were urgently needed by working women. The labor movement, however, wanted government-funded child-care centers incorporated into the public school system with professional personnel (organized by existing teacher's unions) responsible for their administration. Women's groups, for the most part, wanted child-care centers controlled by the local community with parents setting policy for the centers and playing a major administrative role. Disagreements between women's groups and labor unions over ways to organize child-care centers have remained a major stumbling block in the formation of an effective coalition behind child care.

In one area, coalition building has been quite successful. New women's movement groups have found allies among the older, more traditional women's organizations such as Business and Professional Women, the Association of American University Women, the League of Women Voters, the National Council of Negro Women, and various other women's social service organizations. While the older and newer women's groups may have differing positions on some of the more controversial issues such as abortion, they have formed mutually beneficial coalitions on the ERA and various antidiscrimination policies. The older women's organizations have provided the newer groups tangible assistance in terms of political contacts and organizational support and, perhaps even more important, have lent them an aura of legitimacy in their search for official recognition. The newer groups have given the older groups new issues and bases for expanding their membership.

Leadership

While public awareness of women's issues has increased dramatically over the last 15 years, the same awareness is not found among most national policy makers who, generally speaking, place a low priority on women's issues when compared to issues such as the economy, foreign policy, and defense. Leadership on women's issues has rested with a small handful of women and men in Congress and in the executive.

Leadership in Congress has suffered from a dearth of women members and from the fact that the few women members serving are often divided by political ideology, partisan allegiances, and regional loyalties as well as their own attitudes regarding women's concerns. The Congresswomen's Caucus has been unable to achieve consensus on many issues and, until recently, has served mostly as a forum for discussion. As a result, leadership has become the responsibility of several individual congresswomen who are too few to carry the burden in all relevant areas of policy. Several male members of Congress have also devoted themselves to leadership on women's issues such as the ERA and abortion but, even with male allies, the numbers of congresspersons concentrating on women as a primary concern is very small. Moreover, leadership on women's issues, by women or men, has made officeholders vulnerable to campaigns by organizations of the far right seeking their political demise, as was seen in the defeat of several liberal senior senators in the 1980 election.

Leadership on women's issues has, if anything, been even less visible in the executive than in Congress. While more women were appointed to influential policy-making positions in the Carter administration than in earlier administrations, most served in positions which gave them little opportunity to voice their concerns over women's issues. Female Carter administration officials did speak out as a group against the administration's stand opposing abortion as a possible means of family planning. Challenging administration policy proved dangerous, however, as President Carter's first presidential liaison for women's groups, Midge Costanza, discovered when she was dismissed for her open criticism of the president's leadership on women's issues. Costanza's successor, Sarah Weddington, while serving as an advocate for women within the administration, maintained a very low profile in her public role. Both of Carter's female cabinet appointees, Patricia Harris of HUD and Juanita Kreps of the Commerce Department, had the political support of women's groups, but neither made women a particular constituency in their departments. The conspicuous absence of women in senior administrative positions in the Reagan administration makes any executive leadership on women's issues highly unlikely.

The failure of women in the executive to provide leadership on women's issues is based on two related conditions. First, most women administrators do not have an institutional mandate to address women's issues. Those few women who do work on women's issues have been political appointees confined to working within the administration's policy preferences. Thus, advocates for women in the executive must choose between quietly boring from within with the risk of losing credibility with groups outside, or openly challenging presidential policy making with the risk of losing their jobs.

The only individuals who have fully benefited from their association with women's issues have been members of Congress leading the opposition. Beginning with opposition to the ERA and moving to the issues of abortion and the family, these politicians, secure in the support of their conservative constituencies, have gained national recognition and financial backing for their opposition campaigns. Moreover, given the fragmented nature of the political system, they have established firm footholds in Congress where, particularly on abortion, they have used every conceivable maneuver to obstruct the legislative process. Moreover, while they were once a small minority in Congress, the success of conservative congressional candidates in the late 1970s has made these opposition leaders spokespersons for an increasingly large group of legislators.

Whatever women's groups have gained in terms of lobbying expertise and proficiency in coalition building in the 1970s must be balanced against the failure to develop strong support among political leaders. The changing complexion of Congress to a more conservative cast, the low priority given to women's issues on the executive agenda, and the institutional weakness of women policy makers in either branch of government have made it difficult to maintain or build momentum on a wide range of women's issues. Recently, the constant pressure of opposition leaders seeking to chip away at established policies has forced leaders on women's issues to devote so much energy to defending what exists that they have little reserve energy for new initiatives.

POLICY CHARACTERISTICS

Visibility, Degree of Controversy, Scope

The characteristics of a particular policy also affect its chances for success. In many ways women's policies are no different from policies in other issue areas. If a policy has low visibility, fits with prevailing values, and involves narrow concerns, its chances for success are greater than if it is highly visible, involves controversy, and is wide in scope.

Two issues from the 1980 congressional session illustrate these points clearly. One of the few legislative successes women's groups had in 1980 was the passage of the Foreign Service Act, which entitled divorced wives of foreign service officers a share of their former husband's benefits. Passage of this legislation can in large part be attributed to the policy's characteristics. The issue had little visibility at the grass roots; women's groups rarely mentioned the issue in their communications and the media never gave any attention to it until final congressional passage. The low visibility of the issue is explained in part by its noncontroversial nature. Most people would agree that women who devote a portion of their lives to husbands and families, who live overseas and give up their own opportunities for independent careers, deserve upon divorce to share in benefits earned during the marriage. The low visibility of the issue was also attributable to its narrow scope: the new policy affects relatively few families although it has implications for much larger groups, namely, wives of men in the military and civil services.

Policy on domestic violence provides a clear contrast. While a major domestic violence bill passed both houses of Congress in 1980, the legislation died as the session moved toward adjournment when liberals in the Senate withdrew the conference committee report under the threat of a filibuster from conservatives. Domestic violence, once considered a private matter, became a highly visible public policy issue in the late 1970s as women's groups and the media focused attention on the problems of wife and child abuse. The issue has provoked considerable controversy in recent years. Conservatives have portrayed the policy as further intervention by the federal government into family life and in 1980 rallied their followers to oppose the bill. The scope of the bill was fairly wide in that it authorized several different programmatic approaches to domestic violence and significant amounts of funding for pilot programs. Because lobbying on the Foreign Service Act and the domestic violence bill was organized and effective in both cases, the success of the former and the defeat of the latter can best be explained by the differing characteristics of the two policies.

Policy Types: Distributive, Regulatory, Redistributive

Another way of characterizing policy is to examine the policy's effect on society. Using such an approach, Theodore Lowi has differentiated three types of domestic policy: distributive, regulatory, and redistributive.[3] Distributive policies involve distributing benefits to individuals or groups, essentially in the form of a governmental subsidy. Regulatory policies involve governmental regulation of practices by individuals or groups, most frequently in the private sector. Redistributive policies involve the redistribution of benefits, tangible or intangible, from one broad group to another. Lowi argues that the amount of conflict generated by a policy can be predicted by its type, with distributive policies generating relatively little conflict, regulatory policies generating a moderate amount of conflict, and redistributive policies generating greater amounts of conflict.

Lowi's typology has been widely utilized by social scientists but has also come under some criticism. First, the distinctions among the three types of policy are not always clear: for example, a policy may be regulatory in the short run but have redistributive implications in the long run. Second, while policy makers may view policies as having one kind of impact, the affected groups may perceive the policy differently. With these notes of caution, it is useful to examine women's policies within the Lowi classification scheme.

Considering the array of women's policies proposed in the 1970s, it is interesting that most policies fall into either the regulatory or redistributive categories. The few policies which were distributive in nature, such as providing individual tax credits for child care or subsidies to businesses and labor unions for training programs for nontraditional jobs, did, in fact, generate relatively little controversy. Furthermore, while those policies which were primarily regulatory, such an antidiscrimination policies in the areas of credit or pregnancy benefits, generated some debate, they were also achieved with only moderate levels of conflict. Thus, the typology is useful in explaining why these particular women's policies met with little resistance in the policy-making process.

The typology is less useful, however, in examining other women's policies. On the face of it, affirmative action, the ERA, and Title IX are also regulatory policies in the sense that they regulate behavior by prohibiting discrimination based on sex in law, employment, and education. These policies, however, have generated high levels of conflict because they have been perceived both by policy makers and the general public as redistributive in nature, as taking away benefits (jobs, rights, athletic appropriations) from men and conferring them on women. Indeed, these policies may be redistributive in the long run. While affirmative action regulations do not remove men from eligibility for jobs, if properly enforced, they should open up new employment opportunities for women. The ERA, if ratified, would in all likelihood put women *who qualified* in combat positions alongside men. Certainly, nondiscrimination in athletic appropriations is perceived as taking support "rightfully" belonging to male athletes and reallocating it to women.

Differing policy perceptions and differing short-term and long-term policy implications explain why policy types are not always the most reliable means to predict outcomes in the policy-making process. In the case of women's policies, other distinctions may be necessary to understand why policy proposals meet more resistance in some areas than in others. Recent studies of public policy affecting women have begun to illuminate some of the underlying factors at work.[4]

Role Equity Versus Role Change

A role is a pattern of behavior individuals adopt in response to social expectations. Roles are based on many different characteristics—age, occupation, marital status—and vary considerably from one time period to another and from one culture to another. Sex roles are behavioral patterns based on gender; sex roles prescribe appropriate behavior for males and females in social, economic, and political contexts. Often, sex roles are institutionalized in society by rules and practices established through public policy.

The women's movement has been attempting to redefine sex roles through changes in public policy. In some cases, the changes sought have had the goal of equalizing opportunity for men and women in the *same* roles, or *role equity*. In other cases, the changes sought have had the goal of opening up *new* roles for both sexes and, specifically, of assisting women to move into new roles, or *role change*.

As with other typologies, this distinction is not clear-cut in all cases. Some policies may have role equity as their short-term goal but may result in role change over the long term. For example, policy barring sex discrimination in credit may equalize women's roles as consumers in the short run, while in the long run it may result in some women becoming the principal economic decision makers in the family.[5] Likewise, certain policies may be perceived as effecting role equity by some and role change by others. To illustrate, some individuals may perceive child care as an equity issue, equalizing the employment options of mothers and fathers, while others may perceive child care as an issue of role change, allowing women to move from roles of full-time mothers to full-time workers.

What is valuable about the role equity/role change distinction is that it explains the relatively easy acceptance of some women's policies and the massive resistance to others. Role equity fits with the American political tradition of equality; although equity issues engender some opposition in the policy-making process, they coincide with basic economic, social, and political values. Equity issues address the distribution of power in society but do not disturb basic sex-role definitions. In contrast, role change challenges traditional sex-role ideology. Role change does more than address the distribution of power; it involves the redefinition of sex roles in some areas, the elimination of sex roles in others, and most importantly, it involves role change not only for women but also for men. Thus, policy opening up combat roles to women in the military is far more threatening than equalizing military benefits for male and female military personnel.

A framework for analyzing policy change must include both long-range and short-term variables. Environmental and systemic variables influence the long-range prospects for policy change. Political variables and policy characteristics influence the short-term prospects. While the studies in this volume focus on substantive policy areas, the effects of long-range and short-term variables are discussed across the range of issues. Because policy making is fluid, no single variable or set of variables explains the dynamics at work across the spectrum of policies included. Rather, different variables come into play on different issues and at different stages of policy development.

One theme which is constant in this volume is the interplay between power and policy. Power has been a thorny problem for the women's movement. As an oppressed group, women have suffered from powerlessness. Yet the simple solution of gaining more power in the context of existing power structures has been rejected as perpetuating patterns of oppression. Much feminist thinking has, therefore, gone into seeking ways to restructure power relations so that they are more democratic, participatory, and just.

At the same time it is clear that policy change occurs only when groups seeking change have sufficient power to influence the policy-making process. The women's movement has come to distinguish between power *over* and power *for.* The feminist critique of power has been directed at ways of reducing the power of one group *over* another. The goal of women's groups in the policy-making process has been to achieve and utilize power *for* role equity and role change.

No group can expect to revolutionize power relations in so short a time as the last 15 years; yet there are several examples in this volume of attempts by women to pursue policy goals while simultaneously expanding participation in the policy-making process. If this volume provokes discussion not only about the ends of policy making but also about the means, about the goals of power as well as policy, its purpose will have been accomplished.

Notes

1. These policies are discussed in detail in Chapter 4 of this volume, "Women and Public Policy: An Overview," by Jo Freeman.

2. The relationship of the personal and the political in feminist thinking is well described in "Part One: Power and Change," *Building Feminist Theory: Essays from Quest"* (New York: Longman, 1981).

3. A good summary of Lowi's classification scheme may be found in Randall Ripley and Grace A. Franklin, *Congress, the Bureaucracy and Public Policy* (Homewood, Ill.: Dorsey Press, 1970), pp. 16–18.

4. The distinction between role equity and role change was first made by Maren Lockwood Carden, *Feminism in the Mid 1970's* (New York: Ford Foundation, 1977), pp. 40–43.

5. The role equity/role change distinction is well illustrated in a policy analysis of legislation on credit, education, abortion, and pregnancy benefits by Joyce Gelb and Marian Lief Palley, "Women and Interest Group Politics: A Comparative Analysis of Federal Decision-Making," *The Journal of Politics 41,* 2 (May, 1979), 361–392.

Part II
Power and Policy:
The Record of the Sixties and Seventies

Introduction

In the 1970s feminism evolved from a diffuse social movement to an organized political interest on the national, state, and local levels. This evolution was not always an easy process. Tensions developed within and among women's groups regarding the directions women should follow in trying to improve the status of women.

Some activists believed that women should concentrate their energies at the grass roots, consciousness raising, and developing alternative institutions and lifestyles. Their efforts have yielded a wide variety of local activities for women ranging from women's centers, health and counseling services, and women's shelters to women's theaters, coffee houses, businesses, and communes. Other activists believed that the needs of women could only be effectively addressed by establishing a presence in political power centers and operating as an organized lobby.

These tensions have not been fully resolved and, in all likelihood, never will be. Why not? One reason is that as long as women are competing for limited political resources, there will never be enough time, money, or organizational talent available to accomplish all the goals of either the lobbyists or the grass-roots organizers. A second, more fundamental reason for these tensions is that there are basic ideological differences between the lobbyists and grass-roots organizers. The lobbyists, in becoming part of the policy-making process, must adapt to the rules of the game—decision making by elites, the need to develop allies among other groups, the use of traditional political rewards for supporters, and most significantly, the need to compromise. The grass-roots organizers, in rejecting politics as usual, consciously subscribe to different political principles: democratic decision making, self-determination, occasionally separatism, and the rejection of compromise politics in favor of ideological purity.

Because this volume focuses on policy making, it does not treat the grass-roots organization of the women's movement in any deatil. This lack of attention does not reflect any judgment concerning its importance. Rather, the work of the activists at the grass roots is recognized as critical in expanding the reach of the movement and generating a variety of perspectives on issues. While there is a tension between the grass-roots organizers outside the established political system and the lobbyists inside, the inside/outside strategy provides the movement with a continuing momentum. Moreover, the grass-roots organizers indirectly benefit the lobbyists in that their more radical image contrasts with the more traditional image of the lobbyists, thereby giving the lobbyists the aura of respectability.

Women's groups have had to confront numerous obstacles in moving into the political system. Once they embraced the need to become lobbyists, they encountered various developmental problems: how to gain access to policy makers, how to build alliances with other interests, how to persuade office-holders to represent women's interests, how to build credibility. Costain's Chapter 2 describes the first stage of interest group organization for the women's movement at the national level.

Women's efforts to influence public policy have sometimes been channeled through commissions on the status of women. As Rosenberg shows in Chapter 3, women's commissions at the federal, state, and local levels have met with varying degrees of success. While state and local commissions today are confronting more and more opposition from taxpayer and right wing groups, they also have the potential to play a significant lobbying role in the 1980s as decisions regarding programs and services for women shift from the federal to the state and local levels of government.

Chater 4 provides an overview of women's public policy achievements over the last several decades. Freeman shows how the civil rights movement of the 1960s produced a political climate favorable for women and how the style of incremental policy making facilitated the addition of sex as a basis for nondis-crimination policies. Freeman concludes, however, that these past policy achievements have failed to address fundamental issues concerning women's roles. While nondiscrimination policies attempt to provide economic equity for women, they have had little effect on the traditional sexual division of labor by which men are defined as breadwinners and women are defined as dependents whose primary responsibility remains the home and family. Since the traditional division of labor no longer reflects the reality of most women's lives, the argument is made that far-reaching policy change is necessary in the 1980s to meet the needs of women as independent citizens.

Chapter 2

Representing Women: The Transition from Social Movement to Interest Group*

Anne N. Costain

The challenge posed by new social movements and the response of the political system are dynamic aspects of American policy formation which have been neglected by most political scientists. Yet, interaction between movements and the government has frequently resulted in extending the range of political debate in the United Staes as well as introducing new and innovative policy alternatives. Social movements raise serious questions outside normal government channels, often concerning subjects which are not being treated as topics of political concerns. The response of the government to demands by movements often results in expanding the areas of government interest and involvement.[1] For example, in the 1960s and 1970s the United States government, responding to the demands of the black civil rights movement, the environmental movement, and the women's movement, involved itself in areas of policy such as integrating the schools, eliminating sexism in job recruitment, and monitoring environmental impacts, which were previously considered beyond

* Support for the research on which this study is based came from the Center for the American Woman and Politics of the Eagleton Institute at Rutgers University. In addition, Marilyn Johnson and Ruth Mandel of the Center provided valued encouragement and advice. The author would also like to thank Andrew McFarland, Jeffrey Berry, and Douglas Costain for commenting on earlier versions of the manuscript. Finally, the revisions suggested by Fanny Rinn and Ellen Boneparth were very helpful in preparing the manuscript for publication. An earlier version of this article was published in the *Western Political Quarterly, 34:* 100–113. Reprinted by permission of the University of Utah, copyright holder.

the scope of federal responsibility.

Yet, despite the ease with which one can identify social movements that have introduced important new elements to American politics, little attention has generally been paid to the process by which social movements are incorporated into the political system. What factors determine the success or failure of movements that try to gain access to the political system? This study examines factors which allowed one movement—the women's movement—to make this breakthrough. It compares these factors with what is known about other movements active in the same period.

The importance of such an inquiry is suggested by sociological research that delineates the distinctive characteristics of social movements.[2] This research suggests that social movements typically arise in response to serious disaffection with the current course of public policy. Movements encompass both organized groups and unorganized, and usually indeterminate, numbers of followers. Although movements have boundaries, based on the shared beliefs of their members and exhibit a degree of patterning among their parts, these parts are not integrated in any unified structure. Finally, social movements advocate major changes in the political and/or social systems and are reluctant to rely totally on conventional politics to achieve these changes.

Movements, then, are partially organized expressions of severe social discontent. As such, their success in becoming a represented interest provides a significant test of the openness of the political system to new interests. Movements are hard for the government to preempt by incremental policy shifts because movements emphasize radical change. For the same reason, they are difficult for the system to accept since they are likely to contain elements which challenge the system itself and thus question traditional power relationships. Their inclusion or exclusion from the political process is an important indicator of the system's ability to accept change.

The women's movement is a large interest with the *potential* to exercise strong political influence based on the size and geographic dispersion of its members and the *reality* of serious organizational difficulties in bringing the diverse needs and priorities of these members together into an acceptable unified position.[3] It provides an interesting example of the problems generally faced by social movements in organizing as national interests.

METHOD

Factors affecting the ability of the women's movement to organize to lobby the political system are drawn from 65 interviews conducted in the period between Fall 1974 and Summer 1977. Principal reliance is on material gathered in structured interviews with 17 individuals representing 14 organizations active in starting a lobby to represent women's interests in Washington.[4] These interviews are supplemented by less formal discussions with 12 lobbyists who worked with the women's movement in national lobbying campaigns.[5] In addition, 36 members of Congress and congressional staff involved in considering legislation lobbied by women's interests were questioned in a less structured format concerning their contacts with and impressions of the women's lobby.[6] Information concerning the experiences of other social movements seeking to establish Washington lobbies is used to examine the generality of factors which are found to be important in the case of the women's movement.[7]

From these sources, three factors affecting movement access to the political system are identified: (1) a major change in the external environment of the movement sufficient to break down membership opposition to lobbying; (2) primary or secondary groups in society willing to assist the movement in starting to lobby; and (3) supportive members of Congress available to help direct early lobbying attempts. The experience of the women's movement suggests that these factors in combination were sufficient for this movement to achieve access to the political system.

PROBLEMS FOR SOCIAL MOVEMENTS IN ORGANIZING TO LOBBY

Like most new interests the first problem for social movements in developing a national lobby is organizational. In starting to lobby, decisions must be made rapidly about which issues to pursue, how to allocate scarce resources, and when to compromise or hold firm on pending legislation. Social movements, which are only partially organized interests, cannot undertake such efforts without substantial transformation. Consequently, it is the most organized parts of social movements that first become active in lobbying. Without this initial involvement by groups within a social movement, it is unlikely that a movement will channel major effort into conventional interest group politics.

Although the emphasis of social movement organizations on change might suggest that they would move naturally into lobbying activity, several critical components of their organizational makeup exert pressure in the opposite direction. First, movement groups tend to rely primarily on purposive incentives to maintain and expand their memberships.[8] Members are attracted to the group because of its purposes and goals and because they feel that they, through their participation, can contribute to attaining valued outcomes. Yet this may create a variety of problems when the group begins to lobby. By lobbying, a group creates a situation in which specific tactical priorities must be set, risking factional splits within the movement as the purposes which attracted some individuals to the movement are modified to achieve legislative success. In the case of the women's movement, women had been an unorganized interest for so long that this was a particular concern for many of its groups. One of the movement's greatest challenges was to bring women together. Women were similar to other minority groups in their reluctance to adopt collective consciousness, but differed in their more intense resistance to developing a sense of unity. Resistance stemmed from women's close relationship with the dominant group—males—and from women's diversity of social and economic circumstances.[9]

Since women's groups had already experienced both the difficulty of educating women to view themselves as possessing shared interests and the factionalizing which often resulted from policy disputes in the movement, lobbying was initially unappealing to most movement groups as yet another potential cause of movement fragmentation.[10] The organizational transformation which is necessary for effective lobbying particularly threatened a key feminist value, commitment to nonhierarchical organization.[11] No successful lobby can function without centralized direction. Yet the dependence of women's movement organizations on the goodwill and trust of their members made the development of hierarchical organizational structures risky because many movement members thought that such structures betrayed the purpose of the organization. As Jo Freeman suggests:

> These problems reflect the classic dilemma of social movement organizations; the fact that the tightly organized hierarchical structures necessary to change social institutions conflict directly with the participatory style necessary to maintain membership support and the democratic nature of the movement's goals.[12]

A second general characteristic of social movement organizations also creates pressure not to lobby. Movement groups are more likely than most formal organizations to utilize unorthodox or noninstitutionalized means to achieve their objectives.[13] This tendency is partly a function of the difficulty of initiating major changes in policy by traditional means and partly a reflection of the goal of most movements to change institutional structures as well as policy. By lobbying, an organization chooses to direct a major effort through established political channels. This choice, in effect, acknowledges the legitimacy of existing structures and may jeopardize the movement's ability to continue using protest tactics to push for change.[14] Since much of the attention focused on the women's movement in the 1960s had been the product of what Theodore Lowi refers to as "disorderly" politics—picketing, sit-ins, demonstrations, civil disobedience, and even national strikes—the fear was that the thrust of the women's movement could well be blunted by its becoming "just another" lobbying group.[15]

These difficulties associated with purposive incentives for membership and commitment to unorthodox political tactics quickly came to the fore when the two largest women's movement organizations began national lobbying in 1973. The National Organization for Women (NOW) and the National Women's

Political Caucus (NWPC) were particularly hard hit by membership anger over developments associated with lobbying in each organization. Conflict in both NOW and NWPC centered on the relationship between the national offices of the organizations and state and local chapters. Since lobbying requires a uniform organizational posture on specific issues and centralized decision making, the initiation of lobbying was a factor in mobilizing membership opposition to leadership and central direction within both groups.

Dissent within the NWPC centered on the funding of the national office, of which the lobbying staff is a part. Although state and local caucuses were supposed to pay the national caucus at least one dollar per member in dues each year, many refused to pay. In 1973, 14 state organizations paid no dues to the national while ten others paid 50 dollars or less.[16] This nonpayment of national dues was the state and local organizations' method of protesting what they viewed as the unnecessary concentration of power in the national office.[17]

Far from bringing the national office and the grass-roots members together, national lobbying emphasized the division between them. The Caucus, after beginning congressional lobbying in 1973, did little in the next few years to expand its efforts. Although members of the national staff of NWPC expressed in interviews their belief that it was important to follow up the election campaign work of the Caucus with political pressure to ensure that individuals helped into office by the Caucus voted correctly once they got there, this side of NWPC's work was allowed to stagnate at the national level.[18] Instead, the Caucus focused its energy on activities like supporting women candidates which could be decentralized more easily.

NOW's problems in initiating lobbying in 1973 were more severe than those of the Caucus. Like the Caucus, NOW was plagued by the refusal of state organizations to pay dues to the national headquarters during this period. Although NOW's national office was in Chicago and its legislative office in Washington, this nonmonolithic national organization did not adequately allay membership mistrust. In 1974, several of the largest state organizations placed their national dues in escrow in protest over actions of the national leadership. The thrust of criticism directed toward leadership and staff was that NOW was becoming too reformist under the domination of a small elite.[19] The culmination of criticism of the national legislative staff came at NOW's 1975 convention when the entire staff was fired in response to pressure from more politically and organizationally radical NOW members. In an interview several months prior to this convention, a member of the Washington legislative staff described pressure which she saw building in the organization: "A number of crazies are trying to end the legislative activity of NOW. Rather than lobbying against abortion laws they want to teach self-abortion."[20]

As these experiences suggest, movements' reliance on purposive incentives for membership and their use of noninstitutionalized political channels make it difficult for them to initiate congressional lobbying. Without strong outside motivation, it is unlikely that women's movement organizations would have begun national lobbying.

PRESSURES TO ENTER THE LEGISLATIVE ARENA

The first significant factor in initiating lobbying by the women's movement was the substantial change taking place in the movement's outside environment in the early 1970s. Although pluralist theory stresses the importance of negative external stimuli for the emergence of new interest groups,[21] the case of the women's movement suggests that positive events are also powerful in providing incentives to break down resistance to lobbying activity. The women's movement organizations that initiated formalized lobbying in the early 1970s did so in apparent response to two significant changes in the external environment: (1) positive change in public attitudes toward the goals of the movement and (2) passage of favorable legislation by Congress in several areas of great concern to the movement. These related changes are closely tied to aspects of a movement organization's environment which have been shown to be particularly important to groups: the attitude of society as a whole toward the movement and the number of potential movement supporters in society.[22] Taken together, these factors are influential in determining the ability of a movement group to recruit new members and to achieve its goals.

Increased support for the goals of women's liberation, coupled with public opposition to many of the tactics used by the women's movement to achieve these goals, pushed the movement toward conventional lobbying activity. From a sizable minority of men (44 percent) and women (40 percent) who favored efforts to strengthen women's status in society in 1970, by 1974 a solid majority of men (63 percent) and women (57 percent) favored this change according to a Virginia Slims poll.[23] An earlier Virginia Slims poll showed, however, that despite substantial agreement by both sexes with the statement, "If women don't speak up for themselves and confront men on their real problems, nothing will be done about these problems" (women, 71 percent agree, men, 67 percent agree), widespread uneasiness existed about some of the tactics used by women's movement groups.[24] The politics of disorder as used by women's groups seemed to engender strong disapproval among some segments of the population.

The extent of this disapproval is especially apparent in responses to a question concerning "sympathy with efforts of women's liberation groups." In the 1972 Virginia Slims poll, a sizable percentage of women (49 percent) were unsympathetic.[25] Many potential recruits for the movement were obviously unimpressed with the activities of women's liberation groups. The situation was one in which sizable segments of the population favored a change, but found the women's liberation movement itself unsuitable. One option, therefore, for the movement to attract these potential members was by changing its image from one of protest to one of working within the system for change.

At the same time, the Ninety-Second Congress was passing an unprecedented amount of legislation strengthening the status of women.[26] The ERA in particular seemed to provide the single most important catalyst for groups to accomplish the transition to legislative politics. The amendment itself has the advantage of addressing the central issue of the denial of women's rights under the law. In addition to the legal advantages of passing such an amendment, which would put discrimination based on sex on an equal footing with racial discrimination as a suspect classification, the ERA proved an important rallying point for a variety of groups which had previously shunned the feminist label.[27]

In Washington the fight for congressional passage of the ERA was largely orchestrated by members of Congress, particularly Representative Martha Griffiths, but a number of individuals and organizations joined together to support this legislation. An Ad Hoc Committee formed to coordinate lobbying for the ERA began patterns of cooperation and resource sharing that would prove invaluable in later lobbying efforts. Several of the women within this Ad Hoc Committee recognized the need for continued congressional lobbying and founded Women's Lobby Inc. in 1972.[28] Other women affiliated with existing movement organizations encouraged those groups to commit resources to continuing pressure on Congress after the passage of the ERA. In 1972 Women's Equity Action League (WEAL) moved its headquarters from Ohio to Washington. In 1973, as noted previously, NOW and NWPC opened Washington legislative offices.

Passage of the Equal Rights Amendment by Congress provided this kind of stimulus for further lobbying efforts for several reasons. First, it demonstrated the receptiveness of Congress to women's movement goals. Second, it showed skeptical social movement groups the potential of legislation for initiating far-reaching social and political change. Third, it showed both social movement and more traditional voluntary organizations that they could work together to achieve common goals. Finally, since the ERA is a constitutional amendment and must go to the states for ratification and even if ratified will not be implemented for at least two years, this long process highlighted the continued need for interim legislation to end the most blatant cases of legal discrimination.

These positive changes in political and social conditions helped break down the resistance of movement group members to organized political lobbying. The passage of the Equal Rights Amendment by Congress in particular was a stunning demonstration of the level of policy change that could be achieved by lobbying on behalf of movement goals.

STARTING A NEW LOBBY

In starting a new lobby, three capabilities must be developed rapidly: (1) an ability to obtain reliable information on pending legislation; (2) a network of contacts on Capitol Hill to get this information circulated; and (3) links to congressional constituencies (a) to mobilize pressure through the district, and (b) to assure that the lobbyist is reflecting the interests of these constituents. When NOW, NWPC, and WEAL came to Washington in 1972 and 1973, they had neither the resources nor the network of congressional contacts to begin full-fledged lobbying activity. What they did have was a number of groups, primarily women's voluntary organizations, that were sympathetic to the goals of the women's movement and available to help develop a women's rights lobby. The availability of secondary groups willing to assist the women's movement is the second factor of importance in allowing a successful women's lobby to form.

The development of this lobby suggests a pattern of social movement growth similar to that described by Maurice Pinard in his study of the Social Credit Party in Quebec. Pinard found that intermediate social organizations, such as voluntary associations, can facilitate the spread of social movements. According to Pinard, when "pre-existing primary and secondary groupings *possess* or *develop* an ideology or simply subjective interests congruent with that of a new movement, they will act as mobilizing rather than restraining agents toward that movement."[29]

In the case of social movement lobbying, these ties are quite apparent. The ability of new interests to start lobbying depends heavily on the aid of established organizations with compatible goals. In the case of more conventional interests, like Common Cause and the Consumer Federation of America, such assistance has been shown to be important.[30] But this assistance is essential in the case of social movements because most movement groups lack resources and have difficulty getting access to the political system without a "sponsor."[31]

Why did relatively traditional organizations like the National Federation of Business and Professional Women (BPW) and the American Association of University Women (AAUW) become involved in joint lobbying efforts with women's movement groups? Why were they so receptive to feminism? Part of the answer lies in the origins of these women's groups. The AAUW, BPW, and League of Women Voters were all founded out of concern for participation by women in society.[32] Other traditional women's groups like the National Council of Jewish Women and United Methodist Women began out of feminist protest.[33] Feminism was not new to many of these organizations, although it may, in some cases, have been dormant for a number of years.

The membership characteristics of these traditional women's voluntary groups are similar to those of the women's movement groups, with the exception of age. As Carden[34] and Freeman[35] both discover in their data on women's movement followers, these women are predominantly white, middle class, and well educated. This is similar to studies of membership in voluntary organizations generally.[36] Comparing Freeman's report of the results of the 1973 *MS* magazine subscriber poll with the findings of the League of Women Voter's 1974 self-study reveals interesting similarities between the two groups, along the directions predicted by studies of participation.[37] Education levels are similar for the two groups. Ninety percent of the *MS* subscribers have some college education compared with 92 percent of the League members. Socioeconomic status is also comparable. The median household income of *MS* subscribers is $17,740 per year. Although there is no income figure for League members, their husbands are primarily professional men (35 percent are doctors, lawyers, or governmental officials; 15 percent are in education—11 percent at the university level—and 27 percent are in business). The most significant difference between the two groups is age. Seventy-two percent of the *MS* subscribers are under 35 while only 7 percent of the League members are under 30 with another 30 percent between 30 and 39.

The rising age and stable number of members in many traditional women's voluntary associations cause some concern to these organizations.[38] Involving themselves with feminist causes seemed to have the payoff of attracting younger members to organizations such as the AAUW and BPW.[39] Cooperation between traditional women's groups and women's movement groups has also been easier because many of their members are already working together in the states on ERA coalitions.[40]

Why the women's movement needed voluntary organizations is equally clear. Many of the traditional groups such as the AAUW, the National Council of Jewish Women, and the League of Women Voters have long engaged in legislative activity. These groups provided training and contacts on the Hill to the newer movement organizations. Also, many of the older organizations have memberships which dwarf the combined figures of all the social movement groups. A large active membership in the districts together with the legitimacy and experience of the voluntary groups provided sufficient incentive for the movement organizations to seek cooperation. The availability of secondary associations with interests congruent to the new movement made it possible for the women's movement to develop a Washington lobby in a relatively short period of time.

The legislative successes of the women's lobby are impressive, particularly for such a new lobby. In 1974, the lobby persuaded Congress to add a minimum wage for domestic workers to the Fair Labor Standards Amendments and to pass bills providing educational equity for women and granting women equal access to credit.[41] In 1975, the lobby's efforts gained women admittance to American military academies, established a National Commission on the observance of International Women's Year and directed it to convene a National Women's Conference, and defeated congressional attempts to weaken Title IX of the 1972 Education Amendments Act, which prohibits most forms of sex discrimination in federally funded educational programs.[42] The women's lobby also met with defeats, chiefly in its efforts to continue federal funding for abortions and to pass comprehensive day-care legislation. Yet, on balance, for a new and untested interest, the lobby accomplished a great deal.

VOLUNTARY VERSUS ECONOMIC INTERESTS

The importance of traditional voluntary groups in helping women's lobbying succeed is reinforced by the movement's early inability to attract support from economic interests, particularly labor unions. Highly sought after by movement groups, labor unions were rarely willing to work with movement groups in the early 1970s. Their disinterest seemed to stem from the conditions William Gamson described as leading to the "stable unrepresentation" of interests in America. "Unrepresented groups tend to be poor in resources and rich in demands, making them poor [lobbying] coalition partners. They will expect to share in the rewards of a coalition disproportionately to the resources they contribute to it."[43] Women's rights lobbyists in the early 1970s had little to offer economic interests but they wanted much from them. Interviews revealed agreement between the women's group representatives and the union lobbyists that only rarely did the interests of both sides coincide sufficiently for joint action to be feasible. Although unions sometimes endorsed a women's issue, on the national level it was quite infrequent that this endorsement would be backed by any action. One women's movement lobbyist said "The AFL-CIO really has not done a damn thing for the Equal Rights Amendment on the national level. They have had very little involvement with any feminist issue."[44]

The case of the women's movement strongly highlights the importance of noneconomic voluntary organizations as facilitators of new group entry into national lobbying activity. Without this type of secondary group, sympathetic to the goals of the new interest and willing to provide resources and expertise to help it develop, it is less likely that a new interest will succeed in becoming a national lobbying group. Just as the emerging women's lobby received essential aid from established groups such as the American Association of University Women and the Business and Professional Women, so too have other recent social movements found similar benefactors. Church organizations and liberal groups such as the Americans for Democratic Action and the American Civil Liberties Union aided the development of a civil rights lobby. The environmental movement gained from the political expertise of conservation and nature groups such as the Audubon Society, the Sierra Club, and the National Wildlife Federation. The pattern of existing voluntary associations facilitating the entry of social movements into the policy-making process seems well established in American politics.

CONGRESS AND SOCIAL MOVEMENTS

The third factor affecting the ability of social movements to gain access to the system is the necessity of having allies in Congress willing to help direct and organize early lobbying by the interest. Like having secondary groups which will assist the movement, this factor helps assure that lobbying by movement groups will produce some rapid successes. Given the aforementioned likely opposition to lobbying by some vocal movement members, such early success is almost essential in formation of a national lobby.

In the case of the women's movement, the passage of the ERA by Congress put the spotlight on several members of Congress who would welcome and work with a women's lobby when it organized. Most notable among these early supporters were Representative Martha Griffiths (D-Mich.) and Senator Birch Bayh (D-Ind.). In addition, the women's movement had a readily identifiable additional source of help in the persons of the other women members of Congress. Although the representatives of women's organizations who were interviewed reported little face-to-face contact with most members of Congress, the overwhelming exception was in the case of congresswomen.[45] There appeared to be a high level of contact and trust between those seeking to form a women's lobby and the women in Congress. One lobbyist noted: "When I need the lowdown on a pending bill and its chances, I call the women in Congress."

Women members of Congress were the chief sponsors and floor managers of most of the legislation supported by the women's lobby in its first years. Representative Patsy Mink (D-Hawaii) steered the Women's Educational Equity Act through the House of Representatives. The Equal Credit Opportunity Act was the combined product of the work of Representative Leonor Sullivan (D-Mo.), Representative Margaret Heckler (R-Mass.), and Representative Edward Koch (D-N.Y.)[46] Pressure to extend the minimum wage to domestic workers, an early legislative priority of the women's movement, was coordinated by Representative Shirley Chisholm (D-N.Y.). Women as a new interest and as outsiders in the legislative process needed this congressional direction to employ their scarce resources as effectively as possible.

It has long been noted in literature on lobbying that interests are most effective when working under the direction of congressional offices. As Bauer, Pool, and Dexter write in their classic study of reciprocal trade legislation: "The congressman who told us that he had to telephone 'his' lobby to get them going is not telling us a man-bites-dog story. He was describing a usual state of affairs."[47] The experience of lobbying by the women's movement simply suggests that such direction takes on a particular importance in the case of new interests.

The existence of at least a minority of members of Congress who feel intensely enough about a social movement to coordinate and guide its early lobbying seems necessary both for the movement to get a hearing before the legislative body, and more importantly, for it to have a chance for success within that body. The recent influential social movements—the black civil rights, environmental, and women's movements—have had identifiable groups of supporters within Congress who have championed, publicized, and led their earlier legislative battles. The impact on Congress of these movements was, in an important way, created by the members of Congress themselves.

CONCLUSIONS

The early, largely unheralded days when social movements or other emerging interests are trying to organize and gain the ear of government decision makers, are often ignored by those describing the policy process.[48] Yet the ability of government to design policy responsive to new interests, as well as old, hinges critically on the ease with which new interests seeking change in existing policies gain an initial hearing from government decision makers.

The case of the women's movement suggests three factors which appear necessary for social movements to gain this access to the policy system. First, an external stimulus must impact on the movement with sufficient force to break down the resistance of movement members to lobbying. Second, primary or secondary groups must be available and willing to help develop such lobbying. Third, at least a minority of members of Congress must be willing to provide direction for early lobbying efforts.

These linkages between societal conditions and the organization of social movements as new interests have several implications for system responsiveness. First, there is no guarantee within this framework that new change-oriented interests appearing initially as social movements will gain access to the political system. Many of the organizational characteristics of the most developed segments of social movements indicate exactly the opposite. It appears that the transition from social movement to represented interest will not occur without significant sources of external pressure on the movement. The stimulating effect of positive governmental action in this regard suggests that governmental intervention is useful and sometimes even necessary for maintaining the openness of the system to this type of interest.

Second, these links also indicate the need to examine further the role of voluntary organizations within American society. Existing secondary associations seem to have an important role in determining which social movements will be integrated into the policy system. If secondary associations like the

League of Women Voters and the National Council of Jewish Women play as major a part in the transition from unrepresented to represented interests as is suggested by the experience of the women's movement, their organizational goals would establish a kind of value parameter determining which new interests in fact gain acceptance within the American system and which are excluded. Analysis of existing groups could provide a kind of rough prediction concerning future directions of policy change within the system.

Third, these factors suggest a more significant role for Congress in maintaining the openness of the system to new interests than many modern scholars have assigned it.[49] The importance of having representatives of unrepresented groups in Congress is also underscored since in the cases of the black civil rights and women's movements, at least, these representatives were influential in allowing social movement groups to gain access to the legislative body.

Although lobbying by women's movement groups has not brought about radical change in American public policy, it has stimulated innovative policies to eliminate sex discrimination and expand opportunities for women.[50] This change although incremental is not insignificant either in its impact on society or in its origin. For without national lobbying on behalf of women, most of this legislation would not have been passed by Congress. The development of a national women's lobby resulted in changes in policy which otherwise would not have taken place.[51]

The experiences of the women's movements in this regard suggest the need for further study of the transitional phase of interest access to the political system. Such access is directly linked to policy formation and by evaluating the factors affecting access, it may be possible to anticipate future directions of policy more clearly.

Notes

1. Jack Walker, "A Critique of the Elitist Theory of Democracy," *American Political Science Review 60* (June 1966): 293.

2. These characteristics of social movements are taken from the following works: John Wilson, *Introduction to Social Movements* (New York: Basic Books, 1973); Ralph Turner and Lewis Killian, *Collective Behavior* (Englewood Cliffs: Prentice-Hall, 1957); Rudolph Heberle, *Social Movements* (New York: Appleton-Century-Crofts, 1951);

Neil Smelser, *The Theory of Collective Behavior* (New York: Free Press, 1963); and Mayer Zald and Roberta Ash, "Social Movement Organizations: Growth, Decay and Change," *Social Forces 44* (March 1966): 327–40.

3. Although large, geographically dispersed interests possess the greatest potential for political influence, they are often the least likely to mobilize effectively to achieve this influence. As Mancur Olson in *The Logic of Collective Action* (New York: Schocken Books, 1968) and others have noted, it is rarely to the advantage of individuals to spend time in groups whose benefits they are likely to receive regardless of personal contribution to the group. This "free-rider" problem associated with the types of nondivisible benefits, like lower prices and less discrimination, typically sought by large interests, limits their ability to attract members into the formal organizations necessary to achieve real political influence. As E. E. Schattschneider notes in *The Semisovereign People* (Hinsdale, Ill.: Dryden Press, 1960): "Special interest organizations are most easily formed when they deal with small numbers of individuals who are acutely aware of their exclusive interests" (p. 34).

4. Interviews were conducted with representatives of 14 organizations meeting the following criteria: (1) each has an on-going interest in women's rights which is central to the organization's purpose; (2) each makes a systematic effort to influence congressional policy relating to women; and (3) each has offices in Washington, D.C. Initial interviews, lasting from forty-five minutes to two-and-a-half hours were conducted between September 1974 and January 1975. In most cases the director of the group's legislative office was interviewed. In a few of the organizations either a lobbyist or the president of the group was interviewed instead. Less structured follow-up interviews were held through March 1976 with selected organizations to check on current legislative activities. The groups whose representatives were interviewed are: American Association of University Women, November 19, 1974 and August 11, 1975; B'nai B'rith Women, November 19, 1974; Federally Employed Women, December 30, 1974 and May 7, 1975; Federation of Organizations for Professional Women, January 3, 1975 and July 30, 1975; General Federation of Women's Clubs, October 17, 1974; League of Women Voters, October 8, 1974 and August 14, 1975; National Council of Jewish Women, November 1, 1974; National Federation of Business and Professional Women's Clubs (BPW), September 20, 1974 and October 1, 1974; National Organization for Women, October 31, 1974 and August 5, 1975; National Women's Party, January 23, 1975; National Women's Political Caucus, October 22, 1974; United Methodist Women, November 4, 1974; Women's Equity Action League, November 25, 1974; Women's Lobby, December 3, 1974. Two additional organizations seeming to meet these criteria declined to have representatives interviewed: The National Council of Negro Women and the National Council of Catholic Women.

5. Representatives of 12 other groups were also interviewed. These groups, which did not meet all of the criteria specified at the time the initial interviews were conducted, but which were active in joint lobbying on some women's issues, are: the International Union of Electrical, Radio and Machine Workers, April 13, 1977; Common Cause, October 30, 1974 and March 2, 1976; American Civil Liberties Union Women's Project, April 24, 1977; Network, March 16, 1975; Women's International League for Peace and Freedom, January 9, 1975; Center for Women Policy Studies, October 21, 1974; American Alliance for Health, Physical Education and Recreation, September 27, 1974; National Association for Girls and Women in Sport, September 27, 1974; Coalition for Labor Union Women, January 3, 1975; National Organization for Women Legal Defense and Education Fund (PEER), August 19, 1975; Association of American Colleges Project on the Status and Education of Women, July 22, 1975;

Women's Legal Defense Fund, April 28, 1977.

6. The following members of Congress, who served on subcommittees handling women's issues, were interviewed about the impact of the women's lobby: Representatives William Steiger (R-Wis.), December 19, 1974; Patsy Mink (D-Hawaii), June 26, 1975; William Clay (D-Mo.), December 11, 1974; Augustus Hawkins (D-Calif.), December 10, 1974; Leonor Sullivan (D-Mo.), July 24, 1975; Stewart McKinney (R-Conn.), July 16, 1975; Fortney Stark (D-Calif.), July 14, 1975; Clair Burgener (R-Calif.), July 11, 1975; Margaret Heckler (R-Mass.), July 23, 1975; Edward Koch (D-N.Y.), June 25, 1975; Henry Gonzalez (D-Tex.), July 10, 1975; and Matthew Rinaldo (R-N.J.), July 28, 1975. Twenty-four members of congressional staffs were similarly questioned.

7. Among the sources which proved most useful were: Gary Orfield, "Congress, the President and Anti-Busing Legislation, 1966-1974," *Journal of Law and Education 4* (January 1975): 81-139; William Gamson, *The Strategy of Social Protest* (Homewood, Ill.: Dorsey, 1975); Lewis M. Killian, *The Impossible Revolution? Black Power and the American Dream* (New York: Random House, 1968); John Herbers, *The Lost Priority* (New York: Funk and Wagnalls, 1970); Hubert M. Blalock, *Toward A Theory of Minority-Group Relations* (New York: Capricorn Books, 1967); J. Criag Jenkins and Charles Perrow, "Insurgency of the Powerless: Farm Worker Movements (1946-72)." *American Sociological Review 42* (April 1977): 249-68.

8. Zald and Ash, "Social Movement Organizations."

9. Helen Mayer Hacker, "Women as a Minority Group," in *This Great Argument: The Rights of Women,* ed. Hamida Bosmajian and Haig Bosmajian (Reading, Mass.: Addison-Wesley, 1972), pp. 127-45.

10. Jo Freeman, *The Politics of Women's Liberation* (New York: Longman, 1975), provides an excellent overview of the ambivalence felt by many members of movement groups toward direct lobbying.

11. Cellestine Ware, *Women Power: The Movement for Women's Liberation* (New York: Tower Publications, 1970), p. 26.

12. Freeman, *The Politics of Women's Liberation,* p. 100.

13. Roberta Ash, *Social Movements in America* (Chicago: Markham, 1972), p. 1; John Wilson, *Introduction to Social Movements* (New York: Basic Books, 1973), pp. 229-39.

14. Paul Wilkenson, *Social Movements* (New York: Praeger, 1971), p. 30.

15. William H. Chafe, *The American Woman* (New York: Oxford University Press, 1972), pp. 226-7.

16. Susan Carroll, *Women's Rights and Political Parties: Issue Development, the 1972 Conventions and the NWPC* (Master's thesis, University of Indiana, 1972), p. 62.

17. Ibid.

18. Ibid., p. 55. Interview with a representative of the National Women's Political Caucus conducted on October 22, 1974 in Washington, D.C.

19. Interview with a representative of the National Organization for Women conducted on August 5, 1975 in Washington, D.C.

20. Ibid.

21. See for example, David B. Truman, *The Governmental Process* (New York: Knopf, 1951), pp. 104-5.

22. Zald and Ash, "Social Movement Organizations."

23. The following figures from the *Virginia Slims American Women's Opinion Poll.* Vol. III, p. 3, conducted by the Roper Organization in 1974, detail this change in attitude:

FAVOR/OPPOSE EFFORTS TO STRENGTHEN OR CHANGE WOMEN'S STATUS IN SOCIETY

	1974		1972		1970	
	Women	*Men*	*Women*	*Men*	*Women*	*Men*
Favor	57	63	48	49	40	44
Oppose	25	19	36	36	52	39
Not Sure	18	18	16	15	18	17

24. The following figures from the *Virginia Slims American Women's Opinion Poll,* Vol. II, p. 6, conducted by Louis Harris and Associates in 1972 illustrate this dissatisfaction:

STATEMENTS ABOUT ACTIVIST WOMEN'S GROUPS

	WOMEN			MEN		
	Agree	*Disagree*	*Not Sure*	*Agree*	*Disagree*	*Not Sure*
Women who picket and participate in protests are setting a bad example for children. Their behavior is undignified and unwomanly	60	32	8	57	35	8
Women are right to be unhappy with their role in American society but wrong in the way they are protesting	51	34	15	44	40	16

25. Ibid., p. 4.

26. Freeman, *The Politics of Women's Liberation,* pp. 202–5.

27. The following are dates when some of the leading women's voluntary organizations first endorsed the ERA: American Association for University Women 1971; Business and Professional Women 1937; General Federation of Women's Clubs 1944; League of Women Voters 1972; National Council of Jewish Women 1923.

28. Flora Crater, "Women Lobbyists Incorporate for Full Scale Action for Women," *The Woman Activist 2* (November 1972): 1.

29. Maurice Pinard, *The Rise of a Third Party* (Englewood Cliffs: Prentice-Hall, 1971), p. 186.

30. John E. Sinclair, *Interest Groups in America* (Morristown, N.J.: General Learning Press, 1976), p. 45.

31. Jenkins and Perrow, "Insurgency of the Powerless."

32. The AAUW was started in 1882 to expand educational opportunities for women. BPW was established in 1919 to improve women's role in the business world. The League, founded in 1920, the year women's suffrage was written into the constitution, sought to teach the newly enfranchised women how to use their vote.

33. The National Council of Jewish Women was founded in 1894 after Jewish women had asked to participate in the Columbia Exposition's Parliament of Religions, to celebrate the four-hundredth anniversary of the New World, and were admitted only as hostesses. (Bernice Grazian, *Where There Is a Woman, 75 Years of History as Lived by the National Council of Jewish Women.* McCall Corporation, 1967). The National Woman's Party, originally named the Congressional Union for Women Suffrage, was started by Alice Paul in 1913. The Congressional Union organized White House demonstrations, mass marches, and hunger strikes in support of women's suffrage. Miss Paul and several of her followers were jailed in 1917, producing angry public response over their harsh treatment in jail. (Elizabeth Chittick, "Biographic Material—Miss Alice Paul." Mimeographed. National Woman's Party. 144 Constitution Avenue, N.E., Washington, D.C. 20002.) The United Methodist Women began as part of the missionary movement in the Methodist Church. After the male leadership of the church refused to allow single women to become missionaries, a women's missionary division was established to sponsor these women. (Interview with a representative of the United Methodist Women conducted on November 4, 1974, in Washington, D.C.).

34. Maren, Lockwood Carden, *The New Feminist Movement* (New York: Russell Sage, 1974), pp. 19–21.

35. Freeman, *The Politics of Women's Liberation,* pp. 36–38.

36. Sidney Verba and Norman H. Nie, *Participation in America* (New York: Harper and Row, 1972), pp. 200–205. James Q. Wilson, *Political Organizations* (New York: Basic Books, 1973), p. 56.

37. Freeman, *The Politics of Women's Liberation,* pp. 36–37. League of Women Voters, *The Report of the Findings of the League Self-Study* (League of Women Voters, 1730 M. Street, N.W., Washington, D.C. 20036, 1974), p. 4.

38. As data from Abbott L. Ferriss, *Indicators of Trends in the Status of American Women* (New York: Russell Sage, 1971), p. 404, and from interviews with representatives of the League of Women Voters (October 8, 1974), the Business and Professional Women (October 1, 1974), and the American Association of University Women (November 19, 1974) indicate, all of these organizations have reason to be concerned about their future levels of membership. The League of Women Voters had 156,800 members in 1968 and 157,000 members in 1974. Forty percent of the League's 1974 membership was 50 or older. The Business and Professional Women declined from a membership of 178,300 in 1968 to 168,000 in 1974. The American Association of University Women is one of the few traditional organizations experiencing a period of growth, from 173,200 members in 1968 to 182,000 members in 1974, but the average age of AAUW members in 1974 was 49.

39. Interview with a representative of the American Association of University Women conducted on November 19, 1974, in Washington, D.C. Interview with a representative of the Business and Professional Women conducted on October 1, 1974, in Washington, D.C.

40. Groups which were reported working actively in state ERA coalitions in nine unratified states include:

	Number of States
AAUW	4
American Nurses Association	5
BPW	9
Common Cause	5
League of Women Voters	8
NOW	9
National Women's Political Caucus	8

These results are taken from a telephone poll conducted by Common Cause during June 1974, covering the states: Utah, Arizona, Georgia, Alabama, Arkansas, Florida, North Carolina, South Carolina, and Indiana. Only organizations mentioned in four or more of these states are included in the list above.

41. Fair Labor Standards Amendments of 1974. Public Law 93-259, Section 7, April 8, 1974. Women's Educational Equity Act. Public Law 93-380, Title IV. Section 408, August 21, 1974. Equal Credit Opportunity Act. Public Law 93-495, Title VII, October 28, 1974. For descriptions of some of the lobbying for this legislation, see Joyce Gelb and Marian Lief Palley, "Women and Interest Group Politics," *American Politics Quarterly 5* (July 1977): 331–52 and Anne N. Costain, "Lobbying for Equal Credit," in *Women Organizing,* ed. Bernice Cummings and Victoria Schuck (Metuchen, N.J.: Scarecrow Press, 1979), pp. 82–110.

42. Department of Defense Appropriation Authorization Act, 1976. Public Law 94-106, Title VIII, October 7, 1975. Public Law 94-167, December 23, 1975 (To organize and convene a National Women's Conference). For a description of efforts to combat congressional moves to weaken or amend Title IX of the 1972 Education Amendments Act, see, Anne N. Costain, "Eliminating Sex Discrimination in Education: Lobbying for Implementation of Title 9." *Policy Studies Journal 7* (Winter 1978): 189–95.

43. William A. Gamson, "Stable Unrepresentation in American Society," *Group Politics, A New Emphasis,* ed. E. J. Malecki and H. R. Mahood (New York: Charles Scribner's Sons, 1972) pp. 60–75.

44. Although several of the lobbyists interviewed suggested that the Coalition of Labor Union Women (CLUW) established in 1974 might either pressure organized labor to lobby on women's issues, or might lobby these issues itself, these expectations do not seem to be realistic. In interviews with two activists from CLUW, it was clear that the thrust of CLUW's activity is to increase representation of women in union leadership, not to push for action on specific legislation. This preference is confirmed by the absence of any CLUW presence in Congress during the period of this research.

45. Listed below is the number of organizations within the emerging women's lobby whose representatives reported contact with each woman member of the 93rd Congress. (See note 4 for the list of organizations surveyed.)

Number Reporting Contact (N = 14)		*Number Reporting Contact (N = 14)*	
Martha Griffiths (D-Mich.)	14	Yvonne Burke (D-Calif.)	10
Patsy Mink (D-Hawaii)	14	Elizabeth Holtsman (D-N.Y.)	10
Bella Abzug (D-N.Y.)	13	Edith Green (D-Ore.)	8
Pat Schroeder (D-Colo.)	12	Leonor Sullivan (D-Mo.)	8
Shirley Chisholm (D-N.Y.)	11	Ella Grasso (D-Conn.)	7
Corrine Boggs (D-La.)	10	Cardiss Collins (D-Ill.)	6
Margaret Heckler (R-Mass.)	10	Marjorie Holt (R-Md.)	6
Barbara Jordan (D-Tex.)	10	Julia Butler Hansen (D-Wash.)	5

46. Gelb and Paley, "Women and Interest Group Politics."

47. Raymond Bauer, Ithiel DeSola Pool, and Lewis Anthony Dexter, *American Business and Public Policy,* 2nd ed, (Chicago: Aldine, 1972), p. 441.

48. Exceptions to this generalization include: Walker, "A Critique of the Elitist Theory of Democracy"; John Kingdon's discussion of the predecision stage of congressional policy making in *Congressmen's Voting Decisions* (New York: Harper and Row, 1973), pp. 242–60; and Roger W. Cobb and Charles D. Elder, *Participation in American Politics: The Dynamics of Agenda-Building* (Baltimore: Johns Hopkins University

Press, 1972).

49. Once again there are exceptions, including Gary Orfield, *Congressional Power: Congress and Social Change* (New York: Harcourt, Brace, Jovanovich, 1975); and Jack L. Walker, "Setting the Agenda in the U.S. Senate. A Theory of Problem Selection," *British Journal of Political Science 4* (October 1977): 423–46.

50. For a good evaluation of sources of strength and weakness in lobbying on behalf of women, see Joyce Gelb and Marian Lief Palley, "Women and Interest Group Politics: A Comparative Analysis of Federal Decision-Making," *Journal of Politics 41* (May 1979): 362–92.

51. For a fine view of the impact of lobbying by women's groups on the state level, see Janet K. Boles, *The Politics of the Equal Rights Amendment* (New York: Longman, 1979).

Chapter 3

Representing Women at the State and Local Levels: Commissions on the Status of Women

Rina Rosenberg

One response to the demands of women for changes in public policy has been the creation of commissions on the status of women (CSWs). The commission movement originated at the national level and has filtered down over the last 20 years to the state and local levels. Because women's commissions have the potential to influence the policy-making process in various ways, it is important to evaluate their record and to explore ways in which they might increase their effectiveness in the future.

NATIONAL COMMISSIONS

The commission movement began in 1961 when President Kennedy rewarded his female political supporters by creating the President's Advisory Commission on the Status of Women with Eleanor Roosevelt as its chair. The commission was instructed to study the role of women in American society and to make recommendations for new federal policy. The Kennedy and Johnson Commission's report, *American Women,* issued in October 1963, reviewed several critical areas of public policy but concerned itself principally with employment. It lauded the president's support for the passage of the Equal Pay Act and for increasing female participation in the public sector; reflecting the traditional trade union position, however, it did not support the ERA or the enforcement of equal opportunity in the private sector.[1] While the Kennedy

Commission had relatively little impact on public policy, it encouraged women to enter the mainstream and spurred the creation of CSWs at the state level. By 1967, CSWs existed in some form in all 50 states, and by 1979 the number of state and local women's commissions was estimated at 175.

Like Kennedy and Johnson, Richard Nixon also found it useful to reward women active in his presidential campaign by appointing a Presidential Task Force on Women's Rights and Responsibilities. The report of that task force, *A Matter of Simple Justice,* released in 1970, went considerably further than the Kennedy Commission's report in that it demanded action on the ERA, executive enforcement of antidiscrimination regulations, and new policies in the areas of employment, education, and child care.[2] These policy recommendations, however, were treated at first with benign neglect and later with hostile administration vetoes.

The most recent in the series of presidential commissions was Jimmy Carter's Presidential Advisory Committee on Women. The executive order creating the committee included a section stating that "the Committee may request any agency of the Executive Branch of Government to furnish it with such information, advice, *funds* and services as may be useful for the fulfillment of the Committee's functions under this order."[3] As Lynda Robb, chair of the advisory committee, interpreted this, "The Committee will take tin cup in hand and proceed from door to door to try to eke out its existence."[4] It is a tribute to the advisory committee's dedication and initiative that without a budget (the President's Council on Physical Fitness had a budget of $800,000, and the Committee on the Agenda for the 80's, over a million dollars) it was able to produce the final report, *Voices for Women.* The report includes 165 recommendations, most of which reaffirm policy recommendations of earlier commissions which have not been achieved. New areas of concern ranged from women's health to housing to combatting sexual harassment on the job. Pay equity—the notion of paying equal wages for work of comparable worth—was boldly recommended.

Another significant addition was a recommendation that the Office of Management and Budget require federal agencies to assess the effects of their programs on women as part of the regular program review process. Unfortunately, this excellently documented report was presented to President Carter only weeks before he left office and the present administration is unlikely to follow up on the recommendations. The recommendations, however, may well yet have a significant impact as state and local commissions use the documentation to effect change in their own communities.

STATE AND LOCAL COMMISSIONS

Most commissions on the status of women are units of government—they are created and mandated to work on behalf of women, either by executive order or by legislation in the form of statutes, county ordinances, or municipal laws. Since they are sanctioned by government, they enjoy the same rights as other government agencies, and therefore acquire the prestige and aura associated with officialdom, position, and power. This distinguishes them from nongovernmental organized women's groups such as NWPC, NOW, and the League of Women Voters, which share many goals, including ratification of the ERA.

Since they enjoy the authority and power of government, the question posed by this chapter is: how effective have they been in exercising their power and influencing public policy?

State and local commissions perform several basic functions: (1) education; (2) lobbying; (3) administrative or budgetary oversight; and (4) a very few commissions receive and resolve complaints alleging sex discrimination. The commissions devote the greatest portion of their time to educational activities—sponsoring conferences, holding hearings and workshops, publishing newsletters, and distributing materials on women's concerns. Educational activities serve two purposes: they raise the awareness of women's issues in the community, and they gain visibility for the commissions. Educational activities have the advantage of being relatively noncontroversial and therefore they attract little political opposition.

Many of the educational functions, especially as they relate to Title IX (Education Amendments Act), have the additional advantage of raising the consciousness of men and winning them over in support of the women's movement. More recently, the distribution of pamphlets such as ones on the new sexual harassment guidelines or "What to do if you are a battered woman," have resulted in calls of help from men who are concerned about protecting their wives, sisters, and daughters. Numerous men have been enlightened by discussions of sex-role conditioning which limits both sexes' options. In a recent newspaper article, a male commissioner, a political scientist and feminist, commented that "Men are oppressed, too, and some of man's oppression is also women's oppression. When women are liberated, then men also will be liberated."[5]

State and local commissions also devote substantial amounts of time to lobbying. State commissions monitor the state legislative process, occasionally initiate policy proposals, direct grass-roots lobbying campaigns, and lobby office holders directly; local commissions occasionally lobby at the state level as well. Lobbying occurs more informally at the local level as commissions work with local officials for changes in government operations. One specialized form of lobbying performed by both state and local commissions is for the appointment of more women to public office, both elective and appointive. Several commissions maintain talent banks of women willing to serve in order to expedite the appointment process.

In performing the oversight function, CSWs monitor state and local government operations as they affect women. They engage in a variety of activities ranging from investigation of personnel procedures and law enforcement practices, to review of government publications for sexism, to monitoring of government contract awards for discriminatory practices, activities which usually provoke resistance on the part of the bureaucracy. While several commissions have made progress in revising job tests or eliminating veterans' preference points, only limited progress has been made in hiring or promoting women to high-level positions in local government.

The function of complaint resolution is probably one of the most successful ways for commissions to bring about change. If CSW staff who process the complaints are professional, the commission acquires professional recognition and respect in the community. Most people against whom complaints are filed, whether related to employment, credit, or education, are anxious not to be found in noncompliance with governmental rules. If the complaint has sub-stance they are relieved to have a local agency assist them to rectify the discrimination. This provides staff with an excellent opportunity to raise the consciousness of management, banking officials, and administrators. The Santa Clara County CSW, which has acquired this kind of rapport through complaint resolution, reports that many of the industries against whom com-plaints have been filed are very supportive of the commission. They frequently provide financial support, in-kind contributions, and request the commission to hold workshops for them on such subjects as "Women and Men Managing Together Effectively," and "How to Deal with Sexual Harassment on the Job." If social change is to occur, it is important that the change agents find avenues through which to carry their messages. Complaint resolution can and has provided such a vehicle.

Another common concern of CSWs is violence against women. Numerous commissions have worked for reform of rape laws and offer crisis counseling for rape victims. Several commissions have established shelters for battered women. CSWs also work in the field of education, examining sex bias in public school materials, monitoring Title IX implementation, and providing school programs on nontraditional careers for women. Other issue areas frequently mentioned by commissions are child care, displaced homemakers, women's health (including abortion), welfare reform, ERA ratification, and programs for women offenders.[6]

Many CSWs have supported the ERA boycott of unratified states. Others have supported reproductive freedom as well as the gay rights movement. They have thus become targets of opposition groups who seek their abolition and/or defunding. Such political opposition has resulted in energy, expertise, and resources being expended simply to ensure a commission's continued existence. It is not surprising that, as the taxpayers' groups, the antiabortion movement, and the Moral Majority mount their repetitive attacks on CSWs, executive directors and commissioners suffer from burn-out symptoms. The fast turnover of staff and commissioners as a result of such efforts is both time-consuming and enervating. Staff have to be retrained and frequently find themselves reinventing the wheel, reorganizing the fragmented community, and reestablishing their power base. This lack of continuity and gap in sustained effort slows down the process of change.

CHALLENGES TO THE COMMISSION MOVEMENT

The establishment of a women's commission does not guarantee its survival. The willingness of state and local commissions to involve themselves in controversial issues has aroused strong political opposition in recent years from groups opposed to the women's movement. These groups have used a variety of strategies in their attempts to dismantle the commission.

One source of vulnerability for CSWs has been their structure. Only 11 state commissions have independent statutory authorization; the remaining commissions either report to the governor or to a state administrative agency. These commissions have been jeopardized by changes in political leadership, as evidenced by the fate of one of the longest-operating and most active state commissions, Wisconsin's, which was dissolved by a strike of the new governor's (Leo S. Dreyfus—R.) pen in 1979. In Massachusetts, the newly elected governor (Edward King—D.) used the appointment process to eliminate the commission's feminist orientation. In 1979 he dismissed all 40 members of the commission and appointed 25 new members, several of whom were distinguished by their leadership of anti-ERA and antiabortion groups.[7] Even when commissions are independent, they operate under the limitations of the statute or ordinate which created them. As an example, very few commissions can effectively investigate complaints because they lack subpoena power.

The Santa Clara County CSW, which has the authority to obtain subpoena powers, if necessary, from its board of supervisors, has never had to resort to such a procedure. The commission has found that an employer, bank manager, landlord, or school administrator who is unwilling to cooperate in an investigation can easily be persuaded to do so if the legislation mandating the CSW gives it authority to seek subpoena powers. The mere threat on the part of the CSW to place the matter on the public agenda is in most cases sufficient to coerce the party subtly to be more cooperative. In Santa Clara County the complainant is assured confidentiality; similarly, the person or agency against whom the complaint is lodged is accorded the same courtesy. It is only when the latter is unwilling to cooperate that the CSW will be reluctantly forced to "go public" by seeking subpoena powers. Unfortunately, most local and state governments have been unwilling to include such an option in their ordinance.

Another critical problem for state and local commissions is funding, which has generally been more limited for women's commissions than for other types of commissions. Only 12 state commissions have budgets over $150,000; the remainder receive support ranging from $2,000 to $100,000, with four state commissions receiving no funds at all.[8] Of 38 local commissions responding to a 1980 survey, only eight had budgets of $50,000 to $300,000; the remaining commission budgets ranged from $175 to $40,000, with five commissions reporting no funding. While CETA funds, federal grants, and private donations have been used to supplement commission activities, these sources of funds are temporary and are regularly threatened by the termination of federal programs.

Recent austerity trends among state legislatures and voters have further jeopardized CSWs. The Utah legislature totally eliminated funding for the commission. The Washington commission went out of existence after the voters rejected a proposal for the statutory establishment of a commission in a referendum. The Colorado commission was terminated by a legislative committee during "sunset" hearings. (Such hearings are often required by legislators, during which time the policy makers evaluate the performance of boards and commissions as well as the need for their continued existence.) In all three states the commissions were strongly opposed by right wing and right-to-life groups which used budget-cutting appeals, as well as attacks on the commissions' "immoral" activities, to defeat them.[9] In all, between 1977 and 1980, nine state commissions were abolished and several more are threatened.

Most recently, responding to pressure from the Moral Majority, a California senate finance subcommittee voted to eliminate funding for the California CSW. Just a few weeks before this action, a very conservative anti-ERA and antiabortion senator from Orange County was appointed to serve on the California CSW. One wonders why a senator who is totally committed to the elimination of a CSW would want to serve on it, except to use it as a platform to oppose its work?

Even when commissions are free from external threats, they are often beset by internal divisions as a result of the selection process for commissioners. Criteria for appointment to CSWs usually include the requirement that commission members should reflect diverse socioeconomic backgrounds. Commissioners as a whole come from varying classes and occupational, age, and ethnic groups and must bridge their background differences in working together.[10] This has frequently resulted in conflict and in heated discussions about what priorities ought to be judged the most important. Sometimes the debates have been so protracted that the commission has taken considerable amounts of time to set priorities and goals. Commission appointments are frequently used as political patronage with the result that appointees have loyalties to the people who put them in office and are reluctant to oppose them. More seriously, because many commissioners are political appointees, they often lack exposure to the women's movement and experience in working on women's concerns.

The selection process has had some very negative consequences for CSWs. While some commissions report a high level of solidarity, others are beset by factionalism. The lack of awareness of women's issues on the part of many appointees has made it necessary for the commission staff to spend valuable time on consciousness raising with the members. The inexperience of many commissioners puts a tremendous strain on staff who must be prepared not only to implement decisions but also to educate members about the issues and to work with them in developing policy positions.

Commissioners have the advantage of gaining experience in the political process, learning how to influence public policy, and how to function in a bureaucracy. The commissioners acquire expertise by participating in public hearings, advocating for legislative change, and working toward getting more women elected to public office. Many of them have gone on to elected or higher administrative offices as a result of involvement at the commission level.

Can CSWs continue to play a significant role in promoting women's concerns? Women's commissions have the potential to perform several critical roles in relation to the women's movement. First, because women's commissions are governmental bodies, they speak with greater authority than private interest groups both to office holders and the public. While they are not able to use the normal political rewards and punishments to pressure office holders because they are governmental bodies,[11] they have the tool of publicity, positive and negative, to persuade politicians, bureaucrats, and private interests such as employers to attend to women's concerns.

Second, CSWs provide a link between women's interest groups and political actors. Commissions provide access for interest groups to public officials. Equally important, they may be used as a vehicle for public officials seeking to reach out to the grass roots, although, in fact, commissions have not made much use of their ability to facilitate communication in this direction.

Last, CSWs are a means of institutionalizing women's concerns in the policy-making process. While individual interest groups attempt to influence policy in their particular areas, women's commissions, by virtue of their location in government, are privy to the broad range of governmental activity, most of which has an impact on the status of women but which is rarely scrutinized from that perspective. Clearly, CSWs are not the only agencies which might perform this role; as President Carter's advisory committee recommended, policy makers could be required to produce women's impact statements as part of the program review process. Women's commissions have a greater stake, however, than regular bureaucrats in performing this function as well as potentially greater expertise.

Speaking with authority, facilitating two-way communications, monitoring policy making—the performance of these roles is an enormous potential benefit to the women's movement. While some CSWs have performed effectively in these roles, others have failed to establish themselves as anything more than study groups or have encountered such intense political opposition that their existence has been jeopardized.

Yet the 1980s may, more than ever, be a time for women's commissions. Why? As the economic and political environments favor a move away from large centralized federal programs toward greater state and local control over government services, CSWs at the state and local levels will have the opportunity to influence increasingly important policy decisions. In particular, President Reagan's proposal to consolidate numerous social programs into block grants to the states will shift the focus of decision making on many issues to state legislatures and executives. Some of the many programs affecting women to be included in block grants are family planning, child welfare services, Title XX social services, community action programs, and the Women's Educational Equity Act Program. Strong state CSWs could play a vital role in overseeing the budgetary process and lobbying for appropriations for women.

A second critical role for CSWs in the 1980s is to generate support for new issues at the state and local levels. Many developing policy concerns such as pay equity, alternative work patterns, sexual harassment, and treatment of female offenders need to be communicated more broadly to policy makers and women activists. CSWs are in an excellent position to perform this role through their publications and hearings.

If CSWs are to survive the onslaught of right wing and taxpayers' groups they must develop a stronger base of grass-roots support. They need more cooperative working relationships and endorsements from local and statewide women's groups. State CSWs need to develop a mutual support base with local commissions so that local commissions will pressure local legislators to rally behind them; in return, state CSWs need to highlight the work of the local commissions. Lastly, state CSWs need to get out to localities with programs so that more women activists learn what they are doing. It would be a sad irony if women's voices were removed from the scene just when state and local governments are becoming more significant decision-making arenas for women. Thus, commissions must use both the threat from the right and the new spotlight on state and local government to mobilize support for their continued existence.

Notes

1. Irene L. Murphy, *Public Policy on the Status of Women* (Lexington, Mass.: Lexington Books, 1973), p. 21.

2. Ibid.

3. Lynda Robb, in a speech before the National Association of Commissions for Women, Biltmore Hotel, New York City, June 12, 1980.

4. Ibid.

5. *Peninsula Times,* May 5, 1981, p. 11.

6. *Commissions for Women: Moving into the 1980s* (Washington, D.C.: U.S. Department of Labor, 1980), p. 8.

7. Anita Miller, "The Uncertain Future of Women's Commissions," *Graduate Woman* (May/June, 1980), pp. 13–14.

8. *Commissions for Women: Moving into the 1980s,* p. 5.

9. Anita Miller, "The Uncertain Future of Women's Commissions," pp. 13–15.

10. Jennifer Dorn Oldfield, "A Case Study on the Impact of Public Policy Affecting Women," in *People and Public Administration,* ed. Phillip E. Present (Pacific Palisades, Calif.: Palisades Publications, 1979), pp. 112–120.

11. Some commissions, in fact, are required to get permission from the board of supervisors or city council before lobbying.

Chapter 4

Women and Public Policy: An Overview*

Jo Freeman

The emergence of a body of federal policy aimed at improving the status of women is a recent phenomenon. Except for the suffrage amendment, ratified in 1920, no laws in which sex was a major concern were passed prior to 1963. There were, however, a plethora of state statutes, common-law precedents, and judicial interpretations which defined the status of women rather explicitly. Woman's position in society—her rights and responsibilities, opportunities and obligations—was essentially determined by her position in the family, i.e., her role as a wife and mother.

A brief overview of the laws and judicial interpretations which have affected the position of women amply illustrates the way in which their family status formed the basis for their social status. Not surprisingly, laws on women are most frequently found under the rubric of "family law." The basic principle of family law derives from Blackstone's codification of the English Common Law. This provided the primary precedent for American judicial interpretation of the marital relationship. That relationship was succinctly summed up by Justice Black in 1966 when he defined it as resting "on the old common-law fiction that the husband and wife are one . . . [and] that . . . one is the husband."[1] The fundamental basis of the marital relationship is that husbands and wives have reciprocal, not equal, rights. The husband must support the wife and children, and the wife must render services as a companion, house-wife, and mother in return. While this doctrine is largely unenforceable in an ongoing marriage (the courts have held that they should not intervene in an intact relationship[2]) and only occasionally applied in divorce,[3] the courts have found it so fundamental to public policy that contracts before or during marriage altering the nature of these reciprocal duties have been held illegal.[4]

* Copyright © 1982, by Jo Freeman.

While the division of labor in the marital relationship has never been successfully challenged in the courts, most of the traditional disabilities of the married woman were chipped away by the activities of feminists in the 19th century. The substantive and procedural disabilities incurred by women upon marriage in that century were sufficient to make her legally nonexistent. When Edward Mansfield wrote the first major analysis of *The Legal Rights, Liabilities and Duties of Women* in 1845, he summed up:

> It appears that the husband's control over the person of his wife is so complete that he may claim her society altogether; that he may reclaim her if she goes away or is detained by others; that he may use constraint upon her liberty to prevent her going away or to prevent improper conduct; that she cannot sue alone; that he may maintain suits for injuries to her person; and that she cannot execute a deed or valid conveyance without the concurrence of her husband. In most respects she loses the power of personal independence, and altogether that of separate action in legal matters.[5]

The passage of many married women's property acts eventually

> granted married women the right to contract, to sue and be sued without joining their husbands, to manage and control the property they brought with them to marriage, to engage in gainful employment without their husbands' permission, and to retain the earnings derived from the employment.[6]

Nonetheless, a plethora of minor and major disabilities remained prior to the start of the current feminist movement. There have been many changes in the last decade, but the rights and responsibilities of married men and women have yet to be equalized.[7]

As the courts have made clear, the traditional concern of public policy with women's family role formed the basis of her legal existence.[8] One of the earliest cases of sex discrimination to reach the Supreme Court was instigated by Myra Bradwell who had been refused a license to practice law by Illinois. The court ruled against her in 1872 and a concurring opinion by Justice Bradley explained that

> The constitution of the family organization, which is founded in the divine ordinance, as well as in the nature of things, indicates the domestic sphere as that which properly belongs to the domain and functions of womanhood. The harmony, not to say identity, of interests and views, which belong, or should belong, to the family institution is repugnant to the idea of a woman adopting a distinct and independent career from that of her husband. . . .
>
> It is true that many women are unmarried and not affected by any of the duties, complications, and incapabilities arising out of the married state, but these are exceptions to the general rule. The paramount destiny and mission of woman are to fulfill the law of the Creator, and the rules of civil society must be adapted to the general constitution of things, and cannot be based upon exceptional cases.[9]

This rationale has persisted until the last few years. What it reflects is a refusal to see women as individual people apart from their identity as members of a class with a specific social role. Most of the similar state and Supreme Court cases on women used language which did not talk about the rights of individual persons under the Constitution, but the rights of "the sex." The judges have not discussed the rights of citizens but the rights of "women as citizens." The Constitution nowhere mentions the rights of "women as citizens" or even differentiates between different rights of different citizens, but judicial opinion has established such a differentiation.[10]

This was especially evident in the long fight at the turn of the century to pass protective labor legislation in an attempt to curb sweatshop conditions. Originally intended to apply to men and women, the Supreme Court declared a violation of the right to contract those laws which applied to both sexes, but in 1908 allowed those that applied only to women on the grounds that women's

> physical structure and a proper discharge of her maternal functions—having in view not merely her own health but the well-being of the race—justify legislation to protect her. . . . The limitations which this statute places upon her contractural powers . . . are not imposed solely for her benefit, but also largely for the benefit of all. . . . The reason . . . rests in the inherent difference between the two sexes, and in the different functions in life which they perform.[11]

With this precedent, the drive for protective legislation became distorted into a push for laws that applied to women only—on the principle that half a loaf was better than none. While this policy was also favored by male labor leaders who saw the "protection" of women as a way to limit competition, it is safe to say that the Supreme Court contributed significantly to the proliferation of state protective laws for women only. The court has long since rejected the thinking that prevented protective legislation for men, but it expanded its 1908 decision to restrict the activities of women further. The specific case was concerned only with protecting women from strenuous labor but it has been cited in support of the barring of women from juries,[12] different treatment in licensing occupations,[13] and the exclusion of women from state-supported colleges.[14]

The attitude that women's family role made sex a legitimate basis for classification was expressed by the court as late as 1961 when it upheld the conviction of a Florida woman by an all-male jury for murdering her husband by assaulting him with a baseball bat. When she argued that the state law's provision that women were not required to serve on juries unless they registered such a desire with the clerk of the circuit court virtually ensured their elimination from the jury pool and thus violated her Fourteenth Amendment rights, the court replied that

Despite the enlightened emancipation of women from the restrictions and protections of by gone years, and their entry into many parts of community life formerly considered to be reserved to men, woman is still regarded as the center of home and family life. We cannot say that it is constitutionally impermissible for a State, acting in pursuit of the general welfare, to conclude that a woman should be relieved from the civic duty of jury service unless she herself determines that such service is consistent with her own special responsibilities.[15]

It was not until after the start of the current feminist movement that the courts began to display a different attitude. The majority of cases exhibiting this turn-around were those generated by Title VII of the 1964 Civil Rights Act, which prohibited discrimination in employment on the basis of race, color, religion, national origin, or sex.[16] Subsequently, when many employers continued to refuse to hire or promote women to some jobs on the grounds that their working conditions violated state protective laws, women often took them to court. Typical was the judgment of the Fifth Circuit in 1969 when it refused to adopt a "stereotyped characterization" that few or no women could safely lift 30 pounds:

Title VII rejects just this type of romantic paternalism as unduly Victorian and instead vests individual women with the power to decide whether or not to take on unromantic tasks. Men have always had the right to determine whether the incremental increase in remuneration for strenuous, dangerous, obnoxious, boring or unromantic tasks is worth the candle. The promise of Title VII is that women are now to be on equal footing.[17]

The promise of Title VII was not made by Congress with full knowledge of what it was doing. When the 1964 Civil Rights Act was being debated, one of the most controversial sections was that prohibiting discrimination in employment. In one of many ploys by its opponents, Rep. Howard W. Smith of Virginia proposed a floor amendment to add "sex" to the protected groups. While this provision was strongly supported by the women of the House, especially Rep. Martha Griffiths (D-Mich.) who claims she intended to make such a proposal herself, most of the House liberals opposed it, as did the Women's Bureau of the Labor Department. Nonetheless, neither side felt strongly enough to spend more than a few hours in debate (the "sex" amendment had never come up in committee) and little of this was serious. Instead, both Smith and the liberal opponents played the provision for all the laughs it was worth and the ensuing uproar went down in congressional history as "Ladies Day in House."[18]

Looked at from the perspective of a decade later, the prohibition of employment discrimination on the basis of sex is one of the most profoundly redistributive decisions of our century. According to Lowi, redistributive policies are the most far-reaching and least understood of the different types of public policies. They involve the redistribution of social resources from one major group to another.[19] Given the highly sex-segregated nature of the job market,[20] much of it due to direct discrimination, accomplishment of the idea embodied in Title VII would significantly change the employment opportunity structure of our society in favor of women.

The opportunity structure would be altered even more radically if the idea of affirmative action, as required by Executive Order 11246 amended by Executive Order 11375, would actually see fruit. This order, which prohibits discrimination on the basis of race, color, religion, or national origin by all holders of federal contracts (covering one-third of the labor force), was issued by President Johnson on September 24, 1965 as the latest in 25 years of executive orders on racial discrimination by federal contractors. While the addition of "sex," in Executive Order 11375, was not made until over two years later, it was done relatively effortlessly, in large part owing to the precedent of Title VII. The executive branch sought to bring its policies into conformity with those of Congress.[21]

If we ignore for the moment issues of implementation, the nonchalance with which this major redistributive decision was made by both the executive and legislative branches raises the question of how this could happen. There was no organized women's movement in 1964, not much of one in 1967, and little pressure from other women's organizations. Only the most naive would assume either that the men of the Eighty-eighth Congress and the Johnson administration were sufficiently sympathetic, or the women sufficiently powerful, to effect this policy with minimal opposition.

True, the Equal Pay Act had finally passed Congress in 1963 preceded by hearings on the economic problems of women. But not only is the Equal Pay Act barely if at all redistributive, it is more indicative of congressional negligence than interest. First proposed in 1868 at the National Labor Union Convention, equal pay did not become a federal issue until World War I, when many women were encouraged, even required, to move into jobs that had formerly been held by men during the national emergency. Since women traditionally worked for less money than men, the two to four million women suddenly added to the work force created a concern that they would depress wage rates and that men would be forced to work at lower rates after the war. Actions were taken to preclude this by requiring that women replacing men be given equal pay. Some of this momentum carried over after the war, and in 1919, Montana and Michigan enacted the first state equal-pay laws. It was many years before others followed their lead. World War II saw a repeat of what had happened in the first war, and the introduction of the first equal pay bills into Congress. But it was not until 1945 that a major bill with broad coverage was debated and it took "eighteen years of persistent, unsuccessful efforts to get an equal pay bill to the floor of Congress"[22] before the federal government was added to the roster of 19 states that prohibited wage differences on the basis of sex. Even this law applied to only 61 percent of the labor force.

Throughout all the early agitation for equal pay, the major concern of Congress and the supporting unions was the "prevention of women's wages from undercutting the wages of men."[23] Women's unions and feminists supported equal pay out of dedication to principle and feelings of working-class solidarity but always with the proviso that there would be training programs for "working girls" to provide women with the same opportunities as men to earn decent wages.[24] For the most part they never achieved decent wages because male unions continued to exclude women from membership and apprenticeship programs while employers,[25] when faced with a choice between male and female employees, chose women only if they would work for lower wages. Then as now equal pay was irrelevant without equal job opportunity. If anything, the Equal Pay Act *"increased job security for men* by discouraging the replacement of men with lower paid women."[26]

Thus, it was left to Title VII and Executive Order 11375 to begin, almost unnoticed, a major revolution in public policy. Why it was initially unnoticed, at least by those who passed it if not by those who were affected by it, lies in the disregard that women have normally experienced from political leaders and in the routine nature of the addition of "sex" to the pantheon of prohibited discriminations.

It is practically a truism among political scientists that most policy making in the United States is incremental. Great decisions are rarely made; in fact they are often strenuously avoided by our legislators. Instead policy changes are made incrementally, adding a little bit here and there. Congress had been debating and passing legislation to curtail race discrimination in employment since the 1930s.[27] What the early legislation lacked was a means of enforcing this prohibition. The most controversial aspect of Title VII was not the idea of prohibiting discrimination, but that of creating an independent enforcement agency, the Equal Employment Opportunity Commission (EEOC). And, needless to say, while the EEOC did come into existence with Title VII, it did so without any real enforcement powers (until amended by another incremental change in 1972).[28]

Adding "sex" to "race, color, religion and national origin" as a prohibited discriminatory practice, was, from the perspective of white, male legislators in the early 1960s, only another increment. Women may have comprised more than half the population and at that time more than one-third of the labor force, but it was Congress' failure to be cognizant of this fact and not their sensitivity to it that permitted sex discrimination to be prohibited so easily. In fact, the only people apparently aware of what the addition of the word "sex" might mean were some women, in and out of Congress, who approved of it, and blacks with their white supporters, who were quite hostile to the idea. In their view, women were well off and should not be allowed to compete with minority groups for a share of the slim federal pie.[29]

Ironically, it was overcoming the hostility of civil rights activists, not Congress, that was the first major battle of the new feminist movement. In fact, this hostility was a major contributor to the formation of the movement. From the very beginning, the EEOC sought to ignore the sex provision as much as possible. The first executive director, Herman Edelsberg, even stated publicly that it was a "fluke" that was "conceived out of wedlock." He felt "men were entitled to female secretaries."[30] Not everyone within the EEOC, however, was opposed to the sex provision. Two of the five EEOC commissioners and at least one of its lawyers argued that it would be taken more seriously if there were "some sort of NAACP for women" to put pressure on the government. As government employees they could not organize such a group but they spoke privately with those whom they thought could do so, including Betty Friedan and many members of the state commissions on the status of women. Partly as a result of their urgings, the National Organization for Women (NOW) was formed in 1966 and directed a good portion of its initial energies toward changing the guidelines of the EEOC.[31]

Even before NOW's organizing conference in October 1966, the temporary steering committee had fired off telegrams to the EEOC urging it to change its ruling that help-wanted advertisements listed under separate male and female columns were not a violation of Title VII. In the following months, NOW added two more demands: (1) that the *bona fide occupational qualification (bfoq)* exemption of Title VII[32] not be interpreted so as to permit employers in states with "protective labor legislation" to use those laws as rationales for denying equal job opportunity; and (2) that the *bfoq* specifically not be interpreted to allow airline requirements that stewardesses must retire upon marriage or reaching age 32. While the EEOC ruled favorably on the latter demand, the first two issues were resolved by the courts years later. After much waffling, the EEOC finally decided on August 14, 1968 that sex-segregated want ads were illegal but found itself powerless to enforce that ruling until the Supreme Court acted five years later.[33]

The EEOC's initial attitude toward "protective labor legislation" was contrary to that of most feminists, and in line with that of organized labor. While these laws differed from state to state, the bulk of them limited the hours a woman could work, usually to 48 per week, and the amount of weight she could lift on the job, generally to 35 pounds. Feminists had long opposed these laws, arguing that their major use was to prevent women from earning overtime pay, from being promoted to jobs in which overtime might be required, and from gaining access to jobs which occasionally require lifting more weight than the limit.[34] Most labor unions, including the women within their leadership ranks, had long supported these laws, believing that they were a necessary protection for women. The EEOC supported this perspective and refused to investigate several complaints made by women when their denial of job opportunities was justified by employers on the basis of state protective laws. Many women took their cases to court where the decisions were repeatedly in their favor. Concomitantly, the attorneys general of several states ruled that their states' protective laws were succeeded by Title VII and therefore void.[35] As a result, the EEOC was forced to change its interpretations to keep them in accord with judicial rulings, and by 1969 "concluded that such laws and regulations . . . will not be considered a defense to an otherwise established unlawful employment practice."[36]

These court rulings not only changed the EEOC guidelines but paved the way for passage of the Equal Rights Amendment. The ERA was the only feminist-supported proposal which had a long political history, and opposition, behind it. First proposed in 1923 by the National Women's Party as a means to eradicate sex-specific laws, it was introduced into every subsequent Congress. The Senate passed it in 1950 and 1953, but only with the addition of the "Hayden rider" that the amendment "shall not be construed to impair any rights, benefits, or exemptions now or hereafter conferred by law, upon persons of the female sex."[37] Such an amendment was anathema to feminists, but demanded by organized labor as they did not want protective labor legislation undermined.

By 1970, however, not only had numerous court decisions preempted this argument by voiding protective labor laws in favor of Title VII, but extensive research was beginning to disclose that labor laws applying to women only probably caused them greater harm than benefit. Thus, at the very time the emerging feminist movement was turning its attention to ERA, its only major organized opposition was fading from the field.

In February of that year, roughly two dozen NOW members disrupted hearings on the 18-year-old-vote amendment being held by the Senate Judiciary Subcommittee on Constitutional Amendments to demand that hearings be scheduled on the ERA. At the same time the official Citizen's Advisory Council on the Status of Women endorsed the ERA and issued a definitive legal analysis originally written by a founder of NOW. As momentum gathered, the Senate Judiciary Subcommittee called hearings on the ERA in May, and the White House released the report of the President's Task Force on Women's Rights and Responsibilities with its endorsement of the ERA. Then at the 50th anniversary conference of the Women's Bureau on June 13, Secretary of Labor-designate James D. Hodgson added the Labor Department's endorsement. The Women's Bureau and the Labor Department had traditionally opposed the ERA out of deference to organized labor.[38]

The pivotal move, however, had occurred two days before when Rep. Martha Griffiths (D. Mich.) filed a petition to discharge the House Judiciary Committee from further consideration of the amendment as it had not been considered during the previous 20 years. Griffiths was one of the few members of Congress who had both the interest and resources to make such an audacious move. This rarely used procedure requires the signatures of a majority (218) of House members and is generally opposed as upsetting the routine procedures of Congress. Griffiths was not only a long-time supporter of women's bills, but had sat for several years on the powerful Ways and Means Committee. In this position she had accumulated a lot of political favors which she had not used up for home district bills. Consequently, she was not only able to get the requisite number of signatures, but they included most of the chairmen of the standing committees, people who normally disapprove of such petitions. The House passed the ERA in August, as the result of a strenuous lobbying campaign by several women's organizations. The Senate proved more obdurate, and added a rider to permit prayer in public schools. This killed the amendment for the Ninety-first Congress.

The Ninety-second Congress saw the beginning of an enormous 15-month campaign by a potpourri of feminist, women's, establishment, and liberal organizations covering most of the political spectrum, allied with women in several congressional offices and adminsitrative bureaus. Two to three dozen volunteer lobbyists virtually lived in the halls of Congress for the duration, and Congressman Tip O'Neill (D.-Mass.) was quoted as saying that the ERA generated more mail than the Vietnam War.[39]

During this time the ERA's strongest opponent, the AFL-CIO, ceased its active opposition. This change was a result of the voiding of protective labor laws by Title VII, and the efforts of the director of the Women's Bureau to convince women unionists to support the ERA. Consequently, by the time the ERA was sent to the states for ratification, on March 22, 1972, its opposition consisted largely of the John Birch Society, the Communist Party, the National Council of Catholic Women, and only a few members of Congress.

For the first year the ERA appeared to have clear sailing as 28 states quickly ratified it. Then, in January 1973, a national "Stop ERA" campaign surfaced, headed by noted right-winger Phyllis Schlafly. Her initial efforts were not taken seriously by the pro-ERA organizations, but when only a few more states ratified it in the next couple years they gradually realized they could not take support for granted. They also began to realize that "Stop ERA" was not an isolated movement, but part of a resurgence of right wing sentiment which was additionally opposing busing to achieve racial integration in the schools, and the legalization of abortion.[40]

These realizations did not bring immediate action by feminist groups. At the time the ERA was sent to the states, the movement had not yet made an impact in southern and rural states, and these were more than the one-quarter needed to prevent passage of a constitutional amendment. As the movement had always been highly decentralized, looking upon national direction of local activities as something to be avoided, the coalition that passed the ERA on the national level could not be easily replicated in the states, and the national coalition did not have the foresight and support to recruit and train "outside agitators" for those states that could not generate sufficient resources within. Not until 1977, with three states to go and only two years left to gain them, did the women's movement begin a nationally coordinated effort.

Regardless of the outcome of the ERA, the two-year final battle to get it through Congress had some very beneficial side effects. Primary among them was the climate it created in Congress that there was serious constituency interest in women's rights. The ERA was probably the easiest of all the legislative issues to generate mail about from a wide cross section of the population. Once the question of the value of "protective" legislation was out of the way, courtesy of Title VII, there was something vaguely immoral about the inequitable application of the Constitution. Since there was as yet little organized opposition to women's rights legislation in general, this mail created the impression that there was strong support for the whole policy area. As Clausen points out, there is no simple explanation of congressional decision making. Of the five major policy areas he analyzed, he found that constituency pressure was the most significant in the area of civil rights and liberties.[41] While his analysis was done before there were women's rights issues, it is reasonable to assume that as they are basically civil rights issues, and as there was minimal opposition from the parties and the major interest groups, they would follow the same pattern.

The other major side effect of the ERA struggle was the establishment of liaisons between feminist organizations and congressional staff. The ERA lobbying effort both provided an excellent excuse to establish working relationships with and to educate staff, and facilitated the discovery of sympathizers among them. The incipient network this created made it easier to know whom to approach for information and/or support for other bills.

With this impetus, the Ninety-second Congress passed a bumper crop of women's rights legislation—considerably more than the sum total of all relevant legislation previously passed in the history of this country. In addition to the 1972 Equal Employment Opportunity Act and the ERA, there were: (1) Title IX of the Education Amendments Act which prohibits sex discrimination to federally aided education programs; (2) the addition of sex discrimination to the jurisdiction of the U.S. Commission on Civil Rights; (3) a Child Development Act that would have provided free day care for children in families of four or more with an annual income of less than $4,300, and a sliding fee scale for families with higher incomes, if it had not been vetoed by Nixon; (4) an amendment to the Revenue Act that allowed parents with combined incomes of up to $18,000 per year to make income tax deductions of up to $400 a month for child care; and (5) a plethora of anti-sex discrimination provisions to several federally funded programs including health training, revenue sharing, Appalachian redevelopment, and water pollution.

For our notoriously slow-moving Congress, this is a very impressive achievement. When one considers the 95 years it took for equal pay to go from idea to act, and the decades spent fighting for civil rights legislation, it barely seems possible. Even if one allows for the strenuous lobbying and letter-writing campaigns, and the lack of an organized opposition, the relatively easy manner in which the women's liberation movement achieved higher legislative gains so quickly requires some explanation.

The answers lie with several major assets that the movement had which have never been properly credited for its success. The first was the incipient network of supporters referred to earlier. This network provided the movement with easy access to many key points of decision making—a major goal of any interest group. Most such groups, especially if they emerge from dissident social movements, spend years developing sympathetic contacts on key committees and in key agencies. Because of the many women in government in a position to give information, if not always to make decisions, who were potentially sympathetic to the feminist cause, the movement had to invest comparatively little time in acquiring access. Together, the women in government and those in feminist and related groups formed a ready "policy system"—a phenomenon common to any significant policy area.[42]

The second contributing factor is incrementalism. Virtually all of the relevant legislation in the early 1970s involved amendments to or parallels of minority civil rights legislation. Minority civil rights organizations have spent decades trying to enact into law bills which the women's movement achieved in only a few years. Other, predominantly white, interest groups have spent equally long amounts of time trying to achieve their legislative goals. In effect, the civil rights movement broke the ground for the feminist movement. It created both a precedent for and a model of action in the area of sex discrimination. Once the main redistributive decision had been made about the addition of sex discrimination as an area of federal policy, all that was really necessary was pressure to apply it consistently.

Third, politicans are always looking for ways to please their constituents that will not cost them support from other quarters. Since half the voters in their districts are women, and there were, in the early 1970s, no major differences of opinion among those groups claiming to represent women's interests, it was easy to persuade legislators that a vote for the feminist position would please their female constituents without incurring the wrath of other groups. The momentum begun by the Ninety-second Congress was sustained by subsequent Congresses. In the late 1970s dozens of bills passed Congress prohibiting sex discrimination in virtually all Federal programs—particularly those which also prohibit discrimination on the basis of race, religion, and national origin.

Later Congresses, however, saw some divergence from the pattern of incrementalism, as well as the first serious successes by a growing opposition. The Ninety-third Congress saw passage of the first law prohibiting sex discrimination for which there were no parallel prohibitions for race: the Equal Credit Opportunity Act. The disabilities women experienced in obtaining credit were first brought to national attention at the 1972 hearings of the National Commission on Consumer Finance.[43] It became clear at these hearings that outmoded assumptions made it more difficult for single women to get credit than men, and virtually impossible for a married woman to obtain credit in her own name—even when she was the major provider of her family's financial support. Creditors were also unwilling to count a wife's income to determine eligibility when a married couple applied for credit jointly.[44]

Although credit discrimination had not previously been prohibited on the basis of race, this area was otherwise similar to those for which discrimination was prohibited in the Ninety-second Congress. There was a "policy vacuum," i.e., few established positions and no real opposition. Even the credit industry was aware that its practices eliminated from borrowing consideration people it would otherwise consider credit-worthy. It confined its lobbying to minimizing the paperwork requirements of the law.[45] No public expenditures were required. Women's groups were able effectively to mobilize support and technical expertise through use of the "policy system." Those women and couples most likely to benefit from additional eligibility for credit were those most likely to be politically active or to contribute to campaigns.

Although the initial bill was introduced by Rep. Bella Abzug (D.-NY), the bill which was eventually passed was sponsored by a Republican senator from a southern state—William R. Brock (Tenn.). At the time he was a presidential hopeful, and no doubt thought his sponsorship of such a bill would bring him the support of women's groups on what was essentially a conservative issue. Precisely because he was a conservative, his unswerving support was crucial to the eventual passage of the bill, despite opposition from some unexpected quarters. The source of this opposition was a female Democratic member of the House—Leonor Sullivan (Mo.)—who was chair of the subcommittee scheduled to hold hearings on the bill. She refused to hold hearings on the grounds that the most appropriate legislation would prohibit discrimination against all groups. This obstacle was overcome through some parliamentary maneuvering, and the final bill passed overwhelmingly. Two years later prohibitions of discrimination on the basis of race, religion, and national origin were added to the act.

The same Congress saw the other major departure from the pattern of incrementalism in the passage of the first laws aimed directly at eliminating sex-role stereotyping, not just prohibiting discrimination. The Women's Educational Equity Act provides grants for the design of programs and activities to eliminate stereotyping and to achieve educational equity. The funding is not extensive (and of the initial products from these grants only a few look promising) but the mere existence of such a program represents a federal commitment to social changes of which the policy makers are probably not aware. Support for eliminating sex-role stereotyping in vocational education was added two years later.

Of somewhat less significance than the Women's Educational Equity Act, but reflecting a similar departure from simple incrementalism were laws to create a National Center for the Control and Prevention of Rape and an amendment to the Foreign Assistance Act requiring that particular attention be given to "programs, projects and activities which tend to integrate women into the national economies of foreign countries."

As a general rule, equalizing access to various institutions and prohibiting discrimination may assist sex-role changes but does not really instigate them. A major exception to this are those policies which gradually integrate women into the military. Women have served intermittently in the armed forces for most of this century but their participation has been highly restricted. Until 1967 there was a quota on women of two percent of the armed forces, and the requirements for their enlistment were higher than those for men.

With the passage of the ERA by Congress in 1972, the abolition of the draft in 1973, and the continuing decline in the birth rate which was depleting the supply of young men, the Pentagon decided to expand women's participation. The military then began what has been the only truly successful affirmative action program for women. In only four years women's participation in the armed forces increased to five percent, the occupations open to female enlisted personnel expanded from 35 percent to 80 percent, and the proportion of women assigned to traditionally male jobs quadrupled.[46]

Most of these changes were achieved administratively, but a few required amending the relevant statutes. Thus, the ages at which men and women could enlist were equalized in 1974, women were admitted to the military academies in 1975, and benefits for spouses were equalized by a Supreme Court decision in 1973. Since most of the restrictions on women's participation in the armed forces are not incorporated in the law, the Pentagon has been able to pursue its policy changes without congressional approval.

Yet these policies are not anticipated to lead to a female participation rate of greater than seven percent, and while women can legally serve in most combat positions—in fact they are trained for many—there is no expectation that they will actually be put in these positions in the forseeable future. Needless to say, the reinstitution of the draft, or another war, could radically change the current projections either way.

Objections to the possibility of drafting women or putting women in combat have been a significant argument in preventing ratification of the ERA. Detractors have ignored the fact that while the ERA would require women to be drafted if men were, it would not require that women actually face combat. Women can currently be drafted into combat positions if Congress and the military so desire. Yet this issue was raised again when the ERA returned to Congress for the first time in seven years. It returned because the National Organization for Women was afraid that the seven-year deadline for ratification would arrive on March 22, 1979 without the necessary three-fourths of the states having voted their support. Consequently, NOW asked Congress to extend the deadline.

Such a request was totally unprecedented. Of the 26 amendments to the Constitution, only five of those proposed in the last 60 years have had deadlines—always seven years—before which the states had to ratify. The deadlines were always met, and since there was no vocal opposition to the ERA in the early 1970s, the inclusion of such a deadline in this proposed amendment was not an issue, until it became apparent that it probably would not be met.

The idea of extending the deadline was actually conceived by two feminist law students in Los Angeles who were writing a term paper. They reasoned that if Congress had set the deadline, Congress could extend it, and furthermore, since the deadline was specified in the enabling resolution, not the proposed amendment itself, extension should only require a majority vote, not the two-thirds required for constitutional amendment. They brought their idea to the attention of the editor of the *National NOW Times,* who lived in Los Angeles; she sold it to NOW president Ellie Smeal, who in turn persuaded Rep. Elizabeth Holtzman (D.-N.Y.), a member of the House Judiciary Committee (which considers constitutional amendments) that it was feasible. Everyone else thought it was absurd.

Despite initial negative reactions by representatives, journalists, and other opinion makers, logic and lobbying eventually prevailed. In its attempt to extend the deadline, NOW essentially tapped the anger of an enormous number of women who felt the movement was declining after having achieved only some of its goals, but who felt personally powerless to do anything about it. NOW channeled this anger and energy into letters and marches on Washington. Only July 9, 1978, the anniversary of the death of Alice Paul, author of the ERA, NOW organized a march of 100,000 women on the Capitol, despite so little advance publicity that many feminists did not know it was being planned. Three months later, after the House had passed the extension but when it appeared that the Senate would adjourn without doing so, NOW brought over 5,000 people into Washington on five-days notice to rally at and lobby in the Senate. Less than two weeks later the Senate passed the extension. In the interim NOW had maintained a fully staffed lobbying operation on the Hill, with local chapters collecting signatures on petitions and encouraging people to write letters.

This originally impossible victory may still prove to be a pyrrhic one. First of all, to gain the necessary votes, NOW compromised its initial demand of a seven-year extension into one of three years, three months, and eight days. (June 30, 1982 was agreed on to meet the exigencies of state legislative schedules.) NOW organizers already knew that they would probably not get the remaining three states to ratify by lobbying alone. There just were not any "undecideds" left among the current state legislators. This meant that success required an electoral strategy: pro-ERA forces would have to identify and defeat enough "antis" in marginal districts to gain the votes necessary when each state legislature met again. In the United States, it is very hard to make significant changes in the composition of a legislature in only one election, unless there is an issue of overwhelming importance. The states which have not ratified are by and large conservative states which react strongly to national pressure. Thus, while an electoral strategy might work over the period of two or three elections, trying to achieve it in only one was a real gamble. It was a gamble that lost. Since 1979, there was only a slight increase in "pro" legislators, but not a significant one.

Second, the spin-off effects of the original ERA campaign were not duplicated by the campaign for the extension; in fact it may have had the opposite result. Instead of viewing the outpouring for the ERA extension as generalized support for the entire women's rights policy area, members of Congress appear to be interpreting it as indicating that women will sacrifice other issues in exchange for support on the ERA.

This attitude, and the reasons for it, were particularly evident when Congress debated President Carter's proposals for reorganizing the civil service. The only major proposal to be defeated was that modifying the preference given to veterans when they seek civil service jobs. The proposed modification would not have abolished the preference for hiring veterans; it would merely have restricted it to a one-time use within 15 years of discharge (and this was a compromise from the original proposal of 10). Since 98 percent of all veterans are male, this gives men a decided advantage over women when competing for civil service positions. As the statistics indicate, veterans preference has resulted in significantly fewer women (and minorities) being hired or achieving high grades than would have been the case had they competed on equal terms. Women comprise 41 percent of those who pass the entry-level professional and administrative exam, but only 27 percent of those who are hired. Male veterans comprise 20 percent of those who pass but 34 percent of those actually hired. Women constitute 41 percent of the civilian labor force, but only 30 percent of the civil service. Veterans are 25 percent of the labor force, but hold 48 percent of all federal civil service jobs. Since many veterans are career military officers, retired after only 20 years with excellent pensions, training, and experience, they hold 65 percent of the three highest grades in the civil service, while women hold only three percent.

The modification proposals were defeated, despite strong administration backing, because the veteran's organizations opposed them vigorously; and NOW's attention was diverted to the ERA extension. While the other national feminist groups strongly supported modification of veterans' preference, they were not able to educate and mobilize their members on this issue sufficiently to have an impact.

Increasingly successful opposition to feminist positions has been emerging around abortion and is likely to spread to other issues. The pro-choice movement preceded and was independent of the women's movement, but once abortion was recognized as an important feminist issue, the overlap among supporters of each movement has been enormous. Similarly the anti-choice movement, which emerged with pro-choice victories in the late 1960s, and crystallized with the January 1973 Supreme Court decision abolishing most abortion laws, began independently of the anti-ERA forces but has merged significantly with them.

Since the Supreme Court's decision was a constitutional interpretation, it would take a constitutional amendment to change it totally. Anti-choice congressmen have proposed several, but none of them has gotten out of committee. The strategy of the anti-choice groups has therefore focused on whittling down the use of abortion.[47] Most of their efforts have been on the state level, as it is state laws that regulate medical procedures. On the national level, they have focused on eliminating the use of federal funds to pay for abortions. Thus amendments have been passed to prohibit the use of foreign aid or family planning funds for abortions, and to deny them to military personnel or Peace Corps volunteers. But the biggest battles, and the most significant results, have been over the use of Medicaid funds for abortions. Medicaid pays for health care of those individuals and families considered to be living in poverty. Each year, funds for Medicaid must be made available by Congress as part of their budgetary appropriations for the departments of Labor, and Health, Education, and Welfare (now Health and Human Services). Each year there has been an amendment prohibiting the use of these funds for abortions. The first year this amendment failed to pass. But in 1976 funds were denied for abortions except in cases of rape or incest or for those necessary to save the life of the mother. Legal action charging that this was discriminatory against poor women—the only ones who depend on Medicaid for health care—was initially successful. But when the lower court's decision was appealed to the Supreme Court, it held—to the surprise of pro-choice forces—that while the government could not prohibit abortions, it was not required to pay for them. Every vote over Medicaid appropriations since then has seen eligibility defined still more narrowly. Today Medicaid pays for virtually no abortions.[47] Most abortions are still covered through private health care plans, but with the possibility of national health insurance becoming greater, it may well happen that abortions will be available only to those who can pay for them.

Although encroachments on the availability of abortion have been the major success of antifeminists, this is not their only area of attack. Their greatest concerns, and feminists' greatest failures, are on almost any issue that touches on the family. In fact, even before abortion became a national issue, laws to provide child-care services were vetoed by two presidents on the grounds of their "family-weakening implications." Since then, Congress has been less than enthusiastic about promoting federally sponsored child care.

These failures point out the biggest challenge to developing future public policy affecting women: breaking the tradition that a woman's obligations and opportunities are largely defined by her family circumstances. While most of the legislation, administrative decisions, and court rulings of the last decade have ignored women's family status, they were able to do so because the particular issues were economic ones, and in a time of an expanding economy and expanding welfare rolls, it seemed expeditious, even conservative, to enhance a woman's right to support herself.

But if present trends continue, the next few years should see more and more women competing with men and each other, for fewer and fewer jobs. The lack of jobs and the declining birthrate may well lead national policy makers to decide, as they did in the Depression, to restrict employment opportunities to "one per family." (This was proposed in the public service employment component of Carter's welfare reform program, but was not passed by Congress.)

It is still assumed that the principle economic unit is the two-parent family, *one* of whom is the primary wage earner, with the other a dependent. It is this assumption that feminist theory must challenge. Feminist proposals must recognize that all adults should have responsibility for the support of themselves and their children, regardless of their individual living situation, and that all are entitled to policies that will facilitate carrying out this responsibility regardless of sex, marital, or parental status. Acceptance of this idea would require an entire reconception of women's role in the labor force, of what is a family and of what our social obligations to it are.

The current attitude toward the employment of women can best be characterized as supporting "equal employment opportunity." Though much improved over earlier views, this one asserts that women who are like men should be treated equally with men. It accepts as standard the traditional male lifestyle, and that standard in turn assumes that one's primary responsibility should and can be one's job, because one has a spouse (or spouse surrogate) whose primary responsibility is the maintenance of house and family obligations. Women whose personal lifestyle and resources permit them to fit these assumptions, could, in the absence of sex discrimination, succeed equally with men.

Most women cannot, however, because our traditional conception of the family, and women's role within the family, makes this impossible. Despite the fact that only 20 percent of all adults live in units composed of children plus two adults, only one of whom is income producing, our entire social and economic organization assumes that this is the norm. Consequently, couples who share family responsibilities, or singles who take them all on, pay a price for deviancy. The fact that a majority of the population is paying this price has brought about some reforms, but a total reorganization is necessary.

This reorganization must be one which abolishes institutionalized sex-role differences, and the concept of adult dependency. It needs to recognize the individual as the principle economic unit, regardless of what combinations individuals choose to live in, and to provide the necessary services for individuals to support themselves and their children. In pursuit of these goals, programs and policies need to make participation by everyone in the labor force to the full extent of their abilities both a right and an obligation. They should also encourage and facilitate the equal assumption of family responsibilities without regard to sex, as well as develop ways to reduce conflict between the conduct of one's professional and private lives.

Unfortunately, there does not exist in either the government or the women's movement any means to translate these ideas into specific policies, coordinate their passage, or oversee their results. With few exceptions, policy development is generally a patchwork of individual ideas, group preferences, and chance events. It is rare that one sees an attempt at long-range strategy by any interest group or institution; the few groups that do develop such strategies rarely have the resources to carry them out. This means that those policies on women most likely to appear in the future and those that build on the precedents of the past are unlikely to transform sex roles or change the traditional division of labor.

Given that antidiscrimination as a focal point will only take the movement so far, the reactive nature of policy formation, the lack of coordination among feminist groups, and the general antiintellectualism of American society, the likelihood is all too great that we will enter another blind alley like that of "protective labor legislation." As should be clear from its history, protecting women from some of the working conditions that men faced seemed like a good idea to most at the time, but in the long run only served to hinder women's progress. Not only did such policies encourage sex segregation of jobs, but they also discouraged even those employers who might have been willing, or pressured, to put women in the occasionally more strenuous but always better paying jobs.

While the outlines of the next blind alley can already be seen, few people are pointing it out. This blind alley is one which sees the married couple as the basic economic unit. It starts from the assumption that it is socially desirable for one class of adults to be economically dependent on another, and seeks to reform some of the difficulties and uncertainties that dependency might create. The classes I am referring to are those of "breadwinners" and "dependent spouses." While in theory members of either sex can be members of either class—or even change classes occasionally—in practice the sex of each class is largely predetermined, as is the fact that few men will opt to be dependent spouses if they can avoid it. Since the high divorce rate and the greater longevity of women make it very likely that those who choose to be "dependent spouses" will not always be spouses, policies are emerging to facilitate a transition. Such a transition is necessary, but transitional programs should be ones which eventually eliminate the need, i.e., eliminate the class of "dependent spouses." They should not be programs which permanently transfer dependency from "breadwinners" to society in general, nor should they encourage dependency for a major portion of one's life by extolling its benefits and minimizing its costs. Instead, transitional policies should educate women to the reality that they are ultimately responsible for their own economic well-being, and are entitled to the opportunities to achieve it.

Needless to say, the consequences of revising our policies to focus on the individual rather than the family as the basic economic unit, deliberately eradicate the sexual division of labor in both the family and the work force, establish equal participation in the labor force as a right as well as an obligation, and institutionalize the support services necessary to achieve the above, would not be felt only by women. Such policy changes would reverberate throughout our economic and social structure. Thus, one should not anticipate their achievement in the near future. But one will not be able to anticipate their achievement at all until the ideas are raised and the need for change understood. To do this the women's movement needs to return to its origins and begin the process of questioning and consciousness raising over again.

Notes

1. *United States* v. *Yazell* 382 U.S. 341 (1966) J. Black dissenting.

2. *McGuire* v. *McGuire* 157 Neb. 226, 59 N.W. 2d 336 (1953).

3. Citizen's Advisory Council on the Status of Women, *The Equal Rights Amendment and Alimony and Child Support Laws* (Washington, D.C.: U.S. Government Printing Office, 1972), cites cases and statistics indicating that alimony is rarely given (in less than 2 percent of the cases) and then usually only for a few years. Child support is similarly honored more in the breach than in the action. According to one study, 62 percent of those fathers ordered to pay child support are out of compliance within a year, and 42 percent never make any payments. Stuart Nagel and Lenore Weitzman, "Women as Litigants," *Hastings Law Journal 23* (1971): 190.

4. A good discussion of this is to be found in Lenore J. Weitzman, "Legal Regulation of Marriage: Tradition and Change," *California Law Review 62* (July–September 1974): 1259–63. The relevant cases include *Miller* v. *Miller* 132 Misc. 121, 228 N.Y.S. 657 (Sup. Ct. 1928); *Graham* v. *Graham* 33 F. Supp. 936 (E.D. Mich 1940); *Vock* v. *Vock,* 365 Ill. 432, 6 N.E. 2d. 843 (1937); *Norris* v. *Norris,* 174 N.W. 2d 368 (Iowa Sup. Ct. 1970); *Garlock* v. *Garlock,* 279 N.Y. 337, 18 N.E. 2d 521, 522 (1939); *Mathews* v. *Mathews,* 2 N.C., App. 143, 162 S.E. 2d 697, 698 (1968).

5. Edward Mansfield, *The Legal Rights, Liabilities and Duties of Women* (Salem, Mass: Jewett and Co., 1845), p. 273.

6. Leo Kanowitz, *Women and the Law: The Unfinished Revolution* (Albuquerque: University of New Mexico Press, 1969), p. 40.

7. Women's Bureau, U.S. Dept. of Labor, *Handbook on Women Workers* (Washington, D.C.: U.S. Government Printing Office, 1975). ch. 9.

8. Jo Freeman, "The Legal Basis of the Sexual Caste System," *Valparaiso Law Review 5* (Spring 1971): 211–12.

9. *Bradwell* v. *Illinois,* 83 U.S. (16 Wall.) 130, 141–142 (1872) (J. Bradley, concurring). See also *Ex Parte Lockwood,* 154 U.S. 116 (1893).

10. Blanche Crozier, "Constitutionality of Discrimination Based on Sex," *Buffalo University Law Review 15* (1935): 723.

11. *Muller* v. *Oregon,* 208 U.S. 422 (1908).

12. *Commonwealth* v. *Welosky,* 276 Mass. 398, 414, 177 N.E. 656, 664, (1931), *cert. denied,* 284 U.S. 684 (1932).

13. *Quong Wing* v. *Kirkendall* 223 U.S. 59, 63 (1912); *People* v. *Case,* 153 Mich. 98, 101, 116 N.W. 558, 560 (1908); *State* v. *Hunter,* 208 Ore. 282, 288, 300 P. 2d 455, 458 (1956).

14. *Alldred* v. *Heaton,* 336 S.W. 2d 251 (Tex. Civ. App.), *cert. denied,* 364 U.S. 517 (1960); *Heaton* v. *Bristol,* 317 S.W. 2d 86 (Tex. Civ. App.), *cert. denied,* 356 U.S. 230 (1958).

15. *Hoyt* v. *Florida,* 368 U.S. 57 (1961).

16. 42 *U.S.C.* 2000e.

17. *Weeks* v. *Southern Bell Tel.,* 408 F. 2d 288, 236 (5th Cir. 1969).

18. For a thorough documentation of this event, see Caroline Bird, *Born Female: The High Cost of Keeping Women Down* (New York: David McKay, 1968), ch. 1. For a blow-by-blow account of the floor happenings, see *Congressional Record,* House, February 8, 1964.

19. For an analysis of his three major categories of public policy—distributive, regulatory, and redistributive—see Theodore J. Lowi, "Distribution, Regulation, Redistribution: The Functions of Government," in *Public Policies and Their Politics,* ed. Randall B. Ripley (New York: W. W. Norton, 1966) pp. 27–40.

20. Edward Gross, "Plus Ça Change . . . ? The Sexual Structure of Occupations Over Time," *Social Problems 16* (1968): 198–208; Francine D. Blau, "Women in the Labor Force: An Overview," in *Women: A Feminist Perspective,* ed. Jo Freeman (Palo Alto, Calif.: Mayfield, 1975) p. 211–26.

21. Jo Freeman, *The Politics of Women's Liberation* (New York: David McKay, 1975), pp. 193–94.

22. Bessie Margolin, "Equal Pay and Equal Employment Opportunities for Women," *New York University Conference of Labor 19* (1967): 297; see also Morag MacLeod Simchak, "Equal Pay in the United States," *International Labour Review 103,* 6 (June 1971).

23. Elizabeth Baker, *Technology and Women's Work* (New York: Columbia University Press, 1964), p. 412.

24. Alice Henry, *Women and the Labor Movement* (New York: George H. Doran, 1923), p. 129; Edith Abbott, *Women in Industry* (New York: D. Appelton, 1910).

25. Gail Falk, "Sex Discrimination in Trade Unions," in *Women: A Feminist Perspective,* ed. Jo Freeman (Palo Alto, Calif.: Mayfield, 1975), pp. 254–76.

26. Caruthers Gholson Berger, "Equal Pay, Equal Employment Opportunity and Equal Enforcement of the Law for Women," *Valparaiso Law Review 5* (Spring 1971): 331.

27. The principle of equal job opportunity was first passed by Congress in the Unemployment Relief Act of 1933, (48 *Stat.* 22). It provided "that in employing citizens for the purpose of this Act no discrimination shall be made on account of race, color, or creed."

28. See Freeman, *The Politics of Women's Liberation,* pp. 177–84. Prior to 1972, the EEOC could only investigate and conciliate complaints. Afterwards, it had the option of taking recalcitrant violators to court.

29. For an example of this thinking, see U.S. Commission on Civil Rights, *Jobs and Civil Rights,* by Richard P. Nathan, Clearinghouse Publication No. 16 (Washington, D.C.: U.S. Government Printing Office, April 1969), pp. 50–55.

30. Herman Edelsberg, at the New York University 18th Conference on Labor, cited in *Labor Relations Reporter 61* (25 August 1966): 253–55.

31. Freeman, *The Politics of Women's Liberation,* pp. 54–55.

32. Sec 703 (e) of Title VII reads: "it shall not be an unlawful employment practice for an employer to hire . . . on the basis of his religion, sex or national origin in those certain instances where religion, sex or national origin is a bona fide occupational qualification reasonably necessary to the normal operation of that particular business." The EEOC has interpreted this exemption narrowly.

33. *Pittsburgh Press Co.* v. *Pittsburgh Commission on Human Relations,* 93 S.Ct. 515 (1973).

34. Susan Deller Ross, "Sex Discrimination and Protective Labor Legislation," in *The Equal Rights Amendment,* Hearings before the subcommittee on Constitutional Amendments of the committee on the Judiciary, U.S. Senate, pp. 5–7 May 1970, p. 408.

35. Equal Employment Opportunity Commission, *Laws on Sex Discrimination in Employment* (Washington, D.C.: U.S. Government Printing Office, 1970), p. 10.

36. Commission guidelines of 19 August 1969.

37. 96 *Cong. Rec.* 872–3 (1950); 99 *Cong. Rec.* 8954-5 (1953).

38. Freeman, *The Politics of Women's Liberation,* pp. 209–13.

39. Ibid., pp. 213–18.

40. Most abortions were legalized by a Supreme Court decision in January 1973 that laws restricting abortions in the first trimester and most in the second trimester were an unconstitutional violation of the right to privacy. *Roe* v. *Wade,* 410 U.S. 113, *Doe* v. *Bolton,* 410 U.S. 179.

41. Aage R. Clausen, *How Congressmen Decide: A Policy Focus* (New York: St. Martin's Press, 1973), p. 221.

42. Ralph K. Huitt, "Congress, the Durable Partner" in *Lawmakers in a Changing World,* ed. Elke Frank (Englewood Cliffs, N.J.: Prentice-Hall, 1966), p. 19; Douglass Cater, *Power in Washington* (New York: Random House, 1954), p. 22; Ernest S. Griffith, *The Impasse of Democracy* (New York: Harrison-Hilton Books, 1939), p. 182.

43. Joyce Gelb and Marian Lief Palley, "Women and Interest Group Politics: A Case Study of the Equal Credit Opportunity Act," *American Politics Quarterly 5* (July 1977): 331–52.

44. National Commission on Consumer Finance, *Consumer Credit in the United States* (Washington, D.C.: U.S. Government Printing Office, 1972), pp. 498–99.

45. Gelb and Palley, "Equal Credit Act," p. 336.

46. Martin Binkin and Shirley J. Bach, *Women and the Military* (Washington, D.C.: The Brookings Institution, 1977), ch. 2.

47. Nadean Bishop, "Abortion: The Controversial Choice," in *Women: A Feminist Perspective,* ed. Jo Freeman (Palo Alto, Calif.: Mayfield, 1979), pp. 64–80.

Part III
Economics:
Changing Directions

Introduction

Since the end of World War II, revolutionary changes have occurred in American women's family and work lives. These changes, which began slowly, escalated dramatically in the 1970s. In terms of family life, women have been moving away from patterns of early marriage and childbearing to longer periods of "singleness." In 1970, the median age of women at first marriage was 20.8 years; by 1978, it had risen a full year to 21.8 years.[1] In this same period the number of women aged 25 to 34 who had not married increased by 111 percent as compared to a mere 17 percent increase in the number of women who were married and living with a husband.[2] These patterns among younger women are associated with rising levels of education leading to the choice of a career as an alternative to early marriage.

Many younger women have also been delaying childbearing until their 30s. While population experts are debating whether the delay of childbearing will result in a temporary or permanent lowering of fertility rates, recent studies have shown that the longer a woman postpones childbearing after marriage, the less inclined she is to have a child.[3]

The trends toward later marriage and childbearing have been accompanied by a dramatically increasing divorce rate resulting from the liberalizing of divorce laws and the greater social acceptance of divorce. Between 1970 and 1978 the number of divorced women of all ages increased by 94 percent; the number of divorced women in the 25- to 34-year-old age group increased by 170 percent.[4] The rising divorce rate has not been accompanied by a rising rate of remarriage.[5] Widowhood is also on the rise owing to increasing female longevity.[6]

Later marriage, rising divorce rates, and increasing widowhood have all created a rapidly expanding group of single women whose economic needs are different from those of single women 40 years ago. Most significantly, the rising divorce rate has greatly increased the number of female single heads of households; from 1970 to 1978 alone, the number of female heads of households increased by 46 percent as compared to 27 percent for male heads of households.[7] Over 80 percent of all single-parent households are headed by women.

The most disturbing aspect of these statistics is that families with female heads of households represent the largest, and only increasing, category of families below the poverty line. Female-headed families with no husband present make up only 15 percent of families but 48 percent of all poor families.

71

The percentage of families headed by black females below the poverty line (55 percent) was more than twice that of families headed by white females (27 percent).[8]

Housing data further illustrate the plight of the female head of household. In 1978, while 76 percent of married couples and 63 percent of men with no wife present owned or were purchasing homes, only 48 percent of families headed by women with no husband present resided in nonrental housing.[9] Whether owning or renting, single women pay a larger proportion of their incomes (57 percent) for shelter than single men (30 percent) or married couples (22 percent).[10]

The revolution in women's family lives has been accompanied by a revolution in women's work lives. From the end of World War II until 1980, the participation rate of women in the work force has almost doubled from 27 percent to 52 percent. The largest increase has been among married women with children under 18; from 1970 to 1978 alone, there was an 11 percent increase in the number of working mothers.[11] This expansion of the female labor force is expected to continue; projections for 1995 based on current rates indicate a labor force increase of 34 percent for all female workers as compared to 14 percent for males.[12]

The movement of women into the work force has been occasioned by many factors: the necessity of supporting a family as a single head of household, the need to supplement a husband's income, increasing levels of education among women, and greater acceptance of working women. Although most women work out of economic necessity, they have generally high levels of job satisfaction. Not unexpectedly, job satisfaction is highest among younger women, women at the higher occupational levels, women who perceive their husbands as favorable toward their working, and women whose children are over six years of age.[13]

The movement of women into the work force has not, however, brought any improvement in women's economic status relative to men. The earnings gap between full-time male and female workers has actually increased over the last 25 years. In 1955, women earned 64 percent of what men earned; by 1980, women dropped down to 59 percent. While the earnings gap decreases with higher levels of education, college-educated women in 1977 earned only two-thirds as much as college-educated men and had, on average, lower incomes than men with only high school educations.[14]

One of the primary causes of the earnings gap is occupational segregation by sex in the U.S. labor force. While women have been entering the labor force at a rapid rate, almost 80 percent work in clerical, service, or unskilled industrial jobs which are low-paying and low-status. In recent years, the labor force has become more sex-segregated rather than less. As an example, in 1972 there were three female clerical workers to every one male; by 1978, female clerical workers outnumbered males by four to one.[15] While there have been impressive *percentage* increases of women in some high-paying, predominantly male job categories such as craft workers and managers, the *absolute numbers* of women in these positions remains very small.[16]

What impact have these revolutionary changes in women's lives had on American economic policy? As seen earlier, women's economic status has become a growing public policy concern. The main thrust of public policy in the 1960s and 1970s was to ban sex discrimination in pay, hiring, training, and promotion. These policies have provided greater equity for a small number of women workers but they have done little to change the general condition of working women as a "secondary labor market."[17] The few programs which were initiated to educate, train, and recruit women for nontraditional jobs have done more to raise awareness about occupational segregation than to change the status quo.

Unless new policy directions are taken in the 1980s, the female work force of the future will have the same characteristics as today, except that it will be larger. The chapters in Part III describe new policy approaches to improving the economic status of women. Since 1963, equal pay for equal work has been official government policy. While considerable effort has gone into enforcing this policy, it has not succeeded in decreasing the earnings gap between men and women because men and women are not typically in "equal" jobs. Because the work force is highly sex-segregated, women's groups are now seeking to achieve pay equity, a policy which states that when women's work is of *comparable value* to men's work, pay should be equivalent. Chapter 5, by Kahn and Grune, describes the evolution of the issue, the lobbying and coalition-building efforts on behalf of pay equity, and the political obstacles to achieving pay equity as national policy.

Another relatively new policy approach involves alternative patterns of employment which are one means of enabling women to integrate their family and work roles better. As examples, job sharing and flexitime have been introduced in both the public and private sectors to allow individuals greater flexibility in arranging their work lives. While not aimed exclusively at women, these policies have profound implications for women attempting to manage dual roles as workers inside and outside the home. In Chapter 6, after surveying the literature on experiments with these policies, Stoper assesses the prospects for their broader adoption.

Housing policy directly affects the status of women as homemakers, mothers, and consumers. Women are caught in the bind of declining incomes relative to men and rapidly escalating housing costs. Rental discrimination against families with children has hurt female heads of households especially. Diamond examines women's housing needs and suggests new directions for housing policy in Chapter 7.

These policy approaches transcend issues of discrimination against women workers. They address fundamental concerns such as the value of "women's work," the need to integrate work and family roles, and the needs of women workers for housing as well as for employment. The policies described here are only a sample of the new thinking on women's economic needs. Other important issues include reform of the social security system to recognize the value of women's labor in the home and of the welfare system to end the dependency of low-income women. Finally, women's needs as workers are integrally associated with their needs as mothers. Economic policies must be developed in conjunction with policies concerning reproduction and child care; these will be considered in Part IV.

The struggle in the 1980s for new economic policy to keep pace with the revolution in women's lives will be waged in an environment hostile to policy innovation and government spending. Acceptance of new policy approaches necessarily involves educating policy makers regarding women's contributions to the general economic well-being. Ways to promote these new policies will be suggested in the conclusion of this volume.

Notes

1. *A Statistical Portrait of Women in the U.S.: 1978,* (Washington, D.C.: Bureau of the Census, U.S. Department of Commerce, February, 1980), p. 24.
2. Ibid., p. 21.
3. *San Jose Mercury News,* February 8, 1981.
4. *A Statistical Portrait of Women,* p. 5.
5. Ibid., p. 24.
6. Ibid., p. 25.
7. Ibid., p. 22.
8. Ibid., p. 95.
9. Ibid., p. 22.
10. Ibid., p. 22.
11. Ibid., p. 50.
12. Ibid., p. 43.
13. *Women and Work,* (Washington, D.C.: U.S. Department of Labor, 1977) pp. 16–17.
14. *A Statistical Portrait of Women,* p. 70.
15. Ibid., p. 54.
16. Ibid., p. 59–60.
17. *Women and Work,* p. 1.

Chapter 5

Pay Equity: Beyond Equal Pay for Equal Work

Wendy Kahn and Joy Ann Grune

Equal pay for equal work is now well established in American law. This principle, however, does not meet women's needs for economic equity because relatively few women hold jobs equal to men's. Patterns of job segregation have locked women into occupational ghettoes that are characterized by low wages. The principle of equal pay for work of comparable value seeks to raise wages for work performed predominantly by women which is comparable, though not identical, to work performed by men.

The easiest way to understand pay equity or comparable worth is to compare it with "equal pay for equal work." If a woman and a man are both sales clerks and are paid the same salary, that is "equal pay for equal work." If the woman is a sales clerk and the man is a stockroom clerk and they are paid the same salary because the value of their work is thought comparable, that is pay equity.

This chapter will focus on the role of public policies in the push for pay equity and their relationship to organizing. It will describe and evaluate national and state policies with an emphasis on litigation, agency enforcement, and new legislation.

BACKGROUND: OCCUPATIONAL SEGREGATION AND WAGE DISCRIMINATION

There are many reasons why one person might be paid more or less than the next: the effects of technology on the work place, the old traditions of wage setting, fluctuations in the work force itself, and discrimination. Although all these factors can adversely affect men as well as women, there is no question that women are much more frequently the victims of pay inequity.

Full-time year-round working women earn, on the average, 59 cents for every dollar earned by men. In 1979, the starting salary for a teacher in Montgomery County, Maryland (a predominantly female job requiring a bachelor's degree and two years' experience) was $12,323, while a starting salary for liquor store clerks in the same county (a predominantly male job requiring a high school degree and two years' experience) was $12,779.[1]

Studies which evaluate jobs on the basis of knowledge, skill, mental demands, accountability, and working conditions show that predominantly female jobs are paid roughly 20 percent less than predominantly male jobs of comparable worth. For example, a 1978 study of jobs in the state of Washington revealed the following:[2]

Evaluation Points	*Female Job—Salary*		*Male Job—Salary*	
93–94	Food Service Worker	$637.00	Truck Driver	$ 969.00
120	Key Punch Operator	$703.00	Stockroom Attendant	$ 816.00
192–197	Library Specialist (192)	$946.00	Carpenter (197)	$1,241.00

Studies by economists and other social scientists which control for such factors as education, training, years of experience, and overtime find similar "unexplained" disparities between men's and women's salaries.[3]

The overall disparity is the same as it was 15 years ago when women earned 59.6 cents of every dollar earned by men.[4] And this is despite successes in implementing the three major federal laws prohibiting sex discrimination in employment: the 1963 Equal Pay Act, Title VII of the 1974 Civil Rights Act, and Executive Order 11246.

Why does that basic disparity exist? Because, as columnist Ellen Goodman put it, "For every first woman construction worker, there are thousands of secretaries." She adds that 80 percent of the women in this country work in 25 job categories which are overwhelmingly "women's jobs."[5] The list is familiar: secretaries, clerks, librarians, nurses, retail salespeople, household workers.

Obviously, those jobs are low paid in comparison to "men's jobs." And obviously "equal pay for equal work" is not going to help a secretary, even if it does help a woman construction worker. The cause of the problem is as basic as the disparity in wages: job segregation by sex is a major characteristic of the work place.[6]

There are numerous sources of this segregation. A major source can be traced to federal and state governmental policies. Many state laws have excluded women outright from "men's jobs" such as mining, bartending, and police work. Such exclusions were upheld by the Supreme Court as late as 1948;[7] informal exclusion continues today.

"Protective laws" prohibiting night work and setting maximum hours for women, and limiting weights that women could lift were enacted by many states. These laws may have improved working conditions for women on the job, but also had the effect of disqualifying women for certain jobs or limiting their ability to perform those jobs fully. "Protective laws" were not struck down as inconsistent with Title VII of the Civil Rights Act of 1964 until the late 1960s.[8]

Federal antinepotism legislation in the 1930s pushed working wives out of the federal civil service. The enactment of veterans preference legislation, recently upheld by the Supreme Court in *Feeney, et al.* v. *Massachusetts,*[9] also limits women's employment opportunities.

Although many of the federal and state laws which limited employment opportunities for women have been changed, the impact of these laws cannot be erased overnight.

Despite recent affirmative action efforts, training for women in nontraditional occupations, and the increase in the number of working women, the extent of occupational segregation has not decreased. Between 1940 and 1970 the number of occupations with a high proportion of women (70–80 percent) rose markedly. By 1970, half the women were concentrated in only 17 occupations while half the men worked in more than 63 occupations.[10] In the late 1960s one-quarter of all employed women worked in just five jobs: elementary school teachers, secretaries, stenographers, household workers, bookkeepers, and waitresses.[11] The U.S. Department of Labor reports that of the 441 occupations identified in the Census' occupational classification system, women are concentrated in just 20 of them.

Another way of looking at the extent of occupational segregation is to compare the percentage of women in an occupation with the percentage of women in the total labor force. In November 1977, women represented 41 percent of the total labor force; they were 98 percent of all secretaries, 97 percent of all nurses, 94 percent of all typists, 95 percent of all household workers, more than 75 percent of all clerical workers, 64 percent of all service workers, less than 10 percent of skilled workers, less than 5 percent of top managers, and 3 percent of engineers.

In a 1978 report, the U.S. Commission on Civil Rights estimated that for men and women to be doing the same work, about two-thirds to three-fourths of the working women would have to change occupations.[12]

In 1979, for the first time in history, a majority of American women were in the labor force. Although many women have provided themselves with a measure of economic independence never before experienced, women's labor is still widely undervalued.

THE STRATEGIES: A FOCUS ON PUBLIC POLICIES

There are a number of possible strategies for dealing with women's low wages. Equal pay laws, upward mobility programs, and improved access to nontraditional jobs are essential components of an equal rights strategy, as are job supports such as child care, flexitime, and vocational training. But they are not enough.

Relatively few women hold jobs equal to men's. The absolute number of women in nontraditional occupations remains small and many nontraditional jobs are in industries that are not growing. While upward mobility programs have created new opportunities for thousands of women, there are thousands more entering the labor market via traditionally female jobs. Comparable worth is not a replacement for mobility programs. Instead, it is a way of addressing the economic crisis faced by the millions of women in feminized occupations who cannot or will not move up or over into traditionally male jobs.

The roots of the movement for pay equity can be traced at least back to World War I when the War Labor Board applied the principle of equal pay for work of comparable value in over 50 disputed cases. During World War II, the National War Labor Board again supported the principle. In 1942, the Board issued an order which authorized employers to make voluntary adjustments equalizing wage or salary rates paid to men and women for comparable quality and quantity of work on the same or similar occupations. This was at a time when a wage freeze was in effect. Later, the board applied the principle on a mandatory basis it had to decide. As was true in World War I, when the war ended, the program died.[13]

The beginnings of a national movement for pay equity did not emerge until the late 1970s with the spread of often independent initiatives to raise wages for women's work. These initiatives have been at state, local, and federal levels. They include legislation, lobbying, government enforcement, litigation, organizing, collective bargaining, research, job evaluation, public relations, publications, education, and coalition building. They have occurred through the determination of working women, unions, women's and civil rights organizations, researchers, lawyers, reporters, and government officials.

Job Evaluation Systems

Many mechanisms combine to lower wages for women's work. Among them are biased job evaluation systems, violations of labor laws by employers and unions, biased techniques used to determine wage rates, employer collusion in wage fixing, manipulation of potential labor pools, arbitrary depression of wage rates, and the expectation that women will work for less money than men.

To date, many comparable worth initiatives have focused on the role of biased job evaluation systems in reducing wages for women's work and on the potential of less biased systems in assessing comparable wage rates. A job evaluation system evaluates the worth of a job on the basis of criteria such as skill, effort, knowledge, mental demands, responsibility, physical effort, experience, and working conditions. Jobs are ranked according to their worth, and wages are set correspondingly, usually in reference to prevailing market rates.

Many public and private employers use job evaluation systems in salary setting. But in theory and in practice, job evaluation systems have discriminated against "women's jobs." Recent research has uncovered a number of ways in which sex bias enters job evaluation. These include: (1) the selection and weighing of factors for evaluation which tend to undervalue those skills, responsibilities, etc. utilized in predominantly female jobs (e.g., including "lifting" but not "manual dexterity" in the definition of "physical effort"; emphasizing "strength" rather than "visual acuity"); (2) the subjective nature of many decisions involved in job evaluation, which invites sex-biased judgments; and (3) employers often using more than one job evaluation system (e.g., one for plant jobs, another for office jobs) and therefore not being able to compare the worth of jobs across occupational groupings.[14]

Pay equity activists have researched and criticized job evaluation systems for their discriminatory content and have tried to develop and apply less biased systems for purposes of salary setting.[15]

Public Policies

On the federal level, pay equity activists have used public hearings, lobbying, education, and litigation to argue that existing law, (mainly Title VII of the 1964 Civil Rights Act and Executive Order 11246, amended by Executive Order 11375 to cover sex discrimination) applies to wage discrimination. At the state level, pay equity work has concentrated on new legislation mandating job evaluation studies of public employee jobs.

These efforts have occurred in conjunction with efforts to negotiate equity increases in collective bargaining contracts, to pressure for employer policy changes where there is no union, and to promote the clout of women through organizing. These different approaches have usually complemented each other, and many organizations promote all of them as they would all ultimately increase women's salaries.

Activities at the federal level. Many pay equity activities at the federal level have centered on the Equal Employment Opportunity Commission (EEOC), which is the federal agency that enforces Title VII of the Civil Rights Act passed by Congress in 1964. Pay equity advocates argue that since Title VII provides, among other things, that it is unlawful for an employer to discriminate with respect to compensation because of an individual's sex, the depression of wages for predominantly female jobs is a clear violation of *existing* law. Employers argued that Title VII could not be used to enforce comparable worth, claiming that its application should be restricted to identical jobs. For this argument, they cited the Bennett Amendment, which reads:

> It shall not be an unlawful employment practice under this Title for any employer to differentiate upon the basis of sex in determining the amount of wages or compensation paid or to be paid to employees of such employers if such differentiation is authorized by the provisions of §6(d) of the Fair Labor Standards Act of 1938, as amended, 29 U.S.C. §206(d) (i.e., the Equal Pay Act).

The Bennett Amendment was adopted near the end of consideration of Title VII by Congress, to ensure that the Equal Pay Act, which requires equal pay for equal work performed by women and men, could be reconciled with Title VII of the Civil Rights Act.

The June 1981 U.S. Supreme Court decision, *Gunther v. Washington,* resolved the Bennett Amendment controversy in finding that Title VII can be applied to jobs which are not identical. This decision and others are reviewed following this brief history of the government's enforcement efforts.

Enforcement Agencies. Under the leadership of Eleanor Holmes Norton, Chair of the EEOC appointed by President Carter, the EEOC began developing the basis for an enforcement policy on pay equity, although it did not initiate investigations of its own and never claimed that new EEOC guidelines were necessary. Both Norton and Dan Leach, Vice Chair of the EEOC, claimed in their public speeches that the sex-linked depression of wages for occupations was a violation of Title VII. The EEOC filed pro-comparable worth *amicus* briefs in the *Christiansen, IUE v. Westinghouse, Fitzgerald v. Sirloin Stockade* and *Gunther* cases. The EEOC also commissioned the National Academy of Sciences to analyze and evaluate existing methods of wage setting with a focus on job evaluation systems, including the extent to which current systems are biased by traditional stereotypes. The NAS issued an Interim Report to EEOC in February 1979, and a final report in August, 1981.

The EEOC also held Public Informational Hearings on Job Segregation and Wage Discrimination on April 28-30, 1980.[16]

These moves were in response to a number of pressures and influences, including the continuing wage gap between women and men, the cases filed under Title VII referred to above, and the increasing visibility of and organizing around the issue all over the country. Particularly important was the influence exercised by a nationwide network of lawyers and activists from unions, and women's and civil rights groups whose contact with Norton, as well as other EEOC staff, often predated her appointment as chair, and who created the momentum within which the EEOC began to formulate its positions.

During the Carter Administration, two other federal agencies, both within the U.S. Department of Labor, were also active on the pay equity front. The Women's Bureau, headed by Alexis Herman, worked both inside and outside the government as a clearinghouse on the issue. The Office of Federal Contract Compliance Programs (OFCCP) did its part, too. It has responsibility for enforcing Executive Order 11246 prohibiting discrimination by most federal government contractors. The Executive Order does not contain Bennett Amendment language, arguably limiting the reach of anti-sex discrimination language to situations involving equal pay for equal work. Under the executive order, OFCCP filed a complaint against Kerr Glass, alleging discrimination in pay. Male, unskilled, entry level carton stackers received higher pay than female, unskilled, entry level packing inspectors. At this writing, no decision has been issued in this case.

On December 30, 1980, after it received comments from both pay equity advocates and opponents, the OFCCP published regulations stating that "compensation practices with respect to any jobs where males or females are concentrated will be scrutinized closely to assure that sex has played no role in the setting of levels of pay."[17] On January 28, 1981, one day before these regulations were to be effective, the Reagan Administration published a notice deferring the effective date of these and other OFCCP regulations.[18] As of this date, advocates and opponents are presenting their positions to OFCCP on this regulation. The current administration is considerably less sympathetic to the position of pay equity advocates than was the Carter Administration. The direct effect of a change in administration on a change in policy positions is vividly reflected in this deferral action. The action also highlights the need for pay equity advocates to be mobilized at the federal level, but not to put all their eggs in the federal "basket."

Litigation. The meaning of the Bennett Amendment has been the subject of much litigation. On June 8, 1981, the United States Supreme Court decided *Gunther v. County of Washington, Oregon*.[19] In that 5-4 decision, the Supreme Court rejected the employer's argument that the Bennett Amendment restricts Title VII to equal work situations and the restrictions of the Equal Pay Act.

The plaintiffs in the *Gunther* case were prison matrons whose jobs were not identical or "equal" under the law to the all-male correctional officer position since the matrons, having so few female prisoners to guard, had a lower prisoner-guard ratio and also spent more of their time on less demanding clerical duties. The matrons alleged that the employer evaluated both jobs, determined that matrons should be paid 95 percent as much as correctional officers, but then only paid the matrons 70 percent as much.

The *Gunther* decision was not a green light to file suits based solely on an employee's claim that a predominantly female occupation is "comparable" to a predominantly male occupation, i.e., straight "comparable worth" claims.

The allegation in *Gunther* that the employer apparently ignored its own evaluation system in setting wages, to the disadvantage of the female job, was very significant to the Supreme Court. In effect, the Court concluded that the employer's ignoring the results of its own study was evidence of *intent* to discriminate against the women.

Prior to the Supreme Court agreeing to decide the Bennett Amendment issue in the *Gunther* case, some lower courts had held that the federal laws do not prohibit sex-based wage discrimination except when the women and men were doing "equal" work. These courts have been reluctant to interfere in what is perceived as the operation of a free market economy. The decisions in a Denver, Colorado case upheld a $100 a month wage advantage of tree trimmers over nurses. In ruling against the nurses who claimed their jobs were comparable to certain male jobs, the judge proclaimed the case "pregnant with the possibility of disrupting the entire economic system of the United States of America" (*Lemons v. City and County of Denver* [D. Colo. 1978].[20]).

In *Christensen v. Iowa,* the 8th Circuit Court of Appeals found that the University of Northern Iowa did not discriminate when it paid secretaries less than physical plant employees, even though the University's own internal study had placed the two categories in the same labor grade. The court accepted the University's justification that a higher pay scale for physical plant workers reflected the prevailing wage rate, stating:

> We find nothing in the text and history of Title VII suggesting that Congress intended to abrogate the laws of supply and demand or other economic principles that determine wage rates for various kinds of work. We do not interpret Title VII as requiring an employer to ignore the market in setting wage rates for genuinely different work classifications.[21]

On the other hand, even prior to the *Gunther* decision, other lower courts had concluded that women might be able to prove a violation of Title VII in wage discrimination cases even if their jobs were not "equal" to any men's jobs under the Equal Pay Act. In all those cases, there was evidence of something more than merely the women's claim that their jobs were "comparable" to some men's jobs.

For example, in *IUE v. Westinghouse,*[22] the employer's 1939 Wage Administration Manual, explained the practice of lowering the wages for women's jobs on such grounds as "the relative shortness of their activity in the industry," and "the general sociological factors not requiring discussions herein."

And in *Taylor v. Charley Brothers Company,*[23] the court found discrimination where the employer had maintained sex-segregated job classifications, had failed to consider female applicants for certain job categories and promotions, and had paid women less for work of comparable value to the employer. (In one department, women warehouse workers handled certain kinds of products, while in another department, men warehouse workers handled different kinds of products.)

The *Gunther* case opens the door to cases similar to the *Westinghouse* and *Charley Brothers* cases, but does not guarantee that the *Lemons* or *Christiansen*-type cases would be decided differently.

Thus, the *Gunther* decision was a very narrow one. It opens the door to bringing compensation discrimination claims under Title VII without the necessity of showing equal work. It does not establish what must be shown to prove discrimination. And the Court made it quite clear that it would not look with favor upon straight "comparable worth" cases. Very careful litigation strategy will be especially important to avoid the dangers of making bad law and closing the door which *Gunther* pushed open.

Already, a network of organizations and attorneys is being organized by the Litigation Task Force of the National Committee on Pay Equity to share information and attempt to coordinate litigation efforts and ideas.

Pay equity activists are hopeful that the victory for the plaintiffs in the *Gunther* case, will provide a mandate to employers to raise substantially the wages of millions of women in traditionally female occupations. It could also encourage employers and others to attempt to introduce federal legislation to amend Title VII expressly to exclude sex-based wage discrimination claims. If employers do so, supporters of pay equity will have to mobilize all of their resources to defeat the legislation.

The fact that the *Gunther* decision left unanswered so many questions about the scope of existing federal law reinforces the need for pay equity initiatives in addition to litigation and reinforces the danger in relying too heavily on litigation alone. State and local grass-roots campaigns with an emphasis on organizing, collective bargaining, and perhaps on new state legislation remain essential.

Activities at the state level. At the state level, as we indicated earlier, action on pay equity is as much a matter of forging new laws as it is of enforcing or interpreting old ones.

The language of many state antidiscrimination laws does not appear to exclude the concept of pay equity. To the best of our knowledge, however, there have been only two pay equity court cases filed under state law. Both were unsuccessful. A 1972 charge filed by the secretarial staff at Austin Community College in Austin, Minnesota, with the Minnesota Department of Human Rights, alleged that the state violated the Minnesota Human Rights Act by paying unskilled building and grounds workers in the community college system more than it paid secretaries, whose jobs required more education, skills, and responsibility. In the second case, *Tacoma-Pierce County Public Health Employees Association v. Tacoma-Pierce County Health Department,*[24] a group of nurses and therapists lost their claim that the county violated the state of Washington's antidiscrimination law by paying male employees working in sanitation positions more for jobs of comparable worth.

But there have been important policy initiatives in the states. The most frequent type is legislation or executive orders designed to identify the extent of wage discrimination against women. In 1974, Washington's Governor Dan Evans signed an executive order making Washington the first state to conduct a study with the explicit purpose of documenting sex discrimination in pay rates. A follow-up study was performed in 1976. Both studies found that "women's jobs" were paid approximately 20 percent less than "men's jobs" of comparable worth. Little remedial action has been taken, however. The cost required to bring the salaries of the predominantly female jobs up to the "comparable worth" line was estimated to be 30 million dollars in the mid-1970s—an amount that increases annually. After the 1976 study, Governor Evans requested 7 million dollars in his proposed 1977 budget to begin implementation of comparable worth. But the newly elected governor, Dixie Lee Ray, one of two women governors at the time, deleted the budget request. Governor Ray said that the consultant "compared apples and pumpkins and cans of worms and they are not comparable."[25]

Job evaluation studies have also been done in Connecticut, Michigan, Minnesota, and Nebraska, and may be done in Maryland, New York, and California. Unfortunately, pay equity increases have not yet been implemented as a consequence of this research. Nevertheless, these policy initiatives have served to raise the issue, heighten consciousness, build new coalitions, and provide a first step to achieving pay equity.

Other states—Idaho, New Jersey, Wisconsin, Iowa, and Georgia—have not only performed job evaluation studies, but have also implemented new compensation and classification systems. The process was not done with the explicit intent of identifying sex discrimination. In some instances, however, the wages in "women's jobs" have been raised as a result of the new systems. Reactions to these studies have been mixed. Some strategists argue that the chance of achieving the desired result—increasing women's wages—from a process (such as reclassification) is higher if less attention is paid to the fact that the process is designed to reduce sex discrimination. Others disagree.

In Washington and the other states which have done pay equity studies, activists outside of government played an essential role in raising the issue through hearings, organizing, research, and publications, as well as in introducing, securing passage, and implementing the job evaluation mandates. In some states, such as Connecticut, the Commission on the Status of Women played a leading role.

Attempts have also been made to introduce new state legislation dealing explicitly with pay equity. For example, a Michigan bill to amend the Civil Rights Act read in part: "An employer in this state shall not maintain differences in wages between male and female employees who are performing work of equal value." The bill did not pass.

A Wisconsin statute covering public employees was enacted in February 1978. It read: "The administrator shall apply the principle of equal pay for work of equivalent skills and responsibilities when assigning a classification to a pay range." Subsequently, clerical jobs were studied and reclassified but, as observed by Barbara Lightner, "the new clerical classifications do not address the statutory mandate to the state to compensate its employees according to the principle of 'equal pay for work of equivalent skills and responsibilities.' "[26] In other words, call her an office manager, but keep paying her like a secretary. The state employees' union and others are challenging the classifications.

In conclusion, it is important to note again that policy initiatives at the state and federal levels did not occur in isolation from other activities. The bargaining, research, organizing, and litigation work done by labor organizations such as the International Union of Electrical Radio and Machine Workers (IUE), the American Federation of State, County, and Municipal Employees (AFSCME), the Communications Workers of America (CWA), the United Electrical Radio and Machine Workers of America (UE), the American Nurses Association (ANA), the Coalition of Labor Union Women (CLUW), the Connecticut State Employees Association (CSEA), and the California School Employees Association (CSEA), by such professional organizations as the American Library Association (ALA) and by other nonunion organizing groups such as Working Women have helped the cause of pay equity. Likewise, the education, media, and related activities initiated by women's organizations and others are critical.[27]

THE STRUGGLES

Pay equity activists are being prompted to move beyond—but not abandon—the movement-building phase and concentrate more strategically on how to raise wages. The new emphasis is due to the political realities created by the Republican victories in November 1980, the Supreme Court's resolution of Title VII's applicability, and perhaps more importantly, by the emergence of organized opposition.

The most organized and well-directed opposition to pay equity has come from employers. Most employers have not been known for their voluntary and speedy compliance with the Equal Pay Act or with Title VII. It will be no better, and perhaps worse, with equal pay for work of comparable value. Employers are well versed, have invested heavily in legal defense, lobbied and testified at the EEOC hearings, and worked cooperatively to maximize their impact through such organizations as the Equal Employment Advisory Council, which sponsored a conference in November 1980 and also published a book in opposition to pay equity.

Employers have developed a variety of arguments. These include orthodox defenses of the free market and the sanctity of supply and demand in wage setting; objections to the possibility of objective job evaluations systems which would permit a measure of comparability; legal objections based on interpreta-tion of the Bennett Amendment; and a refusal to recognize any legitimate government role in determining the worth of jobs. Interestingly enough, in reaction to the pay equity movement, some employers have promoted upward mobility programs as a more effective (and less costly!) remedy to women's low wages.

Some unions have also opposed pay equity, and, as collective bargaining agents, have been jointly responsible with employers for negotiating wage increases which fail to reduce the wage differential between predominantly female occupations and predominantly male occupations. Unions' objections to pay equity include resistance to any policy that would increase the role of government in the wage-setting process and thereby interfere with collective bargaining; the perception that a dramatic increase in wages for women's work may ultimately mean fewer jobs for women; and membership resistance or perceived resistance—more likely in male-dominated unions—to a bargaining position that would give a larger share of the economic pie to women who represent only a minority of the membership.[28]

On the other hand, some unions have taken the lead in pay equity activities because they have many women members, because they perceive that exploita-tion of one group of workers inevitably invovles exploitation of other workers, and because new organizing opportunities appear to be more fruitful in predominantly female occupations than in predominantly male occupations. Thus, unions, as others, are using pay equity as an organizing tool. After three years of struggle, male and female members of AFSCME, the San Jose Municipal Employee Federation, went out on strike in July 1981. The strike lasted eight days. Their employer, the City of San Jose, refused to implement the findings of a job evaluation study which found that traditionally female jobs received 15 percent less than male jobs of comparable worth. The strike resulted in a settlement for 2,000 city workers of $1.4 million to upgrade women's jobs including a general wage increase of 7.5 percent for the first year and 8 percent for the second.

The National Committee on Pay Equity, which came together as a conference-organizing committee in Spring 1979 and held its founding conven-tion in October 1980, is attempting to develop coordinated strategies among its diverse constituencies including unions, women's groups, lawyers, educators and minority groups. It has organized two national conferences on pay equity, supported local organizing efforts, lobbied and testified at national levels, produced educational and training materials, and engaged in specific advocacy projects. The committee has 13 organizations on its board. It consists of task forces: organizing and bargaining, litigation, education and legislation, federal sector, and research.

The exceptionally broad scope of pay equity's appeal and impact gives a clue to its potential power. But it also indicates both the need for and some of the difficulties of coalition building. Lawyers, organizers, and researchers, for example, often bring different strategic and pragmatic considerations to bear: organizers may want to file a lawsuit as part of the organizing strategy for a particular group of workers, while the lawyers may counsel that that particular case runs too high a risk of resulting in a bad decision which could hurt the development of the law as well as the fortunes of the workers. It is hoped that the National Committee on Pay Equity will be capable of addressing the scope of wage inequities in a way single organizations cannot.[29]

CONCLUSION

The movement for pay equity is new, creative, experimental, growing, and decentralized. It is not institutionalized, but it does have a heart which consists of the communications and enthusiasm connecting people and organizations through conferences, phone calls, media, personal contact, and increasingly, through coalition networks. There is no single strategy for achieving pay equity in the United States. There is a myriad of discovered and yet to be discovered ways of approaching the issue, organizing support, identifying tactics, and building organizations. Local, state and national policies are playing a critical role in this process.

Pay equity carries with it an intuitive and emotional appeal. Progams of upward and lateral mobility have been affected by an ambivalence about the value of traditional women's work. Pay equity frames the problem and solution in a way that permits working women to demand more financial recognition by expressing their pride in being office workers or nurses. This resolution of ambivalence, an ambivalence whose source is sometimes inaccurately attributed to the women's movement rather than the society which created it, gives pay equity activities their mixture of hope, freedom, and fire.

The issue of pay equity has assumed qualities of both role equity and role change. On the one hand, the litigation strategy has argued that the principle of equal pay for work of comparable value is an instrument of incremental policy change since existing law already incorporates it. Similarly, by focusing on women in female-dominated occupations rather than moving women into nontraditional male occupations, it is a strategy which does not involve sex-role change. On the other hand, pay equity identifies a source of women's economic inequality and offers a collective, not individual, solution—the economic empowerment of millions of women in traditional women's jobs. Surely this represents fundamental sex-role change.

Notes

1. Carol Krucoff, "Money: The Question of Men, Women and 'Comparable Worth'," *Washington Post,* (November 13, 1979).

2. Helen Remick, "Beyond Equal Pay for Equal Work: Comparable Worth in the State of Washington," *Equal Employment Policy Strategies for Implementation in the United States, Canada, and Europe* (New York: Temple University Press, 1979). Jobs designated as female jobs in this study are ones in which 70 percent or more of the incumbents were women.

3. *The Earnings Gap between Women and Men* (Washington, D.C.: U.S. Department of Labor, Women's Bureau, 1976), p. 2. See also Ruth Blumrosen, "Wage Discrimination, Job Segregation and Title VII of the Civil Rights Acts of 1964," *University of Michigan Journal of Law Reform 12* (Spring 1979): 397. Blumrosen's article gathers much historical, anthropological, economic, sociological, and legal background relating to occupational segregation and wage discrimination. Her thesis is that minorities or women who demonstrate they have occupied traditionally segregated jobs have established a *prima facie* case under Title VII of the Civil Rights Act that the wage rate paid for those jobs is discriminately depressed, thus shifting the burden of demonstrating that the rate is not influenced by discriminatory factors to the employer. For a response to Blumrosen's article, see Bruce A. Nelson, Edward M. Opton, Jr., and Thomas E. Wilson, "Wage Discrimination and the 'Comparable Worth' Theory in Perspective," *University of Michigan Journal of Law Reform 13* (Winter 1980).

4. *The Earnings Gap between Women and Men,* p. 6. In Leviticus, we learn that a female worker was worth 30 shekels, while a male worker was worth 50 shekels; Leviticus 27:3-4.

5. Ellen Goodman, "Earning Less for Women's Work," *Washington Post,* October 16, 1978).

6. H. Kahne and A. Kohen, "Economic Perspectives on the Role of Women in the American Economy," *Journal of Economic Literature 13* (1975): 1249, 1274.

7. *Goesart v. Cleary,* 335 U.S. 464 (1948).

8. Since 1969, EEOC guidelines on sex discrimination have taken the position that state laws which prohibit or limit employment of women violate Title VII of the Civil Rights Act.

9. 442 U.S. 256 (1979).

10. *Staff Report, U.S. Commission on Civil Rights, Women and Poverty* (Washington D.C.: 1974).

11. Hedges, "Women Workers and Manpower Demands in the 1970's," *Monthly Labor Review 93* (1970): 19.

12. *Social Indicators of Equality for Minorities and Women* (Washington, D.C.: U.S. Commission on Civil Rights, 1978), pp. 42, 44-46.

13. Statement by Donald Elisburg, Assistant Secretary of Labor, Employment Standards Administration, U.S. Department of Labor before the Equal Employment Opportunity Commission, April 29, 1980.

14. See Helen Remick, "Strategies for Creating Sound, Bias-Free Job Evaluation Plans," in *Job Evaluation and EEO: The Emerging Issues* (New York: Industrial Relations Counselors, Inc., 1979).

15. Ibid.

16. Hearings have been published by EEOC.

17. §60-20.5(a) published in 45 Federal Register 86216 (December 30, 1980). Pt. 60-20 is codified in Vol. 41 Code of Federal Regulations.

18. 46 Federal Register 9084 (Jan. 28, 1981), deferring effective date until April 29, 1981; 46 Federal Register 23743 (April 28, 1981), deferring effective date until June 29, 1981, to permit additional consultation with interested groups.

19. 49 U.S.L.W. 4623.

20. 17 FEP Cases 906 (D. Colo. 1978), *aff'd.,* 620 F.2d 228 (10th Cir. 1980), *cert. denied* 101 S. Ct. 245 (1980).

21. 563 F.2d 353, 356 (8th Cir. 1977).

22. 631 F.2d 1094 (3d Cir. 1980), *cert. denied* (U.S. June 22, 1981) (No. 80-781)

23. 25 FEP Cases 602 (W.D. Pa. 1981)

24. 586 P.2d 1215 (Wash. Ct. App. 1978).

25. Helen Remick, "Beyond Equal Pay for Equal Work: Comparable Worth in the State of Washington," p. 6.

26. "Observations on Women and Employment in Wisconsin State Government Service," prepared for the Center for Public Representation, Inc., in Madison, April 1979.

27. For a review of pay equity activities on all fronts through 1979, see Joy A. Grune, ed., *Manual on Pay Equity: Raising Wages for Women's Work* (Washington, D.C.: Committee on Pay Equity and Conference on Alternative State and Local Policies, 1979).

28. In fact, a union which negotiated for a salary study and then for salary increases based on the results of that study so that most females averaged an 8 percent salary increase while most men averaged a 3 percent increase, was legally challenged for taking those actions by an unhappy male member. A hearing officer of California's Public Employment Relations Board upheld the union's actions. *Rodyney Coffron* v. *California School Employees Ass'n, Redwood Chapter 88,* Calif. PERB, Case Nos. SF-CO-80, 81 (May 28, 1980).

29. For those interested, the address of the National Committee on Pay Equity is 1201 16th St., N.W., Room 615, Washington, D.C. 20036.

Chapter 6

Alternative Work Patterns and the Double Life

Emily Stoper

Every woman in America leads a double life. She is shaped by a double socialization; she is torn apart by a double pull; often she carries a double burden. One side of her duality turns inward to the world of the home, children, "inner feelings"—femininity, in a word. The other side faces outward to the world of work, achievement, power, money, abstract thought—the "man's world."

A few women yield wholly to the inward pull, immersing themselves in home life, only to find that they are powerless against the manifold and pervasive ways in which the rest of the world shapes their lives and their children's lives. A few other women yield wholly to the outward pull, engaging totally in money and power pursuits, but with an increasing sense of hollowness. For these opposite extremes, one side of the double life is lived fully, the other side is a shadow.

But the vast majority of women, whether they are called housewives or career women, traditionalists or feminists, have their lives shaped at least to some degree by both sides of the duality. The experience of doubleness is generally an unpleasant one. Whenever a woman turns to one side, she tends to feel alienated from the other; it is difficult for her to experience her life as integrated. She constantly faces impossible choices—between heart and head, between love and work, between children and career. Worse, since she is relatively powerless in both realms, circumstances often make choices for her.

The powerlessness also leads to a combination of overwork and underreward. Women are overworked because they are trying to serve both sides. They are underrewarded at home because their work at home is cut off from what is most valued in the rest of society. They are underrewarded at work because, being women, they are assumed not to be fully committed to the world of work and so are assigned a secondary place within it. And, indeed, most women are unwilling to give as little of their lives as men have to the world of home and children or, more broadly, the world of interpersonal relations and emotional meaning. Our society would surely be a worse place to live in if they did. And yet, women seem permanently relegated to second-class citizenship as long as they yield to the inward as well as the outward pull.

Feminists, seeking to deal with this dilemma, have looked at many aspects of women's lives, as discussed in the various chapters of this book. This chapter will examine an intriguing approach that has emerged in the 1970s: alternative work patterns. This is a catchall phrase that includes such innovations in work patterns as flexitime, staggered hours, compact work week, job sharing, and flexiyear.

THE PROMISE OF ALTERNATIVE WORK PATTERNS

Most alternative work patterns were pioneered in Europe in the late 1960s and early 1970s as an attempt by management to make the best use of labor during a shortage. In the United States, with its perennial unemployment, the adoption of new work patterns has been more gradual. They have been seen by American management as ways of dealing with declining worker morale and a slowdown in the rise of productivity and of attracting special categories of workers, especially women.

From the point of view of women, the new patterns have been seen primarily as offering more flexibility and opportunity for self-management on the job. Easier integration of work and family life has been viewed as one of a list of incidental benefits that also includes easing traffic congestion and permitting weekday access by employees to shopping, recreation, and education.

Alternative work patterns fall into three broad types: those that rearrange the hours at which work is done, those that reduce the total number of hours worked, and those that alter the place of work in life.[1] All three types have the potential of helping women to combine the two sides of their lives more easily.

Rearranging the Hours of Work

The first type of alternative work pattern includes flexitime, staggered hours, and the "compact" or "compressed" workweek. All of these are still sufficiently unusual that they require definition. *Flexitime* (sometimes called flextime) means an extension to the employee of the right to choose, within certain limits, on a day-to-day basis, when the hours of work will begin and end. In the minimum form, it merely means that the employee can choose at what time to start work within a band of two or three hours in the morning and at what time to finish work within a band of two or three hours in the afternoon;

everyone has to work certain core hours in the middle of the day. For example, a flexitime day could look like this:

Flexible hours	7–9 A.M.
Core hours	9–11:30 A.M.
Flexible lunch period	11:30–1:30 P.M.
Core hours	1:30–4 P.M.
Flexible hours	4–6 P.M.[2]

In a more advanced form of flexitime, employees can bank hours from day to day, sometimes for an indefinite period of time, sometimes limited to a single week or a single month. "Banking hours" means working extra hours on one day and then taking time off on another day chosen by the employee.

In 1978, Congress passed Public Law 95-390, sponsored by Representative Stephen J. Solarz (D-N.Y.) and Senator Gaylord Nelson (D-Wis.), temporarily (for three years) suspending obstacles in labor legislation to the banking of hours, so that experiments could be conducted with flexitime and compressed work weeks.

Staggered hours differ from flexitime in that, once chosen, they do not vary from day to day. If chosen by the employer, staggered hours can actually make it more difficult for an employee to combine work with family life—if, for example, a parent is assigned a late work schedule that overlaps after-school hours and dinner preparation time. In most workplaces where they are used, though, staggered hours are chosen by the employee, so that they have some of the advantages of flexitime.

The *"compact"* or *"compressed"* *work week* involves a full-time job done in fewer than five days, usually four ten-hour days but occasionally three twelve-hour days, or, over a biweekly period, eight nine-hour days and one eight-hour day. One might have expected that women would dislike this schedule because neither child care nor housework can easily be postponed from day to day. Both skinned knees and dirty dishes have a way of crying out for immediate attention. Studies show, however, that at least some women on this schedule like it, sometimes even more than men do, perhaps because it gives them a day to catch up on home-related tasks like shopping and sewing.[3] One study[4] did find that people with children at home saw the compact week as having unfavorable consequences for home life, and increasingly so over time. But men complained about this more than women. In any case, the 4/40 (4 days, 40 hours) work week peaked in popularity around 1975 at 2.2 percent of the workforce and has been declining since then, for reasons that have little to do with the impact on family life and much to do with disappointed expectations about raising productivity and cutting costs, largely owing to worker fatigue and the increased complexity of scheduling and other management tasks.[5]

Flexitime, however, has been steadily increasing in use throughout the 1970s to the point where in 1980 about 17 percent of nongovernment organizations with 50 or more employees and 237 government agencies had flexible schedules.[6] Some 6 percent of all American employees were on flexitime in 1977.[7]

Flexitime is difficult (but not impossible) to use in work situations like an assembly line that involve interdependent functions, a buildup of work that must be handled by another person or a high degree of specialization of functions.[8] Flexible schedules are nothing new for many self-employed, professional, managerial, and sales persons who are accustomed to setting their own hours. Office workers are the most important part of the workforce for whom flexitime is a genuine new benefit—and, of course, a highly disproportionate percentage of these are women. Some 40 percent of employed women are clerical workers and many others are in jobs such as supervisor or social worker that lend themselves easily to flexitime.

Flexitime and the Double Life

In a series of informal interviews with workers on flexitime, the author found that it offers a number of advantages to mothers—and, of course, to fathers who want to play their parental role more actively. By starting the workday very early, a parent can be home when the children return from school or soon after. This is an advantage especially if the other parent is able to take responsibility for getting them off to school in the morning. Parents can also take time off during the day without using personal leave. Not having to arrive at work at a specific time can also ease the morning rush at home. Even on a normal day the morning rush at home is often the highest-pressure work of the day, and the parent is lucky to arrive at work on time, though exhausted.

Some ways in which flexitime helps everybody are particularly crucial for mothers. For example, the fact that flexitime often cuts down on travel time by enabling people to avoid rush hours is particularly helpful to mothers who cannot squeeze in much commuting time in an already overloaded schedule. The greater choice of times for college classes often benefits mothers, since they are a disproportionate number of the adults in college, having dropped out earlier in order to have children.

Flexitime also encourages greater self-management in routine office jobs since it is incompatible with petty, moment-to-moment supervision, if only because supervisors cannot be there during the entire expanded workday. And it encourages "cross-training"—that is, learning parts of other people's jobs because the other people will not always be there to do them. Thus, clerical work under flexitime tends to become more autonomous and varied.

In all these ways it would seem that flexitime could help many working parents. Yet the interviews reported here, like much of the research on flexitime, are subjective and unsystematic. A controlled study by Halcyone Bohen of 700 employees on flexitime in two federal agencies found that flexitime actually made little difference in assisting people who were trying to combine work and parental roles. (The study was done before the implementation of Public Law 95-390 permitting the banking of hours, so it refers only to the most limited form of flexitime.) Bohen found that the main beneficiaries of flexitime were not mothers (who experienced equal amounts of stress on flexitime and on a standard schedule) but women without children, for whom flexitime meant less stress.

Since flexitime has been touted not only as a way of easing the load of employed mothers but also as a way of encouraging fathers to spend more time with their children, Bohen also compared fathers on flexitime with those on standard schedules. When she looked at fathers whose wives are employed, she found that those on flexitime do not spend significantly more time on family work than those on standard time. But when she turned to fathers whose wives are not employed, she found that those on flexitime do spend more time on family work than those on standard times, though not more than men with employed wives on both schedules.

Bohen found that there were three kinds of people for whom flexitime made a measurable difference in the ease with which they could take care of personal and family chores and activities: fathers with nonemployed wives, employed married women without children, and single people. All of these are people who do not have primary child-care responsibilities! Single mothers and employed parents with employed spouses did not find that flexitime made any measurable difference.[9]

Another study, however, found that workers who had young children were somewhat more likely to use flexitime and also that workers who changed their hours under flexitime increased their time with their children more than did workers who chose not to change their schedules.[10] Obviously, more research is needed but it appears that flexitime's impact on easing the double pull will be small at best.

Reducing the Hours of Work

An obvious shortcoming of flexitime and the other variant schedules mentioned above is that the total number of hours to be worked is not reduced. No matter how one juggles them, 35 to 40 hours a week are likely to be hard to combine with major child-care responsibilities.

Given the double pull, many mothers of children under 12 do not want to work full-time unless it is economically necessary.[11] The 1977 Quality of Employment Survey done by the Survey Research Center at the University of Michigan found that 51 percent of wives and 42 percent of husbands with children under 18 preferred to reduce their work time in order to spend more time with their families. About 35 percent of workers with children under 18 experience significant interference between their jobs and their family lives.

This was especially true of families with preschool children. Both men and women complained of excessive work time; women also complained of scheduling incompatibilities, especially between work hours and child-care hours.[12]

Besides making scheduling easier, part-time work satisfies mothers' needs in many cases for a balance between home life and work life. Part-time work offers parents many hours a day with their children to establish a strong emotional relationship and to get fully acquainted with them—something which may be difficult for some parents working full-time. Moreover, parents who are part-timers can offset the weaknesses of the child-care facility; for example, offering stimulation if the child-care center is very quiet or quiet if it is very stimulating.[13] Part-time working parents also find it easier to participate as volunteer aides in cooperative nursery schools or grade schools, thus helping assure the quality of the institutions provided by the community to help raise their children.

Part-time employment is also often better for the parents as people. Full-time employment combined with child-rearing leaves many people perpetually frazzled and exhausted. Full-time parenting is also a strain on many people, especially those who feel the outward pull strongly. One study[14] of mothers of young children found the following pattern:

- Employed full-time: highest stress
- Not employed: medium stress
- Employed part-time: lowest stress and greatest satisfaction as worker *and* parent.

Only 42 percent of women (and about two-thirds of men) in the work force now work full-time all year round. Some 22 percent of the work force are part-week, including one-third of all women in the work force, and one-eighth of all men.[15] Close to half of the women part-timers give "home and family responsibilities" as the reason for not working full-time.[16]

This sounds as if the labor market is accommodating itself to mothers' needs. But in truth mothers are accommodating themselves to what the labor market has been willing to offer. There are plenty of part-time jobs in the sales, clerical, and service fields that have become pink-collar ghettoes—and very few in managerial and professional fields, least of all the better paid ones. The effect is to reinforce the sex segregation of the labor market.

When women ask why such jobs cannot also be part-time, they are told that the jobs do not lend themselves to being performed on a part-time basis. But what does this mean? Surely the 35 to 40 hour week does not appear in holy writ. In fact, in 1977, only about 42 percent of employed Americans worked an average of 40 hours a week (31 percent worked fewer hours, 27 percent worked more).[17] One begins to suspect that the real meaning of those who say that managerial and professional jobs are unsuitable for part-timers is that most serious workers are full-time.

A further assumption is clearly that most serious workers are men. Forty hours a week has been a comfortable average work week for men who do not take on major child-rearing responsibilities. Men now hold most of those jobs which are said to be unsuitable for part-timers.

These responsible jobs are also the jobs that are paid well enough to support some people, even with a child or two, on a part-time basis. Most existing part-time jobs are so low-paid that they are useless except as supplements to the family income. Hence, they remain job ghettoes for women.

The unavailability of better jobs on a part-time basis is, however, only half the problem. After all, not all working mothers can have managerial and professional jobs, just as not all working fathers can have such jobs. Women in part-time jobs have another disadvantage: their jobs are usually thought of as temporary and carry no job security. Part-time workers cannot usually get any kind of job tenure or seniority. This fact encourages the prejudice that part-timers are less than fully qualified. There is no inherent reason why the categories part-time and temporary should be confounded in this way—except perhaps that it is convenient for employers to be able to "let go" part-timers easily during slack seasons, as a way of keeping their wage bill lower.

This practice goes far toward explaining why many women who have been in the work force all or most of their adult lives still think of themselves as working temporarily. But the psychological basis for long-term "temporary" work is eroding, as women see increasingly that given the realities of inflation and unstable marriage, they are likely to be in the work force most of their lives.

Along with lack of job security sometimes goes lack of fringe benefits—paid vacations, sick leave, health insurance, workers' compensation, a retirement plan, and so on. Almost half of all Americans working under 35 hours a week do not receive fringe benefits.[18] This lack of fringes means that part-time workers are in effect not getting equal pay for equal work—even with other workers in the same job categories who are full-time. Personnel departments, oriented toward full-time workers, are often stymied by the complexities of prorating benefits or making up an equitable package of benefits for part-timers. These technical difficulties have often been used as a reason for not giving part-timers any fringe benefits at all. Actually, a major study shows that equitable fringe benefits need not cost more.[19]

So there are two main problems with part-time jobs as they exist today: better-paid jobs are usually not available on a part-time basis, and part-time jobs lack job security and fringe benefits. An end to these conditions is unlikely to occur without a change in our social norm which dictates that all serious, long-term work must be done on a full-time basis.

There is a social and political movement trying to effect just such a change in social norms. Organizations like New Ways to Work in San Francisco, Catalyst in New York, and the National Council for Alternative Work Patterns in Washington are trying to stimulate the creation of more and better part-time jobs and to match them to workers.

A bill was introduced in Congress in 1977 that would have required the federal government to increase the number of part-time jobs in every agency at every grade level by 2 percent a year until the total reached 10 percent. In its final 1978 version as Public Law 95-437, it was substantially watered down, merely requiring each federal agency to promote part-time career employment at all grade levels and empowering the Office of Personnel Management to oversee them.

But this was partly because the Office of Personnel Management (then called the Civil Service Commission) saw itself as genuinely committed to further expansion of part-time jobs and merely disliked the idea of having rigid quotas imposed on it.[20] In response to the law, it did make strong recommendations to the federal agencies, including the setting of annual goals and timetables.

The Comprehensive Employment and Training Act (CETA) was also amended in 1978 to permit part-time, flexitime, and other alternative work plans in CETA jobs. In addition, at least ten states in 1978 alone established programs for experimenting with alternative work patterns.[21]

All this federal and state action was an attempt to respond to a situation in which many more workers are presumed to want part-time jobs, especially if they offer responsibility, good pay, fringe benefits, and job security, than there are such jobs. Not only women (or men) attempting to combine child-rearing and work roles, but also students, older people who want to phase into retirement, disabled people, people considering midlife career changes, and so on, would like to work part-time. Since most of these population categories are increasing, the pressure to improve the status and increase the number of part-time jobs is also growing.

Some interesting variations on part-time jobs are being developed, of which the best known is job sharing. In job sharing, two people hold a job that was formerly a single full-time job. This is, of course, desirable only if it is voluntary and only if it includes fringe benefits for both workers. The two workers may "split" the job—by hours or days, by task, by area of responsibility—or they may "share"it, working collaboratively. The collaborative pattern is surprisingly common. In one study by Gretl Meier[22] of 238 job sharers, 70 percent considered their jobs to be shared rather than split. An even larger proportion saw their partner's skills as complementary to theirs. The same study found that over half the teams tended to become more collaborative over time.[23] The study covered a variety of occupations including teachers, administrators/program developers, secretaries/receptionists/clericals, counselors/social workers/psychiatrists, and researchers/technicians.[24]

Job Sharing: Pros and Cons

What are the advantages and disadvantages of job sharing? According to Meier's study, the greatest advantage—one which should apply to any part-time person—was more energy on the job. No fewer than 91 percent of the respondents reported that they had more energy for work.[25]

Advantages from the employer's point of view included the ability to call on job sharing workers for emergency or temporary jobs and to train new people without disrupting the flow of work. Employers, of course, also benefited from the higher energy and the lower incident of "burn-out," especially among helping professionals.[26]

Permanent part-time employment has been found to reduce labor costs, improve job performance, and raise the quality of the work force.[27] Part-time employees have been found to have no less commitment and dedication than full-time ones.[28] Part-time work has also been touted as solving labor-recruitment[29] and scheduling[30] problems.

Employers of large numbers of women might be most willing to offer permanent part-time employment at all levels, as women seem to find job sharing particularly advantageous. Seventy-seven percent of the respondents in the Meier study were in teams of two women, 19 percent in teams of one man and one woman (which were rarely husband and wife, except in academia), the remaining 4 percent in all-male teams. Women's preference is probably best explained in terms of their mothering responsibilities. Fifty-five percent of all the respondents had children aged one to eleven at home, and 81 percent were married, many of them probably with older children at home. Respondents reported that of the time not devoted to their paid job, 32 percent is spent caring for their family, and 25 percent on caring for their home.[31]

Women also seemed to like job sharing better than men did. Asked whether job sharing "enhanced the quality and success of their work," 68 percent of those on all-female teams said yes, whereas only 50 percent of mixed teams agreed. The figure was even lower among the small number of all-male teams.[32]

It is probable that the chief reason for dissatisfaction with job sharing was financial. Some people in the study had left their job sharing arrangements for full-time work; the main reason they gave was money. For only 6 percent of the sample was the shared job the only source of family income.[33]

Related reasons for dissatisfaction were the loss of job security and of opportunities for promotion, perceived by a little under half the sample. Higher-level jobs were rarely available on a job sharing basis and the inability to claim full credit for one's work, as well as slower accrual of seniority, might also impede promotion.[34] For employers, also, the blurring of accountability and responsibility was sometimes unwelcome.[35]

A different kind of problem was that although the jobs were genuinely half-time, many people, especially professionals, had a strong commitment to them and felt frustrated by the lack of time to act fully on their commitment. They tended to work very hard during the time they had or to take work home.[36] This was advantageous from the employer's standpoint, but it poses a real danger that job sharing (or part-time jobs in general) may lead to exploitation of women even when the jobs are well paid and carry fringe benefits and job security. Another study in fact found strong feelings of economic exploitation among job sharing married couples.[37]

One final disadvantage to job sharing is that it may undercut the movement for part-time jobs in general by implicitly conceding that work naturally breaks down into 40-hour-a-week blocks (though there is no reason why two people could not share, say, one and a half jobs, as occasionally is done). Job sharing is not the only desirable form of part-time work, and there are some practical obstacles to it that do not exist for other part-time jobs. The most obvious of these is the need to find a compatible pair; this need could limit the expansion of job sharing. Nevertheless, a major study found that job sharing and work sharing (part-timing as a substitute for layoffs) are the most likely modes for career part-time employment in the future.[38]

Rethinking Work Time

It is extraordinarily difficult for Americans to break the mind-set that thinks of "full-time" (35–40 hours) as the normal work week and that sees two kinds of workers: full-time (serious) and part-time (temporary, just earning a few extra dollars). In West Germany, experiments are being done, primarily in retail trade, with something called "flexiyear," a plan under which every employee contracts annually with management for a certain amount of work time (hours per day, days per week, months per year, or however they want to break it down).[39] Management can then plan to have a work force of appropriate size for slack and busy times, while workers can strike a continually changing balance between work time on the one hand and time for family, education, travel, starting a small business, and so on, on the other. The distinction between part-time and full-time workers then breaks down into a series of gradations. Workers need no longer forfeit any claim to "seriousness" if they want to work less than every day or even every month.

An even more radical idea along these lines, the "full cyclic plan," has been developed by Fred Best.[40] Under this plan, education, work, and leisure would be much more evenly distributed over the life span, instead of being concentrated in youth, the middle years, and old age respectively. Best did an informal survey of workers' preferences and found that 46 percent preferred the full cyclic plan, while only 20 percent preferred the traditional linear model. The third choice was a "moderate cyclic plan," concentrating education in the younger years but redistributing leisure and work over the middle and later years. One device for doing this would be sabbaticals (every seventh year off, usually at reduced pay), a benefit now available to few workers other than teachers.

One writer has proposed a national economic security fund, one percent of which would be set aside to pay for periods of "self-renewal" lasting up to two years.[41] Presumably, procreation and the care of a baby could be interpreted as a form of self-renewal. The governments of Hungary, Czechoslovakia, and Sweden now offer payments to workers who take time off for child-rearing.

A different kind of approach to part-timing is to divide work into "modules" of various lengths, permitting each worker to put together a package of modules of various kinds. This pattern would make possible the kind of balance among mental, physical, and manual work of which Marx dreamed. Some 10 percent of the work force already does this in a way by moonlighting.[42] But making available large numbers of part-time jobs of a great variety of types and lengths would enormously increase flexibility, to the great benefit of parents. It would also contribute to more flexibility and fluidity in labor markets, as well as providing a remedy for boredom and burnout.

IMPLICATIONS AND COMPLICATIONS

It is important to emphasize that we are talking here not merely about changes in options available to workers but about changes in social norms about the place of work in life. Without a change in norms, the new options will be used primarily by women and by a few marginal male workers and thus will only serve to reinforce the marginality of whoever uses them. Only if the norms about the place of work in life begin to change, so that significant numbers of men want to work less and differently, will women to able to continue to respond to both of their dual pulls and not be at a disadvantage in both worlds.

The Unions' Perspective

A major obstacle to the adoption of all of the alternative work patterns described thus far—from the most timid rearrangement of hours to the most radical rethinking of work time—is the skeptical and in some cases hostile attitude of those institutions which have been the chief advocates of American workers: the unions.[43] The attitude of most unions (with some notable exceptions)[44] has been skepticism about flexitime and downright hostility to efforts to upgrade and expand part-time employment.

The fact that alternative work patterns have usually been initiated by management arouses the suspicions of organized labor. Sometimes the motive of management has been to increase productivity (through flexitime and compact work weeks, for example), sometimes to respond to pressures from people who are not seen by unions as primary workers (women, people about to retire, students). These motives arouse the suspicion in union officials that increases in productivity will not be passed on to the worker and thus that alternative work patterns will become a new form of "speedup."

This suspicion is not entirely baseless. Workers under alternative work patterns do tend to be more productive. Overwhelmingly, firms or agencies that adopt flexitime report increases in productivity ranging from 5 to 15 percent.[45] These increases, however, are rarely caused by pressure on workers but rather by benefits to them, such as the opportunity to adjust their schedules to their biological clocks ("night people" do not have to report to work at 8 A.M. and doze away the first few hours), or to quiet times in the office, or to the length of the projects they work on, or to the times when work flow is heaviest. In these ways, flexitime tends to lead to more self-management and higher morale, which in turn reduces absenteeism, tardiness, and turnover. Not surprisingly, flexitime is overwhelmingly popular among employees.

It is true though that a frequently reported "benefit" to management from flexitime is reduction in overtime, presumably at least partly because workers voluntarily adjust their schedules to work flow. (Premium pay for overtime work done by flexitime workers who can bank hours is paid only if the extra hours are requested by management.) Reduction in overtime may not be seen as a benefit by workers, especially if they had come to depend on a predictable amount of weekly overtime pay.

Part-time workers often also have higher productivity, even after one takes into account extra administrative and training costs and extra time needed for communication in the case of shared jobs. In one study, people working a six-hour day were generally producing as much as, or more than, those working an eight-hour day.[46] Part-time work offers some of the same morale and schedule-flexibility benefits as flexitime, and in addition has its own special virtues. People on part-days or even part-weeks suffered less from fatigue and the slackening of attention that often occurs after many consecutive hours or days of work. Probably even more important is Parkinson's Law, which is that work expands to fill the time available. Full-time workers have more time available, so they may simply draw out the work to fill that time, usually unconsciously.

A final factor that applies to part-time professional and some managerial workers is that these people are not really being paid for their time but rather for their expertise, imagination, problem-solving ability, etc. These often cannot be "turned off" when the work day ends, so that the employer may be getting a full-time mind at half-time pay.

An even more fundamental problem with alternative work patterns, arising from the fact that they are not usually initiated by unions, is that they threaten to alter the traditional relationship of workers with management and unions. To begin with, they may increase worker identification with management (though there is no hard evidence of this), mostly by encouraging worker self-management but also because workers on alternative schedules may see themselves as having a special, privileged relationship with management. This may lower their self-protective alertness against management's pressures for higher output or for worker-chosen schedules that are really for the convenience of management—both of which management should be paying for.

Moreover, the kinds of workers who are attracted by alternative work schedules are marginal workers, in the eyes of most unions. Most unions see primary workers as adult males who are heads of families. These are the people seen as most in need of good wages, fringe benefits, and job security and also most likely to be committed to unions who push for such things. For 100 years, unions have put most of their energies into fighting for the "family wage" with which a man could support his wife and children. The assumption behind this fight has been that neither wives nor children will be in the work force themselves except in marginal roles. Unions were major backers of legislation banning child labor and they have cooperated fully with management in the sex segregation of the work force (for example, pushing for protective labor legislation providing different work rules for men and women). They did not make serious efforts to organize into unions the occupations that employ most women (clerical work, teaching, nursing) until about 15 years ago.

The family wage would, of course, be paid to a full-time worker who could reasonably be expected to work all day, every week day, throughout his adult life, except when he is ill, on vacation, or unemployed. The assumption behind the family wage for full-time workers is the traditional patriarchal family—the father at work, the mother at home taking care of the children. In resisting alternative work patterns, unions are still working on this assumption. But with 51 percent of all women in the work force (compared to about 78 percent of men[47]), with the divorce rate at an all-time high, with half or more of the college-age population going to college, most of them wanting to work at the same time, with increasing numbers of vigorous elderly people wanting part-time work, with a new norm for training and employing the disabled—how realistic is that assumption?

At the same time, the structure of the economy is changing so that the traditional blue-collar occupations that have been heavily unionized for many decades are declining relative to the overall economy. Assembly-line workers are now only about 5 percent of the work force. And many of the new occupations—clerical jobs, service jobs, computer-related work—lend themselves much more easily to flexible or part-time schedules. Three-quarters of the workers in Meier's study of job sharing were nonunion.[48]

Unions understandably fear the loss of their central role in setting standards for American working conditions. Such fears are exacerbated by talk of individuals, not unions, bargaining annually with management over work schedules, as in flexiyear, or of people working more than eight hours a day or 40 hours a week, so as to have the "privilege" of banking hours. The tendency to bypass or tamper with collective bargaining agreements or labor laws, for which unions have struggled hard, in order to facilitate alternative work patterns, alarms many union leaders. Even when labor laws are not altered, unions often fear that flexible schedules will make them more difficult to enforce.

While objecting to the erosion of the gains they have made for American workers, most unions have been unwilling to take the lead in introducing alternative work patterns in a manner that did not jeopardize what "primary" workers already have. Some unions, usually under pressure from their rank and file, have begun to play this role. The resistance of the other unions can probably be explained in large measure by their attachment to the idea of the family wage as their central goal.

By challenging the family wage, part-time work raises the possibility of a whole new social norm about the relationship between paid work and family life. Part-time work is now used primarily by women as a way of getting them through the difficult years when the children are small and the family budget is tight. As increasing numbers of mothers of small children enter the work force, the pressure for part-time jobs increases. Women applicants for one job-sharing program outnumbered men by five to one.[49] Overall, the ratio of women to men part-time workers is 1.84, up from 1.63 in 1970.[50]

This is very unfortunate because if part-time work continues to be used primarily by women, its main impact will be to reinforce the sex segregation of the work force by enhancing the differences between the way men and women work and thus making it more difficult for each sex to enter the other's occupations. The last thing women need is another wall around the pink-collar job ghetto in which they have less pay, status, influence, autonomy, and room for advancement than men. Only the use of the part-time option by substantial numbers of male workers can make its use by women truly desirable.

This means that the new patterns must be promoted not only as women's rights but as rights for all workers, not only as women's liberation but as workers' liberation. With the slowdown of economic growth, more part-time work for everyone may be the only way of accommodating all the new people who want to enter the work force. Making a virtue of necessity, many workers may come to see the shorter work time as a form of liberation. But it is going to be hard to promote a movement for workers' liberation without the support of the unions, who are the main organized spokesmen for American workers. Though that support has not yet been forthcoming, it must be sought and it can be won.

First, the unions' fears—some of which are quite legitimate—must be addressed. Unions must be reassured, for example, that management will not abuse flexitime. Reassurance might be in the form of laws forbidding pressure on workers to select hours to suit management and providing appropriate penalties (as Public Law 95-390 does), and in the form of studies showing that the exercise of pressure is in fact rare. Unions' fears that part-timers are not good union members can also be assuaged by showing that this is true only insofar as part-timers have been marginal workers. The alternative work patterns movement can play a role both in urging the new breed of part-timers to show more of an interest in unions and in urging unions to show more of an interest in part-timers and their concerns. Unionized part-timers do have better wages and fringe benefits than nonunionized ones.[51]

Probably the most serious concern of unions about job sharing is that rather than being a way of spreading around employment, it is merely a way of spreading around unemployment. To meet this concern, the job-sharing movement should focus initially mostly on full-time jobs reduced voluntarily to part-time and on relatively high-paid jobs which could support individuals and even some families on a part-time basis. In the long run the movement needs to hack away at unions' assumptions about the patriarchal family.

Besides attempting to address the concerns of unions, the alternative work patterns movement should work to see to it that unions are fully included in all moves to introduce or expand flexitime or job sharing in unionized workplaces. Where there is collective bargaining, the reforms should be part of the contract. Where there is a grievance procedure, grievances arising from the new patterns should be covered under it. Where there are genuine and unavoidable hardships to individuals—say, during a period of transition to more part-time jobs—the unions can play a vital role by insisting that management and/or the government cushion those hardships. For example, full-time workers who are reduced involuntarily to part-time status should be made eligible for partial unemployment insurance, as they are in some European countries and in a few places in the United States. This reform could mitigate the hardship of layoffs by encouraging reductions in hours rather than the brutal severing of junior employees—a disproportionate number of whom are, of course, women and minority males.

In general, the movement for alternative work patterns, as it grows, should offer more support to the unions in some of their favorite causes—most notably, a shortening of the work week. That reform is certainly fully compatible with the others discussed here. In fact, the alternative work patterns movement should probably be arguing from the outset that someone who works, say, half-time, should get, say, 60 percent of pay, on the grounds that part-time work is more productive. Thus, part-time work should not be in competition with the shorter work-week; the two causes should be natural allies.

A Feminist Perspective

Union leaders, of course, are not the only ones who assume that the only serious and important workers are male heads of families, who will of course want full-time work. This view is endemic in management as well. So is the releated view that the large majority of workers will consider work the central activity of their lives, either because of the intrinsic value of what they do or because of the money they earn, or a combination of the two.

This world view is not seriously challenged by flexitime and the other schedules that merely rearrange the hours worked without reducing them. Perhaps for this reason flexitime is relatively uncontroversial (one manager called it a "motherhood apple pie" issue),[52] and also has little or no significant effect on easing the burden of employees with major child-care responsibilities.

Part-time work could mean much bigger changes if more men were to choose it. But why would substantial numbers of male workers choose to work part-time? Presumably because they had some other rewarding and important way to spend much of their time and they were assured that a wide range of jobs, with full fringe benefits and job security, were available to them.

What other socially useful, rewarding, and important way is there for men to spend their time? The only one that is comparable in the strength of its pull to paid work is raising children. Yet raising children has been so cut off for so long from the "man's world" of paid work that most men have long since ceased to feel a major pull toward it (if they ever did). They serve their children by abandoning them daily when they leave for their jobs. The world of "real" (paid) work and the world of child rearing are connected only by the flimsy bond of cash.

Housewife-mothers attempt to raise their children for the world of work without any participatory sense of what that world is about and with only the barest and most indirect influence on that world. Meanwhile, worker-fathers toil daily in order to earn money for the sustenance of children they barely know, especially if, as is increasingly so, they do not even live in the same household because of divorce.

What is clearly needed is a reintegration of the worlds of home and work, in which both men and women will be drawn to both but will experience this double pull not as tearing their lives apart but as weaving them together, as reuniting two halves. Work and love, Freud's famous pair, can serve each other instead of battling each other from their fortresses in men's and women's worlds.

Men who attempt to do this will find themselves at a competitive disadvantage in the world of paid work, as "Dustin Hoffman Kramer" soon found, and as employed mothers have known all along. In the face of this disadvantage, they are likely to make the change only if they experience a radical change of values, away from ever-expanding material wealth and toward a recreation of meaning and wholeness in their lives.[53] Such a revolution in values would have profound implications for the entire economic system. There were foreshadowings of that revolution in the "counter-culture" movement of the 1960s and there are new harbingers in the alternative work patterns movement of today.

Without a transvaluation of values, alternative work patterns are mere gimmicks. Flexitime is likely to make little difference in easing the strain of women's double lives. Job sharing may bring short-term gains for women workers while making the long-term breakdown of the sex-segregated job market less likely. Only with a profound shift in social values will women—and men—be able to experience the double life not as doubly burdened but as doubly enriched.

Neither the unions nor the alternative work patterns movement is likely to bring about such a shift in values. The only social movement that is likely to do so is the women's movement. A major part of that movement has always defined its purpose as freeing men and women from the prison of sex roles. Moreover, at the very core of its goal is the empowerment of women in all their roles. Feminists know that women cannot be liberated in the "man's world" without also being liberated at home, nor can they be liberated at home while they are powerless everywhere else. Thus, feminism can give the movement for alternative work patterns a clear sense of purpose.

A political alliance among the unions, the alternative work patterns movement, and the women's movement offers the best hope that alternative work patterns can make a significant difference in the future of Americans.

Notes

1. Good descriptions of the advantages, drawbacks, and detailed functioning of the various types of flexible schedules can be found in Pam Silverstein and Jozetta H. Srb, *Flexitime: Where, When, and How?* (Ithaca, N.Y.: Cornell University, 1979); Virginia Hider Martin, *Hours of Work When Workers Can Choose* (Washington, D.C.: Business and Professional Women's Foundation, 1975); George W. Bohlander, *Flextime—A New Face on The Work Clock* (Los Angeles: UCLA Institute of Industrial Relations, 1977); Albert S. Glickman and Zenia H. Brown, *Changing Schedules of Work: Patterns and Implications* (Kalamazoo, Mich.: W.E. Upjohn Institute for Employment Research, 1974).

2. Silverstein and Srb, *Flexitime,* p. 2.

3. Glickman, *Changing Schedules of Work,* pp. 24–5, 27, 32.

4. Ibid., pp. 24–5.

5. Silverstein and Srb, *Flexitime,* p. 10; Stanley D. Nollen and Virginia H. Martin, *Alternative Work Schedules, Part 3: Compressed Workweeks* (New York: AMACOM, 1978), p. 39.

6. *Newsweek,* May 13, 1980.

7. Nollen and Martin, *Alternative Work Schedules,* Part 1, p. 6.

8. Ana L. Bishop, "Flexitime in Manufacturing," *American Machinist* (April 1979).

9. Halcyone H. Bohen and Anamaria Viveros-Long, *Balancing Jobs and Family Life: Do Flexible Work Schedules Help?* (Philadelphia: Temple University Press, 1981).

10. Unpublished study by Dr. Richard A. Winett, Institute for Behavioral Research, Silver Spring, Maryland.

11. Personal communication with Lynne McCallister, author of an extensive survey of middle-American mothers.

12. Joseph H. Pleck, Graham L. Staines, and Linda Lang, "Work and Family Life: First Reports on Work-Family Interference and Workers' Formal Child Care Arrangements, From the 1977 Quality of Employment Survey," Working Paper No. 11, Wellesley College Center for Research on Women, 1978, p. 9.

13. Personal communication with Lynne McCallister.

14. Cited in Gretl S. Meier, *Job Sharing: A New Pattern for Quality of Work and Life*

(Kalamazoo, Mich.: W. E. Upjohn Institute for Employment Research, 1979), p. 7.

15. Nollen and Martin, *Alternative Work Schedules,* p. 3.

16. *A Statistical Portrait of Women in the United States, 1978* (U.S. Census Bureau, Current Population Reports, Special Studies, Series P-23, No. 100), pp. 54, 56.

17. Silverstein and Srb, *Flexitime,* p. 1.

18. Joann S. Lublin, "Mutual Aid: Firms and Job Seekers Discover More Benefits to Part-time Positions," *Wall Street Journal,* October 4, 1978, p. 1.

19. Stanley D. Nollen, Brenda B. Eddy, and Virginia H. Martin, *Permanent Part-Time Employment: The Manager's Perspective* (New York: Praeger, 1978), p. 126.

20. Personal communication with Barbara Fiss of the Office of Personnel Management.

21. *National Council for Alternative Work Patterns (NCAWP) Newsletter* (Winter 1979), pp. 4–6; Meier, *Job Sharing,* pp. 15–22.

22. Meier, *Job Sharing,* pp. 48, 61.

23. Ibid., p. 61.

24. Ibid., p. 36.

25. Ibid., p. 62.

26. Ibid., p. 83.

27. Nollen and Martin, *Alternative Work Schedules, Part 2,* p. 4.

28. Ibid., p. 5.

29. Research Institute of America, "One Answer to Hard-to-Fill Jobs: Let Two People Share the Work," *Alert* (April 20, 1977); and "Job Sharing as a Way to Hold the Work Force," *Alert* (February 7, 1979), W. F. Thompson et al., "An Answer to the Computer Programmer Shortage," *Adult Leadership* (January 1970), *Jobs for the Hard-to-Employ: New Directions for a Public-Private Partnership* (New York: Committee for Economic Development, 1978).

30. Nollen, Eddy, and Martin, *Permanent Part-Time Employment,* p. 145.

31. Meier, *Job Sharing,* pp. 42, 45.

32. Ibid., pp. 72–4.

33. Ibid., pp. 60, 44.

34. Ibid., p. 84.

35. Ibid., p. 80.

36. Ibid., p. 78.

37. William Arkin and Lynne R. Dobrofsky, "Job Sharing," in *Working Couples,* ed. R. and R. Rapoport (New York: Harper & Row, 1978), p. 132.

38. Nollen, Eddy, and Martin, *Permanent Part-Time Employment,* p. 155.

39. Silverstein and Srb, *Flexitime,* p. 42; Willi Haller, *Flexyear: The Ultimate Work Hour Concept* (New York: Interflex, 1977); Bernhard Teriet, "Flexiyear Schedules— Only a Matter of Time?" *Monthly Labor Review* (December 1977) pp. 62–65.

40. Silverstein and Srb, *Flexitime,* p. 43.

41. Glickman, *Changing Schedules of Work,* p. 68.

42. Ibid., p. 72; *NCAWP Newsletter* (Winter 1979), p. 12.

43. See Silverstein and Srb, *Flexitime,* pp. 33–7; Bohlander, *Flextime,* pp. 49–57; Martin, *Hours of Work,* p. 50; Nollen, Eddy and Martin, *Permanent Part-Time Employment,* pp. 128–36, 171.

44. Glickman, *Changing Schedules of Work,* p. 66.

45. *Newsweek,* May 13, 1980.

46. *NCAWP Newsletter* (Summer 1979), p. 4.

47. *Statistical Portrait,* p. 46.

48. Meier, *Job Sharing,* p. 39.

49. "Project JOIN: Final Report Available Shortly," *NCAWP Newsletter* (Spring 1979), p. 3.

50. *Statistical Portrait,* p. 50.

51. Nollen, *Permanent Part-Time Employment,* pp. 133–4.

52. Carl Selinger, past manager of the Port Authority of New York and New Jersey Staggered Work Hours Project, quoted in *NCAWP Newsletter* (Winter 1979), p. 11.

53. Glickman, *Changing Schedules of Work,* pp. 55, 80–83.

Chapter 7

Women and Housing: The Limitations of Liberal Reform

Irene Diamond

During the 1970s housing policy was not an important issue for American feminists. Though feminist architects and planners did study how prevailing household design failed to meet the needs of women, the only housing problem that feminist groups placed on the national public agenda was that of mortgage discrimination, a problem specific to dual-earner families and a small group of upper-income and professional women.[1] Yet, during this same period women in working-class and minority communities in the nation's cities have tended to see housing issues as concerns which affect them directly.[2] If organized feminism in the 1980s is to broaden its class and racial base, as many believe it must in order to survive, the issue of affordable housing suitable to the needs of women with children must become an integral component of feminist policy goals. In the absence of serious consideration of what values and principles should guide feminist housing strategies, the development of present housing trends may very well contribute to the breakdown of the patriarchal household in ways which intensify, rather than diminish, class divisions and social isolation among women. My purpose here is to point to some of the trends and policy questions that will need to be considered in that debate.

CHANGES IN HOUSEHOLD
FORMATION AND COMPOSITION

It is somewhat ironic that housing has been a minor issue for feminists because one of the contributing conditions to the emergence of American feminism in

the late 1960s was the decentralized urban space, with its single-family de-
tached units, that national housing policy has favored since World War II. The
isolation and alienation of suburban living made many middle-class women
receptive to feminist criticisms of the traditional household. Yet at the very
same time that this household was being criticized, it underwent transforma-
tions that amounted to a partial revolution. As a consequence of the postpone-
ment of marriage, lower fertility, increased labor-force participation of
married women, and an increased rate of divorce, the traditional family household with a wage-earning husband and a full-time homemaker wife became a
relative rarity: by 1978 one-earner, husband-wife families constituted only 13
percent of all households (Table 7.1). Such figures at a particular point in time
tend to exaggerate the demise of the patriarchal household, concealing as they
do the continuity of women's work and familial lives. For example, most
women still marry over the course of their lives; the proportion of women
between the ages of 30 and 34 who have never married was considerably higher
in 1900 (16.6 percent) than in 1975 (8.2 percent); wage-earning women's
contribution to family income has not risen for at least 20 years; and among
working couples in 1978 women spent an average of 20 hours more per week on
family care than men.[3] Nevertheless, significant changes have occurred. The
question I want to explore here is how these familial changes have affected the
overall structure of housing opportunities in a political system where individualism reigns supreme and the biggest housing "program" consists of tax
incentives for homeowners.[4]

Table 7.1. Composition of Households, * 1978.

Type	Percent of Total
One-earner husband-wife families	13.0%
Two-earner husband-wife families	21.0
Single-parent families	8.0
Childless couples	30.0
Single-person households	21.0
Cohabiting couples	1.5
Other households	5.5

Source: U.S. Bureau of the Census
*A household consists of one or more persons occupying one dwelling unit. The Census
definition of families is "two or more persons related by blood, marriage, or adoption."

The number of separate households in the United States has increased at a
much faster rate than the population itself has grown, as a consequence of
several trends: the generation born since 1940 moving away from home but not
directly into marriage; an increase in the level of divorce across all age groups;

and an increase in widows among the older generations.[5] (Between 1960 and 1970 the number of households increased by 20 percent and between 1970 and 1979 it increased by 22 percent, but between 1960 and 1970 the population itself increased only by 13 percent and between 1970 and 1979 only by 7.7 percent).[6] The conjunction of these changes in household formation, with the delay in childbearing and the increased labor-force participation of married women, has resulted in considerably more diversity of household structures than was true in the past. In 1978, one- and two-person (adult) households constituted over 50 percent of all households—mostly married couples with no children at home and men and women living alone. Households with children are declining as an overall proportion of all households while at the same time the proportion of single-parent households—mostly women—has increased (Table 7.2).

Table 7.2. Composition of Households, 1960–1978.

Type of Household	1960	1970	1978
All households (thousands)	52,799	63,401	76,030
Percent	100.0	100.0	100.0
Nonfamily households	14.7%	18.8%	25.1%
Persons living alone	13.1	17.1	22.0
Other nonfamily households	1.6	1.7	3.1
Family households	85.3	81.2	74.9
Married couple with no children	30.3	30.3	29.9
Married couple with children	44.1	40.3	32.4
One parent with children	4.4	5.0	7.3
Other family households	6.4	5.6	5.3

Source: U.S. Bureau of the Census

FEMALE PARENTS AND POVERTY

While this diversity of household types has undoubtedly generated greater diversity of needs with regard to housing, not all household types have been in the same position to express their housing "preference." In 1977, 41.8 percent of all female-headed families with children lived in poverty, while among black female heads the figure was three-fifths.[7] This income problem means that a central need for most of these single parents is affordable housing. Using average housing costs and household income measures, 1976 estimates indicate that while 80.3 percent of all households could obtain adequate uncrowded housing with 25 percent of their income (the traditional standard for measuring affordability), only 64.7 percent of female-headed multiperson households could afford to do so.[8] Though we do not have actual housing expenses for female-headed families, we can infer from these data that most women cope with their situation by one of three strategies: (1) applying for one of the limited number of slots in federally subsidized housing programs;[9] (2) cutting down on basic necessities in order to obtain housing; or (3) "choosing" housing that is inferior in some way—perhaps a unit that is physically defective, a neighborhood with inferior public services, or one with a high crime rate. Annual housing survey data only deal with the physical characteristics of units, but they indicate that in 1976, 15.1 percent of all female-headed multiperson households lived in units that were physically defective in some way, as opposed to 9.7 percent of all households.[10] It is no wonder, then, that case studies have consistently shown poor women to be the leaders in rent strikes and neighborhood and tenant organizations.

THE RENTAL MARKET

Inadequate incomes—and for black women, income and race—continue to be the major constraints on the housing opportunities of female-headed families. But, today, women with children face additional problems which grow out of assorted market responses to the growth of the new household types we have been discussing. Because women householders rent their housing units (53 percent) more frequently than the general population (35 percent), their fortunes are intimately linked to the housing situation in the rental market where, since the mid-1970s, vacancy rates have declined to new lows.[11] Paradoxically, one of the major reasons for the declining availability of rental units has been the increased attractiveness of the tax benefits of homeownership for higher-income families as inflation has moved such households into ever-higher tax brackets. This increased demand for homeownership—in part attributable to the growth of dual-earner families—has dramatically driven up the price of housing.[12] (Sixty percent of households buying housing for the first time in 1977–78 had two earners.)[13] As a consequence, households with lower incomes have had to turn to the rental market where the stock has not grown substantially, largely because investors have found the homeownership market more profitable. During the 1970s the pressure on the rental market was intensified in many cities by the conversion of existing units to cooperatives and condominiums, a form of housing increasing popular among singles and dual-earner couples who want to combine the tax advantages of homeownership with the locational advantages of center-city living.[14]

NO CHILDREN WANTED

Perhaps the most noteworthy feature of the overall rental situation, both because of what it tells us about American individualism and because of its direct impact on the lives of women, is the rental market's response itself to the growing numbers of one- and two-person households. In an attempt to cater to this new market landlords throughout the 1970s instituted "adults only" policies. A 1980 national survey of renters and the managers of their rental housing estimated that in that year 26 percent of all rental units in the nation were in buildings or complexes which did not allow children, while in 1974 the rate was 17 percent. This change has occurred because existing buildings have established new policies and because newer units are much more likely to be constructed with such policies in place—33 percent of all complexes constructed since 1977 accepted no children.[15] While the national average for exclusionary practices is high, the rates are even higher in certain regions of the country. For instance, a 1979 survey of units advertised in newspapers in California cities found that 71 percent of the complexes in Los Angeles excluded children.[16] Though the available evidence is inconsistent as to whether female-headed families are more likely to encounter restrictive practices than other types of families who are in the rental market, the emotional toll is much greater for women who are alone with their children and do not even have the possibility of sharing their frustrations and protracted searches with other adults.[17]

The one pattern that a variety of different studies consistently document is that exclusionary practices, as well as restrictive practices—forbidding two children to share a room or forbidding children of the opposite sex to share a bedroom—are more common in predominantly white neighborhoods and complexes.[18] Because the net effect of such practices is to reinforce patterns of racial segregation, civil rights groups have argued that these practices constitute a new form of race discrimination.[19] While I am not disagreeing with such an interpretation, I would suggest that these developments should also be understood in terms of the differences between black and white communities regarding the collective responsibility toward children.

TOWARD NEW DEFINITIONS: COLLECTIVE RESPONSIBILITIES AND URBAN SPACE

Clearly the trends that I have just outlined do not bode well for women with children. While scholars have observed that gentrification is occurring because of the breakdown of the patriarchal household, the crucial question is whether the new patterns of household organization permit women more control over their lives.[20] For a black woman with children living in the central city, the fact that greater numbers of single women can now purchase condominiums provides little solace.[21] And for the recently separated white woman who—after a series of different housing moves in order to reconcile her competing needs for supportive arrangements for her children, new social contacts, and a reasonable commuting range for her job-training program—receives an eviction notice telling her that she most move once again because the management has instituted a no-children policy, the new patterns are also ambiguous.[22] The new divide would almost appear to be between women with children and women without.

Are these problems an inevitable part of the process of change? Can they be attributed to unique features of American political life? Or have they arisen precisely because the household changes have only been partial ones? The fact that most other industrialized nations in the world today have experienced with the United States many of the same changes in household formation and composition, yet in no other country do we find widespread and explicit exclusionary rental practices regarding children, lends support to the hypothesis that for this particular problem America may actually be unique.[23] I would argue that while other nations vary considerably in their sense of collective responsibility for those who are perceived as disadvantaged, and thus differ both in the comprehensiveness of their social welfare policies and the degree to which the social consequences of private market activity is regulated, few countries in the world approach the United States in terms of the primacy that is placed on individualism. Whereas in Denmark the sense of collective responsibility for the next generation is such that social authorities have a special responsibility to find housing for single parents, and individuals who want to avoid children fend for themselves, in the United States, the social relations that permit individual existence are obscured by discussions of "balancing" the individual rights of everyone—including those who do not want to live near children.

As I have demonstrated throughout this discussion, the housing problems of women are the result of a complex web of structural relationships and would not be eliminated if federal legislation forbidding discrimination against families with children were enacted tomorrow.[24] The importance of such actions should not be dismissed; a focus on children which at the same time forces public recognition that women need greater control over the conditions of their lives is potentially revolutionary. In conjunction with any such actions, however, attention must also be paid to the political and economic interests which determine for whom housing will be produced. The subtle shift in recent years within subsidized housing programs toward housing for the elderly may have more to do with racism and fear of female-headed families than with the power of the Grey Panthers.[25] I would argue that feminists must begin here—on the issue of affordable housing for families with children—for to do otherwise necessarily increases divisions among women. Yet for feminists this demand must be made within a larger agenda. Because the home has historically been assumed to be the province of women and public work the province of men, a variety of different practices and policies—from kitchen designs which inhibit the sharing of tasks, to land-use regulations which prohibit communal spaces for child care, to transportation systems and the setting of hours of social-service institutions—have all been predicated on and therefore reinforced the traditional division of labor.[26] When any woman with a child tries to navigate across the boundaries between work and home the difficulties are immense; when she is the only adult in a household, they approach the impossible. The plight of female-headed black families in many public housing projects in the nation's cities provides moving testimony that affordable housing which is disconnected from supportive community services does not permit women to gain control over their lives.

In summary, housing policy goals for feminists must be multifaceted. These goals cannot rest exclusively with issues of either access or production; liberal reformers might focus on the former and radical reformers, on the latter. If, however, we are eventually to achieve a society in which all persons share in the different forms of productive work that make us persons, in the family and the labor force, political struggle about what constitutes livable housing and urban space for women is essential.

Notes

1. Legislation forbidding such sex discriminatory practices as lenders discounting a woman's income when she was of childbearing age passed the Congress in 1974 with little opposition. Such practices had become untenable in a housing market which could not sustain itself on the demand generated by single-earner families.

2. Ronald Lawson, Stephen Barton, and Jenna Joselit, "From Kitchen to Storefront: Women in the Tenant Movement," in *New Space for Women,* ed. Gerda R. Wekerle, Rebecca Peterson, and David Morley (Boulder: Westview Press, 1980).

3. For marriage data, see George Masnick and Mary Jo Bane, *The Nation's Families: 1960–1990* (Joint Center for Urban Studies of MIT and Harvard University, 1980), Table B.4, p. 149; wage and family-care data cited in Elliott Currie, Robert Dunn, and David Fogarty, "The New Immiseration Stagflation, Inequality, and the Working Class," *Socialist Review,* 1981 No. 54, pp. 14–15.

4. John C. Simonson in "Tax Expenditures for Homeowners," (unpublished study for the Department of Housing and Urban Development, 1981) estimates that the net cost to the Treasury for the tax savings available to homeowners in fiscal year 1981 was 40 billion dollars, approximately four times the total direct outlays for all of HUD's programs in that year.

5. See Masnick and Bane, *The Nation's Families,* pp. 12–37 for more detailed discussions of these trends.

6. U.S. Department of Housing and Urban Development, Office of Policy Development and Research, "Housing Our Families" (Washington, D.C.: Superintendent of Documents, August 1980).

7. Ibid., p. 3.3.

8. U.S. Department of Housing and Urban Development, Office of Policy Development and Research, "How Well Are We Housed? 2. Female-Headed Households" (Washington, D.C.: Superintendent of Documents, November 1978), Table 11.

9. Federally subsidized housing programs are not entitlement programs. Thus, in

1978 only 6 percent of all income-eligible households participated in such programs. Female-headed families constitute the majority of those households who do participate.

10. "How Well Are We Housed?" p. 7. It is important to note that among households with children, for both black and white, female-headed families are more likely to be inadequately housed than male-headed families. On the other hand for every family type blacks are more likely to be inadequately housed than whites. See "Housing Our Families," Appendix B.

11. Ibid., p. 7.

12. Between 1972 and 1978, the price of an average one-family new home increased by 72 percent nationally. Data from U.S. Department of Housing and Urban Development as cited by Currie et al., "The New Immiseration."

13. Michael E. Stone, "The Housing Problem in the United States; Problems and Prospects," *Socialist Review,* No. 52, (July–August 1980), p. 103.

14. The Department of Housing and Urban Development's study of conversion in 12 SMSAs with high levels of conversion activity observes that condominium owners "are predominantly young, single professionals with higher than average incomes" (*The Conversion of Rental Housing to Condominiums and Cooperatives,* HUD, June, 1981). Only 8 percent of the households have three or more persons.

15. "Measuring Restrictive Rental Practices Affecting Families with Children: A National Survey" (Washington, D.C.: Superintendent of Documents, July 1980), pp. 45–46.

16. Doris Ashford and Perla Eston, *The Extent and Effects of Discrimination against Children in Rental Housing: A Study of Five California Cities* (Santa Monica: Fair Housing for Chidren, 1979).

17. The 1980 national survey of renters found that half of all families with children, irrespective of the sex of the household head, reported that when last looking for a place to live they found places where they wanted to live but couldn't because of restrictive practices about children (See "Measuring Restrictive Rental Practices Affecting Families with Children," Table V–2). These data should perhaps be interpreted with some caution because owing to sampling techniques there were only 118 female heads of households with children in the sample. On the other hand an earlier Rand Corporation study of movers over a five-year period in two cities, a sample that contained a substantial number of female heads of households, found that female heads reported encountering discrimination because of children more often than husband-wife families. (These data have yet to be published but for a preliminary discussion, see "Housing Our Families" p. 4-3). And finally a 1980 study of responses to public service announcements regarding discrimination against families with children revealed that female heads were disproportionately represented among callers in comparison with their overall representation in the population of renter families with children. While these data suggest the possibility of more discrimination, I would argue they provide evidence of the greater emotional toll on female-headed families. [See Jane G. Greene and Glenda P. Blake, "How Restrictive Practices Affect Families with Children," (Washington, D.C.: Office of Policy Development and Research, U.S. Department of Housing and Urban Development, 1980).] All of these studies in conjunction with Robert S. Weiss's research on single parents ["Housing for Single Parents" in *Housing Policy for the 1980's* ed. Dale Rogers Marshall (Lexington, Mass.: Lexington Press, 1980)] suggest that while all families with children will be effected by explicit exclusionary and restrictive practices in apartment complexes, female heads are more likely to be subject to the more subtle form of discrimination where landlords or rental agents turn away divorced or separated women with children. It may be felt that such women are financially unreliable, that their social life will be too active or they will be unable to

supervise their children. The response in these situations is to their deviant family status, rather than children *per se.*

18. Ashford and Eston, *The Extent and Effects of Discrimination;* Jane Greene, *An Evaluation of the Exclusion of Children From Apartments in Dallas* (Dallas: J.G. and Associates, Inc., December 1978); "Measuring Restrictive Practices"; Jan Linker and Debra L. Elovich, "An Analysis of the Adults—Only Rental Market Final Report," mimeographed (Atlanta, Georgia: Emory University: September 1980).

19. Children's Defense Fund "Background Memorandum on Housing Discrimination against Families with Children," mimeographed (Washington D.C.: Children's Defense Fund, 1980).

20. "Ann R. Markusen, "City Spatial Structure, Women's Household Work, and National Urban Policy," *Signs Supplement 5,* 3 (Spring 1980): 35.

21. *The Conversion of Rental Housing to Condominiums and Cooperatives* (HUD, June 1981) notes that 36 percent of the owners of converted units are female whereas females constitute only 10 percent of all owner-occupied housing. Interestingly, the proportion of females among *newly* built condominiums is 12 percent.

22. The available research on the housing problems of women who have been recently divorced or separated indicates that countrary to the conventional wisdom that divorced women with children stay put in the family residence, the more typical pattern is a series of different housing moves. Joint Center for Urban Studies of M.I.T. and Harvard University, *Families in Transition* (forthcoming).

23. In Western Germany where much of the housing market is private rental apartments, families with a large number of children may have a particularly difficult time finding housing. Because of the current shortage conditions, families with children are necessarily affected and landlords have been known to turn such families away, but conversations with housing experts indicate that explicit exclusionary practices are not the major barrier for such families. Income and ethnicity appear to be more important constraints.

24. Currently there is no federal legislation forbidding discrimination against families with children in the private rental market. Such discrimination is prohibited through regulation in both federally subsidized and insured rental housing, but there is evidence of restrictive practices in insured housing. Several states and localities have antidiscrimination legislation pertaining to families with children. Enforcement has been a crucial problem as the antidiscrimination regulations often do not provide for monitoring systems. For published discussion of these issues see "Housing Our Families."

25. During recent years federal outlays for public housing have been reduced and outlays for new construction have gone to the Section 8 program. While families with children are heavily represented in public housing, the residents of Section 8 new projects are disproportionately elderly. For data on new reservations in the different subsidized housing programs, see Table 7–1 in "Housing Our Families."

26. For further discussion of these issues, see Dolores Hayden, "What Would a Non-Sexist City Be Like? Speculations on Housing, Urban Design, and Human Work," *Signs Supplement 5,* 3 (Spring 1980).

27. The special housing needs of single parents has been a subject of some discussion in recent years and one policy option that has received increasing attention in the United States, Britain, and Canada is the creation of housing projects with social services exclusively for single parents and their children. While such projects may have a place when immediate relief is needed in crisis situations (e.g., areas with acute housing shortages or refuges for women escaping from violent spouses) and may provide uniquely supportive environments, I would suggest that such housing on a long-term basis reinforces the already disturbing patterns toward segregation by family types.

Part IV
Motherhood: Policy Failures

Introduction

While women's roles as workers have received increasing governmental attention over the last two decades, their roles as mothers, as childbearers and childrearers, have either been ignored or misrepresented in the public policy arena. Why?

Motherhood is the role which ties women to the most traditional of American institutions—the family; which most clearly defines the female personality—nurturing; and which most effectively establishes women's particular sphere of influence—the home. Sexist ideology uses motherhood, even the *capacity* to reproduce, to establish woman's place and to restrict her ability to succeed in nontraditional roles. Thus, it is not surprising that policy makers have resisted measures which would allow women to combine motherhood with other economic, social, and political roles; to do otherwise would be to legitimate the process of role change.

Despite the failure of the political process to assist women in developing a range of life options, women are doing so at a rapid pace. More women than ever before are choosing to combine roles as mothers with roles as workers outside the home. While such choices are usually motivated by economic necessity, most working mothers feel that they combine these roles relatively successfully. In the 1980 Virginia Slims American Women's Opinion Poll, 47 percent of working mothers believe they are as good as mothers as they would be if not working, as compared to 16 percent who do not.[1] Almost one-third of the women surveyed, however, agreed that combining work and motherhood does not leave them enough time for themselves.[2]

The Virginia Slims Poll also showed that Americans have increasingly favorable attitudes toward child care. Seventy-five percent of the women and 66 percent of the men in 1980 favored an increase in day-care facilities, as compared to 63 and 47 percent respectively in 1970.[3] Almost half of the women under 30 who were not working indicated that they would probably look for jobs if day-care facilities were available.[4]

What obstacles do women face in the policy-making process as they attempt to redefine the role of mother? Norgren's Chapter 8 on the failure to achieve a national child-care policy illustrates the power of traditional ideology to counter role change. Historically, child care has rarely been approached as a policy to benefit working women. Child-care facilities were initially established with the goal of reducing social pathology among poor children. Child-care programs were supported in the Depression because of the additional employment opportunities they would provide. Briefly, in World War II, child care was perceived as a program to assist mothers, but only those mothers working in defense-related industries. The near-passage of a national child-care program in 1971 may be attributed to the incremental expansion of earlier programs, such as Head Start, emphasizing early childhood education and day-care programs established to reduce welfare. Nixon's veto of the legislation because of its "family-weakening implications" and the failure of Congress to override that veto illustrated the strength of traditional ideology regarding mother-at-home, as well as the ineffectiveness of lobbying efforts on behalf of child care. Child-care legislation has foundered since 1971 because of internal divisions within the child-care coalition and growing external opposition from the right.

In contrast, the legislative effort in 1978 to ban discrimination on the basis of "pregnancy, childbirth and other related medical conditions" was successful. Opponents of the legislation—primarily business organizations—argued that the provision of pregnancy benefits, besides being costly, would produce irresponsible employment behavior among women workers. The Pregnancy Discrimination Act passed despite these objections both because it represented an incremental change in an accepted field, antidiscrimination policy, and because a broad coalition of women's groups, civil rights groups, and labor unions united behind it.

As Huckle shows in Chapter 9, the passage of the pregnancy benefits legislation cannot be attributed to a new-found governmental view that women should have special rights as workers because they perform a necessary social role, childbearing. Rather, the support for the legislation was based on the principle of equity: if male workers are covered for a wide range of medical disabilities, female workers should not be excluded from disability benefits on the basis of pregnancy.

Thus far public policy on motherhood has failed to address the underlying need of mothers for a variety of work options. While the bearing and rearing of children disrupt a woman's working life, work options adapted to women's roles as mothers rarely exist. Rather, women must adapt their roles as mothers to their roles as workers.

A revealing irony is that, while the Pregnancy Disability Act banned one form of discrimination, it sustained governmental restrictions on women's reproductive choices by allowing employers to refuse to pay the costs of abortions. The antiabortion amendment shows the willingness of policy makers to intervene on the question of motherhood when that intervention upholds traditional values, while rejecting motherhood issues when government intervention would enhance role change.

Notes

1. Roper Organization, *The 1980 Virginia Slims American Women's Opinion Poll*, p. 12.
2. Ibid., p. 13.
3. Ibid.
4. Ibid.

Chapter 8

In Search of a National Child-Care Policy: Background and Prospects*

Jill Norgren

Americans express ambivalence about the desirable role of the state in the upbringing of their children. The imposition of compulsory school attendance achieved between 1852 and 1918 occurred in an atmosphere rife with dissension. Compulsory attendance laws brought unresolved issues of the republic into sharp relief by imposing explicit values, and the resulting costs, on the lives of citizens and their offspring. These education laws not only authorized the state to demand the presence of a child in school but also, once there, to inculcate uniform, increasingly national values and attitudes. While at one level debate centered upon the question of state versus parental custody of the child, the broader issue was the spectre of standardized behavior and thought which threatened the American tradition of "being one's own man"—the liberal value of individualism.[1]

Today Americans have arrived at a consensus concerning the need for compulsory schooling and the acceptability of the government's role in this function. The same cannot be said for child-care programs. Despite the momentum gathered in the Johnson and early Nixon administrations and a monotonically increasing rate of employment among women with small children, a clearly defined national policy in the area of child care has yet to be enacted. Nevertheless, the issue fundamental to the debate concerning day care—one the day-care lobby must address more forcefully—is the same as that presented by the compulsory school attendance controversy: in what ways

---

*An earlier version of this article was published in the *Western Political Quarterly, 34:* 127–142. Reprinted by permission of the University of Utah, Copyright Holder.

do changing social and economic conditions require new relationships between the family and the state? While Americans accept schooling as necessary preparation for an increasingly technological, homogeneous society, rejection of a comprehensive, national child-care policy continues despite conditions which advocates cite as justification for government involvement.[2] Between 1971 and 1979 three major congressional initiatives toward the development of comprehensive child-care policy were defeated—one by presidential veto.[3]

This chapter reviews the history of day care in the United States and examines the political events and ideological backdrop that contributed to the defeat of committed congressional sponsors and a broad coalition of lobby groups over this eight-year period. The specifics of each legislative episode vary, but similar factors undermined all the efforts. Political factors including the cost of potential programs, a diffuse and contentious coalition of lobby groups, and substantive programmatic differences precipitated defeat. Fundamental myths about American life exacerbated by the bleak popular image evoked by day-care centers, however, fed a political atmosphere that permitted these repeated defeats to take place. Political conservatives continue to manipulate these myths as part of their effort to defeat the concept of a national family policy.

THE DEVELOPMENT OF PUBLICLY FUNDED DAY CARE: THE POWER OF IMAGES AND IDEOLOGY

Early Years

In 1971 President Nixon vetoed the first comprehensive child-care legislation passed by Congress.[4] In the message accompanying his veto Nixon referred to the legislation as having "family-weakening implications," suggested that it would "commit the vast moral authority of the National Government to the side of communal approaches to child rearing over against the family-centered approach [sic], and claimed that the legislation before him would be "truly a long leap into the dark for the United States Government and the American people."[5] The severe, even caustic language reflected significant differences between the White House and Congress over technical content—the nature of the means test, the prime sponsor provision, and the level of funding for a comprehensive program. More than this, however, the Nixon veto underscored the negative social and political image long attached to day care in the United States.

Traditionally Americans have viewed day-care centers as bleak, understaffed institutions where children from poor or troubled families could be cared for under the aegis of a charitable organization or the state. More recently, the use of day-care centers in socialist and communist nations has touched the already negative physical image with political tones suggestive of state-controlled, and therefore, critics say, family-weakening child rearing. The images of grim physical surroundings and the incipient communism referred to in the Nixon veto stand in sharp contrast to the generally positive regard for nursery school, kindergarten and, more recently, Head Start, all programs designed for preschool children but perceived as educational rather than custodial.

Day care began as a charitable service for the children of poor, working mothers, perhaps as early as the 1820s or 1830s.[6] Following the Civil War, the number of centers expanded as veterans' widows and an increasing number of immigrant women found it necessary to work. Virtually all day-care histories describe the surroundings as dreary with time devoted to the teaching of moral principles, cleanliness, and useful skills. While this may not present a particularly attractive picture to the twentiety-century mind, the nineteenth-century schoolhouse was similar both in physical appearance and pedagogical goals.

Reforms of various kinds were introduced at the turn of the century. The earliest centered on health and safety conditions with some municipalities initiating procedures for the supervision and inspection of centers. At the same time the effects of the kindergarten movement began to filter down. For the first time trained staff were hired; in more progressive centers this included teachers with training in the methods of Froebel and Montessori. Prior to the 1920s the clientele appears best described as working class with some children from poor or troubled families.

In retrospect, we might expect that day care would have evolved into an institution similar to an all-day nursery school with a relatively positive image. This did not prove to be the case owing in large measure to the influence of newly professionalized social workers, hired by the centers in the 1920s. Their emphasis on the existence of social pathologies among day-care families and their insistence on the use of intake procedures and formal casework eventually imparted the aura of a social welfare service to these programs.[7] As a result fewer families resorted to day care and, in many instances, those that did were in some way or another "troubled families." Reputation and reality chased each other. In the period between World War I and the Depression the public began to build a negative image of day care based on this social welfare orientation, and has sustained this image until the present.

Early Government-Sponsored Programs

Until the 1930s group day care evolved in each community according to need and the response of local philanthropic and social welfare organizations. The Depression strained or bankrupted the resources of these private agencies and forced the closing of most centers. In 1933, however, the federal government inaugurated a day-care program administered by the Federal Emergency Relief

Administration (later the Works Progress Administration). As a result of federal funds, by 1937 nearly 2,000 centers were established by state departments of education. Although the needs of children were discussed, the primary purpose of the program centered upon the creation of jobs for unemployed teachers, nurses, and other school personnel. This was the first of repeated uses of day care as an employment program rather than as a child-focused service. (As we will see, the 1960s "workfare" lobby supported day care as an adjunct to welfare reform. More recently, the AFL-CIO has recognized that expanded day care could provide career opportunities for the growing number of unemployed elementary and secondary school teachers and has become an active, identifiable participant in the child-care lobby.) The employment bias of the federal commitment became more apparent when the economy improved enough to permit the rehiring of center personnel at their original jobs. Rather than move toward a child-focused day-care policy, federal funding was decreased and officials prepared to terminate the program.

The entry of the United States into the war, however, revived interest in day care and triggered a second, brief era of nationally subsidized centers. Congress authorized funds for the care of children of *working* mothers, but official reluctance to encourage working mothers except where required by the war effort resulted in allocations only to defense areas with war-related employment.[8] As a result major population centers including New York City did not qualify.[9] As with the earlier New Deal legislation, this wartime legislation was not the beginning of an ongoing program of nationally subsidized day care. Both programs represented no more than specific responses to the problems of the times—adult problems. Neither involved long-term policy commitments to children.

THE POSTWAR YEARS: TRADITIONAL ATTITUDES AND NEW SOCIAL FORCES

Although women with children entered the labor market in ever-increasing numbers after an initial postwar lull, the federal government made no effort to respond to the needs of children of working parents. Many officials, feeling that a mother's place is at home, discouraged policy discussion. Moreover, nothing on record suggests lobbying by parents of young children to counter this government position.

Despite the wartime experience and contemporary evidence to the contrary, day care was characterized as a social welfare service for problem families. Well into the 1960s articles by psychologists and social workers focused on day care in terms of social or individual pathology. At the 1965 National Conference on Day Care, the Children's Bureau distributed a pamphlet which asked,

Who needs day care?
Giorgi does. When his father deserted the family . . .

Alice does. Her father . . . was seriously disabled in an automobile accident. . . .

Esther does. She is 4 and mentally retarded. Her parents want her to live at home but are finding this . . . difficult. . . .

Paul does . . . and so do his (8) brothers and sisters. . . .
Their father is unemployed, their mother hospitalized. The family lives in two rooms in a slum tenement. . . .[10]

The orientation of the Children's Bureau and many of the other institutions and professionals caught up in this debate mirrored deeper attitudes concerning the American family and maternal roles. Alice Rossi has written of the postwar period:

> For the first time in the history of any known society motherhood has become a full-time occupation for adult women. Why? American woman has been encouraged by the experts to whom she had turned for guidance in childrearing, to believe her children need her continuous presence, supervision, and care and that she should find complete fulfillment in the role.[11]

The growth in female employment over the past quarter-century, however, strongly indicates other social and economic forces at work:[12] the intensification of change from a rural to an urban-oriented economy requiring cash income; an expanding economy, in particular service industries offering employment opportunities to women; higher levels of female education; a dramatic increase in the number of divorced parents and single mothers; the monetary demands of a materialistic society, exacerbated by the rising rate of inflation; and finally, the influences of the feminist movement.

While the social and economic landscape of America was undergoing change, the small, but persistent National Committee for Day Care successfully lobbied Congress for the resumption of federal day-care funding. In 1962, 16 years after the federal government had terminated its funding of day care, Congress tentatively recommitted funds to the program as part of the Public Welfare Amendments to the Social Security Act.[13] This legislation reflected the efforts of traditional day-care advocates with a social welfare, child-focused viewpoint and a new congressional "workfare" caucus that considered day care a necessary adjutant to welfare reform and job training programs. The disparate goals of this legislative coalition were mirrored by the bill it produced, which failed to delineate whether the government's commitment was to the needs of children or to the reduction of welfare dependency.

In 1967, amendments to the Social Security Act were passed establishing an open-ended day-care funding authorization (up to 75 percent of costs) for (1) any parent participating in the government's Work Incentive Program (WIN), and (2) individuals identified by state welfare departments as "past, present or future recipients of Aid for Dependent Children" (AFDC). Whatever the ambiguity of objectives in the 1962 legislation, the intent of the 1967 amendments appeared clear—the equation of expanded day care with a reduction in welfare dependence. As social policy, the 1967 legislation marked the first time since the federal government initiated social welfare programs that "it became acceptable to think of mothers with dependent, small children as proper objects of the effort to get the very poor off the relief rolls and onto the tax rolls."[14]

Ironically, the impact of the 1967 legislation was not on welfare rolls. The funding authorization and liberal eligibility guidelines did encourage substantial growth in the number of day-care centers. Enrollment in New York City's group day-care program, for example, rose dramatically from 8,000 children in 1970 to 15,000 in 1971.[15] The children enrolled, however, were primarily the offspring of already employed mothers of working and occasionally middle-class, professional background. This 1967 legislation initiated an era of rapidly expanding day care and provided a policy base from which a radically reconstituted day-care coalition would work in its struggle to refashion federally subsidized day care into a comprehensive child-care policy.[16]

COMPREHENSIVE CHILD-CARE POLICY: CREEP OR CRESCENDO

Charles Lindblom has described our political process as one which permits only incremental policy change.[17] The politics of child care from 1969 to the present support Lindblom's contention, suggesting that even in a near-ideal policy environment, incrementalism will prevail. The 1971 Comprehensive Child Care Act, which proponents hoped to use as a vehicle for instituting the new era of child care, was considered in such an environment. The country's new preschool program, Head Start, was held in high regard. The 1970 White House Conference on Children had also endorsed the concept of child development. An administration, which might be expected to oppose the intervention of the state in family life, had committed itself to aid children in the first five years of life and specifically supported day care as a program necessary to welfare reform. Several congressmen stood ready not just to sponsor child-care legislation, but to work for it. Public awareness and interest in the use of community programs for community change was growing, as was the impact of the feminist movement. In addition, there was no lobby organized to oppose day care in this period. With all these positive factors operating on their behalf, day-care advocates had only to find a common ground which could command support in Congress and the White House.

With little general congressional debate and even less public dialogue, several measures were considered in committee over this two-year period.[18] The bill ultimately receiving serious attention was the Comprehensive Child Development Act, Title V of the Economic Opportunity Amendments of 1971 (S. 2007). This legislation was backed by a coalition of two dozen interest groups including day care and early childhood education professionals, labor, community control advocates, and feminists coordinated by Marion Wright Edelman of the Children's Defense Fund. These potentially fractious partisans with limited funds and lobby experience, and disparate objectives, nonetheless propelled a major social policy measure through Congress in amazingly little time.[19] Their final bill, S. 2007, outlined an extensive network of federally funded day-care centers with comprehensive medical, educational, nutritional, and social services for preschool and school-age children. The appropriation request for fiscal year 1972–73 was two billion dollars. Originally, congressional sponsors had proposed free day care to families with incomes below $6,900, with sliding scale fees for families above this figure—an attempt to broaden the potential clientele. Eventually the figure for totally subsidized services was dropped to $4,320, a move meant to appease the Nixon administration whose representative, HEW secretary Richardson, had been taken off guard by the celerity of sponsors Mondale and Brademas's efforts and had failed to structure meaningful countermeasures in Congress. The final bill mandated extensive community and parental involvement, including a highly controversial provision for prime sponsorship by communities with populations as low as 5,000. The emphasis in the day-care centers, drawing upon the Head Start model, would be on cognitive as well as social development with all the necessary support services. Short of the universal, free day care somewhat glibly demanded by radical feminists, who did virtually no lobbying, most lobbyists felt S. 2007 represented a fairly satisfactory initiative which would catapult the United States into an era of child development–oriented day care.

S. 2007, adopted by both houses of Congress, became history rather than public law when President Nixon vetoed the bill late in 1971. Explanations for the president's veto abound. First, the nation's governors were virtually unanimous in their opposition to the community control-prime sponsor provisions of the legislation and had communicated this opposition to the White House. Second, the White House was concerned that approval of the bill might further antagonize the conservative wing of the Republican party, already angered by Nixon's new China policy. The veto was intraparty fence mending—a sign that Nixon had not abandoned all conservative standards. Finally, the veto was consistent with the social and fiscal philosophies of the Nixon administration.

POST-1971 POLITICS

Gilbert Steiner has observed that comprehensive child care "had a quick fling" on the congressional agenda and was gone. In his study, *The Children's Cause,* published five years after the Nixon veto, Steiner implied that child-care proponents had ceased to work for child care after the 1971 defeat; that they had failed to consider that success might "ultimately take a decade and that interim failures were not final." In Lindblom's terms, they had failed to learn the lesson of incrementalism.[20] Congressional sponsors and child-care lobbyists did use a confluence of positive attitudes and events to work swiftly on comprehensive policy proposals between 1969 and 1971. This legislative blossoming, however, was the culmination of a decade of social debate and political action concerning child care, child development, and preschool education. Congress passed two day-care bills during the 1960s, reestablishing federal funding for child care for the first time since World War II. Head Start was born mid-decade. The 1969–71 comprehensive child-care legislation married the older tradition of custodial day care with newer concepts of comprehensive, educationally focused programming. These policy increments suggest not a brief fling but sustained political wooing.

While the 1971 legislation is the benchmark of national comprehensive child-care politics, the Nixon veto did not signal the end of lobbying or congressional action: hearings were held in three separate years—1974, 1977, and 1978—and bills considered or sent to committee in 1972, 1975, and 1979.[21] But the political climate did change significantly after the veto. Steiner correctly observes that proponents could not expect the same highly favorable environment. The defeat also strained the solidarity that existed among groups like the Child Welfare League of America, the National Association for the Education of Young Children, the Day Care and Child Development Council of America, the UAW, the National Welfare Rights Organization, religious organizations, women's groups, and the many local community control–oriented organizations.[22] Differences in approach to policy that were adroitly compromised when success appeared imminent reemerged after the propitious moment passed.

The demands of the AFL-CIO that responsibility for the future development of child care in the United States be given to the public schools have been particularly divisive. With the public schools as prime sponsors, longstanding questions of licensing, local versus federal standards, and community versus professional control would be resolved. Child care would be professionalized (absorbing, not coincidentally, unemployed teachers), costs radically increased, and, in all likelihood, the community involvement and control achieved in many centers would end.[23] As a result of the union's uncompromising stance, in many communities unions are now viewed as opportunists with no real commitment to children or their parents. Opponents have outlined four objections to labor's proposal: (1) the irrationality of establishing as prime sponsors institutions that have not proven themselves "to be a model of efficiency or cost-effectiveness by even the loosest standards";[24] (2) a blurring of the distinction between programs for infants or preschoolers and regular schoolchildren; (3) an unwillingness to relinquish community control; and (4) unreasonably high standards, including a far more and unnecessarily professionalized staff and, therefore, greatly escalated program costs which will obviate chances of selling the nation on an expanded program of federally subsidized child care. Paradoxically, it may well be the case that only these big labor unions with their financial resources, regional and Washington lobbyists, and understanding of the media have the ability to promote serious congressional or White House interest.

Even presuming labor's resources and the compromises this might require from other interest groups, the immediate realization of a national child-care policy may now prove beyond reach. First, as one Senate aide recently remarked, "neither Congress nor the White House is in the mood for a new program . . . only cutbacks and fiscal austerity." Second, the strong and longstanding social and political biases militating against a national child-care policy, which were almost neutralized for a few years, have been reasserted, perhaps more vigorously than ever. The next section of this chapter describes current federal child-care policies and explores the importance of these less political reasons for the absence of a national child-care policy. It considers whether, as happened earlier with compulsory school attendance, the imperatives of new social values and economic forces will lead to major changes in eligibility, funding, and governance of child-care programs in the United States in the forthcoming decade.

CHILD CARE POLICY TODAY

President Nixon's veto of the 1971 "Comprehensive Child Care Act" portrayed child-care programs as "family weakening" and likely to "commit the vast moral authority of the National Government to the side of communal approaches of child rearing." "All other factors being equal," Nixon stated, "good public policy requires that we enhance rather than diminish both parental authority and parental involvement with children—particularly in those decisive years when social attitudes and a conscience are formed and religious and moral principles are first inculcated."[25] Conservative rhetoric? It is easy to dismiss it as such, but to do so precludes any understanding of the failure of the United States to develop a national child-care policy, or more broadly, family policy, similar to that found in many of the industrialized nations of Europe.[26] Although couched in particularly forceful language, in fact, President Nixon's sentiments may be shared by a great number of Americans.[27]

Opposition to a national child-care policy has found expression in a variety of arguments ranging from the issue of expense to statements of insufficient evidence of demand, or unwillingness to accept the particular technical language of the bill. The "issues of the moment," it would seem, are vehicles through which underlying biases concerning the relationship of the individual and the family to the state, and the proper role for mothers are expressed. Those who favor a national child-care policy are aware of these biases, but have failed to counteract their influence. As a result, child-care policy currently exists only as a stepchild to welfare policy for the poor and tax policy for the middle class.

The federal government subsidizes child care either directly through social service programs aimed at welfare recipients and families living below the poverty line, or indirectly through the child-care tax credit under the Internal Revenue Code. The government contributes direct payments primarily through Title XX of the Social Security Act. Other direct subsidy child-care programs also aimed at welfare or below poverty income families include Head Start and those administered by the Departments of Agriculture, Interior, Housing and Urban Development, and the Community Services Administration.[28] In contrast, the government's indirect subsidy via the child-care tax credit suggests broader eligibility. In reality, however, because of "the nature of the tax credit and the structure of our tax system—the credit is not refundable and, on the average, four person families with incomes below $7,500 do not pay any federal income taxes—the credit is largely of use to middle and upper-income families."[29] Congressional Budget Office figures indicate that two-thirds of the tax expenditure funds went to families with incomes over $15,000.[30] Thus, despite the estimated $2.3 billion spent on direct and indirect subsidy of child care by the federal government, as it presently stands our child-care "policy" fails to provide any assistance for a large portion of the population, lacks flexibility for many of those families using direct subsidy programs, and provides no service per se for families using the indirect subsidy tax credit.

What most critically mars the current collection of child-care programs in the United States is the dearth of assistance for low-income, working parents. Parents in this population find that the level of their income disqualifies them from Title XX assistance (or that of other programs) while on the other hand their incomes are too low to benefit from the tax credit. The 1979 Cranston bill took particular note of this group and was intent upon providing a remedy.

In contrast, welfare and low-income families qualify for a variety of family or day-care center programs. Critics of these programs, however, argue that they fail to provide for parental discretion and urge a policy of vouchers—permitting the choice of center and encouraging institutional accountability—or a negative income tax option.[31] Waiting lists or total lack of facilities, of course, preclude an unknown number of low-income children from receiving any kind of government-subsidized care. Middle- and upper-middle-income families face yet another set of child-care problems. Like most working-class families, their children are ineligible for government-subsidized family or group day care: they must reach into the private marketplace for suitable arrangements. Limited financial relief from child-care costs is available for middle- and upper-middle-income families as a result of the child-care tax credit.[32] Thus, the net effect of current federal programs may be described as *directly* providing child-care services only for children of the poor.[33]

The record of the United States stands in marked contrast to the child-care policies of other major industrialized nations. France, Czechoslovakia, the two Germanys, Hungary, Israel, Norway, and Sweden, among others, have evolved various child-care, or more accurately, family policies which provide benefits and/or services as a matter of social right. These include family allowances and housing allowances or priorities, maternity and paternity leave with benefits, insurance benefits, and leave to care for sick children, child-care grants for mothers who stay home with prekindergarten children, universal neonatal and child health care, and various kinds of child-care centers.[34] Universal eligibility governs some of the programs; fees and benefits are scaled according to income in most of the countries.

Child-care policy does not follow any set pattern in these countries. Each does combine some form of income maintenance with day-care centers and family day-care programs. The basic—and often bitterly debated—policy question in almost all of these countries concerns the balance of income maintenance and day care. Many societies accept the principle of general child support through paid maternity leave and child allowances, preferring this approach to day care because children will be cared for at home by mothers. Pressure from women's movements, the financial inadequacy of some income maintenance programs, and the inescapable statistics of increased maternal employment have led recently to almost universal expansion of child-care facilities.

Sweden's approach combines the use of child-care centers with a developmental emphasis, family day care—"child-minding" homes, after-school centers, and paid maternity or paternity leave (parenthood insurance). Sweden's more conservative, less industrialized neighbor, Norway, had pursued an income policy that discouraged maternal employment through the inclusion of "family support" in the salaries of men. This changed in the 1970s. In 1975 the Norwegian government laid plans to increase the number of places in day-care institutions from 40,000 (1975) to 100,000 (1981–82). These centers are to be planned and operated by municipalities with financing from the state. Employed women in Norway may use up to eighteen weeks paid maternity leave (part of which may be shared with the father—if married) and take further leave up to a year with full job protection but no pay. Norwegian parents are also entitled to ten days leave for sick children under the age of ten.

Neither France nor West Germany has yet to provide sufficient facilities for the care of very young children, although programs for children over three are more extensive. Both countries have maternity leave or allowance policies.

German women, for example, may take 14 weeks paid maternity leave and have five days leave available each year for the care of sick children. The development of day-care centers appears less urgent in the Federal Republic of Germany where grandparents care for almost half of all children under three with working mothers. Observers in France believe that the expansion of day care will turn on the strength of natalist arguments and those of income-maintenance versus out-of-home care proponents.

Child-care and income-maintenance policies in Eastern Europe are similar but by no means identical. Programs in Hungary and Czechoslovakia appear somewhat more supportive of the working mother than those in Poland. All three countries provide immediate postnatal maternity leave at different reimbursement levels and for varying numbers of weeks, but Poland fails to grant paid child-care leave for mothers of one- to four-year-olds. Hungary permits a grant until the child is three at one-third to one-half of the average salary of the young mother cohort and counts this toward pensionable years; Czechoslovakia gives all "economically active" women birth grants and a maternity allowance after maternity leave for second, third . . . children. Parents—in some cases only mothers—may take many more leave days (up to 60 in Hungary and Poland) to care for sick children than in Western European countries. Approximately 10 percent of children under three in these Eastern European countries attend a day nursery, and two-thirds to 90 percent of three- to six-year-olds are enrolled in kindergartens.[35]

Proponents of comprehensive child-care or family policy in the United States tend to emphasize the client orientation of European programs. They portray these governments as altruistically redistributing resources in order to promote employment, equality, adequate housing, child care, and social security. Family policy may also be a tool for social control. Nations with comprehensive family policies use the family to structure population and employment policies. Governments similarly recognize the importance of the family in the dissemination of social and political values. The sum of these European programs and benefits reflects public concern for, and commitment to, the family as a national resource. In the United States, public concern for the family seems as high, but the commitment of government remains incoherent.

The American position, or more accurately, lack of position derives from the persisting power of several myths about American life that support a deep current of opposition to any national child-care policy. The older of the two myths concerns the individual unfettered by government, and hearkens back to classical liberal thought and the experience of the American frontier. The reality of the American experience, particularly in the twentieth century, impinges and reduces this to rhetoric and encomiums for the Algers, Ingalls, and Lincolns of another era. We adhere to a philosophy that demands freedom for the individual and the family from government interference and extols the virtues of self-sufficiency. Yet the state has intervened in matters of property and the family from the earliest colonial times.

A 1642 Massachusetts General Court educational ordinance, for example, empowered the selectmen of each town to "Take account from time to time of all parents and masters, and of their children, concerning their calling and employment of their children, especially of their ability to read and understand the principles of religion and the capital laws of this country" and specifically authorized them, with the consent of any magistrate or court, to "put forth apprentices the children of such as they shall 'find' not to be able and fit to employ and bring them up."[36] Two hundred years later the stability, predictability, and national social codes sought as a result of industrialization and the Civil War extended such public guardianship to its logical conclusion in the compulsory school attendance laws. C. J. Greer, county superintendent of the Washington Territory, summed up the extreme position stating, "the children belong to the State and the State should see that they are educated."[37] Certainly in the twentieth century the liberal tradition does not manifest itself in the child-state relationship. Compulsory education is only the most visible in a long list of encroachments that include, or have included, registration of births, mandatory immunization, chemical treatment of children's clothing against fire, residential housing, health and safety regulations, prayer and religious holiday celebrations in schools, control of information about, and access to, birth control and abortions, fluoridization of public water supplies, and child labor laws. While most parents view these laws and regulations as benign and protective, they are nonetheless counter to the liberal tradition of individualism.

Opponents of child care, however, often ignore the degree to which the relationship between the individual and the state has changed, and portray child-care programs as antithetical to established values. For this group, day-care centers, with their capacity to socialize the very youngest members of society, represent the shadow of Big Brother. "Day care is powerful. A program that ministers to a child from six months to six years has over 8,000 hours to teach beliefs and behavior. The family should be teaching values, not the Government or anyone in day care."[38] The 1979 Cranston bill openly acknowledged this position in Section 3, "Protection of Parental Rights," which states, "Nothing in this Act shall be construed to authorize any public agency or private organization or any individual associated therewith to interfere with, or to intervene in, any child-rearing decision of parents."[39] In addition, a national child-care benefits and services policy is further opposed on the grounds that such policy is both an admission of, and an encouragement to, a lack of self-sufficiency in the public. Government intrusion, they argue, engenders dependency.

A second, more recent myth, the importance of the mother-at-home acts in concert with the liberal tradition in retarding the enactment of a national child-care policy. In the mid–nineteenth century social and economic revolution altered the lives of middle- and later working-class women. Industrialization and new wealth permitted some women to withdraw from the labor force and remain at home. The nonworking, "pampered" wife became a Victorian male status symbol. After the turn of the century, and particularly after World War I, this liberation from the work force actually resulted in more women becoming educated and entering professions, but the vast majority in this expanded middle stratum of society made homemaking a profession. The Depression militated against this trend, but following the temporary acceptance of female employment during World War II, it was clearly expected that women would return to their homes and families leaving men to be the breadwinners. Most women, particularly mothers, complied. Three years after the conclusion of the war only 18 percent of mothers in the United States worked outside their home. For a decade little change occurred, owing in part to minimal inflation, the growth and demands of suburban family life, and increased mechanization of industry.

Various schools of professionals and intellectuals pressed this norm upon women by arguing the imperative of staying at home with one's child. Among the most influential was British psychologist John Bowlby whose theory of maternal deprivation had an enormous impact on the type of mother-child relationship supported by professionals and adopted by many families.[40] Ironically, as the influence of conservative theorists like Bowlby grew, mothers began returning to work in increasing numbers. Forty-three percent of women with children under 18 were working in 1971 in contrast to 30 percent in 1960; by 1977 a majority of women in this category had entered the labor force. Figures for 1978 indicate that 43.7 percent of mothers with children under the age of six were employed.[41] Inflation, divorce, migration, and the women's movement negated the desirability or opportunity of staying at home. The expansion of service industries, the Vietnam War, the women's movement, and affirmative action created the possibilities. Nevertheless, the myth of the mother-at-home retains enormous power and influences the development of family and child-care policy in the United States.

Both these biases are currently best expressed in the statements of the "new right" which has been characterized as consisting of individuals working for the defeat of ERA, and opposed to abortion, sex education in schools, feminism, and government-sponsored day care. Well organized and aggressive in the assertion of their position, this relatively new political faction has indicated, most recently in connection with the White House Conference on the Family and the Family Protection Act, that it intends to be influential in any dialogue on the role of the state in family life.[42]

CONCLUSION: PROSPECTS FOR A
NATIONAL CHILD-CARE POLICY IN THE 1980s

The history of day care in the United States reflects a society which has moved slowly and reluctantly in the direction of a broad national child-care policy. The constellation of values described here as the myths of individualism and mother-at-home have resulted in social and political resistance which the fragmented and poorly funded child-care supporters to date have failed to overcome.

In their analysis of women's policy issues, Gelb and Palley hypothesize that several factors are crucial to a successful lobby effort: an issue with the image of broad-based support; an issue narrow enough not to challenge basic values or divide supporters; a policy network capable of securing access to decision makers and providing them with information; an ability to compromise with constituents and in the political process; the additional ability to define success in terms of increments of change; and, in the case of policy affecting social relations, an issue which focuses upon role equity not role change.[43] The issues and politics of child care fulfill only a limited number of these conditions. It is not clear that a broad base of support for comprehensive child care exists. Within the coalition of groups currently declared for a national child-care policy, there is no consensus on policy approach. Bitter opposition to the public school–prime sponsor approach of the labor unions may make compromise impossible. Finally, as outlined above, day care challenges basic values and is perceived to imply role change, some argue on the part of the children as well as the mothers. Given this diagnosis, will a comprehensive child-care policy be forthcoming?

Until groups lobbying for a national child-care policy can diminish the influence of the myths of individualism and mother-at-home, new programs and benefits are not likely. Lobbyists have two tasks before them. The first involves convincing a far broader audience of the realities of contemoporary American life. The child-care lobby has suffered a chronic inability to attract serious, sustained media attention. The *New York Times* and The *Washington Post,* for example, devoted little or no coverage to the hearings and debates over the 1971, 1975, and 1979 child-care legislation. Most popular journals and the various television networks are similarly inattentive. Proponents must use the media to show that a domestic revolution has already occurred, that family structure had changed and child-rearing practices have been altered in the wake. Marion Wright Edelman of the Children's Defense Fund has testified that "public policy . . . should proceed from reality. There are mothers who are already working. There are children who are already handicapped. There are children who need to be cared for."[44] Psychologist Urie Bronfenbrenner has written that the family as the "institution bearing primary responsibility for the care and development of the nation's children has suffered progressive fragmentation and isolation in this child rearing role."[45] Both these observers, and many others as well, emphasize that the family should remain primary in child-rearing decisions, but feel that this new structure requires altering the relationship between the state and the family in order to insure family stability.

The second task for the child-care lobby is to convince the public that child-care programs are an adjunct to parental primacy and family stability, not their antithesis. In terms of child-care policy, the myths of individualism and mother-at-home translate into a belief that the content of child rearing is both the duty and the right of parents. Placement of one's children with nonfamily members for any portion of the day introduces children to new and different norms, particularly if parents have limited control and input with respect to the individual care giver or day-care center. Progress in the development of national child-care programs has been significantly hindered by limited understanding of the proposed programs. Many people fail to realize that participation in the programs outlined in the 1971, 1975, and 1979 legislation was voluntary. Even fewer comprehend the breadth of the programs and benefits that come under the child-care rubric—family allowances, tax credits, insurance benefits for parents of sick children, maternity grants as well as family day care and day-care centers. In short, despite existing government intervention in their lives, or perhaps because of it, the child-care lobby cannot underestimate the force of parental and societal fears about who controls the lives of young children. The family may be perceived to be the last frontier of individualism—of individual authority. If so, those lobbying for child-care policy will have to portray more effectively their commitment to the family by emphasizing how child-care possibilities increase, rather than decrease, the cohesion of family units when the adults either need or want to work.

The process of neutralizing these myths will be affected by the political environment of the 1980s. The 1980 election results point to the growth of political conservatism—a desire to limit publicly funded social programs and government regulatory activities. At the same time, social and economic factors that have encouraged maternal employment show no signs of abating. Assuming that these trends continue, the confrontation between conservative political values and the needs of working mothers is likely to be strident. Politicians may find themselves asked why the substantially increased tax revenue derived from this enlarged maternal work force should not be used to support child-care needs. It would be no less an argument than that made by the trucking and automobile industries for government highway building and maintenance programs, or that of the oil companies for the oil depletion allowance. In American politics interest groups have always expected some taxes to be returned to their members in the form of benefits and services. Acceptance of a national child-care policy, or even more broadly, a national policy on families, poses the following question: do taxpayers, particularly parents, want their tax revenue used to support family services at the price of expanded government and, if so, what are the acceptable conditions of intervention?

Notes

1. Such sentiments were formally expressed by various men in public life. The governor of Pennsylvania, for example, vetoed a compulsory attendance bill in 1893 on the grounds that it was un-American. Jack Culbertson, "Attendance," *Encyclopedia of Educational Research,* 3rd ed. (New York: Macmillan, 1960), p. 94, cited in Charles Burgess, "The Goddess," *Harvard Educational Review 46* (May 1976): 213.

2. Foremost among reasons given is the increase in the number of working mothers in the United States in the past 30 years, a trend forecasters believe will continue. The Urban Institute recently estimated an increase of 3.1 million working women with very young children by 1990—a 56 percent increase over the 1978 level. In addition, an increase of 5.5 million working mothers with children between the ages of 6 and 17 is projected (also a rise of 56 percent over the 1978 level). Ralph E. Smith, *The Subtle Revolution* (Washington, D.C.: The Urban Institute, 1979), pp. 14, 19, 133. The growth of one-parent families and the decrease in extended family child care are also cited by proponents of day care. Studies such as Mary Keyserling's *Windows on Day Care* (New York: National Council of Jewish Women, 1972), for example, indicate the need for child care by demonstrating the number of latchkey children in the United States. A totally different argument for day care is offered by those concerned with the increasing number of Americans on public assistance who see child-care programs as a means of decreasing welfare dependency. Another justification for day-care centers and supervised family care rests upon arguments made on behalf of compensatory, developmental education, that is, all-day nursery school or a Head Start–type program. Feminists argue for child-care programs on the grounds that mothers ought to be provided time to develop themselves. Community-focused activists portray day-care centers as institutions capable of enhancing communications and solidarity in neighborhoods, and as agents of social and economic change.

3. In 1971 President Nixon vetoed the Economic Opportunity Amendments bill because of his opposition to Title V, "Child Development Programs." Both the 1975 "Child and Family Services Act," sponsored by Senator Walter Mondale and Representative John Brademus, and the 1979 "Child Care Act" authored by Senator Alan Cranston, failed to emerge from committee. Perceiving a dim future, Cranston even withdrew his bill before the completion of hearings.

4. Title V, "Child Development Programs," Economic Opportunity Amendments of 1971 (S. 2007). For the veto message, see Richard Nixon, "Veto of Economic Opportunity Amendments of 1971," *Weekly Compilation of Presidential Documents,* December 13, 1971, pp. 1635–36.

5. Ibid., p. 1636. The message may have taken its language from the September 9, 1971 comments of New York's Conservative Senator James Buckley, who described the child development bill as one that "threatens to destroy parental authority and the institution of the family." *Congressional Record* (daily ed.), September 9, 1971, p. S.14010, cited in Gilbert Steiner, *The Children's Cause* (Washington, D.C.: Brookings, 1976), pp. 108 and 113–15.

6. For more comprehensive histories of day care as it developed in the United States, see Rosalyn F. Baxandall, "Who Shall Care For Our Children? The History and Development of Day Care in the United States," in *Women: A Feminist Perspective,* ed. by Jo Freeman (Palo Alto: Mayfield, 1979), pp. 134–49; James D. Marver and Meredith A. Larson, "Public Policy toward Child Care in America: A Historical Perspective," in *Child Care and Public Policy,* ed. Philip K. Robins and Samuel Weiner (Lexington, MA: Lexington, 1978), pp. 17–42; National Association of Day Nurseries, "Origins of Day Care Nursery Work" (1970), processed paper on file at the Child Welfare League of

America Library, New York City; Jill Russack Norgren, "Political Mobilization and Policy Input in Urban Day Care" (Ph.D. dissertation: University of Michigan, 1974), in particular chapters 2 and 3; Pamela Roby, *Child Care—Who Cares?* (New York: Basic Books, 1973); Sheila M. Rothman, "Other People's Children: The Day Care Experience in America," *The Public Interest 30* (Winter 1973): 11–27; and Margaret O'Brien Steinfels, *Who's Minding the Children?* (New York: Simon and Schuster, 1973).

7. The fact that day care did not always convey such an image—at least to working-class families—prior to the increased use of social work techniques is suggested by the comments of a day-care center social worker: "In most of the families [she complained], the parents' attitude is that the Nursery is a community resource, such as the public school, and it is, therefore, for them to use as they wish. Families find it difficult to see the need of discussing financial, social and personal factors." *Case Work Programs in Day Nurseries: A Symposium,* Five Papers presented at the Twentieth Biennial Conference of the National Federation of Day Nurseries, New York, April 1937, p. 7, cited in Steinfels, *Who's Minding the Children?* p. 63.

8. In the Community Facilities Act of 1941 (also known as the Lanham Act), Congress instructed the Children's Bureau to make funds available to states on a 50–50 matching basis for nursery schools and day-care centers.

9. The program continued in New York City when that municipality agreed to contribute funds to privately sponsored centers.

10. U.S. Department of Health, Education and Welfare, Children's Bureau, Welfare Administration, *What is Good Day Care?* (Washington, D.C.: n.p., 1974).

11. Alice S. Rossi, "Equality Between the Sexes: An Immodest Proposal," *Daedalus 93* (Spring 1964): 616.

12. Women constituted 35 percent of the labor force in 1944. This figure dropped to 29.8 in 1947, rose to 34.8 in 1960, and increased most dramatically by 1970 (42.6 percent) and in the subsequent seven years (51 percent in 1977). The percentage of women with children under the age of 6 in the labor force registered an even greater increase: 14 percent in 1950, 20 in 1960, 32 in 1970, and 41 percent in 1977. U.S. Department of Commerce, Bureau of the Census, *Statistical Abstract of the United States* (Washington, D.C., 1971), pp. 212–13, and U.S. Senate, Subcommittee on Child and Human Development of the Committee on Human Resources, *Hearings on the Child Care and Child Development Programs, 1977–78* (Washington, D.C.: 1978), p. 682. The Urban Institute projects a steady increase in the number of women with young children in the labor force. See Smith, *The Subtle Revolution.*

13. Congress authorized a modest $5 million for fiscal 1963 and $10 million the following year. Although the authorization called for $25 million to be spent in the first three years, Congress appropriated only $8.8 million from 1962 through 1965. The modesty of these yearly appropriations is illustrated by a comparison with the day-care budget for just the city of New York in 1963: $7,407,203.

14. Gilbert Y. Steiner, "Day Care Centers: Hype or Hope?" *Transaction 8* (July–August 1971): 51.

15. Herb Rosenweig, *Agency for Child Development Fiscal Year 1972–73 Request* (Human Resources Administration, Agency for Child Development: Office of Public Affairs, n.d.), p. E-1. Staff at the Agency for Child Development described a ripple-like awareness process with municipalities like New York first discovering the potential of the 1967 legislation particularly as they were pressed by community control and women's rights groups to expand local child-care programs.

16. "Comprehensive," in this context, implies day care that provides for a child's social and intellectual needs as well as his or her physical and mental health—comprehensive rather than custodial care.

17. Charles E. Lindblom, "The Science of Muddling Through," *Public Administration Review 19* (Spring 1959): 79–88.

18. For a summary and comparison of the various bills, see Day Care and Child Development Council of America, *The Council's 1971 Legislative Analysis* (September 1971, processed).

19. For a detailed discussion of the politics of the 1969–71 bills, see Steiner, *The Children's Cause,* chapters 5 and 7.

20. Ibid., p. 91.

21. The most recent of these, Alan Cranston's "Child Care Act of 1979," emphasized "the availability and diversity of quality child care services for all children and families who need such services." It did not provide for universal entitlement but rather priorities based upon family need. These priorities were not spelled out although two-parent working families and single-parent families are repeatedly discussed. The Cranston bill also provided for a variety of auspices, flexible funding arrangements including vouchers, sliding fee payments, and a strong regulatory mechanism. This child-care program was to be administered by the individual states after the approval of a comprehensive state child-care plan. *Congressional Record,* January 15, 1979.

22. The list of organizations and interest groups which speak to the issue of child care is lengthy. A review of the published hearings for the 1975 Child and Family Services Act or, more recently, Senator Cranston's "Child Care Act" (S.4) indicate additional names, background, and points of view.

23. For a discussion of cost in nonprofit organization-sponsored day care versus public school programs, see U.S. Congress, House and Senate. *Joint Hearings on the Child and Family Services Act,* August 8 and 9, 1974 (Washington, D.C.: U.S. Government Printing Office: 1974), pp. 259–61.

24. Ibid., p. 259.

25. Nixon, "Veto of Economic Opportunity Amendments of 1971," p. 1636.

26. For a discussion of the various uses of "family" policy, see Sheila B. Kamerman and Alfred J. Kahn, *Family Policy: Government and Families in Fourteen Countries* (New York: Columbia University Press, 1978), pp. 3–8.

27. Speculation must satisfy us for the moment owing to the lack of national citizen-opinion data concerning issues of child-care policy.

28. The Department of Health, Education and Welfare estimates that in fiscal year 1977, 800 million dollars of the $2.7 billion appropriation for Title XX was expended for child care. The Congressional Budget Office has estimated that the federal government provides about $1.8 billion in direct spending for child-care or child-care-related services through these various agencies. *Congressional Record,* January 15, 1979, p. S77.

29. Ibid., p. S77.

30. In the introductory comments to S.4 Senator Cranston estimates that the federal government contributes approximately $500 million a year to the cost of child care through the child-care tax credit. Ibid., p. S77.

31. For a brief discussion of the application of the voucher system to child care, see U.S. Senate, Subcommittee on Child and Human Development, *Hearings,* pp. 6–14, 20–32, and 170–75. For an argument in favor of the negative income tax rather than day care, see William V. Shannon, *New York Times Magazine,* April 30, 1972, pp. 13–85.

32. The Tax Reform Act of 1976 provides for a credit of up to $800 a year for child care for families who qualify. The basic formula allows a credit of 20 percent of child-care costs up to $2000 per year for one child or $4000 for two or more. One thousand dollars in child care for one child, for example, would qualify the taxpayer for a $200 tax credit.

33. The federal government also provides limited funds for child care as a preventive

tool where a mother's incapacitation might otherwise require foster care, or where other social pathologies are diagnosed.

34. See the report of the Coalition of Labor Union Women Child Care Seminar, "A Commitment to Children" in U.S. Senate, Subcommittee on Child and Human Development, *Hearings,* pp. 775–809; Kamerman and Kahn, *Family Policy;* Kamerman and Kahn, "The day-care debate: a wider view," *The Public Interest 54* (Winter 1979): 76–93; and Sheila Kamerman and Alfred Kahn's six-country study, *Child Care, Family Benefits and Working Parents* (New York: Columbia University Press, 1981).

35. The above discussion draws upon materials in Kamerman and Kahn, *Family Policy;* Rita Liljestrom, "Sweden," pp. 41–48; Hildur Ve Henriksen and Harriet Holter, "Norway," pp. 54–64; Nicole Questiaux and Jacques Fournier, "France," pp. 145–82; Friedhelm Neidhardt, "The Federal Republic of Germany," pp. 232–38; Walter Vergeiner, "Czechoslovakia," pp. 102–3, 113–14; Zsuzsa Ferge, "Hungary," pp. 73–77, and Magdalena Sokolowska, "Poland," pp. 252–58. See also Zsuzsa Ferge, *A Society in the Making: Hungarian Social and Societal Policy* (Middlesex, England: Penguin Books, 1979).

36. Lawrence A. Cremin, "Family-Community Linkages in American Education: Some Comments on the Recent Historiography," *Teachers College Record 79* (May 1978): 687–88.

37. Burgess, "The Goddess," p. 215.

38. Statement by a member of Oklahomans for Life, the Eagle Forum (Phyllis Schlafly's organization), the Pro-Family Forum and Stop E.R.A.—the "new right." Nadine Brozan, "White House Conference on the Family: A Schism Develops," *New York Times,* January 7, 1980, p. D8.

39. *Congressional Record,* January 15, 1979, p. S80.

40. John Bowlby, *Maternal Care and Mental Health* (Geneva: World Health Organization, 1952). Also, R. A. Spitz, "Hospitalism: An Inquiry into the Genesis of Psychiatric Conditions in Early Childhood," *Psychoanalytic Studies of the Child II* (1945), pp. 53–74. For a critique of Bowlby, see Milton Willner, "Day Care: A Reassessment," *Child Welfare 44* (March 1965). For a broad review of the literature, see a two-part article by Mary C. Howell, "Employed Mothers and Their Families (I)" *Pediatrics 52* (August 1973): 252–63, and II, "Effects of Maternal Employment on the Child," ibid. (September 1973): 327–42. See also, more recently, Ruth Zambrana, Marsha Hurst, and Rodney Hite, "The Working Mother in Contemporary Perspective: A Review of the Literature," *Pediatrics 64* (1979): 862–70. Selma Fraiberg in *Every Child's Birthright: In Defense of Mothering* (New York: Basic Books, 1977), offers a contemporary statement of maternal deprivation theory.

41. These figures translate into 6.4 million children under the age of six whose mothers work and 22.4 million children ages six to seventeen whose mothers are in the labor force. U.S. Senate, Subcommittee on Child and Human Development, *Hearings,* p. 682, Bureau of Labor Statistics, and Smith, *The Subtle Revolution,* chaps. 1 and 5.

42. Brozan, "White House Conference on the Family."

43. Joyce Gelb and Marion Lief Palley, "Women and Interest Group Politics: A Comparative Analysis of Federal Decision-Making," *Journal of Politics 41* (May 1979): 362–92.

44. U.S. Senate, Subcommittee on Child and Human Development, *Hearings,* p. 874.

45. Urie Bronfenbrenner, "The Challenge of Social Change to Public Policy and Developmental Research," Paper presented at the President's Symposium, "Child Development and Public Policy," at the annual meeting of the Society for Research in Child Development, Denver, April 12, 1975, p. i.

Chapter 9

The Womb Factor: Pregnancy Policies and Employment of Women*

Patricia Huckle

Men and women are biologically different—that is not a political statement, but a fact. What does having a womb mean in terms of employment? What are some of the consequences assumed to follow from women's capacity to reproduce, as reflected in public law and policy?

Since the mid-1960s, feminists have acknowledged the importance of public policies and programs in generating opportunities for women and have geared much of their political efforts toward changing existing laws and development strategies which will result in greater social, political, and economic independence for women.[1] In *The Politics of Women's Liberation,* Jo Freeman explores the coalitions and activities of women's groups in assisting in passage of key legislation and implementation of the Civil Rights Act of 1964. This study examines recent legislative and judicial decisions with respect to treatment of pregnancy as a public policy issue. Its context is the interaction of judges, career bureaucrats, lobbyists, and legislative committees as they set the terms by which employers treat women workers.

By reviewing restrictions on women's employment it is possible to see more clearly the relationship between social structure and individual options. It is also possible to examine the development of a feminist political strategy which is both pragmatic (acknowledging the incremental nature of social change) and drastic in its long-range implications for defining work and women's relationship to both production and reproduction.

The issue of employment policies and pregnancy becomes increasingly

*An earlier version of this article was published in the *Western Political Quarterly, 34:* pp. 114–126. Reprinted by permission of the University of Utah, Copyright Holder.

significant as women who might and do bear children join the labor force. Most women in the United States will be employed at some time in their lives. Pregnant women and mothers are employed in dramatically larger numbers today than in the past. The number of working mothers "has increased more than threefold since 1950, and in 1975 the labor force participation rate of mothers was 47 percent."[2] A substantial number of women who are pregnant are now employed, and they are a fair percentage of all women workers. According to the National Center for Health Statistics:

> Of about 3,034,000 women who had a live birth during a 12-month period in 1972–73, an estimated 1,260,000 or 41.5 percent worked during their pregnancy. . . . Such pregnant workers comprised about 8.8 percent of the estimated . . . women of reproductive age in the labor force at the time.[3]

The focus in this study is the way in which employers, lawmakers, and judges deal with the fact that women have the capacity to become pregnant. Implicitly the question comes down to arguments about whether women are just like men, and therefore should be treated the same for employment purposes, or whether women are not only different, but deserve different treatment. This study deals briefly with historical treatment of pregnant or potentially pregnant women, describes the process of amending the Civil Rights Act of 1964 to include pregnancy discrimination as sex discrimination, with an analysis of the central arguments postulated. Conclusions weigh the changing patterns of public policy against prevailing expectations about societal employment patterns of women and men.

SEVENTY YEARS WORTH OF ASSUMPTIONS

A review of U.S. Supreme Court decisions and employer policies can illustrate the attitudes toward women which may affect current policymaking. From *Muller* v. *Oregon*[4] to *Gilbert* v. *General Electric,*[5] the womb factor has affected women's employment opportunities. Quite often, restrictive policies were developed out of an interest in "protecting women." Often these protected women from long hours as well as from overtime pay and advancement.[6] The *Muller* case was one step in the long labor movement struggle to achieve better working conditions for all workers. This Supreme Court decision had drastic long-term consequences for women. The rationale in *Muller* v. *Oregon* for protective legislation was grounded in assumptions about women's bodies and their dependency on males (reinforced by marriage and property laws):

> That woman's physical structure and the performance of maternal functions place her at a disadvantage in the struggle for subsistence is obvious. This is especially true when the burdens of motherhood are upon her. Even when they are not . . .

continuance for a long time on her feet at work . . . tends to injurious effects upon the body, and as healthy mothers are essential to vigorous offspring, the physical well-being of a woman becomes an object of public interest and care in order to preserve the strength and vigor of the race . . . she is properly placed in a class by herself.[7]

The protective rationale and classification by sex have continued to define the boundaries within which women must attempt to provide economic support for themselves, and their families. As a result of these assumptions, the law, employer policies, and judicial interpretations might be summarized as follows: if she is pregnant, woman needs protection; if she is not pregnant, she might someday be, and therefore it is rational to protect (or exclude) her in advance.[8]

Because of their assumed frailty, related to the capacity to reproduce, women have been excluded from a range of jobs. Only when "manpower" has been diverted for other purposes such as war have employers encouraged women to accept the full spectrum of tasks. During the 1920s and 1930s, when jobs were scarce, it was women who were assumed to be disposable workers. Kathleen Williams, testifying before Congress, reports that women were told that they should have as their primary goal home and child rearing. According to Williams, "A National Education Association study in 1930–31 revealed that 77 percent of all school systems surveyed refused to hire wives; sixty-three percent dismissed women teachers if they subsequently married."[9] She also reports that during the Depression whole cities campaigned against working married women and many state legislatures considered bills to restrict the employment of married women.[10] If women were employed, and retained after marriage, they were frequently fired as soon as pregnancy became known.[11] The practice of firing pregnant women was studied by the Children's Bureau in 1942. Their observation was that while protection of the woman and fetus was the formal rationale, there was some indication that "aesthetic and moral" qualms about the presence of pregnant women in the classroom were the informal basis for such firings. In these cases, women lost jobs because their "natural" and primary role offended others.[12] Nancy Erickson notes that women workers were conscious of the discriminatory effect of employer policies and disability laws which excluded pregnancy, pointing to the 1952 effort of the New York Women's Trade Union League to amend the state disability benefits law "to cover disabilities caused by pregnancy and childbirth."[13]

Although there have been some modifications of law since World War II, a heritage lingers. Despite antidiscrimination laws, if women are to be hired at all, employers have felt free to ask them if they are married or plan to be, if they intend to have children, and what form of birth control they use. In the event that they exercise a right to bear children, women have been fired or forced to take extended leaves of absence whether capable of working or not. They have been denied unemployment benefits when fired. Those on leave have lost seniority and had to start over as new employees at lower levels.[14]

Several Supreme Court decisions in the 1970s dealt with the issues of marriage and reproduction as they affect employment. A regulation forbidding employment of married women was ruled illegal under Title VII of the Civil Rights Act of 1964,[15] in *Sprogis* v. *United Air Lines, Inc.*[16] Also declared illegal was the refusal to hire women with preschool-age children, in *Phillips* v. *Martin-Marietta Corp.*[17] In *Cleveland Board of Education* v. *LaFleur*[18] the Supreme Court declared arbitrary, mandatory maternity leave requirements unconstitutional, and indicated that maternity leaves should be determined on an individual basis. In *Turner* v. *Department of Employment Security*[19] the court decided that a state may not exclude pregnant women from eligibility for unemployment benefits solely because they are pregnant. In *Nashville Gas Co.* v. *Satty,*[20] the court decided that a policy of not awarding sick-leave pay to pregnant employees was not prima facie evidence of sex discrimination, but did rule that a policy that employees on pregnancy leave lose all job-bidding seniority resulted in discrimination against women.

Partly in response to the Supreme Court decisions interpreting the scope of Title VII's sex discrimination provisions, partly owing to the development of guidelines by the Equal Employment Opportunity Commission (EEOC),[21] and partly owing to sharpened awareness of employers and employees, employee policies have been altered over the past decade. Summaries of employer surveys were included in testimony before the Ninety-fifth Congress in 1977. Three surveys conducted by Prentice-Hall show the incremental pattern of change in providing consideration for pregnancy. The first survey, conducted in 1965, just following passage of Title VII, reported on more than 1,000 employers, and showed that two-fifths of the offices and three-quarters of the plants had pregnancy leave policies. According to the testimony, most employers who had policies required early leave, and fewer than 20 percent permitted the employee to decide at what point the leave would commence.[22]

By 1972, the EEOC had issued new guidelines for employers under Title VII. These pregnancy guidelines make clear that excluding applicants or employees because of pregnancy will be considered a violation of Title VII. With respect to treatment of pregnant employees, the guidelines continue:

> Disabilities caused or contributed to by pregnancy, miscarriage, abortion, childbirth, and recovery therefrom are, for all job-related purposes, temporary disabilities and should be treated as such under any health or temporary disability insurance or sick leave plan available in connection with employment.[23]

About the same time as the new guidelines were issued, Prentice-Hall conducted a second employer survey. By 1972, three-quarters of the employers surveyed had maternity leave policies, and 60 percent allowed the employee or her physician to determine length of employment.[24] By the time of their 1973 survey, Prentice-Hall was able to report that 90 percent of the employers surveyed had formal maternity leave provisions. They noted:

> The most frequent policy change reported is the switch to paid maternity leaves. Many firms told us their former policies included paid sick leave, but no pay for maternity leave; most of these companies said they now pay accrued sick pay to employees on maternity leave.[25]

These surveys suggest the extent to which employers, by the early 1970s, were beginning to respond to pressures from women employees, and from the courts and administrative agencies to make some provisions which treat pregnancy as a work disability. Most of these changes were occurring in place of employment, not in government subsidy to women.[26]

In 1976, the Institute for Local Self-Government in Berkeley conducted an informal, telephone survey of municipalities in California. There are 412 cities in California, 153 of which responded to this survey (37 percent). Cities of varying population sizes were contacted, the smallest having a population of between 1,000 and 5,000 persons, and the largest with populations over 100,000 (San Diego was the largest city reporting). Representatives of each city (usually in the city manager's office, or in the personnel department) were asked what policies, if any, the city had with respect to pregnant employees. Of those responding, almost 70 percent allow women to use accrued sick leave for absences due to childbirth. Most of these cities said they did not have a "formal" maternity leave policy. Most cities in the survey said they allow a woman to take a leave of absence without pay. In these cases, for the most part, seniority is retained, but does not accrue. In some cities, there are no women employees, or so few that the question has never been raised. The small city of Mill Valley stated that they don't have a maternity leave policy because: "We don't get pregnant."[27]

In spite of the 1972 EEOC guidelines, and in spite of indications that employers had begun to treat pregnancy as a temporary disability, two U.S. Supreme Court decisions of the 1970s have highlighted both resistance to change and the continuing legacy of the *Muller* v. *Oregon* assumptions. At about the same time that the Supreme Court decided in *Cleveland* v. *LaFleur* that mandatory maternity leaves were unconstitutional under the 14th Amendment to the Constitution, they also held in the 1974 decision of *Gedulding* v. *Aiello*[28] that exclusion of pregnancy from disability plans was not denial of 14th Amendment equal protection provisions, since pregnancy is a "condition" and the issue is "not one of gender discrimination."

Several aspects of this latter decision bear mentioning. First, in the *Aiello* decision the Supreme Court gave great deference to the state's claim of legitimate fiscal concerns, unlike their decision in *Reed* v. *Reed*,[29] where the court refused to accept the argument of the state that administrative convenience should permit them to retain a sex preference in selection of estate administrators. Second, the court determined that exclusion of pregnancy from income protection insurance was not discrimination on the basis of sex. Since this reasoning was central to the later Title VII decision in *Gilbert* v. *General Electric,*[30] it is worth repeating:

> The California insurance program does not exclude any one from benefit eligibility because of gender but merely removes one physical condition—pregnancy—from the list of compensable disabilities. . . . Normal pregnancy is an objectively identifiable physical condition with unique characteristics. . . . The lack of identity between the excluded disability and gender becomes clear . . . the program divides potential recipients into two groups—pregnant women and nonpregnant persons. While the first group is exclusively female, the second includes members of both sexes. . . . There is no risk from which men are protected and women are not. Likewise, there is no risk from which women are protected and men are not.[31]

The state could, then, exclude pregnancy from conditions covered by its disability plan without infringing on constitutional rights. Feminists hoped that *Aiello* would not be binding on other cases involving pregnancy brought under Title VII. In 1975, Kathleen Peratis suggested: "Because the scope of Title VII with respect to sex discrimination is far broader than the scope of the fourteenth amendment, it seems unlikely that all of Title VII pregnancy law will be reversed in the wake of *Aiello.*"[32]

This turned out to be a false hope, as the court in 1976, deciding the *Gilbert* case, used almost exactly the rationale from *Aiello* in reaching its decision that exclusion of pregnancy from disability programs was not illegal sex discrimination under Title VII. Comparing *Geduldig* v. *Aiello* with *Gilbert* v. *General Electric,* Justice Rehnquist stated:

> There is no more showing of discrimination here than in *Geduldig* that exclusion of pregnancy benefits is a "mere pretext" designed to effect an invidious discrimination . . . respondents have not made the requisite showing of gender-based effects . . . there is no proof that the package is in fact worth more to men than women.[33]

Other aspects of the decision seemed to take issue with the lower courts' acceptance of EEOC pregnancy guidelines. Six federal courts of appeals and 18 federal districts had accepted the EEOC guidelines, as had the majority of the state human rights agencies.[34]

There were dissenting arguments, including Justice Brennan's opinion that: "A violation is triggered because omission of pregnancy from the program has the intent and effect of providing that only women are subjected to a substantial risk of total loss of income because of temporary medical disability."[35] He further argued that the General Electric plan should have been examined in light of their employment history with respect to women, and the broad social objectives of Title VII. He went on: "Surely it offends commonsense to suggest . . . that a classification revolving around pregnancy is not, at a minimum, strongly sex-related."[36] Speaking to the voluntary aspect of pregnancy, Justice Brennan noted (as have others) that pregnancy is indeed not always voluntary, and further that the General Electric plan covered other voluntary disabilities, and some of these specific to men. These included sports injuries, attempted suicides, cosmetic surgery, venereal disease, prostatectomies, vasectomies, and circumcisions.

Justice Stevens also presented a dissenting opinion, which said in part:

> The rule at issue places the risk of absence caused by pregnancy in a class by itself. By definition, such a rule discriminates on account of sex; for it is the capacity to become pregnant which primarily differentiates the female from the male.[37]

Nevertheless, at the end of 1976, it was clear that the Supreme Court was in some ways permitting disparate treatment of pregnant women, and not identifying this treatment, at least with respect to income protection, as sex discrimination.

THE RESPONSE: THE ONGOING POLITICAL STRUGGLE

The *Gilbert* decision triggered media and organizational response. Surprise and outrage seemed to characterize the initial women's movement reply. Karen DeCrow, speaking for the National Organization for Women (NOW), stated that NOW had been so sure of an opposite conclusion that they had prepared a two-year implementation strategy. Susan Ross, ACLU Women's Rights Project, said, "The Supreme Court today legalized sex discrimination."[38]

Womanpower published a selection of comments from newspaper editorials criticizing the *Gilbert* decision.[39]

> What is legal under the Constitution as interpreted by the Supreme Court may not also be wise. . . . Women should not have to make a choice between job and family. The right to both should be preserved. *(Los Angeles Times)*

> The decision . . . flies in the face of reality, makes little economic sense, and is bad social policy. . . . Asked to carry on the race by bearing children [women] are penalized economically for doing so. (Boston, *Evening Globe*)

> The French exclaim: Viva la difference! when talking about women. The U.S. Supreme Court states on the same subject: Too bad about that difference! (Hartford, *Courant*)

> The ruling is profoundly disturbing. . . . There is, of course, an ultimate remedy. If more of the people who run the corporations, make the country's laws, and sit on the Supreme Court were capable of becoming pregnant, we have no doubt that pregnancy benefits would be the norm. (Hackensack, *Sunday Record*)

In another kind of response, shortly after the *Gilbert* decision, the New York Court of Appeals decided three cases requiring employers to pay disability benefits for absences due to pregnancy-related disabilities on the same basis as other disabilities. They took note of the *Gilbert* decision, but did not concur.[40] The Pennsylvania Human Relations Commission issued a post-Gilbert statement to all employers confirming that the Pennsylvania law included pregnancy in its sex-discrimination provisions, and failure to pay disability-related benefits for pregnancy-related disabilities would be prosecuted. Connecticut and New Jersey issued similar statements. At the time of the *Gilbert* decision, 22 states required employers to pay pregnancy disability benefits.[41] Also, by this time the California law challenged in *Aiello* had been changed so that the state disability insurance program presently includes pregnancy among conditions covered.[42]

Within weeks of the *Gilbert* decision, a coalition of civil rights and women's groups had formed to develop legislation to negate the impact of the Supreme Court analysis. Called the Campaign to End Discrimination against Pregnant Workers, and including 43 representatives of unions, civil rights groups, and legislative groups in Philadelphia, and 70 representatives in Washington, D.C., they identified their purpose as "To secure legislation assuring that prohibitions against sex discrimination in employment also prohibit discrimination because of pregnancy."[43] Two months later, it was reported that a group of businessmen had begun to organize to lobby for elimination of the pregnancy disability coverage required by Connecticut law.[44]

At the federal level, proposed legislation to amend Title VII was considered by the Ninety-fifth Congress. Opening the meeting of the U.S. House of Representatives, Subcommittee on Employment Opportunities of the Committee on Education and Labor in April 1977, Representative Augustus Hawkins suggested that the proposed HR 5055 and HR 6075 "would clearly indicate that the prohibition against sex discrimination . . . includes a prohibition against employment-related discrimination on the basis of pregnancy, child-birth, and related conditions."[45] The Senate Subcommittee on Labor of the Committee on Human Resources opened its hearings on this issue (SB 995) as follows:

> By concluding that pregnancy discrimination is not sex discriminatory . . . the Supreme Court disregarded the intent of Congress in enacting Title VII. That intent was to protect all individuals from unjust employment discrimination, including pregnant women.[46]

Similar arguments weave through the hearings in both the House and Senate and outline basic areas of conflict. Several questions are addressed by both sides which go beyond the particular issue of coverage of pregnancy in income protection programs. These include: (1) What is the role of women as workers in the United States? (2) Who bears the responsibility for child bearing in this society? (3) Who must bear the costs for social change or status? (4) What is the appropriate role of government in regulating employment?

Among those who spoke in favor of the bill were many who had participated in the *Gilbert* case, many of them also members of the Campaign to End Discrimination against Pregnant Workers. These included in part: Ruth Weyand, attorney, International Union of Electrical, Radio and Machine Workers, and counsel in *Gilbert;* Susan Deller Ross, ACLU; and representatives from NAACP, AFL-CIO, American Nurses' Association, Joseph & Rose Kennedy Institute, United Automobile, Aerospace and Agricultural Implement Workers of America, United Steelworkers of America, Communications Workers of America, American Citizens Concerned for Life, Inc., and the National Conference of Catholic Bishops. Some of the opponents were also familiar from the *Gilbert* case, and included: National Association of Manufacturers; Metropolitan Life Insurance Association of America; American Retail Federation; Chamber of Commerce of the United States. What follows is an attempt to identify patterns in the testimony of these groups and individuals as they speak to the larger societal issues outlined above.

1. Woman as Workers

Advocates for the bill emphasized that women are an integral, not temporary, part of the work force. Most women, in this view, are employed because of economic need; all need income protection just as men do. The social goal articulated is to generate employment opportunities so that the most productive use of human resources can be made. It is argued that employment and career patterns should be determined by individual capabilities and not sex-role expectations. Opponents testified primarily about the negative consequences of providing pregnancy disability benefits to pregnant women. They argue that pregnant women will malinger, will be inclined to stay away from work longer, and will insist on the maximum period of benefits. It is said that they might convince physicians that their condition requires extended leave, and employers will then end up paying much greater benefits than for other employees. Beyond this, they argue that pregnant women will quit after maternity leave, and receive severance pay not available to others.

In response, advocates argue that while data on terminations following pregnancy are incomplete, preliminary evidence from employers who now provide income protection for pregnant workers indicates no serious changes, and that there may be some evidence of incentives to return to employment following pregnancy. They further question the assumption that women are more likely to malinger than men. It is pointed out that male and nonpregnant workers are required to document medical leaves, and that these conditions are likely to continue to apply. In these arguments, it is also noted that these kinds of statements tend to support the traditional view of women as temporary workers, and perpetuate the stereotype of the devious female.

There is tension here between the traditional views and those of advocates for change. One view is that women must be accepted as full members of the labor force, not just the way men are, but as women who are workers and also bear children. The other view is that if women are to be employed, they must expect no more than equal treatment—meaning what a man receives—and must not expect pregnancy to be taken into account.

2. Child Bearing

Those who opposed this legislation followed the line of argument used in the *Gilbert* case. Pregnancy, they argue, is by and large a voluntary condition in these times: "pregnancy is commonly desired and generally planned. The resulting expenses are usually predictable and can generally be planned for."[47] Pregnancy, in this view, is not a disability but rather a unique physical condition. Women who choose to have children are responsible for that decision, and should take it into account in their plans. Since society protects the right to have children, individuals (women) must be responsible for the consequences.

Advocates question the extent to which pregnancy is voluntary. They argue that pregnancy is no more (or less) disabling than many other conditions. A man who breaks his leg can hardly be said to have volunteered, but his condition would be covered by a disability insurance program. In this view, pregnancy is not voluntary or involuntary, but rather a disability like other temporary disabilities. Beyond this is the issue of society's collective responsibility for children as resources. It is pointed out that children are the workers and citizens of tomorrow, and that their contribution goes beyond the individual mother or family. Opponents respond that employers and taxpayers do not own children, but parents do. And, they argue, in this society it is inappropriate to usurp the rights and responsibilities of individuals, or to require employers to bear the consequences of individual decisions.

3. Costs

As is often the case, political issues sooner or later evolve into discussions of money. This is as true of the pregnancy discrimination issue as it is of other redistributive questions. Supporters of this antidiscrimination amendment to Title VII state that equity is the basic issue, not cost. They contend that women have borne both children and secondary status in the work force, and that social justice requires equalization. Advocates argue that there are hidden costs, psychic and actual, in depriving women of a chance to maintain income during pregnancy.

Cost estimates to show the potential impact of the legislation vary widely. Table 9.1 shows a range of projected additional costs estimated to follow from the requirement that pregnancy be included in disability insurance programs

Table 9.1. Costs Predicted on the Basis of Required Coverage of Pregnancy Disability Programs

Source	Duration of Disability	Average Payment Per Week	Additional Women Covered	Total Additional Cost
Chamber of Commerce (Sen. pp. 480–98)	6 weeks	$100	5% of 25 million female workers?	$1.7 billion
Metropolitan Life Insurance Associaiton (Sen. pp. 420–31)	11.3 weeks	$149 (94 percent of average gross weekly earnings, weighted)	435,000	$611 million
Murray Latimer, Industrial Relations Consultant (Sen. p. 499)*	8 weeks	$80.45 (55 percent of 146.28)	364,000	$198 million
AFL-CIO (Sen. pp. 218–19)	6 weeks	$78	276,273	$130 million†
U.S. Dollars (Sen. pp. 554–74)	6 weeks	$80 (60 percent of $134)	208,000	$120.5 million
	7.5 weeks	"	"	$191.5 million
	9 weeks	"	"	$262.5 million

*Latimer is projecting for 1978, and estimates a total for all disability payments of $5.3 billion, so that the increase of $198 million represents an increase of 3.7 percent.

†AFL-CIO estimates this cost to be about $1.50 per worker and represents .004 to 0.01 cents per hour increase in wage rate.

Source: Derived from U.S. Senate Hearings on SB 995, Discrimination on the Basis of Pregnancy, Subcommittee on Labor of the Committee on Human Resources, April 1977.

offered by employers in the private sector. It should be noted that these are not entirely direct costs to employers, since plans frequently require contributions from workers. As the table shows, the range in predicted additional cost per year is from $120.5 million to $1.7 billion. These estimates reach different totals because of differences in fertility rates, average duration of coverage, and average payment level estimated. Using some data from the *Gilbert* case, the Chamber of Commerce cites a total estimate of $1.7 billion per year. Ruth Weyand, IUE counsel in *Gilbert,* suggests that these figures are based on high fertility rates and inclusion of women already covered by pregnancy disability programs, not additional coverage.[48] Metropolitan Life Insurance Association uses the highest estimates for duration of leave (11.3 weeks), for wages (94 percent of the industry average wage, not women's average wage), and an estimated 435,000 additional births expected, for a total additional cost of $611 million per year. Murray Latimer, Industrial Relations Consultant, projected costs for the year 1978, using an eight-week duration of leave, $80.45 average wage (55 percent of 146.28) and 364,000 expected additional births, for a total cost for 1978 of $234 million, or an additional cost of $198 million. This latter figure, he estimates, would be about 3.75 percent of total disability payments made ($5.3 billion). The lowest estimates were provided by the AFL-CIO, with a total additional $130 million cost, which they say would be about $1.50 per worker. Alexis Herman, discussing Department of Labor estimates, states that disability payments for pregnancy represent "only about one-third of one percent of the total lifetime earnings of the average female worker."[49]

These estimates are an interesting example of the manipulation of data to match predetermined expectations or viewpoints. It is probably true that change is costly, both physically and economically. It is equally true that failure to change may restrict opportunities for employment and income for those now without equal options. Who bears the cost for change is a constant political question, as is the question of who bears the cost for not changing, and the question of who decides brings in the traditional conflict over the role of the federal government.

4. Private v. Public Roles: The Government Role

The Civil Rights Act itself is an acknowledgement of government responsibility in providing employment opportunities and addressing questions of discrimination on the basis of sex (and other factors). Business has historically argued for limited (if any) regulation. In the case of the proposed legislation under discussion here, opponents argue that Congress and EEOC would become arbitrators in essentially private matters of labor-management negotiation. Further, they argue, businesses would be required to provide maximum benefits for pregnancy regardless of previous labor contracts. Those employers who do not now have disability programs (about 40 percent) would be discouraged by this legislation from adding them, thus denying all workers additional protection.

Advocates argue that a uniform national policy is required. At present, some states require coverage of pregnancy under disability programs, and some do not. The result is not only confusion, they say, but an unfair situation for employers and employees in different states. In addition, they argue, government regulation is required in this area at the federal level in order to provide guidelines for businesses which have seemed to take little initiative to eliminate discrimination in the past.

THE PREGNANCY DISCRIMINATION ACT OF 1978

Following debate in both the U.S. House and Senate, and committee meetings to resolve final wording, the legislation was passed.[50] As of October 1978, the Civil Rights Act of 1964 was amended so that sex discrimination on the basis of pregnancy is prohibited in employment. The recurring debate over the role of government in reproductive decision making is seen in another light as it moved through Congress. An area of disagreement between the Senate and House versions of the bill was the extent to which abortions, as related to pregnancy disability programs, would or would not be covered. Among supporters of the bill were several groups which identified themselves as "pro-life" or antiabortion. These included Dr. Hellegers of the Joseph and Rose Kennedy Institute at Georgetown University, American Citizens Concerned for Life, Inc., and the National Conference of Catholic Bishops, Committee for Pro-Life Activities. These, and some opponents of the bill, suggest that by providing coverage of pregnancy in disability insurance programs two interrelated goals will be reached. Those women who in the past might have feared loss of income might now become pregnant. Obviously, in this view, this will lead to fewer abortions. Not so, say other opponents of the bill, for if you provide that there shall be no job-related discrimination on the basis of "pregnancy or pregnancy-related conditions," then you automatically require these programs to cover payments for wages lost owing to abortions. That, they argue, makes this legislation proabortion.

As a way of correcting this problem, the Bishops' Committee for Pro-Life Activities proposed to the House of Representatives the following new subsection:

> (k) The terms "because of sex" or "on the basis of sex" include but are not limited to, because of or on the basis of pregnancy, childbirth, or related medical conditions, and women affected . . . shall be treated the same for all employment-related purposes. . . . *Neither "pregnancy" nor "related medical conditions" as used in this section may be construed to include abortion.*[51]

The House of Representatives accepted the substance of this statement, which was proposed by Representative Edward P. Beard (D-R.I.) and approved the final version with the addition: "except where the life of the mother would be endangered if the fetus were carried to term: Provided, that nothing herein shall preclude an employer from providing abortion benefits or otherwise affect bargaining agreements in regard to abortion."[52] The Senate bill (SB 995) contained no such provisions, and the conference report shows the accepted final text, since signed into law:

> This subsection shall not require an employer to pay for health insurance benefits for abortion, except where the life of the mother would be endangered if the fetus were carried to term, or except where medical complications have arisen from an abortion: Provided, that nothing herein shall preclude an employer from providing abortion benefits or otherwise affect bargaining agreements in regard to abortion.[53]

The ambivalence of the conference report reflects the ongoing public debate about the role of government in regulating reproduction, and the complicated patterns of interaction among competing interest groups.

CONCLUSIONS

The passage of the Pregnancy Discrimination Act demonstrates the developing ability of women's groups to organize and present political arguments effectively in the male political arena. The testimony at the hearings shows an understanding of the complexity of sex discrimination issues and the interconnectedness of women's reproductive choices and structural obstacles in employment. The coalition brought together to effect passage combined those who believe women should be protected and those who believe that women need no protection, but rather, a clear recognition that their life circumstances are not the same as those of men. Yet, the process of interpreting and clarifying the scope and intent of the Civil Rights Act has been a long and slow one. The resistance to implementation has been substantial, and is certainly not ended with this incremental change. One strategy for increasing women's economic, political, and social opportunities has been to use the legal/political structure as a catalyst for social change. It is not the only approach, but has led in the past 15 years to increased organizational and political sophistication of increasing numbers of women and of groups with varying ideologies and styles.[54]

Resistance to increased options for women in employment is also clear. It would be a mistake for feminists to underestimate the strength of traditional views and male control. Groups of employers understand the implications of changing the rules so that women are paid equally, and may compete for a wider range of jobs. Groups wishing to control access to abortion are a considerable political force as well. The addition of the modified abortion rider to the bill is a sign of the vigilance and political strength of antiabortion groups. This provision in the bill permits employers to refuse to pay the costs of abortions, but also acknowledges that such provision may be incorporated in bargaining agreements. The Campaign to End Discrimination against Pregnant Workers interprets the language and legislative history of the new statute as making "it clear that women who have abortions are protected by federal law from all discrimination in employment except for the hospital and medical expenses for the performance of the abortion."[55] Whether this provision, or other implementation of the new statute follows this interpretation remains to be seen.

This incremental change in discrimination law represents only one step in the ongoing effort to redefine the implications to be drawn from the increased entrance of women into the work force, combined with the realities of their capacity to bear children, and continuing responsibility for child rearing. There remain conflicting views on how society ought to treat sex differences. The issue of pregnancy and its social consequences is complex. There is now some acceptance that women are entitled to employment opportunities. This has often seemed to mean entitlement as long as women are similar to the "standard, fully developed person who is male as well as white."[56] Although employers may not proceed enthusiastically, they have developed strategies for adjusting to life circumstances which tend to disrupt the work pattern of men. For example, employers have made provisions for retaining the employment status of men who are drafted. These men leave, often for long periods of time, and are able to return to their jobs, seniority retained, or receive veterans' preference in attaining new employment. In this case, employers and society identify as justifiable some compensation for those who are asked to defend the country. No such provision is available to women who are responsible for creating the next generation of workers, citizens, and warriors. In the case of men, flexibility in employment provisions is considered a public good. In the case of pregnant women, the assumption is retained that child bearing is a private decision in which employers and society have only peripheral concern.

Gradually, employment policies and legislation are adapting to the need to accommodate women's employment concerns. It will take far more drastic change however, to move from an employment model which is male-centered and structured to one which takes into account sex differences in life patterns, as well as sex similarities in the capacity to perform diverse tasks.

Notes

1. For the purposes of this discussion, I am borrowing Linda Gordon's definition of feminism: "An analysis of women's subordination for the purpose of figuring out how to change it." *Woman's Body, Woman's Right* (New York: Viking, 1976).

2. U.S. Department of Labor, "Woman Workers Today," 1976, p. 3.

3. U.S. Department of Health, Education and Welfare, "Advance Data," September 15, 1977, p. 1.

4. 208 U.S. 412 (1908).

5. 429 U.S. 129 (1976).

6. Barbara Allen Babcock et al., *Sex Discrimination and the Law* (Boston: Little, Brown, 1975), ch. 1.

7. *Muller* v. *Oregon,* 208 U.S. 412 (at 422).

8. For discussion of these issues, see Jane Roberts Chapman and Margaret Gates, *Women Into Wives,* Vol. 2 (Beverly Hills: Sage, 1977); Ruth Bader Ginsburg, "Sex Equality and the Constitution: The State of the Art," *Women's Rights Law Reporter 4,* 3 (Spring 1978): 143–47; Kathleen Peratis and Elisabeth Rindskopf, "Pregnancy Discrimination as a Sex Discrimination Issue" (California Commission on the Status of Women, Equal Rights Project, 1975); Adrienne Rich, *Of Woman Born* (New York: Bantam, 1977); Ruth Weyand, "Discrimination Because of Pregnancy," *Equal Opportunity Forum* (February 1977), pp. 4–23; and Linda H. Kistler and Carol C. McDonough, "Paid Maternity Leave—Benefits May Justify the Cost," *Labor Law Journal* (December 1975); pp. 782–94.

9. U.S. Senate, "Discrimination on the Basis of Pregnancy, 1977," Hearings before the Subcommittee on Labor of the Committee on Human Resources, 95th Congress, 1st Sess., on SB 995 (April 1977), p. 124.

10. U.S. House of Representatives, "Legislation to Prohibit Sex Discrimination on the Basis of Pregnancy," Hearing before the Subcommittee on Employment Opportunities of the Committee on Education and Labor, 95th Congress, 1st Sess., on HR 5055 and HR 6075 (April 6, 1977), p. 7.

11. In this same time period there was some development of national maternity programs to provide medical aid, counseling centers, and visiting nurses. The Maternity and Infant Protection Act of 1921 provided national funds to local units. The program of family support services is now administered under Title XX of the Social Security Act. See Carolyn Teich Adams and Kathryn Teich Winston, *Mothers at Work* (New York: Longman, 1980), pp. 34–36.

12. U.S. House of Representatives, p. 7.

13. Nancy S. Erickson, "Pregnancy Discrimination: An Analytical Approach," *Women's Rights Law Reporter 5,* 2–3 (Winter–Spring 1979): 83.

14. U.S. House of Representatives, p. 31.

15. 42 U.S.C. Sec. 2000e, forbids all discriminatory employment practices based on sex. Hereafter referred to as Title VII.

16. 404 U.S. 999 (1971).

17. 400 U.S. 542 (1971).

18. 414 U.S. 632 (1974).

19. 96 S. Ct. 249 (1975).
20. 434 U.S. 136 (1977); see Erickson, "Pregnancy Discrimination," pp. 92–93.
21. Hereafter referred to as EEOC. The commission was established by the Civil Rights Act of 1964, and its guidelines and procedures have often been deferred to by the courts.
22. U.S. House of Representatives, p. 457.
23. 29 C.F.R.§ 1604.10 (b).
24. U.S. Senate, p. 244.
25. Ibid., p. 245.
26. Adams and Winston, *Mothers at Work,* p. 33.
27. California League of Cities, "Spot Checks on Maternity Leave Survey," December 1, 1976, p. 1.
28. 417 U.S. 484 (1974).
29. 404 U.S. 71 (1971).
30. 429 U.S. 129 (1976).
31. *Aiello,* note 19.
32. Peratis and Rindskopf, "Pregnancy Discrimination as a Sex Discrimination Issue," p. 5.
33. *Gilbert,* at 421.
34. Susan Ross, ACLU, in U.S. House of Representatives, p. 35.
35. *Gilbert,* at 422.
36. Ibid.
37. Ibid., at 450.
38. "Reaction to the Supreme Court Decision Against Disability Pay for Pregnancy," *Womanpower* (February 1977), pp. 1–5.
39. Ibid., p. 2.
40. "Supreme Court to Hear Maternity Benefit Cases," *Women Today 3* (February 1977): 1.
41. "Civil Rights for Pregnant Workers," *Congressional Clearinghouse on Women's Rights 4,* 5 (April 10, 1978).
42. California Commission on the Status of Women, "California Women: A Bulletin," (November/December 1976).
43. Campaign to End Discrimination against Pregnant Workers, "Fact Sheet" (December 1976).
44. "Reaction to the Supreme Court Decision," p. 3.
45. U.S. House of Representatives, p. 1.
46. U.S. Senate, p. 1.
47. Ibid., p. 399.
48. U.S. House of Representatives, p. 202.
49. Ibid., p. 181.
50. Public Law 95-555, 92 Stat. 2076.
51. U.S. House of Representatives, p. 273. Emphasis added.
52. U.S. House of Representatives, 95th Congress 2d Session, HR 6075, March 13, 1978.
53. U.S. House of Representatives, 95th Congress, 2d Sess., Conference Report No. 95-1786, "Pregnancy Discrimination" (October 1978).

54. See Caroline Bird with Sara Welles Briller, *Born Female,* rev. ed. (New York: David McKay, 1974); Judith Hole and Ellen Levine, *Rebirth of Feminism* (New York: Quadrangle Books, 1971); and Jo Freeman, *The Politics of Women's Liberation* (New York: David McKay, 1975).

55. *Spokeswoman,* December 15, 1978, p. 47.

56. Richard A. Wasserstrom, "Racism and Sexism," in *Philosophy and Women,* ed., Sharon Bishop and Marjorie Weinzweig (San Francisco: Wadsworth, 1979), p. 8.

Part V
Sexuality and Crime: Female Victims and Offenders

Introduction

While the original focus of the women's movement was on economic issues, the movement turned its attention in the 1970s to a wide range of other issues including female sexuality. There are no perfect distinctions between economic and sexuality issues as many sexuality issues have clear economic implications. Sexual harassment on the job has caused many women to suffer humiliation in the workplace out of fear of economic sanctions, or to lose their jobs when they have tried to put an end to it. Prostitution for many women is a choice based on the inability to earn comparable incomes by other means. A battered woman often remains with her male partner out of dependence on his earnings. Thus, sexuality issues involve a concern both for women as victims of male sexual oppression and for the economic causes and consequences of this victimization.

The women's movement has had notable success in raising the public consciousness regarding the sexual oppression of women. In the past female sexuality has been treated either as a private matter or as a morality issue with an emphasis on punishment of women who deviate from traditional norms of behavior. The crime of rape clearly illustrates these tendencies. Traditionally, rape victims have kept their silence. When they did go public, they, as the "immoral" victims of rape, have been subjected to public shame, rather than the perpetrators. In rape prosecutions the burden of proof has often fallen on the victim to prove that she did not seduce the male or provoke the attack, rather than on the rapist to prove his innocence. Given the public humiliation suffered by rape victims and the insensitivity with which they have been treated by the criminal justice system, it is no wonder that most rape victims contribute to the conspiracy of silence.

The women's movement has transformed the issue of rape from a private matter to one of major public policy concern. Services to rape victims ranging from crisis counseling to self-defense training have been supported by public funds. Legal reforms have occurred both in the prosecution of rape cases and in the criminal penalties for rapists. New police procedures and training programs have been instituted to move the criminal justice system toward aiding rather than punishing the victim. While rape remains an urgent, even growing, social problem, women today are confronting and demanding public policy responses to their victimization.

By bringing sexuality issues into the public sphere, the women's movement has been instrumental in exposing the sexist biases of the criminal justice system. For example, while views may differ regarding the criminality of prostitution, prostitution cannot occur without two parties; yet, as women's groups have shown, the prosecution of the crime has fallen far more heavily on the female offender. Domestic violence, like rape, has been regarded as a private matter; women's groups have revealed how law-enforcement officials avoid intervention in domestic strife on the premise that "a man's home is his castle." Recently, feminist groups have spoken out on the issue of pornography, protesting that the "obscene" quality of pornography is not its sexual explicitness but rather its legitimization of violence against women.

Despite the success of the women's movement in raising sexuality issues, proposed public policy responses to these concerns have met serious resistance. In theory the social environment should be supportive of change—who could fail to endorse an end to violence against women? Yet, as the chapters in this part make clear, changes in public policy in this area involve competing values. Bessmer, in Chapter 10, shows how feminist objections to pornography clash with judicial precedents which emphasize sexual explicitness rather than violence, as well as with civil-libertarian objections to censorship of any kind. In Chapter 11, Wexler's study of domestic violence policy reveals how efforts to provide public remedies for battered women clash with the conservative position that any government intervention in family matters is destructive of the family. Moulds (Chapter 12) demonstrates how paternalistic attitudes toward women lead to more lenient treatment of female offenders except when the crime involves sexuality, in which case women receive harsher treatment than men.

The essays in Part V illustrate the need for women to work for public policy change in more arenas of the political system than the Congress which has been the primary target of the women's movement in the last 20 years. In particular, women must try to effect change through the judicial system which remains a male bastion. Only 5 percent of the federal judiciary is female and the number of female appointments to state judgeships is equally dismal, except in a few states. President Reagan's appointment of Sandra O'Connor to the Supreme Court is an important breakthrough but it should be remembered that even if she casts her vote consistently in support of women's issues, it is only one vote out of nine. The number of female attorneys is increasing at a dramatic rate, and it is predicted that by 1990 one-quarter of the nation's lawyers will be women; yet without a sustained educational effort directed at male judges and law-enforcement officials, and close monitoring of the justice system, women's needs as victims and offenders will continue to receive sexist treatment.

Chapter 10
Antiobscenity: A Comparison of the Legal and the Feminist Perspectives*
Sue Bessmer

Any public discussion of the desirability, feasibility, or legality of censoring obscene or pornographic materials, variously defined, is guaranteed to generate heated debate. Support for the censor has long been regarded as the province of the politically conservative, the strongly religious, and those persons deeply convinced of the sanctity of the family and the need to preserve conventional moral norms. Political liberals or progressives, moral relativists, and individuals who either seek or tolerate challenges to conventional standards of sociosexual conduct have traditionally been arrayed against censorship. This easy, if simplistic, taxonomy of the dramatis personae in the obscenity debate, however, has been overset by the genesis of a new political force. This political force, the women's movement, clearly disavows and frequently opposes those values and belief systems which have historically underwritten the drive to suppress pornography. Feminist support for sexual and reproductive freedom of choice, for experimentation with unconventional forms of family organization, and for gay rights exemplify, though they do not exhaust, the areas of disagreement between the women's movement and the traditional champions of censorship. Thus, no comfortable political alliance is possible between them. At the same time, however, feminism as a political philosophy and as a political movement does embody substantial opposition to the "exploitation" by the media of women's bodies and female sexuality as well as marked distaste for much of what might be called, in common parlance,

---

*An earlier version of this article was published in the *Western Political Quarterly, 34:* 143–255. Reprinted by permission of the University of Utah, Copyright Holder.

pornographic presentation of human sexual relations. This fact, in turn, strains the philosophical and political bonds between feminists and the liberal or progressive opponents of censorship who are, in many other respects, their natural allies.

These statements should not be construed to imply that all feminists favor censorship. Indeed, the women's movement is deeply conflicted about the proper response to various examples of obscene or pornographic materials. Considerable controversy exists about what defines, either semantically or in terms of social theory, an obnoxious portrayal of human sexuality and/or an exploitative representation of the female body. Moreover, no single theory which might justify some form of censorship commands anything approaching unanimous assent, except perhaps the liberal consensus that individuals have an absolute right to boycott that which offends them. Yet an active, if sometimes only emotive, opposition to something which might be called obscenity is alive and thriving in the women's movement.

This chapter deals with those areas of controversy. It will attempt to locate, broadly and with several degrees of freedom, what is obscene or pornographic[1] (using these words with a negative connotation) from a feminist perspective. It will also consider how this feminist perspective compares with some other formulations of the concept of obscenity employed by philosophers, academicians, and/or jurists. Finally, the chapter will examine possible theoretical justifications for the suppression, by some means, of that which is deemed objectionable.

Lest the reader be deceived, it must be said that this is not a report of the collected opinions of "feminists."[2] Its success cannot then be measured by its congruence to the previously expressed attitudes of a majority of this population as determined by a survey. Yet neither is this essay purely a work of political theory designed to specify what a feminist view of obscenity "must" be. Rather, it is a reexamination of an issue—obscenity—which has long plagued the courts as well as moral and political philosophers and which promises to be no less irksome for the women's movement. Put simply, the essay considers an old political problem in relation to a new political force.

WHAT IS OBSCENE?

All opposition to pornography or obscenity designed to influence the behavior of others, either juridically or by persuasive argument, requires a definition which distinguishes the objectionable from that which is tolerated or approved.[3] Defining obscenity, in turn, raises questions about the social theory or theories which underwrite this process of creating categories. A grand tour of the diverse linguistic combinations used to delimit the obscene can be most amusing. Yet it is with the social theories underlying these definitions, and not with their language, that this section is concerned. And it must be so, for the most striking contrast between traditional definitions of obscenity, both legal and religious, and feminist definitions lies precisely in their fundamentally different conceptions of the problem.

Legal definitions of obscenity capture most traditional concerns in this area and thus provide a good shorthand device for discussing them. Since the changeable, confused, almost quixotic character of obscenity law is so often emphasized,[4] it is easy to ignore the common properties which lie behind the many legal formulations. Yet such common properties are present. They are articulated in various ways, to be sure, and differentially applied by judges and jurors with divergent tastes and preferences. Yet they remain as central tendencies in obscenity law.

Despite their myriad guises, nearly all legal definitions of obscenity presume its subject matter to be sex. "The law has given 'obscenity' a purely sexual connotation. Material that is merely profane or vulgar, reprehensible, scatalogical, or that portrays violence and sadism is not obscene. Obscenity must be pornography."[5] Materials are obscene because, on the whole[6] or in part,[7] they treat sex in a manner deemed objectionable for any of a variety of reasons, most of which can be grouped into two general and interrelated categories. The first and historically most important category has to do with "that form of immorality which has relation to sexual impurity."[8] "Obscenity is calculated to deprave the morals of the reader by exciting sexual desires and libidinous thoughts."[9] It tends "to lower the standards of right and wrong especially as to the sexual relation."[10] It appeals to "prurient interests."[11] As the late Justice Frankfurter pointed out, the word "obscene" in America law has long referred to "sexual immorality,"[12] which he regarded as "an evil against which a State may constitutionally protect itself."[13]

Because jurists rarely specify what is meant by sexual immorality in this context, it is difficult to say with certainty what that rubric includes. This very omission, however, suggests a reference to some variant of that traditional system of values which deprecates extramarital sex and frowns on certain sex practices, clearly possible between married persons, which cannot, by their nature, result in procreation. Modern judges do appear to be less rigid in their allegiance to traditional sexual mores than were their predecessors. But there is no evidence of a wholesale defection from that old system of values. Neither is there any evidence that contemporary courts have invested new meaning into the concept of sexual immorality such that, for example, materials might be deemed immoral because they promote inequality between the sexes. Sexual immorality means something like what it has meant in the past and is still regarded as some part of the evil of obscenity. This is true despite the fact that judges can and do refuse to censor, on First Amendment grounds, materials which they freely deplore.[14]

The other general category of ills traditionally associated with obscenity is "patent offensiveness" or "indecency."[15] Complaints that materials are lewd, lascivious, or licentious refer to their sexual immorality, while complaints about their coarseness, crudity, vulgarity, or explicitness raise the issue of patent offensiveness. Modern courts have distinguished between these two categories[16] and have judged both to be requisites of obscenity.[17] It has been argued, for example, that the "tendency to deprave," i.e., sexual immorality or an appeal to prurience," is not the characteristic which makes a publication obscene." Patent offensiveness does that. Rather, the tendency to deprave is "the characteristic which makes an obscene publication criminal."[18]

Despite the conceptual and functional differences between them, however, the categories of sexual immorality and patent offensiveness are strongly interlinked. This is not surprising since the accepted yardstick for patent offensiveness is whether the material "affronts contemporary standards relating to the description or representation of sexual matters,"[19] while the measure of a tendency to deprave is "whether to the average person, applying contemporary community standards, the dominant theme of the material taken as a whole appeals to prurient interest."[20] One might well expect prevailing community standards about acceptable levels of candor (patent offensiveness) to be closely conjoined with prevailing community standards about the thing candidly portrayed (sexual immorality). Form and content are not easily divorced.[21]

In summary then, traditional legal definitions of obscenity conceive of it as a portrayal of sexual matters which violates, in a patently offensive manner, some variant of what has been called the "Old Morality."[22] These definitions locate obscenity outside the mainstream of dominant cultural values. Obscenity is then rejected because it is "utterly"[23] or seriously[24] "without redeeming social importance."[25] Thus, for jurists as for most traditional political theorists, obscenity raises the problem of how to protect an important social value, freedom of speech, whilst curtailing the purveyance of materials which offend against the dominant cultural norms in taste and sexual morality.

THE FEMINIST PERSPECTIVE

Certainly many feminists share with their judicial brethren a real concern with protecting free speech from governmental censorship. They also share the difficulties inherent in the articulation of a common and workable definition of obscenity (which they usually call pornography). Yet feminist definitions, like legal formulations, have common properties. A summary of these reveals, at the level of social theory as well as in language, sharp differences between feminist and legal or traditionalist conceptions of the nature and evils of obscenity.

As seen above, sexuality or eroticism are the *sine qua non* of obscenity in law. For most feminists, by contrast, the subject matter of obscenity is not sex. Rather, it is power. Obscenity deals with domineering, aggressive, degrading, or objectifying relations between people, particularly male dominance over females.[26] Certainly, such power relations can be pruriently portrayed and are then rejected. So, for example, one feminist antipornography organization includes among its goals putting "an end to all portrayals of women being bound, raped, tortured, killed and degraded for sexual stimulation or pleasure."[27] A specifically sexual or erotic context is not, however, an absolute requisite of obscenity in feminist circles. Thus, feminist antipornography demonstrations have been directed against such things as a window display in a large Boston department store which featured a battered female dummy sticking out of a trashcan with a par of men's shoes on her head advertised by the caption "I'd kill for these."[28]

But feminists frequently do more than broaden the concept of obscenity to include nonsexual materials. They also generally treat as objectionable certain sexually oriented materials which most traditionalists regard as benign. Scantity treat the "true confession" magazine as benign while feminists often do not. Thus, the Commission on Obscenity and Pornography described these maga- exploitative, and thus pornographic.[29] Similarly, traditional notions of obscen- ity treat the "true confession" magazine as benign while feminist often do not. Thus, the Commission on Obscenity and Pornography described these maga- zines as "fictional accounts of the sexual problems of young women" and reflected traditional concerns in asserting that "they do not explicitly describe sex organs or sexual activity" (patent offensiveness) "and always resolve sexual problems in a moral context"[30] (sexual immorality). Feminist writer Susan Brownmiller takes a grimmer view. She finds them replete with rape themes treated so as to promulgate "a philosophy of submission in which the female victim was often to blame."[31] She notes that the "uppity girl getting her comeuppance from a gang of boys" in the form of rape or threats of rape, with the implication that sexual violence is an appropriate response to female deviation from conventionally prescribed roles, is common in these publica- tions.[32] This might be described as resolving "sexual problems" in a "moral context." But when confronted by titles like "GANG-RAPED BY 7 BOYS— BECAUSE I LED THEIR GIRLS INTO A WOMAN'S LIB CLUB,"[33] neither Brownmiller nor any other active feminist can be expected to endorse the "moral context" in which the "problem" was solved.

Behind their disagreement over the "true confession" magazines lie more fundamental differences between traditionalist and feminist conceptions of the obscenity problem. In traditionalist formulations, explicitness is an important criterion of obscenity. For most feminists, at least in theory, it is not.[34] Indeed, the women's movement encourages women artists, in all spheres, to produce sexually explicit, feminist "erotica."[35] Just as conventional concerns with explicitness are closely conjoined with concerns about sexual morality, so too is the feminist rejection of the explicitness standard closely linked to a rejection of conventional sexual norms. The sexual double standard, the division of women into "good" and "bad" on the basis of their willingness to limit their sexual choices and conform to convention, as well as the reduction of sexuality to its procreative functions are only some of the elements of the "Old Moral- ity" which have come under attack by the women's movement. Ellen Willis, feminist writer, explains why sexual immorality and its colleague, explicitness, have been scrapped as yardsticks for the obscene:

> Historically, obscenity laws have been obstacles to women's liberation. It was obviously harder to combat the double standard, affirm women's rights to sexual pleasure and reproductive freedom, or educate women about their sexuality in an atmosphere where such subjects could not be freely discussed. Those who are tempted to nostalgia by *Hustler* and *Snuff* do well to keep in mind that fifteen years ago newspapers referred to abortions as 'illegal operations' and did not refer to contraceptives at all, while books like *Our Bodies, Ourselves* and *The Hite Report* were unheard of.[36]

Feminists generally deplore the moral values behind antiobscenity statutes and are frequently cynical about the ability of persons imbued with those values to enforce new laws in an acceptable manner.[37] Thus, for many activists in the women's movement, governmental censorship remains anathema.

Yet these feminist opponents of official censorship fall far short of defending unto death the pornographers' rights to ply their trade. Certainly traditional defenses of censorship are regarded as misguided and, in most cases, sexist. Traditional anticensorship arguments, however, are seen as equally obtuse:

> The issue, finally, is not whether sexual permissiveness is a good thing, or even whether the right of individuals to publish or exhibit what they please must always supersede the right of the community to set standards of public decorum. The issue is whether women are obliged, in the name of respect for civil liberties, to tolerate what amounts to a legally and socially sanctioned hate campaign.[38]

In this feminist view, obscenity is not about sex and it cannot be either praised or damned because it questions the "Old Morality," candidly or otherwise. Rather, "obscenity is the undiluted essence of anti-female propaganda."[39] Feminist writers and activists heap scorn on the (putatively) sexist hypocrisy of liberals who cannot or will not see the analogy between pornography and racist or anti-Semitic propaganda of the Hitlerian variety.[40] "Imagine the public outcry that would occur if there were special movie houses in every city where viewers could see whites beating up Blacks, or Christians beating up Jews."[41] Thus, defending the rights of the occasional oddball to spew out an anomalous hate message against some group or another is sharply distinguished from defending the right of a multimillion-dollar industry to profit from a large-scale "anti-female propaganda" campaign.[42]

Feminists emphasize not only the volume of obscenity, but also its congruence to other messages received by citizens in the socialization process. Whereas traditionalists, both pro and anticensorship, tend to regard obscenity as an isolated attack on established cultural values, feminists usually consider it an extension—albeit extreme and vicious—of the dominant values of society. Misogyny, male supremacy, the glorification of power, aggression, and dominance—the very hallmarks of obscenity in the feminist lexicon—are seen as central features of modern American society, permeating all facets of everyday life.[43]

ESSENTIAL DIFFERENCES IN PERSPECTIVE

The crux of the difference between traditionalist formulations of the obscenity problem and feminist reformulations lies in their location of obscenity in relation to other elements in society. Traditionalists generally treat obscenity as a thing apart from other socializing messages, as foreign to and in conflict with dominant cultural values.[44] To some traditionalists, obscenity is both antisocial and pernicious. To others, obscenity is relatively harmless, precisely because it is offset by so many countervailing messages, thus allowing citizens ample choice in a "free marketplace" of ideas.[45] "I have the same confidence in the ability of our people to reject noxious literature as I have in their capacity to sort out the true from the false in theology, economics, politics or any other field."[46] Indeed, most defenses of free speech presume that no body of ideas will enjoy a competitive advantage (let alone a monopolistic position) *a priori*. Jumping ahead, it is precisely the view that obscenity does enjoy just such advantage which distinguishes feminists from traditionalists.

Returning to traditionalist thought, a third strain argues that obscenity has positive virtues stemming from its attacks upon or deviance from conventionality. It is a breath of fresh air which speaks to "natural" human urges repressed by conventional norms[47] and/or a harmless outlet for destructive drives which might otherwise result in antisocial conduct.[48] Although the proponents of these diverse evaluations of obscenity have lively disagreements amongst themselves, they share, generally, a common view of the nature of the obscene. Obscenity is a candid, explicit or offensive portrayal of sex which fundamentally challenges conventional morality and which runs against the grain of entrenched societal values as manifested in ordinary socializing messages.

Feminists tend to see the problem quite differently. For them, obscenity is a degrading and debasing portrayal of power relations between people, in particular male dominance over women, which is, in no fundamental sense, foreign to established social values. Indeed, for many feminists, obscenity is the offspring, perhaps the unacknowledged bastard child, of those conventional values.

Some feminist discussions treat obscenity as a direct, linear extension of conventional norms. Male supremacy in politics, economics and law, extend in pornography into interpersonal relations. The "masculine" attributes of competitiveness, dominance, aggression, and the ability to conquer, command, and control one's space are glorified in obscenity (and help to define it) as they are lauded in other social messages and customs. The sexual double standard, enshrined in the "Old Morality" is as antifemale as obscenity, which simply carries to an extreme the view that degradation and punishment are natural correlates of unfettered sexuality, at least for women. The time-honored, hoary notion that women prefer dominant men and submissive roles[49] grounds the pervasive pornographic fantasy of the (often proud and willful) virgin who is raped and then develops, forthwith, an insatiable craving for endless encores.[50] Examples of elements in popular culture and traditional values which give rise to obscenity are legion in feminist writings and discussions of the subject. Viewed as an adjunct or extrapolation of established social norms, obscenity is not, for feminists, countercultural.

Other feminists see the relationship between established values and obscenity as more dialectic than linear, as in the interaction between Christianity and the obscene. Christianity contains a tradition which rejects the body as imprisoning and debasing the spirit. Denying and mortifying the flesh becomes the route to spiritual freedom and the exhilarating pleasures of salvation. On that road, pain and pleasure merge. Early Christian saints and martyrs displayed remarkable ingenuity for self-torture and described the joys of masochism in glowing terms, while the "most distinctive and disturbing thing about Christian art, especially during the last thousand years, has been its tendency to glorify suffering."[51] Yet a rejection of the flesh can become an obsession with its sinful powers and its degradation can become, for saintly and secular flagellants alike, the source of an ecstasy, an intensity of feeling, which fuses rapture and pain. In Christianity, saints experienced this conjuncture in the willing service of God, while obscenity tells us that women experience this same combination of pleasure and anguish in the service of their earthly "lords."[52] Sadism, too, is present in Christian theology and Christian art. Detailed and inventive depictions of Hell undoubtedly served to drive the people to repentance and to church, hardly a humane or liberal method of social control. But these horrific visions also offered people "a vindictive pleasure at the thought of their enemies or oppressors cast into hell . . . and one of the delights promised the blessed was the sight of the miserable and helpless struggles of the damned."[53] Finally, we can hear the masculine obsession with and anxiety about insatiable female sexuality, so prevalent in pornography,[54] echoed in the Christian treatment of the female as the locus of temptation and the root cause of man's fall from grace.[55] Thus obscenity, with its obsessively detailed treatment of the physical, its vastly exaggerated sense of the power of "natural" urges, its sadomasochistic elements and its conjoining of pleasure and pain, mirrors many traditional Christian conceptions about sex and the human body, and most especially female sexuality.[56]

For feminists, obscenity is intimately interlinked with other social learning. Rigid Christian concepts of physicality and the "Old Morality" as well as conventional notions of appropriate gender-role behavior are seen as antihuman, antifemale and antichoice. They denigrate human sexuality, promote male supremacy, and limit or oppose free and informed choice in sexual and interpersonal relations. The values which underwrite obscenity are not regarded as fundamentally different from the values embodied in these venerated elements of conventional culture.

IMPLICATIONS

Whether obscenity is defined as an explicit, countercultural treatment of sex or as a degrading, misogynist portrayal of power relations buttressed by similar messages in other aspects of the culture has important implications. As noted above, these two models often classify different materials as obscene. When similar items are so classified by both models, these judgments rest on substantially divergent rationales. Moreover, each model prescribes different questions for empirical research and suggests distinct methodological problems.

Consider, for example, the matter of the effects of obscenity, a much debated issue. From a traditionalist perspective, one important question is whether the consumption of "explicit sexual materials" predisposes the consumer to antisocial, delinquent, or criminal conduct. Most research poses the problem in this way. Given the traditionalist conception of obscenity as an explicit portrayal of sexuality, examining the effects of such materials makes perfect sense. It also generates mixed results, ranging from the reports of subject-viewers that these materials increased their knowledge of sexual matters and/or enhanced their marriage to reports that these viewers were seriously disturbed.[57] Feminists, who reject the explicitness standard,[58] might well argue that these mixed results are predictable, since some sexually explicit materials are educational, equitable, and humane (and thus both acceptable to feminists and likely to produce positive responses) while others are violent, debasing, and misogynist. From a feminist perspective, it makes no sense to conjoin these very different types of materials into the category of "obscenity" and it is thus futile to try to demonstrate that they have a single or unilateral effect. Indeed, the methodological differences between the two models are even more fundamental. Although many feminists believe that obscenity, as they define it, encourages violence against women in real life, the feminist paradigm makes that proposition extremely difficult to prove. If it is the case that obscenity is merely an extension of other sociocultural norms, then determining its effects, in isolation, poses what may be insurmountable methodological problems. If, by contrast, obscenity is countercultural, as the traditionalists presume, then it might be possible to disentangle its impact from the welter of other countervailing socializing experiences, although this has yet to be done conclusively.[59]

Finally, these very different formulations of the obscenity problem result in significantly different notions about how to solve it. For traditionalist opponents of obscenity, the problem is one of rendering harmless, nullifying or suppressing a relatively isolated set of antisocial messages. For feminist opponents of obscenity, the problem is much larger. Suppressing obscenity gets at the extreme variants of antifemale "propaganda" but does not, ultimately, reach to the heart of the matter. A broader assault upon a much wider range of socializing agencies, in conjunction with a program of public "reeducation" is called for.[60] Feminists face the awesome task of redefining the terms of public debate on a longstanding and highly emotional issue. Traditionalist opponents of obscenity must be converted to a new and more liberal philosophy while traditionalist defenders of it must be brought to recognize distinctions between benign and progressive explicit sexual materials and violent, misogynist ones.

SOME LINKS AND PERHAPS A BRIDGE

One final aspect of the situation at once complicates and ameliorates it for feminists. All political movements, however radical, are born out of their own social context and are comprised of human beings unable, wholly, to divorce themselves from the values of the culture against which they rebel. The women's movement is no exception. Most feminists find in themselves, to their great dismay, vestiges of the values and practices they deplore. Similarly, when the rage subsides, they often perceive potential allies amongst their apparent enemies, allies who have laid at least a partial foundation for the "new" feminist perspective.

Many feminists are quite uncertain, at least at the boundaries, what a "degrading" or "humiliating" portrayal of female sexuality really means. Feminists have rejected the explicitness standard but many find it difficult to shake off their own conventional upbringing. By this convention, sex is "dirty" and women who participate in it outside of the privacy and sanctity of the marriage bed are soiled. If the women's movement is clear on any point, it is on the rejection of this way of thinking. Yet many feminists admit that they cannot see an explicit depiction of women in a sexual context (particularly when men are present and might apply the "Old Morality" to the women thus exposed) without immediately finding the portrayal "debasing." Naturally this inability to overcome the very ideas which they oppose complicates the obscenity problem for feminists. When one's own "re-education" has yet to jell, reeducating others is more problematic.

On the brighter side, feminists are not nearly so alone as an examination of the diverse positions on the "obscenity" problem might suggest. They have built upon preexisting political foundations and can find allies outside the women's movement. For example, objections to violence in the media, a common vehicle for depicting those aggressive and domineering interpersonal relations which many feminists regard as obscene, is widespread outside the movement. Of course, the problem of media violence has been treated, traditionally, as separate from the problem of obscenity. But the separation has been imperfect. As part of its antiobscenity statutes, New York once punished the purveyance of materials "principally made up of criminal news, police reports, or accounts of criminal deeds, or pictures, or stories of deeds of bloodshed, lust or crime"[61] when these elements were "so massed . . . 'as to become vehicles for inciting violent and depraved crimes against the person.' "[62] The United States Supreme Court, after pointing out that this statute did not require these materials to excite "sexual passion," concluded that what it proscribed was "not indecency or obscenity in any sense heretofore known to the law."[63] In this instance, the Court was enforcing the traditional boundaries between the obscene, which must be prurient, and the merely violent. As noted above, feminists generally reject this distinction, a philosophical disagreement of some importance. But it is also important to remember that many groups in society are becoming increasingly upset about excessive media violence. Even if such people do not incorporate media violence into their conception of obscenity, they do provide feminists with allies on particular issues. Moreover, a shared emotive disaffection from violence in the media, however categorized, could be a bridge to greater communication and perhaps philosophical conversion.

Further, feminists are not forced to settle merely for allies who share some of their emotions while rejecting most of their analysis as to the nature and root causes of the problem. The traditionalist formulation of the obscenity issue has found challengers outside the women's movement. These challenges have come, most notably, from humanist critics of both censorship and that brand of pornography which has raised feminist hackles. Thus, for example, D. H. Lawrence, for all his machismo,[64] despised men who have sex with a woman and then "triumphantly feel that they have done her dirt, and now she is lower, cheaper, more contemptible than before."[65] Lawrence asserted that "even" he "would censor genuine pornography" which "you can recognize . . . by the insult it offers, invariably, to sex, and to the human spirit."[66] Although Lawrence confined his understanding of pornography to materials dealing with sexuality, he nevertheless did share many of the premises which now ground a feminist perspective on the obscenity problem. Significantly, he shared the view that obscenity arises out of precisely that conventional sexual morality which motivated most censorship in his day.

More recently, essayist and philosopher Paul Goodman has suggested that "censorship itself is part of a general repressive anti-sexuality, which creates the need for sadistic pornography sold at criminal profit."[67] He argued that censorship induces guilt and associates "lust with punishment and so creates sado-masochistic thoughts."[68] Like Lawrence, Goodman specified that sexuality was the topic of the pornographic. However, again like Lawrence but here also like the feminists, Goodman distinguished between "innocent and useful" explicit sexual materials and a more virulent breed which he described as "harmful."[69] Some of his statements are reminiscent of that traditionalist school which regards obscenity as useful, and perhaps desirable, simply because it attacks convention and represents an outlet for countercultural messages. Goodman, however, divorced himself from that school by arguing that little, if any, pornography has yet reached the stage of being a healthy socializing experience, by describing much of it as pernicious and by insisting upon the intrinisic unity of conventional morality and obscenity.[70] For Goodman, obscenity is inexorably linked to the culture which spawns it and thus he echoes the feminist perspective. Moreover, what he found destructive about harmful pornography, "its mere sexuality or 'lust,' devoid of any further human contact, drama or meaning; and its very frequent sado-masochism,"[71] approximates common feminist critiques, even down to a recognition that these elements often manifest themselves in women hating.[72] He rejected that "permissiveness" advocated by traditionalist defenders of obscenity (who turn a blind eye to its deleterious effects and see only its "non-conformist virtues") and he called for a strategy of more affirmative leadership just as feminists now call for public reeducation.[73]

Goodman, Lawrence, and other humanist critics of both obscenity and conventional morality, who see the former as a product of the latter, provide a philosophical link between feminists and those liberals whose fear of censorship makes suspect all attacks on the obscene. The women's movement could do worse than to seek out such humanist allies wherever possible.

CONCLUSION

Obscenity is, indeed, a very old problem. Public efforts at its suppression have been met, thus far, with only indifferent success. If the feminists and their humanist allies are correct, this failure was inevitable since the values which animate the censorship drive themselves give rise to the very evil they seek to defeat. Of course, reconstituting the terms of public debate can never be an easy task. Feminist groups, however, do not seem to have yet exhausted their energies or their ingenuity in combating pornography. They are writing, boycotting, meeting, picketing, and marching. Perhaps most significantly, women with a feminist perspective are beginning to enter the professions which have traditionally been the most influential in the obscenity debate: law, politics, journalism, and other media. Whether feminists and their allies, as legislators, jurists, film makers, writers, consumers, and activists, will succeed in reshaping the public discussion of obscenity and pornography remains to be seen. But it may be the case that nothing short of this will usher in a day when our media no. longer glorifies power, aggression, and dominance in human relations, when "sex and violence" are not portrayed as fellow travelers, and when human sexuality in general and female sexuality in particular cease to be commodities in the marketplace.

Notes

1. The terms "obscenity" and "pornography" will be used here interchangeably unless otherwise specified.

2. Certain obvious methodological problems would inhere in reporting the attitudes of feminists. The state of being a feminist is, after all, attitudinal. Defining a population by its opinions and then asking what are the opinions of that population exemplifies tautological reasoning. It might be possible to define feminists in terms of their beliefs on other subjects. But, since it is possible to hold feminist (or liberal or conservative) views on some matters and not on others, this technique contains its own problems. Similar problems arise in relying upon self-selection to define the relevant population.

3. Defenders of absolute freedom of expression can duck this testy issue. Indeed, they are inclined to taunt their less fortunate opponents when, as frequently happens, the latter become hopelessly bogged down in definitional quagmires. See especially Black's dissent in *Ginzburg* v. *United States,* 383 U.S. 463, 476 (1966).

4. See, for example, Harry M. Clor, *Obscenity and Public Morality* (Chicago: University of Chicago Press, 1969); Richard H. Kuh, *Foolish Figleaves?* (New York: Macmillan, 1967); C. Peter Magrath, "The Obscenity Cases: Grapes of Roth," in *The Supreme Court Review,* ed., Philip B. Kurland (Chicago: The University of Chicago Press, 1966).

5. Notes, "The Substantive Law of Obscenity: An Adventure in Quicksand," *New York Law Forum 13* (1967): 84. See also in this regard *The Report of the Commission on Obscenity and Pornography* (Washington D.C.: Government Printing Office, 1970), p. 3.

6. *Halsey* v. *New York Society for the Supression of Vice,* 136 N.E. 219, 220 (1922); *United States* v. *Levine,* 88 F. 2d 156 (1936).

7. The practice of judging the obscenity of a whole work based on examining some part of it was common in the 19th and early 20th century. It then came under heavy criticism, as in *United States* v. *Kennerly,* 209 F. 119, 120 (1913), and has since been abandoned.

8. *Swearingen* v. *United States,* 161 U.S. 446, 451 (1895).

9. *Burton* v. *United States,* 142 F. 57, 63 (1906).

10. *People* v. *Berg,* 272 N.Y. Supp. 585, 588 (1934).

11. *Roth* v. *United States,* 354 U.S. 476, 487 (1957). The court defined prurience as "having a tendency to excite lustful thoughts." Ibid, p. 20.

12. *Kingsley Pictures* v. *Regents,* 360 U.S. 684, 696 (1959).

13. Ibid, 694.

14. See, for instance, Justice Harlan's assertion that "nothing in this opinion of course remotely implies approval of the types of magazines published by these petitioners, still less of the sordid motives which prompted their publications." Harlan pronounced the prevailing opinion for the court's refusal to censor the magazines in question. *Manual Enterprises* v. *Day,* 370 U.S. 478, 495 (1961).

15. Ibid., 482.

16. Ibid.

17. *Miller* v. *California,* 413 U.S. 15, 24 (1973). Thus, for example, scatalogical language could be patently offensive or indecent but it is not obscene in law unless used in a context which appeals to prurience. *Federal Communication Commission* v. *Pacifica, The United States Law Week 46* (June 27, 1978): 5021.

18. *Manual Enterprises* v. *Day,* 485.

19. *Memoirs* v. *Massachusetts,* 383 U.S. 413, 418 (1966).

20. *Roth* v. *United States.* See also *Miller* v. *California,* 413 U.S. 15, 24 (1973).

21. Justice Harlan observed that, in most cases, patent offensiveness and prurience correlate and it is exceptional when they do not. *Manual Enterprises* v. *Day.*

22. Poll data from 1977 suggest that most Americans have not abandoned the "Old Morality" despite more than a decade of "Sexual Revolution." The only category of "liberated" sexual conduct which commanded majority acceptance (52 percent) was cohabitation between unmarried adults. "The New Morality," *Time 110* (November 21, 1977): 111-E8. These data buttress the assumption that the court continues to mean something like the "Old Morality" when it speaks of appeals to prurience (the modern verbiage for sexual immorality) and relies on community standards to flesh out this category.

23. *Memoirs* v. *Massachusetts.*

24. *Miller* v. *California.*

25. *Roth* v. *United States.*

26. Ireme Diamond, "Pornography and Repression: A Reconsideration of 'Who' and 'What,' " unpublished ms. prepared for the Annual Meeting of the Western Social Science Association, April 27-29, 1978, pp. 4-8.

27. Women Against Violence in Pornography and Media, *Newspage,* November, 1977, p. 1.

28. Art Silverman, "No On Nukes and Nooses," *Berkeley Barb,* May 6-12, 1977, p. 7. Explicitly sexual violence is also becoming more prevalent in advertising as is feminist protest against it. "Really Socking it to Women," *Time 109* (February 7, 1977): 58-59.

29. When Industrial Telephone Systems, apparently expecting no trouble, put up a billboard featuring a phone, a bikini-clad woman, and the caption "The Businessman's alternative to Ma Bell," they discovered their error. A coalition of women's organizations got up a letter-writing campaign demanding immediate removal of the billboard and a change in the corporation's advertising policy. The corporation removed the billboard after "angry citizens" defaced it with the message "Exploiting Women *will* stop." Women Against Violence in Pornography and Media. *Newspage,* April 1978, p. 6.

30. *Report on the Commission on Obscenity and Pornography,* p. 14.

31. Susan Brownmiller, *Against Our Will* (New York: Simon and Schuster, 1975), p. 343.

32. Ibid., 346.

33. The subtitle of this article was "I knew I was partly to blame, too—because I tried too hard to change everybody's life." Ibid.

34. Women Against Violence in Pornography and Media "has no objection to explicit sex." *Newspage,* November, 1977, p. 1. Diana Russell, feminist writer, finds "unfortunate" the "equation of 'erotica' with 'pornography.' " "Pornography: A Feminist Perspective," unpublished ms., June 1977, p. 4. Susan Brownmiller divorces herself from those people "who shudder at the explicit mention of a sexual subject." *Against Our Will,* p. 392. While Gloria Steinem asserts that "sexuality itself isn't the source of the almost unbearable feeling of outrage and vicarious humiliation" occasioned by pornography. Gloria Steinem, "Pornography—not sex but the obscene use of power," *Ms* (August 1977), p. 44.

35. See, for example, in the visual arts, Margaret Walters, *The Nude Male: A New Perspective* (New York: Paddington Press, 1978); Jamaica Kincaid, "Art: Erotica!" *Ms 3* (January 1975): 30-33. In this regard, it is interesting to note that the idea of a "women's erotica" which is separate and different from male erotic or obscene writings predates the current feminist resurgence. Steven Marcus finds that Victorian pornography written by women differed from male pornography in having no concentration on organs, paying much more attention to emotions, and containing greater amounts of "contemplation, conscious reverie, and self-observation." *The Other Victorians* (New

York: Basic Books 1966), p. 281. Similarly, Anais Nin, in her introduction to a collection of her erotic writings, argues that she was "intuitively using a woman's language, seeing sexual experience from a woman's point of view" even though she had "only one model for this literary genre—the writing of men." *Delta of Venus* (New York: Bantam Books, 1977). pp. xiv, xv.

36. Ellen Willis, "Sexual Counterrevolution I," *Rolling Stone* (March 24, 1977), p. 29. *Snuff* is a film depicting the brutal murder of a woman as the culmination of orgiastic pleasures. *Our Bodies, Ourselves* is a feminist health and sexuality manual for women emphasizing the need to understand one's own physiology. *The Hite Report* presents in explicit language research findings on the sexual attitudes, preferences, and practices of modern American women.

37. For example, Gloria Steinem fears that proposed laws to suppress the distribution of child pornography, which nearly everyone deems objectionable and in which power is so clearly an issue, will be used by "puritanical judges and communities . . . to suppress the personal freely chosen expressions of teenagers, while letting commercial vice go." Steinem, "Pornography—not sex but the obscene use of power," p. 44.

38. Willis, "Sexual Counterrevolution I," p. 29.

39. Brownmiller, *Against Our Will,* p. 394.

40. Ibid., pp. 394–95.

41. Women Against Violence in Pornography and Media, *Newspage,* November, 1977, pp. 1–2.

42. Brownmiller, *Against Our Will,* p. 395.

43. Anthologies of feminist writings illustrate the wide-ranging aspects of life which are thought to involve sexism, male supremacy, or male dominance. See, for example, Deborah Babcox and Madeline Belkin, eds., *Liberation Now* (New York: Dell, 1971), or Vivan Gornick and Barbara K. Moran, eds., *Women in Sexist Society* (New York: Basic Books, 1971). Gloria Steinem describes child pornography as "one logical, inevitable result of raising boys to believe they must control or conquer others as a measure of manhood." Steinem, "Pornography—not sex but the obscene use of power," p. 44. Ellen Willis describes obscenity as "a sexist, misogynist society's answer to women's demand to be respected as people, rather than exploited as objects." Willis, "Sexual Counterrevolution I," p. 29.

44. The only notable exception to this pattern is found among those religious fundamentalists whose apocalyptic vision includes pornography amongst the many other evils rife in this degenerate modern world. While these groups seem to be able to rally a popular following for such causes an anti-gay rights, they have not been able to capture substantial support in the legal community nor in the mainstream of writers, either religious or legal, in the obscenity field.

45. *Smith* v. *United States,* 97 S.Ct. 1774 (1977) (Stevens, J., dissenting opinion).

46. *Roth* v. *United States,* (Douglas, J. dissenting opinion).

47. See, for example, Michael Perkins, *Modern Erotic Literature* (New York: William Morrow, 1977). Perkins' work was sponsored by *Screw* magazine, long a champion of this perspective on obscenity.

48. See, for example, Earl F. Murphy, "The Value of Pornography," *Wayne Law Review 10* (1964): 661. An earlier proponent of this view was Dr. Benjamin Karpman who asserted that "contrary to popular misconception, people who read salacious literature are less likely to become sexual offenders than those who do not, for the reason that such reading often neutralizes what aberrant sexual interests they may have." *The Sexual Offender and His Offenses* (New York: The Julian Press, 1954), p. 485.

49. This stereotype is reflected in works as popular and diverse as Shakespeare's *Taming of the Shrew,* Ayn Rand's *Fountainhead,* or the characterization of "Fonzie" in

the television program *Happy Days.*

50. For an excellent discussion of this fantasy in pornography, see Steven Marcus, *The Other Victorians.*

51. Margaret Walters, *The Nude Male,* p. 67.

52. *Roget's Thesaurus* offers up as synonyms "paradise," "unalloyed happiness," "beatitude," and "ravishment." Robert L. Chapman, *Roget's International Thesaurus* (New York: Crowell, 1977), p. 865.

53. Margaret Walters, *The Nude Male,* p. 72.

54. Steven Marcus, *The Other Victorians,* passim.

55. Margaret Walters, *The Nude Male,* pp. 66–69.

56. Ibid., passim.

57. *The Report of the Commission on Obscenity and Pornography,* pp. 23–27.

58. Diamond, "Pornography and Repression," p. 10.

59. For a summary of the conflicting research findings on the effects of obscenity, see Clor, *Obscenity and Public Morality,* pp. 136–74. Irene Diamond, feminist writer, also notes the inconclusive nature of existing studies on this issue. She makes the interesting point that the President's Commission on the Causes and Prevention of Violence concluded that media violence can induce violent behavior in consumers while the Commission on Obscenity and Pornography concluded that exposure to pornography does not promote antisocial conduct. Diamond suggests that these findings are contradictory because the former relies on a social learning model of human behavior while the latter rejects that model. She criticizes the Pornography Commission's research for assuming that "its subject of concern involved nothing more than 'explicit sexual materials.' " Yet, having criticized the categories which ground the research, she proceeds to analyze that research on its own terms. At no point does she do more than hint at the possibility that sexually explicit materials, per se, *have* no evil consequences and are so radically different from the misogynist or sexually violent materials which she calls pornographic that conjoining them in a study of the effects of pornography renders the data thus generated utterly useless. She finds the research of the commission so seductively vulnerable on other grounds that she muddies her own argument by treating of it seriously after rejecting it at its foundations. "Pornography and Repression: A Reconsideration of 'Who' and 'What,' " passim.

60. Women Against Violence in Pornography and Media is planning a billboard campaign in San Francisco buses to "get our message out" and to make clear the values behind their critiques of obscenity. Personal interviews with group members, July 27, 1978. This group has also organized a "National Pornography Conference" to be held on November 17–19. *Newspage,* September 1978.

61. *Winters* v. *New York,* 333 U.S. 507, 508 (1948).

62. Ibid., p. 514.

63. Ibid., pp. 518–19. "There have been persistent efforts to frame an obscenity statute that would also proscribe the depiction of violent crime and 'horror.' However, restraints in this area appear virtually outlawed." Notes. "The Substantive Law of Obscenity: An Adventure in Quicksand," p. 88.

64. Lawrence's belief that women who desert their biological function of mothering and take on male roles are doomed to misery would hardly endear him to feminists. D. H. Lawrence, "Cocksure Men and Hensure Women," in *Sex, Literature and Censorship,* ed., Harry L. Moore (New York: Twayne Publishers, 1953).

65. D. H. Lawrence, "Pornography and Obscenity," in *Sex, Literature and Censorship,* p. 76.

66. Ibid., p. 74.

67. Paul Goodman, *Utopian Essays and Practical Proposals* (New York: Random House, 1962), p. 51

68. Ibid., p. 54.
69. Ibid., p. 63.
70. Ibid., passim.
71. Ibid., p. 64.
72. Ibid.
73. "Yet I do not think that moral problems are private problems and can be left alone. . . . On the contrary, it is because moral problems are so publicly important— sexual practice is crucial for family, courting, friendship, education, and culture—that . . . only the manifold mind of all the institutions of society, skirmishing and experimenting, can figure them out and invent right solutions." Ibid., p. 66.

Chapter 11

Battered Women and Public Policy*†

Sandra Wexler

Policy studies often take as their starting point the articulation of a governmental policy or the implementation of a programmatic effort. The relationship between a given program and the initial expressions of demand for the program is frequently not explored or only peripherally mentioned. Yet there is little basis for assuming that the program which is eventually instituted reflects the preliminary definitions of the problem. If policy formation is a process of redefinition corresponding to the interest and set of participating actors, then it is not surprising that the services which are finally made available do not necessarily address the original expression of need.

This chapter therefore begins its exploration of the creation and implementation of a policy experiment for domestic violence by taking a step back, briefly chronicling the emergence of the problem. The perceptual or definitional shift, the transformation of a private event into a public concern, is especially interesting since it necessitated a challenge of many commonly held values and assumptions.

A PRIVATE PROBLEM

The family is traditionally considered one of society's most sacred institutions.

---

*Although a portion of the following chapter focuses on the shelter projects, the general points are applicable to the civil law clinic (See p. 198). This service is unique to its community and, although seen as necessary, existing agencies do not want to provide it.

†Data cited in this chapter were provided by the URSA Institute, Pier 1½, San Francisco, CA 94111, under Grant Award 78-MU-AX-0049 from the National Institute of Juvenile Justice and Delinquency Prevention, Office of Juvenile and Delinquency Prevention, U.S. Department of Justice. The chapter expresses the conclusions and opinions of the author and does not represent the views of the Department of Justice or the URSA Institute.

It is the source of comfort and nurturance for its members. High standards have been set for its functioning. Problems or failures to actualize these ideals are taken as indications of personal inadequacies. Individual fault is thus posed as the source of marital difficulties. The very definition of the family places severe constraints on the ability of its members to go outside of it for help. The ideal family is supposed to contain internal mechanisms for coping with problems. To admit that one cannot resolve a situation is tantamount to a public admission of one's own failure and maladjustment. There are enormous societal pressures to keep one's troubles within the home.

Once the matrimonial door is shut, the actions of the individuals are to a large extent removed from society's gaze. Abusive behavior within a marriage is especially vulnerable to personalization and denial. If a woman is beaten, "she must have been asking for it." While a certain level of violence is socially legitimized, the use of too much force is seen as pathological. At what point force crosses the line from a reasonable to an extreme amount is a difficult question. By denying that the phenomenon of violence within marriage exists, or equating its existence with personal deviance, society has been able to sidestep this definitional question. This very act of denial, however, further sanctions the notion that the use of force is an acceptable form of behavior.

Attempts by abused women to seek outside assistance often have been of little solace. Family and clergy are frequently initial sources approached for aid and support. Taking refuge in the home of relatives may provide a brief respite but few families are prepared or able to accept the woman (and usually her children) indefinitely. The reactions of family members at times echo and reinforce the woman's own doubts. Being counseled that she "unwisely chose her mate," "that a few slaps are a part of marriage," or "that everything would be fine if only she would stop provoking her husband," enhances possible feelings of shame, isolation, and helplessness. Nor are the admonitions of clergy very helpful. Women are not simply urged to return to the abusive partner but to find salvation through complete surrender of their will to their husbands'. Again, the responsibility for the abuse is placed on the woman, who somehow is thought to have earned it by not being the appropriately submissive, "perfect" wife and mother.

This mingling of self-doubt and fear of possible reprisals further hinders the abused woman in interactions with other helping professionals. Hospital emergency rooms minister to the injuries of countless battered wives. Only a small minority of these women identify themselves as victims of abuse. The majority have their wounds treated, return home until the next occasion of abuse, and manage to slip through the medical system unidentified. Similar experiences have been reported by mental health and counseling professionals:

> Most often the busy practitioner deals with the presenting complaint at face value and makes few inquiries about its origin. Mental health professionals have tended to see the problem as a relatively unimportant part of some more general diagnos-

tic entity—depression, schizophrenia, drug abuse, alcoholism, phobias, or marital disharmony.[1]

This tendency by medical practitioners and mental health counselors to treat the presenting symptoms has often led to the prescription of inappropriate and potentially harmful drugs. According to one study, physicians prescribe tranquilizers for one in four battered women, while fewer than one in ten nonbattered women receive tranquilizer prescriptions.[2] While tranquilizers might be an appropriate response in certain circumstances, they do not remedy the abuse which the battered woman experiences.

Finally, the police are perhaps the agency most commonly called upon for intervention. Available 24 hours a day, seven days a week, authorized to "make house calls," they have been characterized as the "poor man's social worker." The traditional attitudes of the police to domestic disturbance calls embody several contradictory tendencies. Generally these calls are considered low-priority, bothersome family squabbles. The reluctance of many officers to respond is in part due to a realistic dose of self-interest in their personal safety, as domestic violence calls often result in police injury.[3] Yet, while the police appear to assess the potential danger of the situation for themselves, this assessment is often not extended to the disputing couple. If and when the police do arrive, they frequently attempt to evoke a "good old boys" connection with the husband. A walk with the man around the block and a promise from him that it will not happen again is a typical police intervention method.

The issue of battered women may also be seen as a private problem in terms of group conduct. The association of violence with race and class leads to the conclusion that it is a problem for "them" but not for "us." It is conventional wisdom that "Latin—or black, or working-class—men beat their wives, but, that is just the way they are—or they do not know any better and what else can you expect." These conceptions serve to justify and reinforce existing stereotypes and to remove white society from the responsibility of having to associate itself with this phenomenon.

Within the last decade the private aspects of domestic violence have slowly come into the public limelight. Having indicated some of the factors which contributed to the perception of this as a private event, we will not turn our attention to the emergence of battered women as an issue on the public agenda. To imply, however, that the issue has both emerged and been completely accepted as a legitimate social concern would be inaccurate. Rather, a tension remains between these private and public orientations toward the problem.

A PUBLIC ISSUE

The "discovery" of spousal abuse should be considered within the context of the late 1960s and early 1970s. Social movements, beginning with the civil rights activists, challenged the validity of many commonly held notions. The antiwar and student movements raised new areas of questions regarding the assumptions and practices of many public and private institutions. In particular, the women's movement,[4] comprised of national and local unaffiliated feminist groups, opened up sex roles, the family,[5] and de jure and de facto sex discrimination to public debate.[6]

"The personal is political"—a popular slogan indicative of the ideology of a large sector of the women's movement—rejected the notion that certain subjects were isolated, individual problems or taboo topics. The events of women's lives became important subjects for discussion and analysis. This sense of experimentation, discovery, and commonality was shared by women throughout the nation. Traditional women's magazines such as *Family Circle* began publishing articles on working women, child care, and women's health issues.[7]

An outgrowth of this was the antirape movement. Again, personal experiences were drawn upon and politicized. "Speak outs" were held in major cities. These forums served several purposes—as consciousness-raising experiences for the participants, as ways to challenge commonly held stereotypes regarding women as victims, and as ways of bringing the issue before the general public.

Crisis phone lines and advocacy services for rape victims were established by feminist organizations in many areas. Yet rape victims were not the only callers. In some instances, women's centers and crisis lines were contacted by battered women seeking assistance. As abused women started identifying themselves as such and seeking assistance the magnitude of the phenomenon slowly became evident.

Parallel with this general interest in women's issues was research being conducted in the related area of child abuse and neglect. During the late 1960s studies provided initial documentation on the incidence, frequency, and severity of child abuse and neglect in the United States. The phrase "battered child syndrome" was coined to draw attention dramatically to the problem and to suggest the need for a systemic or family orientation to remedies. Connections between wife and child abuse were documented in the findings of a study by the National Center for Child Abuse and Neglect (NCCAN) of Los Angeles, California child-abuse programs.[8] This evaluation revealed that approximately 39 percent of the children in the program came from families in which the mother was also abused.

Activities in both of these areas—child abuse and rape—brought forth the underlying issues of violence and power. Dynamics of familial interactions, particularly the use of force within the family, became open to inquiry. The abuse of women within the home slowly emerged from behind the matrimonial door into the domain of sociologists.

Research undertaken by R. Gelles, M. Straus, and S. Steinmetz provides the first glimpse into the scope of this phenomenon.[9] This research has played an important role in documenting and validating battered women as a "real" problem. It is estimated that every year between 1.8 and 3.3 million women experience some form of intraspousal violence. Approximately one in four women who experience violence is beaten while pregnant. Spousal abuse may be one of the truly democratic institutions crossing racial, religious, age, and socioeconomic lines. Incidence, however, is not equally distributed—higher occurrences among lower socioeconomic and minority populations has suggested the influence of societal stress factors, such as unemployment, financial difficulties, inadequate housing.

Providing a backdrop for these statistics was the experience of small, grass-roots shelter projects. Opened in 1971, the Chiswick Women's Aid in England quickly demonstrated the need for services.[10] The concept of providing supportive refuges for abused women and their children crossed the Atlantic and took hold in the United States. In 1976, there were approximately 20 shelters in the United States. By 1979, the number had grown to about 250.[11] As a short-term response, these refuges serve as reminders of the gravity and desperation of the situation. Women involved in abusive relationships have used these facilities, keeping most of them filled to capacity.

In sum, this range of activities served both to identify and to legitimize this issue. As the problem of family violence gained credibility as a social concern, differing suggestions were offered as to its causes and cures.

Recent calls for comprehensive intervention strategies,[12] sweeping plans addressing a myriad of objectives, imply that resolution of the question of causality is not forthcoming and is perhaps impossible. Four separate federal-level hearings[13] on this topic were held within a one-year period. These hearings provided important forums for the presentation of contending claims. These discussions have informed and helped clarify the positions of governmental bodies.[14] A consensus, however, as to what should be done or which direction should be taken has not been reached.

GOVERNMENTAL INITIATIVES

Now that many concur that violence within the home is a "real" problem, what actions have been taken by government? Over the past several years, officials from all levels have slowly begun to articulate policy plans designed to address this issue. Activities on the part of local officials have most frequently been undertaken as reactions to mandates from higher-level decision makers. Those instances in which local officials have assumed an active (as opposed to a reactive) stance have produced highly idiosyncratic responses which makes summation or comparison extremely difficult. Discussions of governmental initiatives will therefore focus on state and federal responses.

State Responses

The primary form of action on the state level has been legislative reform. The array of amendments which have been introduced most often focus on mechanisms to improve documentation and recording practices of local agencies, in particular, those of law-enforcement agencies, and to create or enhance avenues of civil law recourse. Although several states have allocated monies for direct services, this funding has been minimal. Where available, the competition for these funds has been enormous and stands as further documentation of local need.

The legislative modifications undertaken by state government may be partially understood as indicative of constituent demand. In presenting the issue of battered women to state legislators women have constituted themselves as an interest group, offering testimony and providing factual documentation to state committees holding hearings on domestic violence. As of 1978, 33 states either had already passed or had domestic violence legislation pending. With the exception of one statute which was passed in 1973, 32 bills dealing with this issue were introduced and/or approved by state legislatures in the two-year period of 1977 and 1978.[15] The legislation covers changes in such areas as civil remedies, criminal statutes, and to a very limited extent, the provision of shelter services.[16] For illustrative purposes, California's legislative activity will be described.

In 1977 the California state legislature approved SB 91 which has been hailed as a landmark piece of legislation. Sponsored by State Senator Presley, the bill provides for the establishing and funding, on a demonstration basis, of a statewide network of not less than four or more than six domestic-violence project centers. The state Department of Health would be required to contract with public or private nonprofit agencies for the purpose of funding such pilot project centers in designated locations within the state.[17] An appropriation of $280,000 from the state general fund was approved to help finance this program.

There are, however, several limitations to this statute. Designed to fund at the maximum six shelter projects, requests for applications were received from over 250 organizations representing 36 California counties.[18] This flood of response indicates the enormity of local interest and need. Clearly, the amount of funding appropriated to fulfill this task is far from adequate. In describing why this level of allocation was chosen, State Senator Presley stated that the reason for "not putting more money into it, was a veto by the Governor and we didn't want that to happen, we wanted to get the program underway."[19] While these monies may alleviate some of the short-term financial difficulties for a few chosen programs, they provide no assurance of ongoing, continuous funding. This limited demonstration funding by the state reveals a "wait and see" attitude toward the question of long-range solutions, in large part based on the hope that the federal government will supply additional resources.

The same legislative session enacted several other bills addressing domestic violence but none of these bills contains mechanisms for appropriating funds. Thus, while they attempt to modify policy and to an extent local procedures, they make no provision for the financial resources which might be needed to implement these directives. The following synopsis of the major provisions of these bills serves to highlight those areas of policy which are most often being subject to state legislative revision:

- *Chapter 720* changes the requirements for obtaining a temporary restraining order, including cohabitants, eliminating the necessity to have marriage dissolution papers on file before obtaining an order. Violation of a temporary restraining order becomes a misdemeanor, e.g., subject to criminal sanctions by the police.
- *Chapter 908* provides for separate reporting of spousal and child abuse.
- *Chapter 912* makes spousal assault a felony subject to imprisonment for not more than one year. Includes cohabitants within the definition of spousal assult.

Subsequent legislative sessions have witnessed the introduction of additional bills. They are primarily concerned with making revisions in or "fine tuning" existing statutes. For example, the 1980 legislative session enacted laws further specifying civil remedies. Three types of restraining orders now available are:[20]

- A *Temporary Restraining Order (TRO) to Prevent Domestic Violence* offers protection for up to 90 days to women who either are married to the attacker and do not want a divorce or have formerly or are presently cohabiting. The order is issued to prevent a recurrence of domestic violence and to assure a period of separation of those involved. Violation of an order is a misdemeanor punishable by a $500 fine and/or six months in jail.
- A *Civil Harassment Restraining Order* can be issued to a woman who is being harassed by a man with whom she has never lived. Harassment is defined as all forms of abuse except physical violence. A temporary restraining order, effective for not more than 15 days and an injunction (i.e., a permanent restraining order), effective for up to three years, may be obtained. Violation of a harassment order carries the same penalties as violation of a temporary restraining order.
- A *Restraining Order Accompanying a Divorce* is available to women who are filing for divorce or custody of their children. The sanctions for violation previously described also hold in these instances.

Moreover, the 1980 session voted to levy a $10 marriage license surcharge to support domestic-violence programs. Monies generated by this surcharge are to be collected and distributed by each county or by groups of counties that elect to pool their funds. As of August 1980, Florida, Kansas, Missouri, and North Dakota had adopted this funding strategy. Similar legislation is pending in three other states.

A final trend in state legislation enacted in 16 states, although not in California, has been to permit warrantless arrests where there is probable cause that a misdemeanor offense was committed. Formerly, an arrest for a misdemeanor offense could be made if the police officer witnessed the offense. Under these statutes, police officers no longer have to be a witness to the event in order to effect an arrest.

The impact of legislative directives on localities is difficult to gauge. Since the actions required are primarily concerned with recording procedures and legal sanctions, an assessment of the effectiveness and degree of implementation must wait until state-mandated evaluations are completed. One may speculate that since there were either limited or no financial appropriations provided, i.e., no monetary incentives or supports for the local government, implementation of these policies by localities may be very uneven.

Federal Responses

The labyrinthine character of the federal system leaves one wondering where to begin a description of its responses to this issue. There are the federal departments, each with its own guidelines, requirements, and response provisions. There are the regional offices of the federal departments, which if viewed as the source of local information should be considered separately since they at times offer information which differs from that coming from Washington. Then there are the various national commissions (e.g., Civil Rights, International Women's Year) which addressed the issue. Finally, there is the activity of the Congress and its various committees.

A review of congressional legislation provides a backdrop for discussion of existing departmental provisions. These departmental actions may be viewed as competing attempts to stake claim to the issue. Congressional legislative activity illustrates a refinement and narrowing of these competing claims wherein resolution (i.e., adoption of a particular bill) contributes to the formation of an official plan.

The first major domestic violence bills were introduced during the 1978 congressional session. To date, no significant legislation has successfully made it through both houses of Congress. In the 1980 congressional session two bills were introduced in the Senate (S. 1843, 1153), and two in the House of Representatives (H.R. 2977, 3434):

S. 1153 and H.R. 3434 Presently the use of Title XX funds by the states to fund domestic-violence shelters is discretionary. Several states have prohibited the utilization of these funds for this purpose. These companion bills would amend Title XX guidelines so that states would no longer be able to prohibit the use of these funds for shelter activities. While the bills amend standing legislation and thereby broaden the scope and jurisdiction of the act to include domestic-violence victims, they do not provide additional appropriations. Undoubtedly, the effect will be that domestic violence victims will become competitors with other groups presently covered by this act for funds and services.

Of those under consideration, the following two bills are the most significant in terms of allocations and services:

H.R. 2977 "Domestic Violence Prevention and Services Act" (passed by the House on December 12, 1979). For the purposes of this bill, domestic violence is defined as any act or threat of violence. This legislation would provide for a three-year appropriation of seed money for services. It directs the secretary of the Department of Health and Human Services (HHS) to designate a coordinator for this area. The scope of activities eligible for funding includes training programs for personnel, demonstration projects, and shelter services. The formula for allocations provides for 50 percent of the monies to be directly distributed to the states; 25 percent to be distributed to projects by HHS; 15 percent to support state administrative bodies; and 10 percent to support HHS administrative costs. A maximum of 25 percent of the budget of $150,000 may be awarded to each project/activity. The allocation of funds to the states would be based upon applications. States would then be charged with responsibility for the distribution of funds to the localities.

S. 1843 "Domestic Violence Prevention and Treatment Act" (the companion bill to H.S. 2977, passed by the Senate on Sept. 4, 1980). It differs from the House legislation in its formula for allocation. Accordingly, 60 percent of the total appropriation is designated for state use; 25 percent is distributed to projects by HHS; 5 percent is earmarked for research; and 10 percent is to be used to develop state plans to ensure citizen participation.

Subsequent to passage, the bills were sent to conference to reconcile the differences between them. The conference report was passed by the House and sent on to the Senate shortly before the November 1980 election. The report did not come up in the Senate until after the election. At that time, Republicans threatened to stage a filibuster if the bill was brought to a vote. Sixty votes would have been needed to prevent a filibuster. That the bill did not come up until after the election severely hurt its chances of passage. Many of those defeated were simply not around. Liberals in the Senate experienced great difficulty marshalling their forces during the lame-duck session. Several important bills were awaiting Senate action and placed competing claims on voting priorities. In this environment, an all-out effort for domestic-violence legislation could not be mustered. On November 17, Senator Cranston, one of the bill's sponsors, withdrew the legislation.

The demise of this legislation was foreshadowed in earlier Senate hearings. A vocal and strong "pro-family" position was articulated during the August hearings on S. 1843. This opposition, which resurfaced to threaten a filibuster of the conference report, is illustrated by the remarks of Senator Humphrey (R–New Hampshire), ranking minority member of the Subcommittee on Child and Human Development. During the Senate hearings on S. 1843, Senator Humphrey stated:

> Mr. President, I oppose S. 1843, the Domestic Violence Prevention and Services Act, for a variety of reasons. It addresses a broad and disquieting problem, but that is not sufficient to recommend this bill. This bill's approach is both improper and impractical. The methods of S. 1843 are both intrusive and disingenuous. We are not speaking here of legitimate police activities, or the responsibility of government to protect citizens from bodily harm. We are considering federal entailment with psychosocial techniques, and the promotion of ideas on conjugality and on the family. These are the proper concerns of families, churches, universities and private groups. The federal government has no business intruding here. . . .
> . . . What vision would the federal bureaucracy promote? What standards? We are given a startling revelation of the anti-family thinking of the administration in a 700-page report that advocates the type of legislation we are considering. The report is published by the U.S. Commissioner on Civil Rights, and mailed at government expense. I might add that this particular document was much in evidence during the development of this bill. The report, entitled "Battered Women: Issues of Public Policy," repeatedly mocks family life.
> . . . I am concerned that the outside interests who are pushing this legislation are intent on proselytizing at the taxpayers' expense. I fear that the would-be grantees under S. 1843 are opposed to traditional families. Sixty-four percent of the funding under the proposal would go to sustain so-called "homes for battered women." What kind of values and ideas would these "homes" advance? The federal government should not fund missionaries who would war on the traditional family or on local values.[21]

The sentiments expressed in this statement are quite telling. While admitting that violence within the family may exist, the remarks reinforce the privatization of the phenomenon. Government intervention and support for services, particularly shelters, are posited as threats to families. If one extends this logic further, the welfare and safety of individual family members should be sacrificed to the preservation of the unit.

With the public emergence during the 1980 election of the "moral majority," positions such as this are gaining respectability and political mileage. Having been defeated in the three prior congressional sessions, it appears extremely doubtful that federal domestic-violence legislation will be forthcoming. Given the tenor of the times, support for domestic-violence services will have to be secured within existing federal programs.

Several federal agencies have been either actively involved in or generally associated with the issue. A *Handbook of Federal Resources on Domestic*

Violence, compiled by the Interdepartmental Committee on Domestic Violence, provides an excellent overview of available funding sources.[22] In addition to the Department of Health and Human Services, resources can be obtained from such places as the departments of Education, Labor, Agriculture, Housing and Urban Development, and Justice. For example, the Section 8 Housing and Community Development Block Grant programs of the Department of Housing and Urban Development, while not earmarked as domestic-violence programs, are potential resources. These programs, as with those of other departments, reflect the mission and orientation of the sponsoring agencies. Domestic violence programs or individual victims may be entitled to benefits under the agency's definition of eligibility (e.g., Section 8 housing subsidies can be obtained not because one is a battered women but because one is poor). In light of the uncertainty regarding programmatic and funding availability under the Reagan administration, a detailed description of departmental actions may soon be outdated.

Interestingly, since the emergence of domestic violence as a socially recognized problem, only one federal agency initiated services specifically targeted for this issue. The Law Enforcement Assistance Administration (LEAA) within the Department of Justice, provided funding for local domestic-violence programs. In what may be considered an example of an official plan, an LEAA policy initiative for domestic violence offered the first occasion for this issue to be formally recognized.

LEAA AND THE FAMILY-VIOLENCE PROGRAM

That LEAA has assumed a major role in creating programs for intraspousal abuse comes as a surprise to many. As an agency of the Department of Justice, crimes are the major preoccupation of LEAA. By defining a principal aspect of intrafamily violence as criminal activity, LEAA was able logically to extend its jurisdiction into this area. Yet this definition, while providing a necessary justification for action, does not sufficiently explain what led the agency to create its family-violence program.

In understanding the development of this program, one must look to the agency's history. In 1974 the Citizen's Initiative programs were instituted as a national priority program of LEAA. The impetus came from the agency's concern that average citizens had lost confidence in the criminal justice system. An underlying assumption is located in the statement of purpose in which it was postulated that the program could make a "significant impact on the reduction of crime through the active involvement of the citizen in the criminal justice process."[23] The demonstration and research projects funded under this program established the need for expanded and refined services for victims and witnesses of crime.

This concept was inaugurated in 1976 with the establishment of the Victim/ Witness program. A major objective was "To assist in the development, implementation and replication of projects designed to improve the treatment of victims and witnesses and to increase citizen confidence in and cooperation with the Criminal Justice System."[24] Special emphasis was placed on reaching victims of "sensitive crime"—rape, child sexual abuse, battered women, and the elderly. To complement this emphasis, the Center for Women Policy Studies was awarded a grant to gather information on "sensitive crime."

A change in the LEAA administration during 1977 gave rise to speculation that the Victim/Witness program was to be phased out. At that point, the program manager proposed that a special initiative be developed around family violence. The proposal asserted the following rationale for agency action:

In spite of the high incidence of these crimes, the justice system has traditionally given these problems low priority, ignoring, perhaps, the fact that these patterns of violent behavior are being passed on from one generation to the next, often progressing from violence in the home to violence in the street. A new LEAA Initiative directed at "Crimes in the Home" would be very timely, given the media's recent attention to child abuse, wife battering, and community crime prevention. It also is timely in terms of the Carter Administration's interest in strengthening familes.[25]

In the summer of 1977, the program manager testified before the Commission on Civil Rights in a hearing on battered women. This was the first occasion at which the agency was publicly linked to the issue. Subsequent to her appearance, the program manager was given permission to proceed in developing the program, but with a limited commitment of resources. By the fall of that year, six initial demonstration projects, four for intraspousal violence and two for child sexual-assault victims, were funded through the Victim/Witness program. Victim support services as regards domestic violence translates into battered women's serivces. All four of these initial projects contained shelter components as their primary service-delivery mechanism.

The scope of the program was subsequently broadened from the initial victim focus of the Victim/Witness projects to a focus on the whole family. While program goals were formulated, a model for accomplishing these goals was not developed. Rather, initiators were interested in discovering the effectiveness of intervention at various points in both the cycle of violence and in the justice system. In 1978 this expanded demonstration was formalized as the LEAA Family Violence Program. Under this auspice, 16 family-violence projects were funded. Thirteen of these projects in 12 communities are considered here.

Three interesting problems emerge from the analysis of the projects: the role of women's organizations in the genesis of the projects; changes over time in the project decisional strucure; and changes over time in project services.

The Role of Women's Organizations

Who initiated the domestic violence projects? The first two categories of actors may be described as purposive; that is, their actions were based on ideological conception of domestic violence. Their activities had a particular intent, to create programs which they believed correctly intervened in the problem. The third category of actors may be considered more reactive than purposive. In these cases, the initiating actors did not have clearly formulated assumptions about either the causes or cures for domestic violence. The availability of federal money and expressed community interest thrust these actors into involvement with the issue.

The categories of initiating actors may be defined as:

1. *Victim/Witness.* These actors came from the Victim/Witness Assistance Programs, the LEAA-funded projects whose aim was to increase the efficacy of the criminal justice system by offering supportive services to victims and witnesses of violent crimes. The experience of battered-women clients in these projects prompted these individuals to create programs designed to meet the unique needs of these victims.

2. *Women's Organizations.* Formal or informal, self-identified feminist groups. This category spans a wide spectrum from formal, national organizations such as the National Organization for Women (NOW), to quasi-governmental organizations such as commissions on the status of women, to informal, grass-roots groups.

3. *Grantseekers.* This catch-phrase is used to connote those actors who became involved because of the availability of federal funding. These actors lack a defining ideological approach to the issue. There is a mixed commitment to the issue of domestic violence. The cases which fall into this category were all initiated by institutional actors responding to community pressure by bringing in outside money.

Of the 13 projects, women's organizations were instrumental in the genesis of six. Of those remaining, five communities (two projects are located in one community) had women's organizations active in the issue of domestic violence. In these five instances, women's organizations, while not directly taking part in the grant writing, acted to increase community awareness of the issue and maintained varying degrees of contact with the initiating actors. Thus, women's organizations had a direct or indirect influence in the genesis of these programs in 11 out of the 12 communities.

While domestic violence was identified as an issue in the communities through the actions of interest groups (i.e., women's organizations), once defined as a problem, it was presented to the formal structures of government for solution. The LEAA request for proposals may be seen as a first attempt to incorporate this issue into the structure of a federal agency. The actions of women's organizations in initiating local grant proposals represents a continuation of their influence in this policy area. Their presence in 11 of the 12 communities seems to indicate the importance of their role in this issue. On the local level, domestic violence still appears to be predominantly a "women's issue."

The Structure of Decision Making

In identifying the decision-making structures, two main types are evident:

- *Centralized*—administrative functions, policy formulation, and service provision are carried out by a single organizational unit.
- *Decentralized*—predominantly a subcontracting model. Administrative and policy decisions are located within one unit while outside agencies provide services on a contractual basis.

These primary distinctions can be further refined to reflect differences in decision making within types:

- *Centralized Hierarchy*—Lines of authority and responsibility follow a vertical model in which control is vested in the top echelon of the hierarchy.
- *Centralized Cooperative*—within the single organizational unit responsibilities and decision making are democratically shared/dispersed among the participants/staff.
- *Decentralized Hierarchy*—the central administrative unit maintains control of policy formulation and directs the activities of the subcontractors. There is a vertical chain of command with the subcontracting agencies working for the administrative unit.
- *Decentralized Cooperative*—the central administrative unit acts to coordinate activities of the subcontractors. There is greater input by the subcontracting agencies into the overall direction and policy and more sharing of power among agencies.

As the projects proceed, one would expect some fluctuation in the structural arrangements over time. These variations could be created by increases in staffing, expansions of programmatic activities, or adjustments of the structure based on experience. Of the 13 projects, five are undergoing significant changes in their decisional structures. These projects use either a centralized or decentralized cooperative model. All are presently moving toward hierarchical models within respective structural types.

In three cases the cooperative model evolved from feminist preferences for consensual decision making. The experience of the cooperatively structured program indicates the influence of traditional bureaucracy on innovative programs. Community institutions such as the police, department of probation, or the department of social services all use highly refined hierarchical structures. In their interactions with other agencies, the expectation is that similar structural arrangements will be used.

The local police chief, for example, wants to know the name of the project administrator. Putting a name to an organizational position is important since people often want to conduct interagency business with someone holding an equivalent structural position. The notion of a steering committee or shared responsibilities is foreign. Actors in existing hierarchical community agencies do not want to deal with people belonging to what they see as a formless, confusing collective.

The domestic violence projects, which are in the process of establishing themselves within their communities, lack the influence to exert pressure to change on these surrounding bodies. As new organizations, these five projects are all highly dependent on the acceptance and goodwill of established agencies. This acceptance and contact is essential if the project is to fulfill its mission according to the LEAA goals. Thus, the transition from a cooperative to a more hierarchical model may be viewed as a necessary adaptive strategy. By assuming decisional structures which culturally parallel those in their environment, the projects minimize a potential obstacle to interagency cooperation. This capacity to make trade-offs or compromises on particular points is crucial. In particular, the three projects in which ideological concerns motivated their structural arrangements may be viewed as exchanging one manifestation of their political beliefs (e.g., cooperative decision making) for a better opportunity to offer services.

The Implementation of Project Services

What types of services did the projects create and how were they implemented? Of the 13 domestic violence projects, five are undergoing important changes in their service components. All five projects attempted to use mechanisms of the criminal justice system as their primary mode of service. In the remaining projects, seven are offering shelter and one is a civil law clinic. Except for the civil law clinic, the projects which are not modifying their services all operate short-term shelters for abused women and their children. This type of service was not available in these communities prior to the existence of the projects. Since this newly created service is unique in its community, the service domain of these projects does not come into conflict with those of existing institutions. Thus, interagency competition for clients could be avoided or at least greatly minimized.

In contrast to the shelters, the criminal justice projects encountered several obstacles in implementing their service plans. Each of these projects attempted to establish new forms within established criminal justice system mechanisms. Two projects focused on prosecutorial services and tried to have the district attorney's office refer all cases to a special domestic-violence prosecutor. Two projects developed service plans which necessitated not just close working relations with the police, but changes in police practices. The fifth project sought to align itself with and offer services similar to those of the family court probation department.

Competition and rivalries emerged almost immediately. The existing institutions viewed the projects as encroaching on their territories. They saw no reason to change their practices to suit the projects. Nor were they willing to work cooperatively with people seen as offering the "same" services. The projects overlapped with the domains of these institutions and the pressure for them to change commenced.

Being new organizations, the projects lacked the power and authority necessary to modify the practices of the institutions in their environment. In addition, they were extremely dependent on these established agencies for client referrals. Two projects have had virtually no clients because the referring agencies have refused to direct clients to them. In another instance, the project was told that its plan to offer crisis mediation in conjunction with police intervention was unacceptable. The police simply stated that "they didn't want any social workers interfering with them while they were handling dangerous situations." And so the service never got off the ground.

The problems faced by the two prosecutorial projects were similar. The district attorney's offices in both localities exhibited reluctance in referring cases. The criminal courts, which have traditionally treated domestic violence as a personal matter rather than as a crime, were not receptive to this new push to prosecute. And finally, difficulties emerged between the clients and the projects themselves.

The viability of applying criminal sanctions to the problem of domestic violence is open to question. Women who have been the victims of abuse often have ambivalent feelings about prosecuting their assailants, who may be at the same time their spouses/partners. Jails are viewed as punitive, not rehabilitative, institutions. Victims have expressed fear that the men will return and beat them more severely after a short jail sentence. The men are often described as needing help, not confinement which might make them worse. This ambivalence clashed with the projects' notion of "prosecuting to the fullest extent of the law." Many of the clients wanted some sort of legal relief, but not necessarily prosecution. In one case, this discrepancy of purpose became so pronounced that the clients began to view the project staff as acting against their interests.

Given the reality of their environments, these five projects were faced with a choice: either modify their service components or becoming increasingly isolated and ineffective. All have opted to redesign their services. Each project is attempting to find new ways to work within the criminal justice system. For example, the difficulties which one of these projects face in implementing a purely prosecutorial strategy led it to abandon its special prosecution position at the end of the first year. Since the reluctance of victims to testify and associated evidentiary issues had posed major obstacles to the initial service plan, project staff felt that attention should first be concentrated on these areas. The service strategy of the project was modified to emphasize victim support services. This change has been positively described by project staff who view it as an attempt to achieve the goal of increasing prosecution through new, less direct methods.

THE FUTURE: IMPLICATIONS FOR ACTION

The LEAA Family Violence Program may have the distinction of being the first and last federally sponsored program for intrafamily violence. LEAA funding of local projects is being phased out during 1981, approximately a year earlier than originally planned. Most sites are currently engaged in somewhat frantic attempts to secure local and/or private support. It is too early to know if the projects will survive.

What can be learned from this national demonstration? In particular, what might be viable strategies to pursue in the coming period? Several points, though they may seem obvious, are worth highlighting. First, domestic violence as a social problem is a women's issue. As exemplified with the 13 LEAA demonstration projects, women's organizations were involved to various degrees in the genesis of programs in 11 of the 12 communities. Across the nation, women's groups have actively engaged in increasing awareness of the issue and in the provision of direct services.

As women came together to initiate and demand services, they constituted themselves as an interest group. This notion of interest group (i.e., women acting on behalf of their own interest), while commonplace in U.S. politics, is still a somewhat new identification for women. Typically, one thinks of interest groups in terms of men, money, and power. Yet, in the coming period, concerted action by women around "women's problems" may be more important that ever. If women are not prepared to demand what is needed, it is doubtful that anyone else will. This implies a strategic coalescing around a variety of social concerns. Women have been in the forefront of struggles for reproductive rights, high quality, low-cost child care, reentry programs in both educational and economic spheres, and adequate income levels for those not in the labor force. And only women can prevent spousal abuse from being once more quietly withdrawn behind the closed matrimonial door.

Moreover, it is clear that the opposition is out to defeat domestic violence projects by linking them with feminism as seen in the following testimony:

In her testimony, Rosemary Thomson of Family America asked the following question: "To what degree can you guarantee that any grants under this bill, if passed, will be awarded on the basis of merit and community support as opposed to contacts made in the 'good old girl' network of feminists?"[26]

Feminists should therefore strengthen and broaden support for this issue among a wide range of groups.

Secondly, the examination of the 13 LEAA projects illustrates the centrality of basic supportive services. While women who have been subject to abuse by a partner need many types of assistance, a primary need is for safe shelter. Refuges or safe homes for battered women must be viewed as a baseline service. Without the option of leaving a violent home situation, other services (e.g., job training, child care, educational opportunities, or even prosecution) may be superfluous. The provision of shelter services embodies such a common-sense approach that one may forget about or underestimate the opposition. The arguments put forth by Senator Humphrey are representative of a growing body of opinion. Women must be prepared to confront these arguments, to point out their contradictions, and to combat them effectively. Though differences exist amongst women's groups in terms of ideological positions on the nuclear family, they cannot afford to be divided by jingoistic phrases about "threatening traditional family life." In demanding services for abused women, women must continually point out that violence against family members within any type of family structure (e.g., heterosexual or homosexual, nuclear or extended) is damaging and dangerous to the individual and can no longer be socially condoned.

All of which leads to a final point involving identification of arenas for raising these demands. It is highly unlikely that congressional legislation on domestic violence will be forthcoming. Given the resource limitations of most groups concerned with this area, congressional lobbying should not be given high priority.

There are, however, two potential avenues to pursue. First, there must be an increased lobbying effort in state legislatures. As described earlier, a range of legislative modifications has been achieved on the state level. In addition, the Reagan administration is seeking to turn over more authority for social programs to the states.

In terms of the types of state legislative actions which could be undertaken, of highest priority should be those designed to generate and provide funding for direct client services. The marriage license surcharge, currently imposed in five states, offers one model of a fund-raising strategy. To date, this approach has provided a viable mechanism for supporting domestic-violence programs. This strategy could be replicated with minimal difficulties in other states. Those interested in pursuing this or other forms of legislative initiatives may find suggestions for action in the *Response* review of existing state laws.

Secondly, a parallel and complementary strategy involves obtaining support for services for domestic-violence victims via established federal (or state) programs. This would entail investigating the eligibility requirements of a diverse spectrum of federal programs. Objectively, many battered women's programs qualify for a variety of benefits under existing departmental mandates. Unfortunately, many of these potential resource suppliers are hidden within the fragmentary and confusing structure of the federal bureaucracy. The *Handbook of Federal Resources on Domestic Violence*[27] is extremely useful in identifying the diversity of programs which may be tapped.

Since it is improbable that any federal agency will initiate a line item in their budget for domestic violence during the mid-1980s, the redefiniton of eligibility so as to include domestic-violence victims and programs may be the only realistic option available for securing government support. One potential problem in this approach should be mentioned. In a time of shrinking resources, competition for what is available is bound to increase. As the number of social programs is reduced, many interest groups will vie for what remains.

The problem of violence within the family and the concomitant need for services will not disappear. If anything, improvements in identification, documentation, and recording practices will bring ever-increasing numbers of cases into the public domain.

Ironically, one of the foremost opponents of domestic violence legislation put it well when he stated that:

> As the family becomes a major battleground for interest group politics and the quest for federal leverage and power, the domestic violence issue no doubt will continue to be highly controversial.[28]

Notes

1. Bruce Rounsaville, "Battered Wives: Barriers to Identification and Treatment," *American Journal of Orthopsychiatry 48* (July 1978): 487–94.

2. Anne Flitcraft, E. Stark, and W. Frezier, "Medicine and Patriarchal Violence: The Social Construction of a 'Private Event'," *Journal of International Health Services* (August 1979).

3. As cited in the U.S. Commission on Civil Rights, *Battered Women: Issues of Public Policy* (Washington, D.C.: U.S. Government Printing Office, January 1978), p.

8, Federal Bureau of Investigation statistics for 1974 indicate that one out of five officers killed in the line of duty died trying to break up a family fight.

4. A social history of the development of the women's movement and its relationship to the civil rights and new left movements of the sixties can be found in Sara Evans, *Personal Politics* (New York: Vintage Books, 1980).

5. For a discussion of why the women's movement focused on the issue of the family, see Barbara Easton, "Feminism and the Contemporary Family," *Socialist Review* (June 1978), pp. 11–36.

6. An account of the impact of the women's movement on national policy formation is contained in Jo Freeman, *The Politics of Women's Liberation* (New York: McKay Publisher, 1975).

7. The function of traditional women's magazines as social barometers of women's position in society is discussed in Betty Friedman, *The Feminine Mystique* (New York: Norton, 1964), chap. 2.

8. U.S. House Committee on Science and Technology—Subcommittee on Domestic and International Scientific Planning, Analysis, and Cooperation, *Research into Violent Behavior: Domestic Violence Hearings* (Washington, D.C.: U.S. Government Printing Office, 1978), pp. 51–71.

9. Statistics in this paragraph are from the National Violence Survey, 1976. See U.S. House Sci. and Tech. Hearings (1978), pp. 72–7. It should be noted that the survey was based on a sample of over 2,000 couples who are representative of all U.S. couples. Couples were defined as intact, legally married individuals. Excluded from the sample were divorced, separated, or cohabitating people. The narrowness of the sample unit definition may skew the findings downward.

10. E. Pizzey, *Scream Quietly or the Neighbors Will Hear* (London: Ridley Enslow Publishers, 1977).

11. R. Gelles, "The Myth of Battered Husbands," *Ms.* (October 1979), pp. 65–72.

12. *Battered Women: Issues of Public Policy,* pp. 176–78.

13. Public hearings on the issue of domestic violence have been held by: U.S. Commission on Civil Rights, January 1978; U.S. Senate Subcommittee on Child and Human Development, March 1978; U.S. House Subcommittee on Domestic and International Scientific Planning, Analysis and Cooperation, February 1978; U.S. House Subcommittee on Select Education, July 1979.

14. For example, subsequent to the Commission on Civil Rights hearings, the Department of Health, Education and Welfare (now the Department of Health and Human Services) created the Office of Domestic Violence. Operating as an internal working body, the office is charged with making agencywide recommendations for policy and program for this area.

15. *Battered Women: Issues of Public Policy,* Appendix B.

16. An excellent summary of state-level legislative activities may be found in *Response, 3* 12, (Aug./Sept. 1980), the Center for Women Policy Studies, Washington, D.C.

17. After passage, SB. 91 was enacted as Chapter 5 of Part 6 of Division 9 of the Welfare and Institutions Code.

18. U.S. Senate, Committee on Human Resources—Subcommittee on Child and Human Development, *Domestic Violence: Hearings* (Washington, D.C.: U.S. Government Printing Office, 1978), pp. 3–5.

19. Ibid.

20. Enacted as California Code of Civil Procedure Sections 540-549, 527.6 and 4359.

21. *Congressional Record—Senate* (Washington, D.C.: U.S. Government Printing Office, August 25, 1980).

22. Interdepartmental Committee on Domestic Violence, *Handbook of Federal*

Resources on Domestic Violence (Rockville, Maryland: National Clearinghouse on Domestic Violence, December, 1980).

23. U.S. Department of Justice, Law Enforcement Assistance Administration, *Guidelines Manual M4500.1C* (Washington, D.C.: U.S. Government Printing Office, 1978).

24. U.S. Department of Justice, Law Enforcement Assistance Administration, *Guidelines Manual M4500.1D* (Washington, D.C.: U.S. Government Printing Office, 1976).

25. Special Programs Division, Office of Regional Operations, LEAA, April 15, 1977. Internal memorandum.

26. *Congressional Record—Senate* (Washington, D.C.: U.S. Government Printing Office, August 25, 1980).

27. Interdepartmental Committee on Domestic Violence.

28. *Congressional Record—Senate* (Washington, D.C.: U.S. Government Printing Office, August 25, 1980).

Chapter 12

Women's Crime, Women's Justice

Elizabeth Fry Moulds

Women's changing role in American society has been the topic of much recent discussion and analysis. A favorite topic for the last several years has been women's involvement in crime and the criminal justice system. Much of the evaluation of women's criminal involvements comes in the form of media commentary related to sensational trials such as those of Angela Davis, Patty Hearst, and Lynette Fromme. The "new female criminal" and the "new violent woman" are popular subjects for both print and electronic media. The analysis offered the public in most of these stories is, however, questionable. This chapter will examine a series of key issues related to women charged with crimes and their treatment in the criminal justice system.

If we are to establish rational public policy concerning women criminals and their treatment, this policy must be designed in the context of new understanding about the character of women's crime and women's justice. Females, both juvenile and adult, have been no more than a token concern of criminologists until recently. For years, major texts in the field of criminology indexed topics related to women only sporadically and typically devoted only a few pages or an isolated chapter to the subject. Before 1970 a small body of literature did exist concerning the specific topic of women and crime, but the theories posed by most of these early authors have long since been rejected as inadequate analyses of female criminality.[1] Since 1970 there has been a striking increase in the literature on women and crime, and a number of serious works, both journal articles and full-length books, are now available.[2]

It will become evident that women's criminal behavior and treatment by the criminal justice system are very different from the behavior and treatment of men; and although there may have been some merging of these patterns in the last ten years, the convergence has been very slight. In order to examine these patterns in detail, the chapter will be divided into two sections: the first section will deal with women and crime and the second will deal with the handling of accused and convicted women in court.

WOMEN'S CRIMINAL BEHAVIOR

Historically, women's recorded involvement in crime has been miniscule in comparison to that of men, and that pattern has continued into recent times. In 1960, for example, women constituted just 10 percent of those arrested throughout the United States.[3] This limited criminal activity has resulted in a lack of major concern about women criminals. Women criminals have been regarded as anomalies rather than as severe social threats. Theorists focusing on the causes of crime have spent most of their energies, accordingly, attempting to explain male crime. Those who have addressed the issue of female criminality have tended to treat it as something quite apart from criminality in general. Their explanations have stressed factors unique to the female sex.

Cesare Lombroso, one of the earliest criminologists to write on the subject of women criminals saw women's crime as stemming from biological abnormalities or atavism. In addition to studying the physiology of women prisoners, he measured the bones and skull capacities of deceased women criminals and concluded that the measurements and general physiognomy of female criminals more closely approximated those of men than they did those of "normal" women.[4] Sigmund Freud and W. I. Thomas, both writing in the early 1900s, stressed what they saw as uniquely female psychological and social factors, such as a "natural" female passivity as well as biological factors, as the sources of female criminality.[5] For most of this century there has been a distinct tendency for criminologists addressing female criminality "to rely on psychologistic theories that impute some pathological difference to the criminal such as some abnormality of sex-role socialization, identification, or performance."[6]

An apparent increase in female criminality during the last decade has brought about a substantial shift in the literature concerning female criminality. Two new foci have developed in the analysis: one stresses the role of the women's liberation movement in bringing about an increase in women's participation in crime[7] and the other emphasizes the importance of economic factors in explaining changes in female criminality.[8] A major difference between the two foci relates to the assumptions made about the impact of the women's movement on women's behavior and on women's economic condition. Freda Adler, in stressing the importance of the women's movement, foresees the tendency of women's behavior to become more masculine as a result of emancipation and assumes that women are enjoying economic advancement as the result of the women's movement.[9] Those who hold that economic factors are more relevant to women's crime than the women's movement present a rather pessimistic view of women's current economic conditions. They argue that whatever economic progress has been experienced by women has been restricted to middle- and upper-middle-class women,[10] and that the overall economic picture for women is more bleak now than it was in 1960.[11]

It is important in the context of this dispute to examine where American women stand economically so that economic condition can be considered in relationship to changes in women's criminality in the past two decades.

WOMEN'S ECONOMIC CONDITION

Contrary to popular wisdom, the women's movement has not resulted in overwhelming economic advances for American women. It is true that the number of women in the work force has almost doubled since 1960 (23,272,000 in 1960, compared to 44, 493,000 in 1980) and that over half of the adult female population is now in the labor force (51.6 percent in 1980, compared to 37.8 percent in 1960). This compares with a percentage drop for males in the labor force from 84 percent in 1960 to 78.2 percent in 1980.[12] It is *not* true, however, that the increase in the number of women working necessarily represents an improvement in women's overall economic condition. Women today bear a larger share of economic responsibilities than they did in 1960. The number of families headed by women, for example, has almost doubled during the 1960–1979 period (a move from 4.5 million to 8.2 million families for 1979). The 87.7 percent increase in female heads of families for this period compares with a 21.3 percent increase for married couple heads of families and a 29.8 percent increase for other male heads of families.[13] There has been a 34 percent increase in the number of single, widowed, and divorced adult women since 1970.[14] During the same period that women's economic responsibilities increased, their economic status remained relatively weak. In 1979 the unemployment rate for all women 20 years old and over was 5.7 percent compared to a figure of 4.1 percent for men. The unemployment rate for female family heads that same year was 8.3 percent.[15] In 1979 the unemployment rate for black and other ethnic women was 12.3 percent and for black and other ethnic men it was 10.3 percent.[16] In 1978 median earnings for full time workers was $7,464 for women compared to $13,588 for men.[17] The relative earnings of men and women have changed very little since 1970. In 1970 women's weekly earnings were 62.2 percent of men's and in 1979 they were 62.4 percent of men's.[18] During the period of 1959-1979 there has been a drop in the number of persons below poverty level from 39.2 million to 25.2 million. During this same period, however, the percent of those below the poverty level who were female household heads rose from 26.3 percent to 52 percent.[19] As of 1979, 77.5 percent of women workers were involved in sales, clerical, blue collar, service, and farm work.[20] It is in this economic context that we must focus our discussion of changes in female criminality. As will be seen, economic factors may be much more closely linked to changing patterns in women's crime than is the women's liberation movement.

WOMEN'S CRIME PATTERNS

Assessing changes in female criminality is a most difficult task because it involves reliance on arrest data which are filled with methodological discrepancies. The most frequently used data on crime patterns are contained in the annual *Uniform Crime Report* of the FBI. The UCRs contain data collected each year from local law-enforcement agencies across the nation. There is variation from year to year, however, as to the number of agencies reporting and the estimated population for each sample so that trend reporting is likely to be inaccurate. Also, the UCRs report actual numbers of arrests each year rather than factoring in population increases or other demographic changes, thus creating a distorted impression of relative increases in crime. Other factors typically not taken into consideration when UCR data are used include such matters as the increase in law-enforcement officers since 1960, improvement in police technology, improved data-collection techniques, and failure to adjust certain crime categories affected by inflation (changes in classification of particular property crimes from misdemeanors to felonies).[21] Because the press has tended to report these arrest figures directly, the overall impression is one of an overwhelming crime wave in the United States which began its upward surge about 1960.

Reported crime has been increasing in the United States since World War II, but the increase has appeared more dramatic since 1960 than in the immediate, postwar period. Since 1960, reported crime by women has increased more rapidly than reported crime by men. Table 12.1 provides figures pertaining to the increases in all reported crime and in the seven crimes which make up the FBI "crime index": murder and nonnegligent manslaughter, forcible rape, robbery, aggravated assault, burglary, larceny-theft, and motor vehicle theft. The table also contains figures showing the level of women's involvement in total and "index" crime arrests.[22] Table 12.1 shows that there has been an increase in the percent of total arrests of women from 10.7 in 1960 to 15.7 in 1979. The percent of female participation in index crime rose from 10.1 in 1960 to 19.5 in 1979. These totals, however, offer only general impressions about what was occurring regarding women's criminality. It is necessary to examine the data in more detail in order to understand the nature of the crime patterns and their possible relationship to such factors as the women's movement and women's economic conditions.

Table 12.1. Women's Arrest Trends, 1960–1979.

Year	Total Arrests	Total Female Arrests	(% of Female of Total Arrests)	Total Index Crime* Arrests	Total Female Index Crime Arrests	(% of Female of Total Index Crime Arrests)
1960	4,077,596	438,274	(10.7)	541,523	54,748	(10.1)
1965	5,031,393	599,768	(11.9)	834,296	111,972	(13.4)
1970	6,570,473	946,897	(14.4)	1,273,783	215,614	(16.9)
1975	8,013,645	1,262,100	(15.7)	1,901,811	370,711	(19.5)
1979	9,506,347	1,494,930	(15.7)	2,163,302	421,320	(19.5)

*Index crimes are the crimes of criminal homicides, forcible rape, robbery, aggravated assault, burglary, larceny-theft, and motor vehicle theft.

Source: Adapted from United States Department of Justice, *Uniform Crime Reports of the United States for 1960,* pp. 94 , 100; *1965,* p. 115; *1970,* p. 129; *1975,* p. 191; and *1979,* p. 199. (Washington, D.C.: U.S. Government Printing Office).

The figures generally cited as proof of women's increasing involvement in serious crime are the UCR index crime as shown in Table 12.1. There is an inherent problem, however, in using this particular collection of offenses as the indicator of major crime in the United States. One of the offenses included in the index crime category is larceny-theft, which the FBI defines as "the unlawful taking, carrying, leading, or riding away of property from the possession or constructive possession of another. Thefts of bicycles, automobile accessories, shoplifting, pocket-picking or any stealing of property or article which is not taken by force and violence or by fraud."[23] In so defining larceny-theft, the UCRs fail to distinguish between petty and grand theft. Because of this lack of distinction, a distorted impression is created concerning women's involvement in major crime. Darrell Steffensmeier, who has researched this particular point in some detail, pointed out that "the *increase* in arrests of females for larceny is due largely to larger numbers of females being arrested for shoplifting."[24] Steffensmeier recomputed UCR arrest data concerning index crimes for the period 1965 to 1977, *excluding* larceny-theft, based on the argument that crimes included in the category of larceny are not primarily major crimes, and found that "the percent of the total female arrest rate accounted for by serious crimes without larceny shows no increase. . . . These data show clearly that the increase in arrests for larceny accounts for most of the female increase in serious crimes, thereby contradicting the sensational claims about dramatic changes in the kinds of crimes committed by females."[25]

In addition to reporting arrest trends for serious or index crimes each year, the UCRs offer a breakdown of index crimes into violent index crime (murder, forcible rape, robbery, and aggravated assault) and property index crime (burglary, larceny-theft, and motor vehicle theft). The violent crime increases from year to year receive a great deal of public attention, but contrary to popular perceptions, women are not committing a larger portion of violent crimes. It is true that there has been an increase in the number of reported arrests of women for violent crimes each year for the last two decades, but the percent of violent crime which is committed by women each year has remained relatively unchanged since 1960. Table 12.2 provides details concerning both violent and property index crimes for 1960 and 1979; it shows that there has been an increase in the number of reported female violent crimes from 11,324 in 1960 to 44,212 in 1979, but it also shows that the percent of violent crime committed by women has remained constant (10.5 percent in 1960 and 10.2 percent in 1979). The percent of violent crime increase for this 18-year period has been very close for females and males: 290 percent for females and 305 percent for males. These data contrast with Adler's contention that a "masculinization" of women's behavior as a result of the women's movement is bringing about larger portions of female violent crime. Adler's explanation of the trend was: "[A]s the position of women approximates the position of men, so does the frequency and type of their criminal activity. It would, therefore, seem justified to predict that if present social trends continue . . . [women will] compete increasingly in such traditionally male criminal activities as crimes against the person, more aggressive property offenses, and especially white collar crime."[26] As of 1979 this trend toward increasing proportions of female violence had not come about.

Property crime patterns for women in the last two decades are quite a different matter. As Table 12.2 shows, there has been a dramatic increase in both the number of arrests of women for property index crime and in the proportion of these crimes committed by women in the last two decades. While in 1960 women were responsible for just 10 percent of burglaries, larceny-thefts, and auto thefts (43,424 arrests), in 1979 women accounted for 21.8 percent of these arrests (a total of 377,108). The increase for males over this period was 246 percent compared to an increase of 768 percent for females. These figures do confirm the popular perception of women's growing role in crime.

It is important to examine women's involvement in specific property crimes in order to understand fully where the major increases have taken place. Have the increases been in aggressive or in relatively passive property crime? Have

Table 12.2 Violent and Property Index Crime Arrests 1960 and 1979, by Sex.

	1960	(%)	1979	(%)
Violent Index Crime*				
Total	107,722	(100.)	434,778	(100.)
Males	96,398	(89.5)	390,566	(89.9)
Females	11,324	(10.5)	44,212	(10.2)
Property Index Crime†				
Total	433,801	(100.)	1,728,524	(100.)
Males	390,377	(90)	1,351,416	(78.2)
Females	43,424	(10)	377,108	(21.8)

*Violent Index Crimes are the crimes of criminal homicide, forcible rape, robbery, and aggravated assault.

†Property Index Crimes are the crimes of burglary, larceny-theft, and motor vehicle theft.

Source: Adapted from United States Department of Justice, *Uniform Crime Report of the United States for 1960,* pp. 94, 100, and *1979,* p. 199 (Washington, D.C.: U.S. Government Printing Office).

the offenses been primarily those traditional to women (such as shoplifting and bad checks) or have they moved in the direction of white-collar crime? Table 12.3 provides comparisons of women's involvement in each category of property offense reported by the UCRs for 1960 and 1979. Robbery has been included here as the taking of property from a person by force or violence or by fear of force or violence. Table 12.3 shows that relatively small percentage increases have occurred in the more aggressive categories such as robbery and burglary, but dramatic increases have occurred in the more passive categories such as larceny-theft, embezzlement, fraud, forgery, and counterfeiting.

The remaining question is whether the large increases have taken place in offenses which can be considered "white-collar" crime. It is the hypothesis of both Adler and Simon that emancipation of women resulting from the women's movement will bring with it an increase in the amount of white-collar crime engaged in by women. As Simon put it, "Women's participation in financial and white collar offenses [fraud, embezzlement, larceny, and forgery] should increase as their opportunities for employment in higher status occupations expand."[27] This hypothesis is based on the assumption that women will be moving into higher-status occupations as a result of the women's movement, an assumption which has already been shown to be of limited validity to date.[28] The involvement of women in white-collar crime needs scrutiny.

The classic definition of "white-collar crime" offered by Edwin Sutherland is that it is crime committed by a person of high respectability and social status in the course of his or her occupational role.[29] This definition may be appropriate for portions of female property crime, but only for small portions. The four property crimes which can be considered potentially white-collar are larceny-theft, embezzlement, fraud, and forgery-counterfeiting. Larceny-theft has already been described as a shoplifting-dominated offense.[30] Although the UCRs do not distinguish between petty and other theft in their reporting of larceny-theft, other data sources do make the distinction. In California, for example, petty thefts (thefts of amounts up to $200) are recorded separately from thefts of amounts exceeding $200. Eighty-seven percent of women arrested in 1979 in California for thefts were arrested for *petty* thefts.[31] Although there is no means of determining the status of the persons committing these offenses nor of determining whether the thefts were committed in the course of occupational roles, common sense would seem to indicate that thefts of $200 or less do not qualify as classic white-collar crime. There is similar doubt as to whether women's crimes of fraud, forgery-counterfeiting, and embezzlement are appropriately classified as white collar. Steffensmeier takes the position that these are largely petty-theft crimes. He spells out his reasoning for this in some detail:

> The evidence indicates that most arrests of women for fraud are *not* occupationally related but rather involve passing bad checks (e.g., insufficient funds),

Table 12.3. Female Arrests for Property Crimes in 1960 and 1979, shown as Percentages of Total Arrests for Each Crime.

	1960		1979	
	% Female	(N)	% Female	(N)
Burglary	2.9	(3,952)	6.3	(29,674)
Robbery	4.6	(1,495)	7.4	(9,646)
Motor Vehicle Theft	3.6	(2,285)	8.9	(12,814)
Stolen Property: (buying, receiving, possessing)	8.5	(996)	10.7	(11,514)
Embezzlement (includes fraud for 1960 only)	15	(6,276)	25.3	(1,998)
Larceny-Theft	15.8	(37,187)	30.3	(332,536)
Forgery & Counterfeiting	15.6	(3,912)	30.9	(21,961)
Fraud			40.4	(98,276)

Source: Adapted from United States Department of Justice *Uniform Crime Reports of the United States for 1960,* pp. 94, 100 and *1979,* p. 199 (Washington, D.C.: U.S. Government Printing Office).

credit card fraud, theft of services, welfare fraud, and small con games. . . .
Meanwhile, the arrests of women for forgery are largely for forging credit cards,
checks, and related falsifications of identification. In addition, the typical arrestee
for embezzlement fits the broad, but not the narrow definition of white-collar
criminal. He or she is a lower echelon employee in a subordinate position,
principally cashiers, tellers, and clerks . . . , and is *not* a person of high social
standing who commits a crime in the course of his/her occupation.[32]

The major increases in women's crime, then, have been in the realm of
property crime rather than violent crime, and this property crime has been
primarily passive and petty. These patterns do not follow from emancipation
of women brought about by the women's liberation movement as described by
Adler. A far more logical explanation is that these patterns are closely linked to
the relatively poor and worsening economic condition coupled with the increasing economic responsibilities of large numbers of American women today. If we wish to address these "alarming increases in women's criminality"
the logical place to begin is with the gross inequities in the American economy.

TREATMENT IN THE HANDS OF THE CRIMINAL
JUSTICE SYSTEM: WOMEN IN COURT

Now that we have examined the patterns of female criminal behavior in recent
years, it is important to examine the treatment given women as they are
processed by the legal system. In examining women's criminal behavior, we
have had to use arrest data as the indicator of relative amounts of male and
female crime. Arrest data are the official measure of police officers' decisions
to arrest a suspected criminal on a particular charge. These figures may not be
an accurate reflection of women's levels of participation in crime because of the
role played by law-enforcement officers. Police officers employ a relatively
large amount of discretion in the decision to arrest in many circumstances, and
there are no means of determining whether women benefit from this discretion
to a different extent than from men. Once the arrest has been made, however,
the processing of the individual through the system becomes a matter of public
record. The handling of the case by the prosecution, the resolution of the case
in court (if it goes to court), and sentencing of the convicted are all matters that
can generally be traced. This section focuses, therefore, on disparities in the
treatment of men and women in court.

California data pertaining to the outcome of felony arrests give an indication of the general treatment accorded males and females in court. For both
males and females there is a reduction in the number of cases at each step in
processing through the courts. A very large number of felony arrests each year
are subsequently charged as misdemeanors or are dropped altogether from the
courts. These cases never reach California superior courts. Table 12.4 shows

Table 12.4 Superior Court Dispositions,* Convictions in Superior Courts and Sentences to Death or Prison in California in 1979, by Sex, Shown as a Percentage of Adult Felony Arrests.

	Adult Felony Arrests (N)	Superior Court Dispositions* (N)	Felony Convictions (N)	Sentences to Death or Prison (N)
Male	100% (221,962)	15.6% (34,686)	13.9% (30,863)	3.7% (8,293)
Female	100% (34,505)	13.1% (4,512)	11.3% (3,906)	1.5% (524)

*Disposed of in superior court by dismissal, acquittal, or conviction.

Source: Adapted from State of California Department of Justice, *California Criminal Justice Profile, 1979.* (Sacramento, California: Bureau of Criminal Statistics), pp. 31, 88.

the percentages of male and female felony arrests reaching California superior courts in 1979 and the comparative results of the prosecutions. The comparative arrest percentages in 1979 were 15.6 for males and 13.1 for females. Once a case reaches superior court in California it is resolved by (a) conviction, (b) acquittal, or (c) dismissal. Table 12.4 shows the comparative California felony conviction percentages (13.9 percent for males and 11.3 percent for females). The last column on the table, sentences to death or to prison, offers a comparison of the percentages of males and females receiving the harshest possible sentences from California courts in 1979 (3.7 percent for males and 1.5 percent for females). The pattern clearly shown in this table is that at each measured step in the criminal justice process where discretion is exercised, females were more frequently favored by the system than were males.[33]

SENTENCING PATTERNS AND PATERNALISM

A detailed analysis of sentencing patterns will reveal the consistency of the pattern of gentler treatment of women in court.[34] The starting point for an examination of sentencing patterns is a study from the early 1960s done by Stuart Nagel.[35] Nagel obtained a nationwide sample of state cases for the year 1962 and data for all federal criminal cases decided in 1963. The federal data have been recomputed and the results are reproduced in Table 12.5. (The pattern found in Nagel's nationwide sample of states' data was similar to that found in the federal data although the differences between the sentences given males and females were not as substantial in the state sample data.)[36] Table 12.5 highlights the very different treatment of the sexes in showing the relatively high proportion of women receiving light sentences (probation with and without supervision was given to women twice as often as to men—65.2 and 37.3 percent respectively) and the relatively high proportion of men receiving harsh sentences (8 percent of the men receiving sentences of five or more years in prison compared to 4.7 percent of the women).

More recent California data reveal a very similar pattern of differential treatment of the sexes. Table 12.6 presents felony sentencing figures for both 1974 and 1979. This table enables us to examine comparative sentences under two different types of sentencing laws. For years, persons convicted of felonies in California were sentenced to "indeterminate" prison terms. The indeterminate sentence was based on the premise that prisons existed, at least in part, for the purpose of rehabilitation and a sentence to prison for an indefinite period allowed the system flexibility with regard to the needs and rehabilitation progress of each prisoner. A Men's Adult Authority Board and a separate Women's Board of Terms and Parole reviewed the case of each prisoner eligible for parole every year and determined whether or not the individual was ready to be returned to the community. The indeterminate sentence (and the rehabili-

Table 12.5. Comparison of Type and Length of Male and Female Sentences in Federal Courts 1963.

	% 5 or more years	% 3–5 years	% 1–3 years	% 6 mos. 1 year	% less than 6 mos.
Male	8.0	11.9	14.6	8.6	10.3
Female	4.7	6.3	10.2	4.5	5.6

	% Fine	% probation after another sentence	% probation	% un-supervised probation	Total
Male	7.9	1.4	36.1	1.2	100 (N = 27,927)
Female	2.8	.7	63.9	1.3	100 (N = 2,417)

Data Source: Inter-University Consortium for Political Research, P.O. Box 1248, Ann Arbor, Michigan, 48106.

Table 12.6. Comparison of Male and Female Adult Felony Sentencing in California Superior Courts in 1974 and 1979.

	Death or Prison	Other Incarceration*	Probation or Fine	Total
1974				
Male	15.9%	63.4%	20.7%	100% (N = 33,481)
Female	6.6%	50.3%	43.1%	100% (N = 3,886)
1979				
Male	26.9%	62.2%	10.9%	100% (N = 30,836)
Female	13.4%	60.1%	26.5%	100% (N = 3,906)

*Other incarceration includes sentences to jail, jail and probation in combination, the California Youth Authority, and civil commitments (to drug or mental health facilities).

Data Source: California Department of Justice, Bureau of Criminal Statistics, P.O. Box 13427, Sacramento, California 95813.

tation programs on which it was theoretically based) were pronounced failures in California in the mid-1970s by both liberals (who saw inhumaneness in the arbitrary nature of the granting of parole) and conservatives (who were anxious for some old-fashioned punishment of criminals). The outcome of this dissatisfaciton with the indeterminate sentence was the passage in 1974 of SB42, the Nejedly Determinate Sentencing Act. The law now requires judges, when sentencing persons to state prison, to use one of three statutorily prescribed sentence lengths and states that "The trial judge shall state the reasons for his sentence choice on the record at the time of sentencing."[37] As can be seen in Table 12.6, females received milder sentences than males in each of the two years shown, but in 1979 there was a much larger proportion of incarceration sentences for both sexes than in 1974. Additionally, it can be noted from this table that the move toward more incarceration was more dramatic for women than it was for men. This trend is best revealed in the figures for probation and fines which dropped for men from 20.7 percent in 1974 to 10.9 percent in 1979 and for women from 43.1 percent in 1974 to 26.5 percent in 1979. Although it is still too early to tell what the long-term results of determinate sentencing will be in California, the short-term results appear to include a closing of the gap between male and female sentences. This may be the result of judges feeling under closer scrutiny with regard to their sentences and the *reasons* for their sentences than was characteristic under the indeterminate sentencing law. Reducing discretion by use of determinate sentencing, then, may result in harsher sentences for women, but it should also encourage sentencing objectivity.

Although the California sentencing data reveal substantial differences in the treatment of males and females, it is possible that these differences, or part of these differences, could be accounted for by factors other than sex. A number of studies have indicated that race was related to the severity of sentence given a particular individual[38] and others have found income or economic class to be related to patterns of sentencing.[39] Other relevant factors are the severity of the crime committed and prior record of the defendant. The 1974 California data were analyzed to determine the effect of several of these variables. Controlling for race, type of crime, and prior record has resulted in the same basic pattern: consistently milder treatment for women than for men.[40] It should be noted that patterns of racial disparity were found in the 1974 data. Although females of all races received milder treatment than did their male counterparts, the data also indicated that white females received gentler treatment than nonwhite females and that white males received gentler treatment than nonwhite males.[41]

If it is true that females have received consistently lighter sentencing in federal and in California courts, the important question remains why? It has been argued that the explanation for preferential treatment is a so-called "Chivalry Factor."[42] The term "chivalry," however, pertains primarily to a code of manners and creates a deceptive impression when used in conjunction with women's treatment in criminal courts. Chivalry is generally viewed positively and this positive explanation may have forestalled more serious analysis of the differential treatment of women. Specifically, the concept of chivalry does not deal at all with the power relationship which exists between men and women, while power is the essence of the legal system. The power relationship at work here is more accurately described by the term "paternalism." Paternalism involves "a type of behavior by a superior toward an inferior resembling that of a male parent to his child . . . [and] since a 'child' is defenseless and lacks property, he requires assistance and support. Second, since a 'child' is not fully aware of his role and therefore not fully responsible, he requires guidance."[43]

The American legal system has historically treated women as inferiors, sometimes subjugating them and sometimes "protecting them in their best interest." The common law of the United States recognized and supported the subjugation of women. It assumed that women were defenseless and in need of support and guidance. It often denied to women the responsibility of political decision making, the right to determine their residence, and the right to property.[44]

Other major historic examples of the subjugation of women in America have been extensively documented.[45] The lengthy denial of women's suffrage, the barring of women from numerous occupations, the passage of protective legislation for women in the labor market, the Supreme Court's approval of special treatment of women, the exclusion of women from political participation in such matters as jury duty, and the continued failure of an Equal Rights Amendment have all served to allot to women a special and less than equal position in the American political arena.

The implications of this paternalism have been most serious. The laws enacted by legislatures and the decisions of courts have set the tone for the inferior regard of women held by much of society. They have contributed to the institutionalization of the assumptions that are the bases of such laws. Judges have participated in the process, and their language has been most pointed on the subject at times. On the issue of the fitness of women for the legal profession 100 years ago, for example, the United States Supreme Court was most explicit: "Man is, or should be, woman's protector and defender. The natural and proper timidity and delicacy which belongs to the female sex evidently unfits it for many of the occupations of civil life."[46] The notion of protecting women from themselves or from some identifiable evil (specifically prison for the purposes of this study) has had continued judicial expression throughout this century. The pattern of California judges in sending a substantially smaller proportion of convicted female felons to prison than males should be viewed as one expression of this paternalistic protection.

Sentencing of men and women has not, however, always followed California's pattern. There have been a number of states which historically have sentenced men and women differently by statute with the result that women have received longer incarceration terms than men. Ironically, a paternalistic rationale has also been offered for this disparity.

DISCRIMINATORY SENTENCING STATUTES

A basis for statutory sentencing distinctions between males and females was established in Indiana in the late 1860s when the state built an incarceration facility (called a reformatory) for women which was quite unlike the prisons to which men were sentenced. The reformatory was designed to accomplish rehabilitation whereas the male prisons were designed for punishment. This model has been followed for most of this century in a number of American states.[47] In order to accomplish rehabilitation, women have been detained in many state "rehabilitation facilities" and "reformatories" according to statute for as long as necessary. Males being sentenced to prison in these same states have been given specific terms of incarceration by separate statutory provisions.[48] Frequently the result has been that females have served longer sentences than males for the same offenses. The basic premise involved in the differential treatment was expressed quite clearly in a recent court challenge of New Jersey's differential statutory sentencing: "[F]emale criminals [are] basically different from male criminals, and they [are] more amenable and responsive to rehabilitation and reform which might, however, require a longer period of confinement in a different type of institution."[49] In a 1968 challenge to a Connecticut differential sentencing statute the state made a lower-court argument that women's institutions were rehabilitative in character and were not intended to be penal institutions. The facilities, they argued, were designed differently from those of men in order to provide for "women and juveniles a special protection and every reformative and rehabilitative opportunity." The state further explained that this "reformative and rehabilitative opportunity" justified longer imprisonment for women.[50] The expression by the state that women and juveniles require special protection fits the classic definition of paternalism. It is "in the best interest of women" and "for their protection" that the state provided them with "rehabilitative opportunities" which kept them locked away for longer periods of time than their male counterparts.

Carolyn Temin points out that court challenges in the various discriminatory sentencing statutes have resulted in inconsistent positions from state to state and contends that the only real hope for total elimination of the statutes lies with the Equal Rights Amendment. Short of an ERA, egalitarian public policy in the area would involve individual state elimination of the differentials inherent in the statutes. A determinate sentencing statute for all adults in each state is a logical response to the inequities built into the differential sentencing statutes. The California determinate sentencing model is not a perfect solution, but it is a move in the direction of egalitarian treatment.

JUVENILE FEMALE TREATMENT:
THE DOUBLE PATERNALISM

Statutes providing harsher sentences for women than for men have a corollary in the treatment of juveniles. Just as longer sentences were provided for women by some states in the name of "rehabilitation," more severe sanctions have been meted out to juvenile females "for their own protection."[51]

Paternalistic attitudes concerning youth have been present for both males and females for the entire history of the United States' juvenile justice system. In addition to establishing special juvenile court procedures purporting to help rather than punish children, the court has placed itself firmly in the role of parent since the late 1800s in determining what is the most appropriate treatment for a particular child.[52] As such, the practice of the court in acting *in loco parentis* is routine for those cases in which the child is declared a dependent child or ward of the court. The court is expected to provide for the child the custody, care, and discipline as nearly as possible equivalent to that which should have been given by his or her parents. This model of treatment fits precisely the classic definition of the term "paternalism" offered earlier in this chapter.

In its "protection" of juveniles, however, the juvenile justice system has gone at least one step further for females than it has for males. In effect, juvenile females are subjected to a *double* paternalism (for their femaleness as well as for their youth). The reasoning behind this differential treatment can be traced to specific cultural concerns about young girls. Meda Chesney-Lind has described the concern: "The traditional American family has always exerted great control over their daughters' behavior in order to protect their virginity (or virginal reputation). This control is necessary because of what is known as the sexual 'double standard,' which suggests that the 'good' adolescent female is never sexual (although she must be sexually appealing). The healthy adolescent male, on the other hand, must prove his masculinity by experimenting "sexually."[53] Sexual activity (often referred to as "waywardness") in girls is repeatedly cited as a major cause for concern on the part of the courts. An interesting piece of evidence of the court's concern with the sexuality of young women was found by Chesney-Lind in her study of the Honolulu juvenile courts. During the period studied (1929–1955), the Honolulu juvenile courts issued special court orders for physician-administered physical examinations for selected juvenile offenders. Seventy to 80 percent of the female juvenile offenders were ordered examined compared to 12 to 18 percent of the male juvenile offenders. The health of the youths, however, was only one concern of the court:

> The court's specific interest in these examinations was made explicit by the doctor's comments on the forms with regard to the condition of the hymen. Notations such as "hymen ruptured," "hymen torn—admits intercourse," and "hymen intact" were routine despite the fact that the condition of the hymen is usually irrelevant to

health or illness. Further, gynecological examinations were administered even when the female was referred for offenses which did not involve sexuality such as larceny or burglary.[54]

Judicial enforcement of the sexual double standard is most clearly visible in male and female juvenile arrest rates for different types of behavior. Male arrest rates have been consistently higher than female arrest rates for behavior which would be criminal if committed by an adult.[55] Young females, on the other hand, are arrested at a much higher rate than young males for offenses which would *not* be considered criminal were the individual an adult. This latter category of offenses which frequently is termed "unruly," "delinquent tendency," or "status" offense, includes matters such as running away from home, promiscuity, incorrigibility, and curfew violations. For example, 72 percent of juvenile female arrests in California in 1960 were for status offenses while 56 percent of juvenile male arrests were for status offenses.[56] In some states, Connecticut and New Jersey, for example, the figures have run as high as 80 percent for females brought to court for unruly or status offenses.[57]

Judicial enforcement of the sexual double standard extends beyond arrest practices. Incarceration rates and length of incarcerations are relevant factors also. The Female Offender Resource Center found that "female juveniles are more likely to be confined for status offenses than males and more likely to be confined in jail settings."[58] For example, in 1971, 75 percent of juvenile females held in detention centers nationally were in detention for status offenses while the comparable figure for juvenile males was between 20 and 30 percent.[59] "Not only are female delinquents institutionalized more often than males for less serious crimes, but the latest data available also indicate that girls spend, on the average, two months longer in institutions than do boys. After incarceration, they remain on parole for longer periods."[60]

Detention rates for juvenile females have also been found to be higher than those for males brought to court for serious crime. A study of juveniles appearing before the New York family courts from 1964 to 1974 found that "although several thousand fewer females than males were brought before [the court] for involvement in serious crimes, several thousand more females than males were eventually placed in a rehabilitative setting."[61] This study also determined that juvenile females remanded to New York State training schools were detained there for longer periods of time than were juvenile males.[62] Chesney-Lind had found the same pattern in the Honolulu Detention Home for the period 1954–64. Female juveniles "spent, on the average, three times as long in these facilities as did their male counterparts."[63]

The reasoning for this differential has been revealed in interviews with juvenile court personnel such as those conducted by Peter Kratcoski. Kratcoski found that the court personnel and police officers involved in juvenile cases "viewed the juvenile court as predominantly a protective and service agency rather than a punishment agency and . . . that it was often necessary to hold a girl in detention for her own safety and well being."[64] Paternalism appears again as the rationale for differential treatment.

A major portion of the gender-based differentials just described has been traced to the collection of laws outlining "status" offenses in the various states. The court has become involved in the lives of these status offenders as substitute parent when the family has been unable to control unruly behavior. The court, acting in its paternalistic role, has frequently seen incarceration as the most appropriate means of "protecting" these unruly youth. Alternatives to this pattern of treatment are available and are worth examining.

Sufficient concern has been expressed nationally concerning the handling of status offenders in juvenile justice systems that in 1974 Congress passed the Juvenile Justice and Delinquency Prevention Act[65] encouraging states to keep status offenders out of juvenile detention and correctional facilities. The law was extended in 1977, making funds available to assist communities in developing alternative methods of handling juvenile status offenders. Compliance with the spirit of the act has been uneven, but a number of states have made major changes in their handling of status offenses.[66] California serves as an example here of a state which is making major changes in compliance with the act.

Effective January 1, 1977, California has encouraged the diversion of status offenders into community programs which are in many cases outside the juvenile justice system. Status offenders remaining inside the juvenile justice system are now separated entirely from criminal offenders.[67] The result of the California reform has been a drastic reduction in the numbers of arrests of status offenders and in a change in the handling of those who are arrested. In 1973, prior to the new law, 45,239 juvenile females were arrested for delinquent tendencies (status offenses) in California. This number made up 50.5 percent of all juvenile female arrests that year (the comparative percentage for boys was 21.2).[68] In 1979, after the changes brought about in the handling of status offenses by the new law, the number of female juveniles arrested for delinquent tendencies was down to 23 percent of the total of juvenile females arrested.[69] Community-based programs are now handling large numbers of the California delinquent tendency cases. The young people involved are not processed through the criminal justice system. This appears to be a sensible step forward in the handling of noncriminal juvenile behavior. In an era of fiscal conservatism, the next issue will be whether these community-based services will be able to compete successfully with other demands in the criminal justice system for adequate funding.

PROSTITUTION: THE WOMAN'S CRIME

There is an adult corollary to the pattern of treating females more harshly than males for crimes defined as sexual in the juvenile justice system (promiscuity, incorrigibility, and other status offenses). *The* woman's crime is prostitution. Prostitution is the only crime for which women are arrested more often than men (56,096 women as opposed to 25,992 men arrested in 1979 for the combined crimes of prostitution and commercialized vice).[70] Social concerns about sex for hire have been directed almost exclusively at women. Two areas of differential treatment stand out particularly: female gender-based statutes, and differential enforcement.

Early definitions of prostitution made clear that the crime involved was that of the woman engaging in prostitution, not that of her customer or her brother prostitute. "The practice of a female in offering her body to an indiscriminate intercourse with men for money or its equivalent" was one early definition.[71] Statutes based on such definitions have existed in many American states for most of this century. The number of these states has been declining as a result of challenges based on the equal protection clause of the Fourteenth Amendment, but several states have kept prostitution statutes which apply only to women even in recent years (Indiana, Louisiana, North Dakota, Wisconsin, and Wyoming, for example).[72] In 1972 the state supreme court of Indiana specifically rejected a Fourteenth Amendment equal protection attack on a female-only prostitution statute, saying that the sexual classification in the law rested upon "an inherent and substantial basis for classification."[73]

Even in those states where the statute is *not* gender specific, however, the design of the statute or its enforcement (or both) create a de facto discrimination against women. Given female domination of the prostitution profession (this figure has been put at 90 percent)[74] statutes which criminalize acts of prostitution but not acts of patronizing prostitutes discriminate against women.

The most common discrimination pattern, however, is that of selective enforcement of the prostitution laws. Women are arrested far more frequently under these laws than men even though most of the acts proscribed involve both a male and a female partner. According to UCR data, 73 percent of prostitution and commercialized-vice arrests in 1960 were of women. In 1970 women comprised 81 percent of these arrests, and in 1979 the figure was 67.5 percent.[75] More finite detail as to differential treatment is difficult to obtain nationally, but two local studies of New York City and San Francisco provide some insight. New York City's law regarding prostitution contains two sections: one pertaining to prostitutes and the other pertaining to patrons of prostitutes. During a late 1960 attempt at "cleaning up" Times Square, there were several thousand arrests under these prostitution laws in a six-month period (September 1967–February 1968). The number of arrests under the section pertaining to prostitutes was 3,357, resulting in 1,443 convictions. Patron arrests numbered 127 and resulted in five convictions. In addition, over 2,000 women were arrested for loitering or disorderly conduct during the months of September and October alone.[76] The overwhelming focus of the police and of the courts was on the activities of the women involved and not of the men. The San Francisco study revealed similar disparities. A Women's Jail Study Group studied the handling of prostitution in San Francisco in 1976 and found that of an average 200 prostitution-related arrests each month, 76.5 percent were of females for prostitution, 6.5 percent were of males for prostitution, 8 percent were of males for being customers, and 6.5 percent were of males for pimping.[77]

A number of approaches have been taken to eliminate the disparities shown by the New York and San Francisco studies. In 1975 one San Francisco municipal court judge received international notoriety when she refused to hear prosecutors' cases against prostitutes unless the customers were similarly charged and brought in.[78] A number of jurisdictions have begun using female police officers as decoys in an attempt at equalizing solicitation enforcement.[79] In Alameda County, California, a court challenge alleging selective enforcement temporarily prohibited prosecution of 252 women charged with violation of prostitution statutes in 1975 and 1976.[80] The Oakland, California police department practice of targeting prostitutes and not customers with an enforcement arrangement that used 20 times as many male decoys as female decoys was later found constitutional by the California Supreme Court. The court held that the enforcement practices were not discriminatory because the focus of police efforts was on the "profiteers" of prostitution rather than upon the customers.[81]

The effectiveness of attempts to equalize enforcement of prostitution laws has been limited. Women are still being arrested for prostitution and related offenses in vastly disproportionate numbers. Prostitution is a crime for which our criminal justice system seems incapable of dispensing equal justice.

One increasingly popular proposal to solve the discrimination problem is the decriminalization of prostitution, excluding perhaps provisions pertaining to public solicitation of prostitution. There are, of course, moral issues involved which leave many offended by this solution. It is worth noting, however, that in California prostitution remains the *only* illegal adult, private, consensual sexual activity; this and the fact that prostitution is primarily a woman's crime reveal a great deal about social attitudes concerning women and sex.

NEW DIRECTIONS FOR THE FUTURE

We have examined here a number of misconceptions concerning female criminality, and we have reviewed a series of issues pertaining to the differential treatment of females in court. Although some of the inequities reviewed operate to the short-term benefit of women (lighter sentences in particular), the inequities cannot be condoned because of the underlying causes and their long-term implications for the status and treatment of women in a democratic state.

The paternalism described here is rooted in historic patterns of subjugation of women in American society. The principles of self-determination and equality are done great damage by permitting paternalism on the part of public officials to continue. Public policy designed with the assumption that women must be specially protected (or subjugated) is also damaging. A commitment to equal treatment requires that several public policy changes be made.

At the outset, the war against women's crime must begin with a war against women's poverty. The fact that property crime by women has increased during a period of worsening economic conditions and increased economic responsibilities for women can no longer be overlooked. Scapegoating the women's movement for increases in women's crime serves to delay relief from the economic problem. It is the failure of the economic goals of the movement rather than the success of the movement that is related to present patterns of female criminality.

Second, two kinds of sentencing reform appear appropriate. Replacing indeterminate sentencing statutes with determinate sentencing statutes provides a means of injecting objectivity into the sentencing process and has the added advantage of providing prisoners with specified release dates. Women may receive harsher sentences under determinate sentencing statutes than under indeterminate sentencing statutes, but this is a reasonable price to pay if women are to move out of a subjugated and protected class. Gender-specific sentencing statutes should be abolished outright. The justifications provided for the continuation of these statutes are direct denials of women's right to be treated equally with men.

The major area in which females have received differential treatment in the juvenile justice system has been the handling of status offenders. Congress has already passed legislation encouraging the states to deinstitutionalize status offenders and to provide instead community-based services to assist young people previously labeled as status-offense criminals. Where compliance with the federal law has taken place, as in the case of California, the result has been a dramatic reduction in the number of girls taken into the juvenile justice system and a greater equality between males and females processed through the system. It is hoped that these new community-based services which are replacing institutionalization will offer flexibility, fairness, and humaneness not typically experienced in juvenile halls and youth-authority prisons. Deinstitutionalization of status offenders and decriminalization of status offenses is a desirable policy goal for all states that have not yet moved in this direction.

Finally, the discrimination against women inherent in many prostitution statutes and in the enforcement of prostitution statutes has not been satisfactorily addressed by reforms attempted to date. The discrimination continues, and the prostitution continues. Morality legislation has always been questionably appropriate in a nation theoretically committed to the separation of church and state, and it has been of very limited success in stopping the acts prohibited. It is time now to decriminalize this private, consensual adult behavior. If we wish to discourage prostitution, an obvious alternative would be to tempt potential prostitutes into other occupations by providing education and job preparation which makes desirable occupational alternatives a realistic possibility. As has been shown, the only way to counter women's crime, including prostitution, is to resolve the economic issues that underly it.

Notes

1. For reviews of the early literature, see Dorie Klein, "The Etiology of Female Crime: A Review of the Literature," *Issues in Criminology 8* (Fall 1973): 3–30; and Christine E. Rasche, "The Female Offender as an Object of Criminological Research," *Criminal Justice and Behavior 1* (December 1974): 301–19.

2. The more extensive recent works have been Freda Adler, *Sisters in Crime: The Rise of the New Female Criminal* (New York: McGraw-Hill, 1975); Richard Deming, *Women: The New Criminals* (Nashville: Thomas Nelson Inc. Publishers, 1977); Rita J. Simon, *Women and Crime* (Lexington, Mass.: Heath, 1975); and Carol Smart, *Women, Crime and Criminology: A Feminist Critique* (London: Routledge and Kegan Paul, 1977). Collections of articles and special issue volumes also to be noted are Freda Adler and Rita Simon, *The Crimonology of Deviant Women* (Boston: Houghton Mifflin Company, 1979); Lee Bowker, *Women, Crime, and the Criminal Justice System* (Lexington, Mass.: Lexington Books, 1978); Annette Laura Crites, ed., *The Female Offender* (Lexington, Mass.: Lexington Books, 1976); Susan Datesman and Frank Scarpitti, eds., *Women, Crime, and Justice* (New York: Oxford University Press, 1980); Winifred Hepperle and Laura Crites, eds., *Women in the Courts* (Williamsburg, Virginia: National Center for State Courts, 1978); "Women and the Criminal Law," *American Criminal Law Review 11* (Winter 1973); "Women, Crime, and Criminology" *Issues in Criminology 8* (Fall 1973); "Criminal Justice to Women: Not Fair!" *Crime and Delinquency 23,* 2 (April 1977); and "Articles on Women," *Crime and Social Justice 12* (Winter 1979).

3. United States Department of Justice, *1960 Uniform Crime Reports of the United States* (Washington, D.C.: U.S. Government Printing Office), pp. 94 and 100.

4. Cesare Lombroso, *The Female Offender* (New York: Appleton and Company, 1900).

5. See Klein, "The Etiology of Female Crime," for a review of these works.

6. Joseph Weis, "Liberation and Crime: The Invention of the New Female Criminal," *Crime and Social Justice 6* (Fall–Winter 1976): 17.

7. Adler, *Sisters in Crime;* Deming, *Women: The New Criminals;* and Simon, *Women and Crime.*

8. Crites, *The Female Offender,* ch. 2; Dorie Klein and June Kress, "Any Woman's Blues: A Critical Overview of Women, Crime, and the Criminal Justice System," *Crime and Social Justice 5* (Spring–Summer 1976); Laurel Rans, "Woman's Crime: Much Ado About . . . ?" *Federal Probation 42* (March 1978); Darrell Steffensmeier, "Sex Differences in Patterns of Adult Crime, 1965–77: A Review and Assessment," *Social Forces 58,* 4 (June 1980); and Weis, "Liberation and Crime."

9. Adler, *Sisters in Crime,* pp. 166–7. Simon, *Women and Crime,* agrees with Adler that the success of the women's movement will bring about increases in women's crime (especially white-collar crime), but she points out that the women's movement had not brought major economic improvements for women, at least as of 1970. See ch. 3.

10. Crites, *The Female Offender,* p. 38 for example.

11. Rans, "Women's Crime," pp. 47-9.

12. U.S. Bureau of the Census, *Statistical Abstract of the United States: 1979,* 100th ed. (Washington, D.C.: U.S. Government Printing Office, 1979), p. 394.

13. Ibid., p. 45.

14. Ibid., p. 41.

15. Ibid., p. 407.

16. Ibid.

17. Ibid., p. 422.

18. Ibid., p. 424. The median weekly earnings of full-time wage and salary workers in 1970 was $151 for males and $94 for females. In 1979 the earnings were $298 for males and $186 for females.

19. Ibid., p. 465. During the same period male heads of families below the poverty line dropped from 73.7 percent to 48 percent.

20. Ibid., p. 418.

21. Rans, "Women's Crime," p. 45-6.

22. U.S. Department of Justice, *Uniform Crime Reports* 1960-78.

23. Ibid., for 1975, p. 6.

24. Steffensmeier, "Sex Differences in Patterns of Adult Crime," p. 1094.

25. Ibid.

26. Adler, *Sisters in Crime,* pp. 251-2.

27. Simon, *Women and Crime,* p. 2.

28. Supra, pp. 207, 208 on women's economic condition.

29. Edwin Sutherland, "White Collar Criminality," *American Sociological Review* 5, 1 (1940): 1-12; or see Sutherland and Donald Cressey, *Criminology, 10th Ed.* (Philadelphia: J. B. Lippincott Company, 1978), p. 44.

30. Steffensmeier, "Sex Differences in Patterns of Adult Crime," p. 1094.

31. State of California Department of Justice, *Crime and Delinquency in California, 1979* (Sacramento, California: Bureau of Criminal Statistics), pp. 116, 119.

32. Steffensmeier, "Sex Differences in Patterns of Adult Crime," p. 1095.

33. In a recent study of Washington, D.C. and Detroit, Freda Solomon discussed the impact that the organization of the prosecutorial process has on the objectivity of defendant treatment. Solomon finds that a formal prosecutorial process with highly structured discretion yields a more objective (less disparate as to sex) treatment than does an informal prosecutorial process. A comparable study is not presently available for California. See Freda Solomon, "Gender Justice: Differential Treatment of Male and Female Felony Defendants." Unpublished paper presented to the Annual Meeting of the Western Political Science Association, Denver, Colorado, March 1981.

34. An earlier study by the author offers a lengthy discussion of this issue and of the findings of other researchers concerned with the same topic. See Elizabeth Moulds, "Chivalry and Paternalism: Disparities of Treatment in the Criminal Justice System," *Western Political Quarterly 31,* 3 (September 1978): 420-9.

35. Stuart Nagel, *The Legal Process from a Behavioral Pespective* (Homewood, Ill.: Dorsey Press, 1969), ch. 8.

36. Data source fo the federal data: Stuart Nagel, *Federal Court Cases,* ICPR 7245. Inter-University Consortium for Political Research, P.O. Box 1248, Ann Arbor, Michigan, 48106; Data source for the sample state data, American Bar Foundation, *State Criminal Court Cases,* Principal Investigators: Lee Silverstein and Stuart Nagel, ICPR 7272. Inter-University Consortium for Political Research.

37. California Senate Bill 42/Chapter 1139, 1975, Penal Code Section 1170.1.

38. See, for example, Henry A. Bullock, "Significance of the Racial Factor in the Length of Prison Sentences," *Journal of Criminal Law, Criminology, and Police*

Science 52 (November-December 1961): 411-17; Green, *Judicial Attitudes,* pp. 56-62 and Tables 27-35; and Nagel, *The Legal Process,* pp. 93-5 and Tables 8-1 through 8-8.

39. Indigence and sentencing is discussed by Nagel, *The Legal Process,* pp. 87-9 and Tables 8-1 through 8-8. See also Dallin H. Oaks and Warren Lehman, *A Criminal Justice System and the Indigent* (Chicago: University of Chicago Press, 1968); and American Bar Foundation, *Defense of the Poor in Criminal Cases in American State Courts: A Field Study and Report* [by] Lee Silverstein [project director]. Chicago, 1965 (Vol. 1).

40. Moulds, "Chivalry and Paternalism," pp. 428-9 and Tables 5, 6, and 7.

41. Ibid., pp. 425-6 and Table 5.

42. Walter Reckless and Barbara Kay, *The Female Offender: Report to the U.S. President's Commission on Law Enforcement and the Administration of Justice* (Washington, D.C.: U.S. Government Printing Office, 1967), p. 16, for example.

43. "Paternalism," in *International Encyclopedia of the Social Sciences,* II ed. David L. Sills (New York: Macmillan, 1968), p. 472.

44. See Leo Kanowitz, *Women and the Law: The Unfinished Revolution* (Albuquerque: University of New Mexico Press, 1969), for a discussion of women's legal status historically in the United States.

45. See, for example, Kirsten Amundsen, *A New Look at the Silenced Majority: Women and American Democracy* (Englewood Cliffs: Prentice-Hall, 1977); Karen DeCrow, *Sexist Justice: How Legal Sexism Affects You* (New York: Vintage Books, 1974); Eleanor Flexner, *The Women's Rights Movement in the United States* (New York: Atheneum, 1972); Kanowitz, *Women and the Law;* and William L. O'Neill, *Everyone Was Brave: A History of Feminism in America* (Chicago: Quadrangle Books, 1971).

46. *Bradwell* v. *The State,* 83 U.S. 130 (December 1872) at 141.

47. For a discussion of these indeterminate sentencing statutes, see Carolyn E. Temin, "Discriminatory Sentencing for Women Offenders: The Argument for ERA in a Nutshell," *American Criminal Law Review 11* (Winter 1973): 355-72.

48. Temin points out that as of 1973 these differential statutes continued to exist in Iowa, Kansas, Maine, Maryland, Massachusetts, New Jersey, and Pennsylvania.

49. *State* v. *Costello,* 282 A. 2nd 748 (1971).

50. *U.S. ex rel. Robinson* v. *York,* 281 F. Supp. at 14 (D.C. Conn. 1968) quoting from respondant's brief at 18. Also see Kanowitz, *Women and The Law,* p. 170, for a discussion of the state's logic in this case.

51. Meda Chesney-Lind, "Judicial Enforcement of the Female Sex Role: The Family Court and the Female Delinquent," *Issues in Criminology 8* (Fall 1973): 51-70; Allan Conway and Carol Bogdan, "Sexual Delinquency—The Persistence of a Double Standard," *Crime and Delinquency 23,* 2 (April 1977): 131-5; Peter C. Kratcoski, "Differential Treatment of Boys and Girls by the Justice System," *Child Welfare 53* (1974): 16-22; Reckless and Kay, *The Female Offender,* pp. 8-12; and Rosemary Sarri, "Juvenile Law: How it Penalizes Females," in Crites, *The Female Offender,* chap. 4.

52. Anthony Platt, *The Child Savers: The Invention of Delinquency* (Chicago, University of Chicago Press, 1969). This work offers an excellent history of the handling of delinquent youth in America.

53. Chesney-Lind, "Judicial Enforcement," p. 54.

54. Ibid., p. 56.

55. Ibid., p. 60; and Kratcoski, "Differential Treatment," pp. 18-20.

56. State of California Department of Justice, *Crime in California, 1957-1960* (Sacramento, California: Bureau of Criminal Statistics), p. 143.

57. Linda Singer, "Women and the Correctional Process," *The American Criminal Law Review 11* (Winter 1973): 298.

58. Female Offender Resource Center, *Little Sisters and the Law,* 1977.

59. Law Enforcement Assistance Administration, U.S. Department of Justice, *Children in Custody: A Report on the Juvenile Detention Facility Census 1971* (Washington, D.C.: U.S. Government Printing Office, 1973), p. 9.

60. Senator Birch Bayh, "Forward," in *Status Offenders and the Juvenile Justice System: An Anthology,* ed. Richard Allison (Hackensack, N.J.: National Council on Crime and Delinquency, 1978), p. x.

61. Conway and Bogdan, "Sexual Delinquency," p. 133.

62. Ibid., pp. 134–5 and Table 2.

63. Chesney-Lind, "Judicial Enforcement," p. 57 and Table 4.

64. Kratcoski, "Differential Treatment," p. 20.

65. Public Law 93-415.

66. "Senate Hearings Show Problems and Progress in Status Offender Deinstitutionalization." *Criminal Justice Newsletter 8,* 20 (October 10, 1977): 1–3.

67. California Assembly Bill 3121/Chapter 1071, approved September 20, 1976.

68. State of California Department of Justice, *Crime and Delinquency in California,* 1973, p. 136.

69. State of California Department of Justice, *California Criminal Justice Profile, 1979* (Sacramento, California: Bureau of Criminal Statistics) p. 49. The N was 13,888.

70. U.S. Department of Justice, *Uniform Crime Reports, 1979,* p. 199.

71. *Ferguson* v. *Superior Court,* 26 Cal. App. 554, 558, 147 Pac. 603, 605 (1915), as cited by Kanowitz, *Women and The Law,* p. 16.

72. Marilyn Haft, "Hustling for Rights," in Crites, *The Female Offender,* p. 214.

73. *Wilson* v. *State,* 278 N.E. 2d 569 (Ind. 1972) at 571, as cited by Charles Rosenbleet and Barbara Pariente, "The Prostitution of the Criminal Law," *The American Criminal Law Review 11* (Winter 1973): 385.

74. Robert Sherwin and Charles Winick, "Debate: Should Prostitution be Legalized?" *Sexual Behavior 2,* 1 (January 1972): 71.

75. U.S. Department of Justice, *Uniform Crime Reports, 1960, 1970,* and *1979,* pp. 94 and 100, 129, and 199 respectively.

76. Pamela Roby, "Politics and Criminal Law: Revision of the New York State Penal Law on Prostitution," *Social Problems* 17, 1 (Summer 1969): 97–8.

77. Gloria Megino, *Prostitution and California Law* (Sacramento, California: California Senate Committee on Judiciary, 1977), p. 50, reporting the results of the Women's Jail Study Group of the Citizens for Justice Committee, San Francisco.

78. Statement by Judge Ollie Marie-Victoire at 1980 Western Political Science Association Meetings (San Francisco: March 1980), Panel "Women at the Top: Political Power in the 1980's."

79. One such San Francisco officer stood on street corners wired for sound for two-to five-hour periods. During the three months she remained on duty, she recorded 150 solicitations and made 100 arrests (this contrasted with the experience of a San Francisco male undercover decoy who was able to make only two to three arrests of women per week—arresting 100 women in two and a half years of work as a decoy). Testimony of Officer Sandra Daly, Record at 112, *People* v. *Richardson,* no. M48961 (S.F. Mun. Ct. Oct. 4, 1975) as reported by M. Anne Jennings, "The Victim as Criminal: A Consideration of California's Prostitution Law," *California Law Review 64,* 5 (September 1976): 1280–1.

80. *People* v. *Superior Court* (Hartway) (1976) 128 California Reporter 519. This decision was vacated when the supreme court of California granted a hearing in the matter; see note 81 below.

81. *People* v. *Superior Court of Alameda County,* Cynthia Hartway et al., Real Parties in Interest (1977) 19 Cal. 3d 338, 349, 138 Cal. Rptr. 66, 71. In dissent Justice Tobriner declared: "Although the majority discern no discriminatory intent in the

action of the Oakland police, I agree with the American Bar Association's section of Individual Rights and Responsibilities which has characterized such police practices as 'one of the most direct forms of discrimination against women in this country today. In accordance with society's double standard of sexual morality, the woman who sells her body is punished criminally and stigmatized while her male customer . . . is left unscathed.' " Ibid., at 357.

Part VI
Foreign and Military Policy: New Policy Arenas

Introduction

The primary programmatic emphasis of the women's movement in the United States was, until the mid-1970s, domestic policy. While most women's groups organized in the 1960s included in their statements of purpose a commitment to work for peace and proclaimed their sisterhood with women around the world, foreign and military policy generally took a back seat to domestic issues.

Yet, American women have historically had a long involvement with issues of war and peace. This involvement reflects two different strains among women: pacifism and service to their country. Organized female opposition to war was first portrayed in ancient times in the *Lysistrata* of Aristophanes, in which Athenian women withheld themselves sexually from their men to force an end to the fighting between Athens and Sparta. Organized female opposition to war in the United States first appeared in World War I when suffragists from the National Woman's Party demonstrated against the war, proclaiming that democracy should be established at home before America set out "to make the world safe for democracy." Jeannette Rankin, the first female member of Congress, cast the only vote against entry into World War I. The pacifist strain among American women has been well documented in public opinion polls which show women consistently taking more pacifist positions than men. One long-established women's organization, the Women's International League for Peace and Freedom, has a distinguished history of working for peace, including spearheading women's opposition to the Vietnam War.

Contrasting with the pacifist strain is the record of women's service to their country in times of war. From the American Revolution to the present, women have served as noncombatant members of the military, as workers in defense industries, as volunteer medical workers, and even, in very rare instances, as soldiers. In World War II, the movement of women workers into industry to replace male workers who were drafted has been identified as one of the catalysts for the dramatic expansion of women in the work force in the postwar period.

Two developments in the 1970s brought the women's movement around to a direct concern with foreign and military policy. First, in the aftermath of the Vietnam War the military draft was discontinued in favor of an all-volunteer army. The inability of the U.S. military to recruit sufficient numbers of qualified male volunteers resulted in a policy decision to admit more women to military service. The increasing number of women in the military has provoked debate both within the women's movement and in society generally on issues of equal treatment of women in the armed services and the use of women in combat.

A second important event in the early 1970s was the coming together of American feminists around the United Nations Decade for Women. While a few activists had in the past established ties with women in other countries over suffrage, human rights, health, and educational issues, the preparations for the first U.S. Conference for Women in Mexico City in 1975 attracted large numbers of women to international concerns for the first time, raising their consciousness of the plight of women in other countries. The recognition of the oppression of women around the globe led to the coining of the phrase "the fourth world" referring to the struggle of women for survival everywhere, in developed, as well as, Third World countries. Concern for the effect of American foreign policy on women in developing countries led to the establishment in 1974 of the Women in Development Office in the U.S. Agency for International Development (AID).

Despite the growing interest of the women's movement in foreign and military policy, it will not be easy for feminists to influence thinking on these issues. Chapter 13, by Holsti and Rosenau, on the foreign policy beliefs of women leaders reveals that few sex differences exist between male and female leaders except on the issue of intervening in the affairs of other countries. It follows that if the women's movement wants to influence foreign policy, it would be well advised to focus on changing the thinking of men *and women* in leadership positions. More specifically, it should seek to counter the occupational socialization of women in business and the military by promoting detente and humanitarianism in international affairs. Such efforts will not, of course, be easily realized, but the women's movement does have some fertile ground in which to work: the greater aversion of women leaders to interventionism could serve as the basis for taking less aggressive stances in Cold War situations. While the women's movement is unlikely to want to restrict its consciousness-raising efforts to women leaders only, the findings in Chapter 13 suggest that women leaders' isolationism may be a common ground on which to begin evolving foreign policy positions more in line with the movement's concerns.

The last two chapters in this section illustrate the difficulty of effecting policy change for women in male-dominated bureaucracies. While the Women in Development Office in AID was established with relative ease, its impact on development policy has been severely restricted by ideological opposition to its goals, severely limited resources, and its marginal position in the agency's power structure. Despite attempts by Women in Development personnel to mobilize a constituency both inside and outside the agency, the effectiveness of the office has been hampered by agency attitudes that women's concerns are either irrelevant or intended to "politicize" the development field. As Staudt shows in Chapter 14, bureaucratic resistance to women within AID translates into a failure to expand women's options around the world.

What is the proper place for women in the military? This question has given rise to conflicting views among military and nonmilitary policy makers, among the population generally, and even among feminists. As Stiehm shows in her analysis in Chapter 15, the arguments against using women in combat have many different attudinal components—chivalry and fear of competition among men, and opposition to war among feminists. Whatever the source of these attitudes, they are inextricably bound up with attitudes toward sex roles and role change. While the implications of excluding women from combat are just beginning to be explored, it seems reasonable to link universal patterns of female exclusion from combat roles to the subordinate position of women around the world. In the United States, the increasing use of women in the military and the issues of equal treatment raised by constitutional challenges to draft registration and by the ERA promise to make women in combat one of the thorniest policy questions of the 1980s.

Chapter 13

The Foreign Policy Beliefs of Women in Leadership Positions*

Ole R. Holsti

James N. Rosenau

Few predictions about social change seem as safe as the proposition that women will play an increasingly important role in leadership positions. However one may judge the pace of change in this respect, there can be little disagreement about the trend.[1] If that premise is valid, how will this development affect politics? Will it bring a higher standard of probity to the political process? A more humane set of concerns into the establishment of political agendas? In the realm of external affairs, will it give rise to more serious concern and a higher priority for undertakings that often fall outside the purview of those espousing or practicing *realpolitik* diplomacy? These questions imply that women may bring a set of beliefs or world views to the political process that differ systematically from those of their male counterparts.

For at least two reasons those seeking answers or clues to these interesting questions will not be wholly satisfied with the existing findings. First, although literature on women in politics is not insubstantial, and it has grown dramatically in recent years, much of it focuses on several areas, including background attributes and political participation, voting behavior, and the like.[2] Other

*An earlier version of this article was published in the *Journal of Politics, 43* (May 1981): 326–47. We are grateful to the editors of the *Journal* for permission to reprint the article. For support of this research we are indebted to the Research Council and the Computation Center, Duke University, and the Institute for Transnational Studies, University of Southern California. Professor Jean O'Barr, Duke University, provided exceptionally helpful comments and suggestions on an earlier draft of this paper, as did four anonymous reviewers for the *Journal of Politics*.

questions, including foreign policy beliefs of women in leadership positions, have received much less attention.[3] For example, two recent surveys of foreign policy views undertaken by the Chicago Council on Foreign Relations included both leaders and members of the public at large. Summaries of the findings do not even report the results for men and women separately, much less analyze the similarities and/or differences between them.[4]

Second, results of the few existing studies have sometimes yielded quite contradictory conclusions, depending upon the groups under scrutiny. For example, Almond's study of *The American People and Foreign Study* found that "more women than men seem to be ignorant of or apathetic to foreign policy issues," but this conclusion received no support in a study of women at the leadership level.[5]

This chapter explores two different lines of reasoning concerning the foreign policy beliefs of American women in leadership positions. These can be stated in the form of competing hypotheses.

Hypothesis I: *The foreign policy beliefs of women in leadership positions differ significantly from those of their male counterparts.*

More specifically, women will tend to have a more benign and optimistic view of the international system, to give priority to social-economic-humanitarian issues rather than to political-strategic concerns, and to be less inclined toward the use of military capabilities and force as a means of dealing with global issues.

This hypothesis conforms to a long tradition, traceable to as far back as *Lysistrata* and earlier, which views women as the less belligerent half of the species. It also finds some support in more recent studies. For example, a summary of polls on the war in Vietnam found that women consistently provided less support for the American war effort, and they were stronger advocates of withdrawal from Southeast Asia.[6] Another review of Gallup and Harris polls revealed that these results were not confined to the Vietnam issues; women were generally found to be less likely to seek military solutions to international problems.[7]

Although such findings appear to provide substantial evidence in support of Hypothesis I, it is important to recall that they are based on sample surveys of the entire public, whereas our focus is upon persons in positions of leadership. The premise underlying Hypothesis I is that sex-role experiences constitute such a potent variable that their effects persist throughout the population, including those in positions of leadership in various institutions. That is, sex-role factors outweigh those linked to occupation and other roles as determinants of foreign policy beliefs and attitudes.

Hypothesis II: *The foreign policy beliefs of women in leadership positions do*

> *not differ significantly from those held by men in comparable roles.*

The second hypothesis is also supported by some previous research although, as indicated earlier, we have relatively few studies drawing upon systematic evidence. An exception is a study of leaders attending a 1958 conference on national security.[8] It revealed that any differences between men and women disappeared after controlling for occupation and party preference. This hypothesis assumes that whatever the differences between women and men among the entire population, their views converge at the leadership level. Stated differently, according to this view leaders have more in common with each other than they have with members of their own gender in the public at large.

DATA AND METHODS

The data used to explore these hypotheses are derived from a mail survey of American leaders, within and outside government, on a wide range of foreign policy issues. Parts of the questionnaire focus upon three clusters of items relating to this nation's experience in Vietnam. In addition to asking respondents to assess the "lessons of Vietnam" and the sources and consequences of American failure in that conflict, we probed for their general orientations toward foreign policy—for example, the appropriate goals of American external relations—and a few domestic issues, as well as data about their personal backgrounds. To permit some cross-survey comparisions we included several foreign policy questions that have also been used in other recent surveys of American leaders: the Harris/Chicago Council on Foreign Relations study, the Harvard-*Washington Post* survey, the Russett-Hanson study of business executives and military officers, and the Barton study of 500 American leaders of major interest groups.[9]

We had initially hoped to construct our sample from a single source that encompasses persons who presently occupy a variety of top leadership roles as well as those in subleadership positions who would have a high probability of occupying the top roles in the years ahead. Unfortunately, no single source met all of our requirements. Thus, the sample was constructed in ways that represented several types of compromises between the ideal and reality.

A random drawing of nearly two thousand persons listed in the 1975–76 edition of *Who's Who in America* provided one part of the sample. *Who's Who* is a useful source because it includes biographical material about each person, as well as home addresses for virtually all biographees. The probabilities of a completed questionnaire being returned were assumed to be greater if it were received at home rather than at an office. If received at home it was also less likely to be passed on to a subordinate or colleague for completion. *Who's Who in America* is not without some significant drawbacks, however. Some groups are very heavily represented, especially business executives and educators. Conversely, military officers, labor leaders, the clergy, media persons, and several other groups of interest are underrepresented. The limited representation of women in *Who's Who* made it especially inadequate for present purposes.

The second part of our sample was constructed on the basis of quotas for leaders from important occupational groups that are underrepresented in *Who's Who:* foreign service officers, labor leaders, politicians, clergy, foreign affairs experts outside government, media leaders, and senior military officers serving at the Pentagon as well as junior officers at one of the service schools. As a partial remedy for the rather meagre representation of women in several sources—98.4 percent of the names drawn from *Who's Who in America* were men—we included *Who's Who in American Women* among the several supplementary directories used to construct the sample. As a result, of the 4,290 persons receiving the questionnaire, 414 were women.[10]

The first mailing in February 1976 yielded 1,899 completed questionnaires. In order to preserve their anonymity, respondents were asked to return the questionnaire to one address (a stamped, addressed envelope was provided for this purpose), and a postal card (also provided) acknowledging its completion to another. Names of those returning the postal cards were removed from the list for a follow-up mailing two months later. The second mailing brought in another 383 completed questionnaires. Limited research funds precluded a third mailing to the remaining nonrespondents.

Over 53 percent, or 2,282 of the 4,290 persons who received it, completed and returned the questionnaire. Return rates were 54.1 percent for women and 53.1 percent for men.[11] Given the length of the questionnaire and the atmosphere of distrust toward social science surveys prevalent in recent years, this return rate seems satisfactory, if not ideal, and it compares favorably with that achieved by similar studies. Analyses of the returned questionnaires yielded some basis for confidence that the respondents constituted a reasonably representative sample of those to whom the survey was mailed. We compared responses to the two mailings, assuming that those who had to be prodded a second time sufficiently resembled those who did not respond at all. If the 383 second-mailing respondents differed significantly from their 1,899 counterparts in the first mailing, concern that the sample was biased would have been heightened. In fact, we found little difference in the responses of the two groups. For example, of the 41 items described in Tables 13.1-13.4 below, significant[12] response differences occurred only on a question concerning the civil war in Angola, an issue that was essentially resolved during the two-month period between the two mailings.

Table 13.1. "Cold War Axioms": Comparing the Responses of 224 Female and 2,009 Male American Leaders (mean scores[a]).

		Women	Men
A.	There is considerable validity to the "domino theory" that when one nation falls to communism, others nearby will soon follow a similar path.	0.16	0.25
B.	A nation will pay a heavy price if it honors its alliance commitments only selectively.	0.42	0.49
C.	Any communist victory is a defeat for America's national interest.	−0.13	−0.13
D.	The major assumptions of détente have been proven false by the events in Vietnam.	−0.05	−0.14
E.	Communist nations have been encouraged to seek triumphs elsewhere as a result of Vietnam.	0.13[b]	0.34[b]
F.	The Soviet Union is generally expansionist rather than defensive in its foreign policy goals.	0.46[b]	0.59[b]
G.	China is generally expansionist rather than defensive in its foreign policy goals.	−0.13	−0.25
H.	Détente permits the USSR to pursue policies that promote rather than restrain conflict.	0.06	0.16
I.	It is not in our interest to have better relations with the Soviet Union because we are getting less than we are giving to them.	−0.36	−0.32
J.	Containing communism [as a foreign policy goal for the United States]*	0.58	0.64
K.	The U.S. should take all steps including the use of force to prevent the spread of communism.	−0.41	−0.28
L.	The U.S. should never try to get by with half measures; we should apply necessary power if we have it.	−0.09[b]	−0.10[b]
M.	Rather than simply countering our opponent's thrusts, it is necessary to strike at the heart of the opponent's power.	−0.08	0.01
N.	When force is used, military rather than political goals should determine its application.	−0.26	−0.20
O.	If foreign interventions are undertaken, the necessary force should be applied in a short period of time rather than through a policy of graduated escalation.	0.48	0.56
P.	There is nothing wrong with using the CIA to try to undermine hostile governments.	−0.37[b]	0.02[b]
Q.	The U.S. fought with a "no win" approach [as a cause of failure in Vietnam].*	0.61	0.66
R.	The use of American air power was restricted [as a cause of failure in Vietnam].*	0.55	0.56

Table 13.1.   (continued)

		Women	Men
S.	Insufficient attention was paid to advice from the military [as a cause of failure in Vietnam].*	0.45	0.46
T.	The U.S. should undertake military intervention in the Middle East in case of another oil embargo.	− 0.52	− 0.48

ᵃResponses scored on a scale of 1.00 (agree strongly) to − 1.00 (disagree strongly). For items marked with an asterisk(*), responses scored on a scale of 1.00 (very important) to 0.00 (not at all important).

ᵇDifferences significant at the .001 level, whether based on parametric (analysis of variance) or nonparametric (*chi*-square) statistics.

Table 13.2. "Post-Cold War Axioms" (Internationalist): Comparing the Responses of 224 Female and 2,009 Male American Leaders (mean scores[a]).

		Women	Men
A.	American foreign policy should be based on the premise that the communist "bloc" is irreparably fragmented.	− 0.30	− 0.25
B.	Revolutionary forces in "Third-World" countries are usually nationalistic rather than controlled by the USSR or China.	0.16	0.19
C.	It is vital to enlist the cooperation of the United Nations in settling international disputes.	0.40[b]	0.18[b]
D.	Strengthening the United Nations [as a foreign policy goal for the United States]*	0.58[b]	0.46[b]
E.	Worldwide arms control [as a foreign policy goal for the United States]*	0.88	0.81
F.	Fostering international cooperation to solve common problems, such as food, inflation, and energy [as a foreign policy goal for the United States]*	0.88	0.84
G.	Helping to improve the standard of living in less developed countries [as a foreign policy goal for the United States]*	0.66	0.65
H.	Combatting world hunger [as a foreign policy goal for the United States]*	0.75	0.72
I.	Helping solve world inflation [as a foreign policy goal for the United States]*	0.76	0.72
J.	The U.S. should give economic aid to poorer countries even if it means higher prices at home.	− 0.10	− 0.04

[a]Responses scored on a scale of 1.00 (agree strongly) to − 1.00 (disagree strongly). For items marked with an asterisk(*), responses scored on a scale of 1.00 (very important) to 0.00 (not at all important).

[b]Differences significant at the .001 level, whether based on parametric (analysis of variance) or nonparametric (*chi*-square) statistics.

Table 13.3. "Post-Cold War Axioms" (Isolationist): Comparing the Responses of 224 Female and 2,009 Male American Leaders (mean scores[a]).

		Women	Men
A.	America's conception of its leadership role in the world must be scaled down.	0.20[b]	0.02[b]
B.	We shouldn't think so much in international terms but concentrate more on our own national problems.	−0.06[b]	−0.26[b]
C.	The best way to encourage democratic development in the "Third World" is for the U.S. to solve its own problems.	0.40	0.26
D.	Military aid programs will eventually draw the United States into unnecessary wars.	0.20[b]	−0.15[b]
E.	Stationing American troops in other countries encourages them to let us do their fighting for those countries.	0.28	0.14
F.	The U.S. should avoid any involvement in the Angolan civil war.	0.51[b]	0.22[b]
G.	It was a serious mistake to agree to locate American technicians in the Sinai.	−0.26[b]	−0.49[b]
H.	The conduct of American foreign affairs relies excessively on military advice.	0.22[b]	−0.01[b]
I.	Americans have relied too much on presidents to define the national interest.	0.41[b]	0.20[b]
J.	The foundations of the American economy were seriously damaged by our involvement in Vietnam.	0.29	0.22
K.	The real long-term threats to national security—energy shortages, the environment, etc.—have been neglected as a result of our preoccupation with Vietnam.	0.55[b]	0.32[b]

[a]Responses scored on a scale of 1.00 (agree strongly) to −1.00 (disagree strongly).

[b]Differences significant at the .001 level, whether based on parametric (analysis of variance) or nonparametric (*chi*-square) statistics.

Table 13.4 Gender, Occupation, and Foreign Policy Beliefs: A Comparison Based on the Responses of 2,282 American Leaders, Classified According to Sex and Occupation.

		Total Number of Items	Number of Items with Significant Differences (.001 level) Between:[a]	
			Sex	Occupation
"Cold War Axioms"	(Table 13.1)	20	4[b]	20
"Post–Cold War (Internationalist) Axioms"	(Table 13.2)	10	3[c]	10
"Post–Cold War (Isolationist) Axioms"	(Table 13.3)	11	5[d]	10
	TOTALS	41	12	40

[a]Results based on two-way analysis of variance. Interaction effects between sex and occupation are significant for none of the 41 items.

[b]Items D, G, P, and S, Table 13.1.

[c]Items C, D, and J, Table 13.2.

[d]Items B, D, F, G, and I, Table 13.3.

FINDINGS

Because the two gender-based subsamples are not identical, it may be useful to describe some of the more notable similarities and differences between the 224 female and 2,009 male leaders.[13]

- A substantial number of the women are clustered in two occupations (educators [26.8 percent] and media leaders [14.7 percent]), whose members are most likely to take a "dovish" position on international issues, whereas a high proportion of the male leaders are to be found in the more "hawkish" occupations (military officers [24.3 percent] and business executives [13.4 percent]).[14]
- The leaders in our sample are highly educated. Among both women (53.1 percent) and men (60.9 percent) the modal respondent holds some type of postgraduate degree, and overall educational differences are only moderate.
- The female respondents are, on balance, younger than their male counterparts. One-third of the women and one-fifth of the men were born since 1940.
- Although both groups of respondents include more Democrats than Republicans, the margin favoring the former among women is more than two-to-one, whereas among men it is about four-to-three.
- The female respondents are more liberal than the males; one-half of the former describe themselves as being on the "liberal" end of the scale, compared to only one-third of the latter who do so.
- Not surprisingly, the most striking difference between men (73.1 percent) and women (10.7 percent) concerns military service.
- The two groups of leaders expressed equal interest in politics, but men were somewhat more interested than women in those at the international level, whereas this situation was reversed with respect to local politics.[15]
- Male respondents engaged more frequently in consulting and travel, but there were no differences between the sexes in other types of political activity: writing or talking to a congressman, senator or local official; making speeches at public meetings; appearing on radio or television; and contributing articles to a newspaper or magazine.[16]

Because the two subsamples differ in several important respects, it will be necessary not only to compare the foreign policy beliefs of men and women directly (as will be done in the next three sections), but also to undertake multivariate analyses that control for some of the more salient intervening variables, such as occupation.

Cold War Internationalist Axioms

An earlier analysis revealed the existence of three clusters of ideas about international affairs that constitute quite well-defined belief systems.[17] These clusters of beliefs encompass not only reactions to American participation in the Vietnam War, but also foreign policy issues that are quite unrelated to Vietnam—for example, on the nature and desirability of détente—as well as preferences about the goals that should guide American diplomacy in the future. More specifically, they differ sharply with respect to the nature of the international system, the character and goals of this nation's adversaries, the role of the Third World, the scope and nature of American national interests, and the means by which foreign policy goals can most effectively be pursued.

The "Cold-War internationalist" axioms depict a conflictual world in which the primary cleavages continue to be those dividing the East and the West, and in which most, if not all, of the salient issues and conflicts are closely linked to each other and to that faultline. As a result, disturbances in one area will reverberate throughout the system. Within that international system the United States faces an ambitious, often aggressive, but always patient coalition of adversaries led by Moscow. The Third World plays a crucial role as both the battleground and the prize in the conflict between contending blocs. The basic problem for the United States therefore is to maintain the territorial and political integrity of noncommunist parts of the world in the face of a highly-armed, expansionist power that harbors an unchanging commitment to achieving a position of global hegemony. The United States thus must accept the responsibilities and burdens of its leadership position within the noncommunist sector, and at a minimum it must restore a balance of power necessary, if not sufficient, to convince the Soviet leadership that aggrandizement will not pay.

Table 13.1 reports mean scores on the "Cold War axioms" for the 224 women and 2,009 men who returned our questionnaire. The most striking finding is that there are significant differences between the male and female leaders on only 4 of the 20 items. Women tend to be somewhat less concerned about the international goals of communist nations in general (1:E) and the USSR in particular (1:F), but they are also less inclined to regard Chinese foreign policy as merely defensive (1:G).[18] Most strikingly, women are more opposed than men to using the CIA to undermine hostile governments (1:P).

But these exceptions notwithstanding, the more impressive finding is that on 16 of the 20 items differences between women and men are negligible, whether the issue is the containment of communism (1:J, 1:K), the validity of the "domino theory" (1:A), or the value of better Soviet-American relations (1:H, 1:I). Even on eight of nine questions relating to the use of force in foreign policy (1:K, 1:M, 1:N, 1:O, 1:Q through 1:T; the exception is 1:L), women expressed views that differed little from those of their male counterparts.

Thus, these data on the "Cold War axioms" provide only the most modest sustenance for the theory—or is it more accurately labeled a stereotype?—that "dovishness" is linked to female roles, whereas "hawkishness" is linked to those of males. Among our respondents the similarities between men and women clearly outweigh the differences.

Post–Cold War Internationalist Axioms

The post–Cold War axioms portray contemporary international relations in ways that differ sharply from those described in Table 13-1. Within a loosely structured international system there exist complex competing interests that do not always find the Western democracies arrayed against the monolithic, Soviet-dominated communist bloc; the linkages between conflict issues are at best modest, with the consequence that their reverberations may be little more than local in scope; Third-World conflicts are more likely to reflect nationalist than communist motivations but, in any case, they rarely pose a serious threat to vital American interests; these interests are sufficiently varied and complex that they cannot adequately be met by employing such simple decision rules as "oppose communism"; and the means by which foreign policy goals can most effectively be pursued are not limited to, or even primarily, military ones.

Embedded within the post-Cold War axioms are two somewhat diverging themes. The internationalist version is informed by three closely related propositions. First, the international system offers a rich and varied menu of both threats and opportunities for creating a viable and just world order. Dangers arising from strategic/military issues remain real, but the roots of future international conflict are located not merely in military imbalances—real or perceived—but also in problems arising from poverty, inequitable distribution of resources, unfulfilled aspiration for self-determination, regional antagonisms, population pressures, technology that outpaces the political means for controlling its consequences, and the like. Second, the Soviet Union is a military superpower but in other ways it is a developing nation. Finally, an active but not overbearing American role in creating an equitable and stable world order is indispensable.

Evidence from several public opinion surveys suggests that women are more inclined than men to support the kinds of social-economic-humanitarian concerns that are included among the "post-Cold War Internationalist" axioms. The alternative line of reasoning, encompassed in Hypothesis II above, is that at the leadership level these differences will tend to disappear.

The evidence summarized in Table 13.2 reveals little support for the hypothesis of systematic differences between female and male leaders. Significant differences are, in fact, limited to two items concerning the United Nations (2:C, 2:D). In both cases, women attributed greater importance to that international organization. Notably absent was any compelling evidence of greater concern by women for such international undertakings as improving the standard of living among less-developed countries (2:G), combatting world hunger (2:H), coping with inflation (2:I), economic aid (2:J), and international cooperation on a broad range of nonsecurity issues (2:F). Moreover, women were *less* inclined than men (although not significantly so) to accept two central items in the post–Cold War Internationalist belief system: that present fissures among communist nations are irreparable (2:A), and that revolutionary movements in the Third World are nationalistic rather than controlled by Moscow or Peking (2:B).

These results, combined with those summarized in Table 13.1, indicate that at least on many of the issues that have dominated foreign policy discourse during the post–World II era, differences among men and women are substantially less impressive than are the similarities.

Post–Cold War Isolationist Axioms

The issues that constitute the isolationist version of the post–Cold War axioms focus less on the state of the international system and more on the appropriate role for the United States within that system. Isolationists recognize the existence of conflicts along both North-South and East-West axes, but they tend to dismiss as a dangerous delusion the belief, widely accepted during the decades following the end of World War II, that there is any compelling practical or ethical imperative for the United States to be centrally involved in the amelioration of all the world's ills; just as every international problem cannot claim American paternity, so it does not necessarily have a unique or effective American solution. Because this country's ability to contribute to the solution of many global issues is limited to the power of example, it behooves the United States to achieve a satisfactory resolution of such problems as decaying cities, racial conflict, inflation, unemployment, cultural decadence, illiteracy, environmental depradation, and the like, before turning its attention and energies to preaching at or materially helping others. Indeed, among some there has been a revival of a theme that has deep roots in American thinking about foreign affairs: an active foreign policy and domestic reforms—if not democratic institutions themselves—are mutually exclusive.[19]

Whereas data on neither of the clusters of axioms described in Tables 13.1 and 13.2 revealed consistent differences between men and women, a rather different pattern emerges from the figures in Table 13.3. On 8 of the 11 items women in the leadership sample responded in a significantly more isolationist manner. Moreover, in the three instances that differences fell short of statistical significance, they were nevertheless in the same direction—that is, women were inclined to favor a more restricted international role for the United States. Thus, it appears that evidence for Hypothesis I is largely limited to greater support for isolationism.

While there are no attitudinal or personality data in this study which might be used to explain this sex difference, it is nevertheless important to speculate on the underlying reasons for greater isolationism among women leaders.

What might account for a sex difference along this dimension when the responses of women and men leaders along the first two dimensions examined here are more similar than different?

Several possible explanations come to mind. First, one commonly held notion regarding personality differences between men and women is that the former are more aggressive and the latter more passive. This difference, whether based on biology or social learning, may account for women's greater reluctance to have the United States intervene in the affairs of other countries. If female passivity were the explanation, however, one would expect women to be significantly more "dovish" along other dimensions as well, which was not the case.

A more likely explanation is based on the finding in public opinion polls that women are more concerned with protection of the hearth than are men. This attitude is revealed in more pacifist foreign policy and military policy positions, in less tolerance for social deviance, and in voting for presidential candidates who are perceived as peace-oriented. Protection of the hearth and home is conservatism in the pure sense, namely, conserving what is. This conservative strain among women can perhaps explain the seeming inconsistency in this study of women leaders supporting a strong defense against known antagonists but also resisting unnecessary intervention in world affairs.

Finally, social learning may also account for sex differences on the isolationism dimension. Men are socialized to be world leaders. As men have a near monopoly on leadership positions in military and foreign policy making, this learning is reinforced by countless numbers of role models. Women are socialized to be civic leaders, community activists whose political concerns are with their immediate community rather than with international relations. Given this difference, it does not seem surprising that women would put a higher priority on attending to domestic problems than on engaging in international involvements. This commitment to domestic concerns, coupled with women's growing recognition of themselves as an oppressed group, might well lead women to place a higher value on eliminating oppression at home than on sustaining a role for the United States as intervenor in world affairs.

Gender and Occupation

Analyses to this point have uncovered some differences, and a greater number of similarities, between men and women in our sample of American leaders. It remains to be determined, however, whether these findings can withstand the introduction of intervening variables into the analysis. As indicated earlier, the two subsamples differ with respect to occupation and several other background factors, thus possibly confounding direct comparison between men and women. Moreover, there appears to be a built-in bias favoring Hypothesis I. The female leaders are younger, more Democratic, more liberal,[20] and they are less heavily concentrated in occupations—the military (4.9 percent versus 24.3 percent) and business (10.3 percent versus 13.4 percent)—that are associated with the "Cold War Internationalist" belief system.[21] As a consequence of these differences further analyses controlling for the possible effects of occupational role and other background characteristics should be undertaken.

Table 13.4 summarizes the results of two-way analyses of variance in which sex is paired with occupation. The results are consistent with the findings reported in Tables 13.1–13.3: differences between women and men in leadership positions are of rather modest proportions on the Cold War and internationalist Cold–War axioms, but they emerge a bit more strongly on the isolationist terms. These results confirm the conclusion that, although some gender-based differences survive even when occupation is controlled, the dominant lines of cleavage among this sample of respondents are those defined by occupation.[22]

It is appropriate to inquire, however, whether the results for these 41 items are representative of the main tendencies within the much larger set of items in the study. Table 13.5 summarizes the findings for 111 items (including those already described in Tables 13.1–13.4) concerning: the sources of failure in Vietnam (21 items), consequences of the war in Southeast Asia (13), the "lessons" of Vietnam (34), goals of American foreign policy (18), the appropriate international role for the United States (7), and appraisals of current foreign policy performance (18). The results are similar to those reported above. Two-way analyses of variance with sex and occupation as explanatory variables reveal significant effects of the latter for 103 of the 111 questionnaire items, compared to only 23 of 111 for the former. It should be reiterated, moreover, that even when gender differences yielded statistically significant results, the underlying scores did not uniformly fit the pattern of "hawkish" men versus "dovish" women.

A more detailed examination of eight key propositions that seem most faithfully to capture the different world views reveals more clearly the nature of cleavages among our respondents. The first six items in Table 13.6 depict a bipolar world in which the United States has primary responsibilities for coping with a variety of threats from implacable enemies. The remaining two propositions are usually included high on lists identifying the "lessons of Vietnam" espoused by critics of Cold War premises. When respondents are classified into 20 subgroups (2 sexes × 10 occupations),[23] evidence of differences between men and women is quite weak, save on the issue of cutting back on America's leadership role in the world. Contrary to Hypothesis I, subgroups with women are found with almost equal frequency among both the strongest and weakest supporters of the Cold War positions. But once more we find that, compared to men, women are more inclined to favor a more restricted international role for the United States.

Compared to this rather mild support for the hypothesis of significant differences between the sexes, a much more consistent pattern emerges from the data on the occupations of the strongest and weakest supporters of the Cold War axioms. Military officers and business executives, *including both men and women,* provide the strongest support for these views—together they account for 29 of the 48 entries in the left-hand column of Table 13.6—whereas media leaders and educators are almost equally pronounced in their skepticism, accounting for 26 of the 48 subgroups in the right-hand column. Stated somewhat differently, for cases in which cross-pressures may be at work—for example, male media leaders or educators, or female military officers and business executives—the impact of occupation clearly tends to override that of gender.

The impact of occupational socialization on women leaders in business and the military is particularly interesting. Given the findings at the mass level that women are less likely to seek and approve of military solutions for international problems, the support of female business and military leaders belies the arguments of some feminists that increasing the number of women in leadership positions would necessarily result in less aggressive postures on the international scene.

Table 13.5. Gender, Occupation, and Foreign Policy Beliefs:
A Comparison Based on the Responses of 2,282 American Leaders,
Classified According to Sex and Occupations

	Total Number of Items	Number of Items with Significant Differences (.001 level) Between:[a]	
		Sex	Occupation
Goals of American Foreign Policy	18	4	18
"Lessons" of Vietnam			
The international system	5	0	5
U.S. adversaries	3	1	3
Role of the United States	9	3	8
Making American foreign policy	9	1	8
Instruments of foreign policy	6	1	5
Uses of the past in foreign policy-making	2	0	2
Sources of Failure in Vietnam			
Actions of others	3	0	3
Vietnam was an unsound undertaking	2	0	2
Military factors	4	1	4
Domestic constraints on U.S. policy	5	0	5
Lack of knowledge and understanding	3	0	3
Others	4	0	4
Consequences of Vietnam War			
Impact on the international system	3	1	3

Table 13.5. Gender, Occupation, and Foreign Policy Beliefs (continued)

	Total Number of Items	Number of Items with Significant Differences (.001 level) Between:[a]	
		Sex	Occupation
U.S. adversaries encouraged	2	1	2
Constraints on future U.S. policy	2	0	1
Types of future U.S. undertakings	3	1	3
Damage to American society	3	0	2
The U.S. International Role	7	4	7
Rating U.S. Foreign Policy Performance	18	5	15
TOTALS	111	23	103

[a]Results based on two-way analysis of variance. Interaction effects between sex and occupation are significant for none of the 111 items.

Table 13.6. Strongest and Weakest Support for Selected Foreign Policy Propositions among 2,282 Respondents Classified into 20 Subgroups (2 sexes × 10 occupations).

	Subgroups with Strongest "Cold War" Positions:			Subgroups with Weakest "Cold War" Positions:		
	Occupation	Sex	Mean Score[a]	Occupation	Sex	Mean Score[a]
There is considerable validity in the "domino theory" that when one nation falls to communism, others nearby will follow a similar path.	Labor	Women	0.63	Media	Women	−0.08
	Military	Men	0.56	Media	Men	−0.05
	Pub. Off.	Women	0.53	Educators	Men	−0.01
	Business	Men	0.46	Educators	Women	−0.01
	Business	Women	0.43	Lawyers	Women	0.00
	Military	Women	0.41	Labor	Men	0.05
Any communist victory is a defeat for America's national interest.	Pub. Off.	Women	0.40	Media	Men	−0.42
	Military	Women	0.27	Media	Women	−0.41
	Business	Women	0.17	Educators	Men	−0.39
	Military	Men	0.13	Labor	Women	−0.38
	Business	Men	0.03	Educators	Women	−0.31
	Clergy	Men	0.02	Lawyers	Women	−0.29
The Soviet Union is generally expansionist rather than defensive in its foreign policy goals.	Military	Women	0.73	Educators	Women	0.34
	Military	Men	0.72	Media	Women	0.42
	Business	Men	0.67	Educators	Men	0.43
	Lawyers	Women	0.67	Labor	Women	0.50
	For. Svc.	Women	0.64	Business	Women	0.50

Table 13.6. (continued)

Statement						
Détente permits the USSR to pursue policies that pro- mote rather than restrain conflict.	Pub. Off.	Women	0.63	Labor	Men	0.56
	Military	Men	0.44	Labor	Women	−0.13
	Pub. Off.	Women	0.43	Lawyers	Women	−0.08
	Military	Women	0.41	Media	Women	−0.08
	Clergy	Men	0.29	For. Svc.	Men	−0.07
	Labor	Men	0.24	Educators	Men	−0.06
	Business	Men	0.23	Pub. Off.	Men	−0.04
The U.S. should take all steps including the use of force to prevent the spread of communism.	Military	Women	0.09	Labor	Women	−0.64
	Military	Men	0.09	Media	Men	−0.58
	Pub. Off.	Women	−0.10	Educators	Women	−0.53
	Business	Women	−0.18	Educators	Men	−0.52
	Business	Men	−0.20	Lawyers	Women	−0.46
	Clergy	Men	−0.21	For. Svc.	Women	−0.41
The U.S. should undertake military intervention in the Middle East in case of another oil embargo.	Military	Women	0.00	Labor	Women	−0.88
	Pub. Off.	Women	−0.06	Media	Women	−0.79
	Business	Women	−0.20	For. Svc.	Women	−0.75
	Business	Men	−0.28	Media	Men	−0.73
	Military	Men	−0.31	Educators	Men	−0.65
	Lawyers	Men	−0.40	Educators	Women	−0.60
Revolutionary forces in "third world" countries are usually nationalistic rather than controlled by the USSR or China.	Business	Women	−0.20	Lawyers	Women	0.67
	Pub. Off.	Women	−0.07	Media	Men	0.40
	Clergy	Men	−0.04	Pub. Off.	Men	0.40
	Military	Men	−0.01	Educators	Men	0.37
	Business	Men	−0.01	For. Svc.	Men	0.33
	Military	Women	0.05	Media	Women	0.30

Table 13.6. (continued)

	Subgroups with Strongest "Cold War" Positions:			Subgroups with Weakest "Cold War" Positions:		
	Occupation	Sex	Mean Score[a]	Occupation	Sex	Mean Score[a]
America's conception of its leadership role in the world must be scaled down.	Military	Men	−0.29	Educators	Women	0.26
	Military	Women	−0.18	Educators	Men	0.25
	Pub. Off.	Men	−0.05	Business	Women	0.22
	For. Svc.	Men	−0.02	For. Svc.	Women	0.21
	Clergy	Men	−0.01	Lawyers	Women	0.21
	Business	Men	0.00	Pub. Off.	Women	0.20

Summary:

Number of Appearances in Each Column

Occupations:	Strongest	Weakest
Military Officers	16	0
Business Executives	13	2
Public Officials	8	3
Clergy	5	0
Foreign Service	2	5
Labor Leaders	2	6
Lawyers	2	6
Media Leaders	0	12
Educators	0	14
Sex:		
Women	23	29
Men	25	19

[a]Mean scores recorded on a scale of 1.00 (strongly agree) to −1.00 (strongly disagree).

CONCLUSION

A single survey provides an insufficient base from which to draw broad conclusions about differences in the foreign policy beliefs of women and men. It may nevertheless be interesting to speculate about the broader implications of the main finding that gender accounts for a rather limited amount of the variance among the American leaders in our sample. At least two not altogether mutually exclusive lines of speculation may be advanced. The first emphasizes both vertical (leaders versus others) roles and horizontal (occupations) ones. The processes of leadership recruitment, socialization, and the like are sufficiently potent to reduce if not eliminate differences between men and women—at least within the same occupation—that persist among the public at large. There is at least scattered evidence in other studies that would appear to support this interpretation. Mueller cites evidence from the Korean-War period that women with somewhat "liberated" views of the female role also tended to have foreign policy beliefs that resembled those of men. Thus, he speculates that "if the effect of women's liberation is to change the attitudes of women, making them more assertive so that they can compete in a male-oriented society, a correlative result may make them more hawkish on war and foreign policy."[24] Another study, focusing on leaders invited to attend a national conference on "The Foreign Aspects of U.S. National Security" in 1958, also suggested the central importance of leadership rather than sex roles: "If a particular opinion-making position compels close attention to foreign affairs, this is not likely to change if it is occupied by a woman rather than a man. Again this reasoning is upheld by the data."[25]

A second interpretation emphasizes broader social change. According to this view, gender differences are tending to disappear across the social spectrum, rather than merely at the leadership level. Time thus supplements and perhaps supersedes occupation as the key variable. There is also some evidence supporting this interpretation. Earlier public opinion studies tended to find significant differences between women and men on foreign policy, a conclusion supported by surveys during the earlier stages of the Vietnam War.[26] But the latter study also revealed that differences based on sex roles narrowed during the later stages of that conflict. Analyses of a more recent public opinion survey also indicate that gender is among the very weakest correlates of foreign policy beliefs.[27] Finally, this interpretation receives support from a recent survey of political sex roles in contemporary America. "Actual differences in political behavior between adult women and men have consistently declined over the last decade. . . . Studies of the 1970s . . . show declining sex differences in political participation and call for new explanations. The most plausible new interpretation appears to be that sex roles are changing, and with them the distinctive character of female and male participation."[28] This evidence, while far from conclusive, is at least consistent with the proposition that our findings may reflect not merely differences between leaders and others, but also a broader trend toward diminishing gender-based differences on issues of international relations and foreign policy.[29]

Notes

1. This seems a safer prediction about the Western democracies. It may even prove to be wrong about communist nations, not one of which has ever seen a woman rise to any important political position comparable, for example, to that achieved by Margaret Thatcher, Golda Meir, Indira Ghandi, or Flora MacDonald. Chiang Ch'ing (Madame Mao) may be the closest exception to the rule, but her prominence derived solely from her position as the chairman's wife, and it did not long outlast Mao's death.

2. Among the many controversies in the enormous literature on the development of sex differences is whether their source is primarily biological (e.g., hormonal) or social (e.g., learned sex roles). That controversy lies outside the scope of the present paper. The use of the term "sex role" in this paper should not be regarded as a denial of any biological differences. Rather, it seems a more appropriate term to use in a paper that deals not only with gender but also with occupation as key variables. For excellent discussions of the various positions on the issue, see Eleanor E. Maccoby, ed., *The Development of Sex Differences* (Stanford: Stanford University Press, 1966). Especially helpful are the chapters by the editor, David A. Hamburg and Donald T. Lunde, and Walter Mischel. Other useful introductions to the literature on sex differences may be found in Arlie Russell Hochschild, "A Review of Sex Role Research," in *Changing Women in a Changing Society*, ed. Joan Huber (Chicago: University of Chicago Press, 1973), pp. 249–67; Martin Gruberg, *Women in American Politics* (Oshkosh: Academia Press, 1968); Rita Mae Kelly and Mary A. Boutilier, *The Making of Political Women: A Study of Socialization* (Chicago: Nelson Hall, 1978); Eli Ginzberg et al., *Life Styles of Educated Women* (New York: Columbia University Press, 1966); and Kathleen Newland, *Women In Politics: A Global Review* (Washington: Worldwatch Institute, 1975).

3. An extensive classified and annotated bibliography on sex differences does not list a single study of foreign policy attitudes or beliefs, either among leaders or the public at large. Roberta M. Oetzel, "Annotated Bibliography," in Maccoby, ed., *The Development of Sex Differences*, pp. 223–351. For an exception, see James N. Rosenau, *Citizenship Between Elections: An Inquiry into the Mobilizable American* (New York: The Free Press, 1974).

4. John A. Reilly, ed., *American Public Opinion and Foreign Policy 1975* (Chicago: Chicago Council on Foreign Relations, 1975); and John A. Reilly, ed., *American Public Opinion and Foreign Policy 1979* (Chicago: Chicago Council on Foreign Relations, 1979). Two secondary analyses of the earlier survey, however, have examined the impact on gender, whereas a third one failed to do so. Barbara Bardes and Robert Oldendick, "Beyond Internationalism: A Case for Multiple Dimensions in the Structure of Foreign Policy Attitudes," *Social Science Quarterly 59* (December 1978): 496–508; Eugene R. Wittkopf, "The Structure of Foreign Policy Attitudes: An Alternative View" (University of Florida: Mimeo, 1979); and Michael Mandelbaum and William Schneider, "The

New Internationalisms: Public Opinion and Foreign Policy," in *Eagle Entangled: U.S. Foreign Policy in a Complex World,* ed. Kenneth Oye, Donald Rothchild, and Robert Leiber (New York: Longman, 1979).

5. Gabriel Almond, *The American People and Foreign Policy,* (New York: Harcourt, Brace and Co., 1950), p. 121; James N. Rosenau, *National Leadership and Foreign Policy* (Princeton: Princeton University Press, 1963), p. 181.

6. William Lunch and Peter W. Sperlich, "American Public Opinion and the War in Vietnam," *Western Political Quarterly 32* (March 1979): 34–5.

7. Naomi Lynn, "Women in American Politics: An Overview," In *Women: A Feminist Perspective,* ed. Jo Freeman (Palo Alto, Calif.: Mayfield, 1975), p. 369.

8. Rosenau, *National Leadership and Foreign Policy.*

9. Reilly, *American Public Opinion and Foreign Policy 1975;* Barry Sussman, *Elites in America* (Washington: Washington Post Publishing Co., 1976); Bruce M. Russett and Elizabeth Hanson, *Interest and Ideology* (San Francisco: W. H. Freeman, 1975); and Allen H. Barton, "Consensus and Conflict Among American Leaders," *Public Opinion Quarterly* (Winter 1974–75), pp. 507–30.

10. In addition to *Who's Who in America* and *Who's Who in American Women,* random samples were drawn from: *Foreign Service List; Who's Who in American Politics; Directory of National Unions and Employee Associations; Biographical Directory, International Studies Association; Episcopal Church Annual; Christian Church Yearbook and Directory; Presbyterian Church in the United States; American Lutheran Church Yearbook; United Presbyterian Church in the U.S.A.; Southern Baptist Convention Annual; Official Catholic Directory;* and *Who's Who in World Jewry.* The last eight sources were used to draw the clergy subsample. In addition, the *Congressional Directory* served as the source of samples for members of the printed and electronic media, as well as for senior military officers in the Pentagon.

Entire populations rather than samples were used in some cases. All chief editorial writers of newspapers with a circulation exceeding 100,000 were identified in the *Ayer Directory of Publications.* The "foreign policy experts outside government" subsample included all editors and authors of articles in the journals *Foreign Affairs* and *Foreign Policy,* excluding only non-U.S. citizens, during 1973–75.

For further information on questionnaire construction and the sampling design, see Ole R. Holsti and James N. Rosenau, "The Lessons of Vietnam: A Study of American Leadership" (paper presented at the 17th Annual Conference of the International Studies Association, Toronto, February 25–29, 1976).

11. Return rates among occupational groups, however, varied more substantially, ranging from lows of 38.7 percent for labor leaders and 47.8 percent for political leaders to a high of 70.6 percent for "foreign policy experts outside government." Thus, aggregate results are less useful than comparisons between groups.

12. Throughout this series of studies we have adopted a moderately stringent standard for statistical tests. Results are reported as significant only if they exceed the .001 level.

13. Forty-nine of the 2,282 respondents failed to identify their sex.

14. For further information on this point, see Ole R. Holsti and James N. Rosenau, "Cold War Axioms in the Post-Vietnam Era," in *Change in the International System,* ed. Ole R. Holsti, Randolph M. Siverson, and Alexander L. George (Boulder: Westview Press, 1980).

15. Women's opportunities for political activity have more frequently been available at the local level (school boards, city councils, etc.) than at the international level. For example, during the half-century ending in 1970, only ten American ambassadors and ministers were women, and as late as 1967, only three of 103 chiefs of U.S. missions abroad were women. Lynn, "Women in American Politics," p. 380.

16. For further evidence that there is little difference between women and men in the level of political activity, see Rosenau, *National Leadership and Foreign Policy*, p. 181; and Sidney Verba and Norman Nie, *Participation in America* (New York: Harper and Row, 1972), p. 181.

17. For further evidence and discussion, see Holsti and Rosenau, "Cold War Axioms in the Post-Vietnam Era"; and Ole R. Holsti, "The Three-Headed Eagle: The United States and System Change," *International Studies Quarterly 23* (September 1980): 339–59. That very similar cleavages exist among the public as well as among leaders is documented in Michael Mandelbaum and William Schneider, "The New Internationalisms."

18. Information in parentheses identifies the table and item. Thus, (1:E) refers to Table 13.1, item E.

19. For an articulate recent statement of this position, see George F. Kennan, *The Cloud of Danger* (Boston: Little, Brown, 1977).

20. Evidence on two domestic issues also indicates that the women in our sample are somewhat more inclined toward "liberal" positions. Asked to assess the pace of racial integration in the United States, one-half of the women responded that it was "not fast enough," whereas only one-third of their male counterparts did so. And, given a choice of concentrating economic policy on combatting either inflation or unemployment, women were divided almost equally between these two options, whereas men favored concentrating on inflation by a margin slightly in excess of two-to-one.

21. See the description of the sample on p. 247.

22. Space limitations preclude extensive discussion on the impact of other intervening variables. It will have to suffice for present purposes to state that comparable analyses pairing sex with party, ideology, age, and military service failed to overturn the main finding that differences between the women and men in our sample are rather weak on the Cold War and post–Cold War internationalist axioms, and somewhat stronger on those dealing with isolationism.

23. This double classification scheme yielded at least 11 respondents in all groups except two; there were only four female labor leaders and none of the clergy were women. Although it would clearly be desirable to have more adequate representation in these two groups, the main thrust of the findings reported in Tables 13.4–13.6 appears to have been affected only minimally by this deficiency.

24. John Mueller, *War, Presidents and Public Opinion* (New York: Wiley, 1973), pp. 146–47.

25. Rosenau, *National Leadership and Foreign Policy*, p. 181; see also pp. 104–14, 151, 220, and 309 for other evidence and discussion.

26. Almond, *The American People and Foreign Policy*, p. 121; Philip Converse and Howard Schuman, " 'Silent Majorities' and the Vietnam War," *Scientific American 222* (June 1970): 22; Lynn, "Women in American Politics," p. 369; and Lunch and Sperlich, "American Public Opinion and the War in Vietnam," pp. 34–5.

27. Bardes and Oldendick, "Beyond Internationalism"; and Wittkopf, "The Structure of Foreign Policy Attitudes."

28. Janet Zollinger Giele, *Women and the Future: Changing Sex Roles in Modern America* (New York: The Free Press, 1978), p. 53.

29. With comparable data from a follow-up survey undertaken recently, as well as with those to be conducted at regular intervals in the future, it should be possible to make assertions about trends with greater confidence.

Chapter 14

Bureaucratic Resistance to Women's Programs: The Case of Women in Development

Kathleen A. Staudt

In the last decade, advocates of sex equity have been accorded some legitimacy on the legislative agenda. Numerous laws now mandate nondiscrimination and imply the possibility of government policy which will be more responsive to women. Indeed, if one looks at recent laws and policy pronouncements alone, one might perceive that significant advances have been made in moving government policy in a direction of greater accountability to women as well as to men. Administrative theorists remind us, however, that real policy may be found in bureaucratic practice.[1]

Limited gains toward sex equity suggest a reality at odds with seemingly fairer policy pronouncements. Although bureaucratic structures are in place to provide for equal wages and equality of opportunity, women's economic position relative to men's has eroded. Enforcement is clearly problematic.[2] Similarly, within bureaucracies, affirmative-action monitoring and advocacy structures are in place yet little progress has been made in achieving the outcomes envisioned in original policy.[3] While nondiscrimination in program allocation is mandated in specific pieces of legislation as well as in broad civil rights legislation, data are not even collected to examine program impact by sex or the degree to which discrimination might exist.[4]

Women's policy studies have alluded to implementation problems but none has systematically examined the implementation process once policy pronouncements are in place.[5] Public administration and policy studies note frequent breakdowns, distortions, and delays in the implementation process and warn that implementation is far from automatic in this highly politicized process.[6] Bureaucratic resistance to women's programs may be greater than the usual resistance to new mandates—as one study argues.[7] The realization of policy responsiveness to women or to equity policy hinges on successful bureaucratic politics and leveraging, the burden for which falls upon structural units within the bureaucracy and constituency pressure from the outside. Such seemingly mundane matters as developing procedures, penetrating training and budgetary processes, monitoring, and collecting data, or what some disparagingly refer to as "paper pushing," are critical to putting policy into practice. Were women's program units to control significant resources, build useful alliances, and create appropriate incentives, other parts of the bureaucracy would be more likely to respond to policy mandates on sex equity.

This study of a women's program examines three matters: first, the legislative and organizational history of Women in Development (WID) within the Agency for International Development (AID); second, the resources available to the Women in Development office within the context of AID politics; and third, the interaction between the office and outside constituencies at the point of interface—the feminist WID political appointee. The data are derived from the author's field notes, internal memoranda and documents, and participation observation.[8]

WOMEN'S WORK: INTEGRAL TO DEVELOPMENT

The vast majority of people in the developing world live in rural areas and depend on food production for family consumption needs and extra cash through the sale of surplus. Women work actively in agricultural production, storage, crop processing, trade, and other income-earning activities. Regional United Nations agencies estimate that women's involvement in agricultural production is highest in Africa and Asia with women contributing 60 to 80 percent of the labor, and next highest in Latin America, with 40 percent of the labor.[9] It is estimated that up to one-third of households around the world are headed by women, a result of migration patterns that have pulled men toward cities.[10]

Although women's economic activities and household maintenance functions fall squarely within development concerns of recent decades, development programs are oriented toward men.[11] Prevailing development patterns favor men, as capital-intensive development strategies push women out of income-earning labor, and as manufactured goods compete with women's income-earning crafts.[12] Women's access to agricultural extension and credit is always less than men's, as case studies demonstrate.[13] Women household heads face particularly acute access problems. New technology bypasses or belatedly addresses women's work.[14] Planners and practitioners assume that men are the sole providers and that modernization hinges on men assuming the primary productive role. Where programs exist for women, they tend to be narrowly oriented toward their roles as mothers and wives, for example, family planning and traditional home economics. Except in the most industrialized countries, gaps exist in literacy and educational achievement between the sexes.[15]

A consequence of these patterns is that men acquire disproportionate access to and control over fundamental information, resources, and opportunities which affect people's life chances, material welfare, and opportunities. Thus, development not only ignores women but also tends to increase disparities between the sexes. Male preference is expected to take its toll on women's productivity, program effectiveness, and ultimately, development.

The essence of a Women in Development approach is to ascertain what women actually want and do within a society and to provide them with opportunities, skills, and resources to enhance that participation. Moreover, when new opportunities are available, they are to be made available to women as well as men, and girls as well as boys. In full knowledge of the tendency to bypass or exclude women and female household heads, a woman-sensitive program would design specific strategies to involve women. The WID strategy rests on creating more rational and even-handed planning which takes into account the sex division of labor, fair returns for labor, and the equitable infusion of new opportunities and resources to all members of a given community.[16]

WOMEN IN DEVELOPMENT POLICY IN AID

In recognition of how women have been excluded, even disadvantaged, by past national and international development efforts, the Percy Amendment to the Foreign Assistance Act in 1973 established as policy for AID that women are to be integrated in development efforts.[17] AID's response to the congressional mandate was Policy Determination No. 60 in 1974, which specified that strategies to include women were to be part of all agency plans, sector assessments, and preliminary and final project papers.

A Women In Development (WID) office was created in 1974. Under the most recent organization it has moved from the highly visible location attached to the administrator's office to the policy bureau of the agency. The WID office is responsible for reviewing agency plans and projects to assure that women are integrated, for monitoring agency progress, and for working with other international donors and organizations. In conjunction with these tasks, its five professionals attend project reviews and track agency budgetary commitments. The office has also sponsored policy-oriented research, conferences, and the development of a roster of experts who can provide technical assistance in project design, implementation, and evaluation. A policy bureau office, such as WID, does not fund projects in the field. Rather, projects are identified in the field (i.e., AID missions in collaboration with host-country governments) and funded primarily through the regional bureaus. Two types of AID projects have been identified in the WID monitoring system: women-specific projects, in which women are the central focus, and women's components of projects, which are strategies to involve women in larger AID projects.

AID: THE ORGANIZATION

AID, the major U.S. bilateral economic foreign assistance organization, was created in 1962. AID supports development projects in over 60 countries; decentralized field missions coordinate these efforts with relevant host-country officials. AID/Washington is organized into nine bureaus, the following six of which are relevant here: four regional bureaus (Latin America-Caribbean, Africa, Asia, and Near East), the Development Support Bureau (the technical assitance bureau), and Program and Policy Coordination (the policy bureau). Several layers of political appointees help to make the agency more responsive to executive and congressional mandates.[18]

In 1973 and thereafter Congress mandated a variety of "New Directions" for AID which ostensibly provide a supportive policy context for women in development. AID was mandated to reach the "rural poor majority" in equitable development strategies designed to meet basic human needs in health, education, and nutrition. What this meant in concrete terms was a shift from capital-intensive orientations, such as large construction projects, to more labor-intensive strategies emphasizing agriculture, farm-to-market roads, water, and elementary education in rural areas.

Integrating women in development promotes the full realization of an equitable development strategy. First, women's proportional economic contribution to household maintenance is highest among low-income families where survival depends on the active participation of all members.[19] Moreover, female-headed households are often disproportionately concentrated among the low-income segments of society. Development strategies which include women tend to address low-income households within a society, whether female- or male-headed. Yet growth with equity should not be conceptualized in terms of economic class alone, but also in terms of sex equity. Any strategy which disproportionately favors men cannot be considered an equitable approach.

AID is a politically vulnerable organization which operates in an extremely uncertain task environment.[20] Knowledge about development is uneven, data on rural areas are nearly nonexistent, and implementation occurs across numerous vertical organizational layers and horizontal national boundaries. Foreign aid has been termed one of those few cases where close to zero growth has been the norm for 25 years.²¹ Massive RIFs (reductions in force) have reduced the number of AID employees from a peak of over 17,000 a decade ago to 6,000 in the current period. Yearly scrambles to "save the budget" and periodic concerns with agency survival itself consume executive energy.

Congress has imposed scores of requirements on AID, a veritable repository of special interests, which pull AID in potentially contradictory directions. Some are designed to protect American interests and others to promote progressive developmental thinking. These diverse goals can be found in the lengthy checklist of congressional requirements attached to each finalized project paper (the second stage of project design). In the late 1970s, these requirements numbered not less than 62 items. WID is one of many new goals, and its monitoring mechanisms coexist with others, all of which culminate in an overburdened system.²²

Besides the widespread, unpopular perception of foreign aid as a "give-away program," AID lacks a strong supportive U.S. political constituency.²³ Owing to limited knowledge about development, AID is subject to easy sniping, and serves "as a target—in a way the State Department never could—for criticism of U.S. foreign policy."²⁴ The absence of a U.S. program-beneficiary constituency has been linked to AID's extensive reliance on outside contracting for technical assistance, to its numerous reorganizations, and to what Anthony Downs terms "excessive rigidity" because it lacks constructive negative feedback from its beneficiaries who are outside the political system.²⁵

While these characteristics imply general difficulties for AID in the congressional authorization and appropriation process, they also suggest a certain receptivity to new constituencies, such as those which advocate women in development. AID seeks and is potentially responsive to groups that support the organization in the legislative process.

AID'S PERFORMANCE ON INTEGRATING WOMEN

The extent to which AID has integrated women in development is measurable but slight. The WID office has survived, but has faced periodic calls for abolition, including one in the 1979 Heritage Foundation report to the new Reagan administration. Each AID project paper is required to have a "woman-impact" statement (rather than a strategy to involve women, as the policy determination states), and the social soundness analysis, required since 1975 for all projects, theoretically considers the division of labor, diffusion, and distribution patterns within communities affected by projects. Woman-impact statements, usually no more than a paragraph, tend to be recycled from document to document and are perceived as "boilerplate," in agency terms. Representatives of the WID office, or WID representatives in the regional bureaus, raise questions about women's involvement in projects at project review meetings, two of which are held for each project. Initially, those comments and questions were greeted with laughter, even from committee chairpersons, but they are now treated more seriously. Guidance on integrating women is found in agency handbooks. Internal training addresses the WID issue along with a host of other new issues mandated by Congress.

Quantitative assessments of agency performance are more difficult to acquire, but they indicate some degree of progress. Women constitute 13 percent of AID-supported international trainees from AID-assisted countries which represents an increase from the 4 percent of trainees who were women at the time of the mandate, but matches the percentage reached in the early 1960s. Regional bureau budgetary commitment to women in development has grown. The WID office tracking system estimates, based on responses from AID field missions on women-specific and women's components of projects, that 3 percent of regional bureau budgets are devoted to integrating women in development. Agriculture, nutrition, and rural development is the largest development sector, to which just over half of AID bilateral resources are devoted. In an assessment of seven agricultural extension and credit document sets, strategies to reach and include women were found in less than 10 percent of those projects.[26] In many of those projects with strategies, premandate emphases on traditional home economics rather than attention to women as producers were common.

Although policy is firmly in place, actual implementation is minimal. An examination of internal power resources, leverage capabilities, and external pressure reveals why.

BUREAUCRATIC POLITICS

According to the "bureaucratic politics" model, government action is a result of bargaining among players who are hierarchically positioned in government. The probability of success in bureaucratic games depends on bargaining advantages, skill, and will in using resources. Biasing the outcome of bureaucratic political games are organizational routines and standard operating procedures.[27]

The Women in Development offices prospects for effective bargaining are dependent upon its power resources, activities, and alliances. The four resources examined here include expertise, control over material resources, structural location, and internal alliance building.

Implementation occurs in response to appropriate incentives. The strength of positive incentives ranges on a continuum from prescription, weakest of incentives, to resource provision alone (what Bardach calls "enabling") to resource provision tied to performance. Negative incentives, such as sanctions in the form of veto capability or funding termination, are potentially strong molders of behavior, but may incur ill will and even new, more subtle forms of resistance. Moreover, they are vulnerable to political pressure and are rendered meaningless if applied inconsistently or infrequently.[28]

Expertise

In bureaucracy expertise implies specialized knowledge about a policy, program, or sector. For the WID office, that specialization is realized in the power to define, monitor, and supply studies on women. The WID office has the power to define, within the boundaries of the legislative mandate, whether projects are legitimately labeled "WID" and it reports this information to Congress. While the supply of studies is primarily an "enabling incentive," the capacity to gather and report data to Congress on agency compliance is an incentive which is more firmly tied to performance. A 1978 congressional amendment to the International Development Food and Assistance Act (Section 108) provided the incentive for the agency to "prove" that it spends $10 million on women in development. The deadlines imposed in quarterly reporting to Congress add more leverage to the WID office information requests than its limited authority warrants. Monitoring with targeted, quantifiable goals provides a stronger incentive to change behavior and increase compliance than mere qualitative improvement. Yet the $10 million is itself a goal representing only minimal commitment, or less than 1 percent of regional bureau spending.

Legislative language on WID in 1974, 1977, and 1978 stresses women's *economic* integration.[29] As defined in the AID Special Concerns Code, a project labeled WID must increase women's participation, opportunities, and income-earning capacities. Explicitly excluded from the WID definition are those projects in which women are recipients of goods (such as contraceptives and health projects) or of food and services for themselves or their children.

The concept has unevenly penetrated central and regional bureaus as well as field missions. This is in part the result of an overload of new special concerns and the periodic revision of definitions. More important, however, is the limited agreement about whether the definition of women in development *should* stress direct participation in productive activity. Because of its small staff and its inability to observe whether mission responses are legitimate WID efforts, the WID office is dependent upon verbiage from AID field missions.

The provision of substantive policy-, program-, and project-oriented data is a potential power resource. With monies budgeted for the funding of small, policy-oriented research, the WID office has emphasized the documentation of women as decision makers, heads of households, employees, and participants in sector-specific development issues such as agriculture, forestry, and water.[30] WID-supported studies, enabling staff to plan, design, and implement projects with more comprehensive information, reduce the burden on missions to fund studies and thus serve as positive incentives to WID permeation. Academic studies also lend legitimacy. Yet there appears to be a tendency toward requiring more data on women than on men or "demanding particularly strong documentation that a program for women is really needed."[31] This pattern can serve to delay implementation of the WID concept.

For all the WID office's attention to scholarly documentation of women's work and decision making as it relates to AID activities, the widespread reaction to WID is not a recognition of expertise but rather an ideological association with some of the more uncomplimentary perceptions of late 1960s feminism. Agency personnel frequently complain that WID is a "woman's lib" issue being used to export American ideas, rather than an issue grounded in development and/or equity justifications. Among those ambivalent about or somewhat receptive to the concept, the recentness of the academic literature, its straddling across several disciplines, and its "ghettoization" in women's studies reduce its credibility. Furthermore, WID is sometimes trivialized. In testimony before Congress, a representative repeatedly tried to prompt and extend the words "male chauvinism" and "male chauvinist pigs" to the WID coordinator's comments, to which she replied, "It's your term, not mine."[32]

Several grounds are used to justify resistance toward WID. First, WID is accused of being "social engineering," a label not accorded other equity-oriented development strategies, family planning, or the encouragement of private investment. This is in part derived from the prevailing "public-private" distinction prevalent in American political culture which lodges women in the "private" sphere and rejects government interference in that sphere.[33] Second, support for WID is assumed to be antifamily. As one regional bureau agricultural officer once commented, "I'm not interested in WID; I'm interested in families." Third, women in development as a concept is distorted and/or personalized. According to the former WID deputy coordinator, AID agriculturalists sometimes perceive women's labor on family farms as "abnormal, an incursion into . . . a male sphere." A senior agricultural specialist in AID once stated, "The happiest day of my life was when my mother no longer had to go out to help in the fields" back on his family's midwestern farm.[34] The term "women in development" also lends itself to tedious joking about the absence of a "men in development" program or comments on how "I'd like to develop a woman."

Complicating the reaction to WID is the gender composition of the office. The WID office is currently an all-woman office in an agency where most professionals are men and most clerical staff are women. Numerous studies of token group members demonstrate the special performance pressures to which tokens or small proportions of physically different people are subject.[35] A woman professional's personal style takes on extraordinarily significant dimensions in determining receptivity to the issue. An earlier WID coordinator is remembered as "abrasive," a characteristic that has lingering association with the issue.

In sum, the power of WID expertise is substantially dimmed in the AID context. While WID has the power to define and monitor agency performance on the issue, and with the 1978 amendment, to tie agency performance to compliance, the vague definition and dependency on mission responses render the resources less meaningful. The emphasis on expertise and legitimacy through academic studies is insufficient to mute the strong ideological and personalistic responses to the issue and its supporters. Implementation analysts have argued that "when oversight is taken seriously, it generates pressures to develop indicators of program performance."[36] AID evaluations, however, rarely disaggregate data by sex. Thus, it is difficult to determine whether women even participate in projects, must less whether project impact is positive, negative, or neutral.

Financial Resources

Although the WID office is charged with the broad mandate to integrate women through project review, studies, linkages with constituents, and international coordination, its annual program budget has been limited to $1 million or less since inception. As a result, WID exhorts other bureaus to commit resources ("jawboning") to implement its mandate. Thus, WID's limited resource base precludes it from playing much more than a prescriptive role, one of the weakest of incentives. Moreover, the existence of an average of five professionals in an agency of thousands is a limited staff resource base for promoting prescriptive efforts.

The "no friends" testimony to Congress illustrates how jawboning alone, without funding reinforcement, is a weak base from which to disseminate new values and concepts. As the WID coordinator testified, "The missions have come to us . . . and we have said no. We have not made friends that way, with things they want to finance, new opportunities.[37] At those hearings, the WID constituency submitted an amendment which would have earmarked $10 million for WID activities to be divided between the WID office and WID projects in sector offices. Fear was expressed that the money designated would be the *only* money spent on women, resulting in a separate program at the expense of an integrated concept. These concerns formed part of the amendment's legislative history and caused some later confusion in interpretation. The AID general counsel's office determined that the amendment constituted minimum funding levels, rather than a financial source for new activities over which the WID office had influence. Had the WID constituency foreseen this interpretation to target a goal rather than supply new resources, a larger goal would have been set. Other confusions resulted from this interpretation; missions perceived that WID was budgeted more generously and were dismayed to have their requests to WID for small projects denied. The WID office continues to lack monetary incentives to promote compliance.

Structural Location

Office locations provide clues about the office's formal authority and the timing of participation in bureaucratic politics. AID periodically undergoes reorganization, and WID has moved from its initial location in the administrator's office to the policy bureau. This movement is logical for new mandates, but location in policy forestalls the possibility of supplying technical assistance and pilot project monies (typically available in technical bureau offices).

A 1974 internal memorandum requested responses from a variety of bureaus about the appropriate location for the WID office. In the six organizational proposals made in 1974, no bureau or office recommended placement in itself. These responses ran contrary to "bureaucratic imperialism" which is said to characterize agency stances, and they suggest an early inhospitability to the issue.[38] Although turf conflict is portrayed in the administration literature as dysfunctional, the absence of conflict over or demand for housing a function suggests a worse fate—that of marginality.

Although the WID office plays a legitimate representative role at project review meetings, it lacks the authority to veto projects as is the case for other special concerns such as environment. WID can raise doubts about the project which may shatter the consensus and delay or forestall the project. WID "success," however, realized in terms of blockage, "wins no friends" among mission staff.

WID's small staff is hard pressed to read all the often more than inch-thick project documents and to attend the hundreds of review committees scheduled in the course of a year for the various bureaus. Massive time requirements have forced the WID office to prioritize attendance into sectors, missions, and project types. One prime priority is the women-specific project, which tends to be a small-scale pilot model focusing on helping women "catch up." By default, the WID office is its prime supporter—support which ties the office to an unpopular project type. Women-specific projects are typically reviewed with particular scrutiny. Detailed questions are raised about what is an extremely low-budgeted project in agency terms ($25,000 to $1 million); reviews take longer and require more justification and rewrites. In a typical example, one bureau spent one and a half hours in a committee over a $50,000 women-specific proposal and a half-hour over a $10 million regular AID project. As a form of "compensatory policy," women-specific projects arouse resentment; nevertheless, the level of relative funding is far less than the heady term connotes.

WID's formal authority and location provide it with few resources for leverage and bargaining. Its responsibilities are indeed more than its limited authority warrants.

Allies

Alliance building is crucial for establishing the base, momentum, and capacity for expanding the incentive structures for compliance. The mandate to "integrate" necessarily requires ties with offices which will draw the issue into their scope of responsibility. Several sets of allies to women in development would be logical in a development-oriented agency, stemming from both their functions and the extent to which AID success aids in advancing their own efforts. Among these are sector-specific offices, process representatives, women, and WID representatives in other bureaus and the missions. Logical allies, however, do not always overlap with actual allies.

Sector-specific offices that oversee areas in which women are active, or in which women's disadvantage is apparent, are logical allies of WID. Yet this alliance depends on the regular supply of data that focus attention on the issue. Although women's involvement in water collection, agriculture, forestry, and rural development is generally extensive, it is unpaid and/or included as undifferentiated "family labor"; no data are regularly supplied to those offices which specify women's involvement. The technicians who dominate those sectors have limited awareness of the social-science or women's studies literature that document that participation. In contrast, the education sector staff, regularly confronted with easily accessible data on sex differences in literacy and educational achievement now mainstreamed into general documents, have an interest in women in development. Those sectors in which traditional women's concerns are addressed, such as health and population, also represent potential allies. Certain new sector issues such as renewable energy have periodically allied with WID because of women's fuel-collection activities and fuel use in cooking. While some technicians continue to doubt whether women farm, trade, earn income, or head households, women's near-universal cooking responsibility requires no alteration of assumptions.

"Process" representatives who are responsible for social analysis in projects and evaluation of impact on people might be expected to serve as allies. Well within their jurisdiction would be analysis of the sex division of labor and differential benefit distribution by sex. Yet these concerns are frequently unrecognized in preference for using the household as a unit of analysis with the assumption that men universally head households. An agricultural program, based on radio communication in Central American highland communities where women are agriculturalists, began shows with *"Buenos Dias, Señor Agricultor."* Not only did communications aimed at men continue throughout the project, but the bias escaped even the evaluation. Moreover, this "successful" project model was further disseminated in a special studies monograph.[39]

As is evident, not all social analysts are familiar with the literature on women and development. Furthermore, measurement tools and indicators on women and women's participation are far from developed. Much of women's work is unpaid, yet agricultural work, water, and fuel collection contribute to production for consumption and sale. Without easily identified monetary labels for work, other methods for assessing work such as time-budget methodology become complex, costly, and time-consuming.

Regardless of their office and tasks, women tend to be more supportive of WID than men. The WID office sponsors briefings, discussions, and lectures on the issue and notifies both men and women. Yet women predominate at meetings. For example, for an August 1979 series of four briefings from policy-oriented researchers, over 100 persons were notified, 53 percent of them men. Approximately 25 persons attended each session, many of whom were consistent attenders of WID briefings. In two sessions, there were no men and in two others, one and three. In an agency where more than nine out of ten senior officials and executives are male, alliances limited to women restrict the pool of powerful supporters.

WID representatives are located in the regional bureaus and in AID field missions. The former are assigned approximately 50 percent of their time to the issue, while the latter, 5 to 10 percent. The WID officers vary in their interest in, commitment to, and knowledge of women in development. The WID office does not formally participate in their selection, and loyalties tend to be with the geographic bureau and mission. Consequently, there is little consensus among WID officers about the meaning of women in development.

Opportunities present themselves for making new allies at meetings, through internal agency media and conferences. Support from top-level administrators can also build support at middle and lower levels and provide incentives for agency staff to respond to the issue. Former AID Administrator Governor Gilligan gave support in the form of speeches to outside groups, but WID never constituted an agency budget priority. A former deputy administrator publicly stated in a meeting where the argument about women being disadvantaged by development was advanced, "Isn't that the silliest thing you've ever heard?"[40] The administrator appointed by President Carter, however, sponsored a guidance cable to missions (drafted for him by WID and its allies) offering several positive incentives, including technical assistance and budget prioritization.

To the extent that other offices take on the responsibility of Women in Development, the burden on a women's program office with limited resources is relieved and the prospects for genuine integration are heightened. Movement toward that integration exists, but is uneven.

CONSTITUENCY LINKS

As Allison and Szanton describe, interests can be vested within a bureaucracy, but influence does not automatically follow from vesting. Rather, it arises from linkage to sources of power outside government.[41]

AID, like other public organizations, depends on constituencies for its health in the authorization and appropriation process.[42] Given its political vulnerability and public unpopularity, AID is especially dependent on diverse constituency support. The strongest constituency group for WID, the Coalition for Women in International Development drew much of its early strength from a key liberal supporter of foreign aid, the League of Women Voters. Women researchers in American universities, particularly in agricultural universities, also represent a significant constituency.

A crucial interface between internal agency offices and outside constituencies is found in leadership, in this case study, a feminist Carter appointee with strong ties to the women's movement. She has engaged in a variety of constituency-strengthening and mobilization efforts which provide leverage for bureaucratic politics within the agency.

The WID appointee is a self-defined feminist who believes women, both in the United States and in developing countries, must be politically empowered to make claims upon government on their own terms. Reaction to feminism within AID is generally negative, and the term itself is assiduously avoided in agency dealings.

Feminists have argued that organizational structure and leadership style,[43] should be participant, nurturant, and sharing of information and resources. Such values place strong performance pressures on feminist appointees responding to a feminist constituency. Compounding that pressure is the performance pressure placed on lone, visible tokens, or small proportions of female professionals in male-controlled bureaucracies, as mentioned earlier. Indeed, the WID appointee faced the triple constraints of being a woman executive vastly outnumbered by men counterparts who is a feminist promoting sex equity policy in a women's program office. She was quite conscious of the divergent pulls of feminist and AID program responsibilities. As she stated in a Radcliffe-sponsored panel on women and power:

> If I am too much of a feminist, I lose credibility as a policy maker and manager. If I am not enough of a feminist, I lose credibility in my job, which is to help women overseas. I lose credibility with those outside whom I need to do my job effectively.[44]

The Coalition for Women in International Development, representing 80 organizations (such as church and women's groups as well as private voluntary organizations) and 50 individual members, creates visibility for WID and affirms outside support for WID both to Congress and to top AID officials. Since 1977, the coalition has made regular visits to top officials in AID to discuss efforts both to integrate women in development and to increase female professional staffing. That year, ten calls were made to bureau heads and office directors. A Task Force for Revisits to AID Administrators and Office Directors plans female delegation visits to administrators with presubmitted questions. In early 1979 a WID office memorandum briefed the head of the policy bureau about the WID Coalition and provided possible responses to their questions. Besides visiting administrators, members of the Coalition testify in hearings before Congress. That testimony tends to be more critical than that coming from the WID coordinator and her deputy, who must demonstrate a certain degree of agency loyalty.

Coalition activities have ripple effects, both in private voluntary organizations which constitute part of the coalition and which run development projects overseas, and in other networks such as those ad hoc coalitions that form around various United Nations conferences, including the FAO World Conference on Agrarian Reform and Rural Development, the Conference on Science and Technology for Development, and the several Decade for Women conferences.

The WID coordinator also extended ties to women researchers and practitioners at American agricultural universities. The WID-sponsored Women and Food Conference in 1978 strengthened the tie between women and a major AID development sector. Later that year, another smaller conference within AID was designed to enhance participants' understanding of AID and the WID literature. Participants at that second conference developed a set of recommendations to the agency, for which an official response was made and later disseminated to missions—activities which heighten WID visibility. Rosters of women-sensitive persons who can serve on project design and implementation teams have been developed at various schools. Women at those schools, however, are often isolated into separate departments and disciplines, making it difficult for them to penetrate the decision-making and allocation processes. Even among potential WID supporters, there is some tension between home economists and social scientists.

The coordinator also attempted to build a constituency among women in development researchers. Such attempts were fraught, however, with the typical problems associated with practitioner-researcher relationships. Policy makers and researchers come from different traditions, with the former operating in a shorter time frame than the latter. They each speak and write a different language, creating reporting barriers which obscure research results.[45] Coming from a political rather than research background, the coordinator had a continuing skepticism about researchers, but recognized the ability of scholarly literature to legitimize the issue to the broader development community.

Unlike the former coordinator who drew research from consultants in the Washington, D.C. area, the current coordinator developed liaison with scholarly researchers from around the country, many of whom were isolated in their own institutions. These efforts were in part a result of the background and orientation of the former deputy coordinator, herself a scholar and valued for the network she brought to the office.

A series of networking sessions, at which discussions were held on research and gaps in the literature, were sponsored in 1977 and thereafter. Little

consensus was achieved, owing to disparate orientations, with some researchers concerned with the New International Economic Order, others with
Third-World women themselves defining gaps, and still others interested in
short-term policy concerns amenable to AID action. WID policy makers,
however, were not in a position to alter the international economic order, and
some researchers were unwilling to participate in an effort that appeared only
marginally to address a wider problem.

A major problem with mobilization strategies is the potential competition
and tension among organizations for limited resources. Already diverse, but
initially diffuse, groups tend toward what has been termed the "hybridization
of interests."[46] The constituency factionalized around special research concerns, sectors, and perspectives, and the WID office was unable to respond and
support that diversity, given its own vulnerability. The WID office was perceived by constituents to have a substantial budget, with high expectations
about probabilities of funding of proposals submitted; the confusion over the
$10 million added to that perception. The existence of program money, what-
ever the amount, stimulates the mentality for getting a "piece of the action,"
which is highly problematic with small sums available and the resulting need to
reject numerous proposals. An acute sensitivity develops over choice criteria in
proposal funding and office priorities. A wide net is cast to build momentum
for an issue, but when there are limited resources, few are satisfied.

CONCLUSION

Clearly, WID resources for influencing internal bureaucratic politics are quite
limited. A program budget of $1 million to turn around a multibillion-dollar
agency is small, as is a professional staff of five in an agency of thousands. The
WID office is constrained in its structural location to an exhorter role, rather
than as a supplier of technical assistance or project monies. Monitoring is
extraordinarily difficult, and the data produced are not always reliable, owing
to dependency on resistant field missions for whom paper compliance is a
developed art. Despite these resource shortages, WID has been able to formulate alliances and generate academic literature which in turn sparks interest and
builds credibility in the agency and in other institutions.

Given these resource limitations, the importance of outside constituencies to
act as catalysts for demands in AID and elsewhere is clear. The energy invested
in mobilization, however, is not without costs. That time detracts from direct
WID efforts within AID. Permanent staff are somewhat resentful about
political "interference" and some perceive WID as "purely political." Moreover, resources spent for outside groups detract from resources available for
missions, technical assistance, and other services to the AID field. Yet, without
outsider constituency ties, particularly given the special attitudinal resistance

which WID seems to encounter, WID could all too easily dissipate. Maintaining an appropriate balance is a delicate matter. The WID office is caught between the fundamental need for diverse constituencies and the need to prove to internal AID offices that its priorities lie in those offices.

While resistance to new mandates is a typical bureaucratic stance, women's programs face special and unique forms of resistance, as this case demonstrates. Detractors personalize their hostility. The effort to legitimate the issue academically is made complex with longstanding research traditions that exclude women and collect little or no data on their work. Adequate resources and staff were not appropriated from WID's inception, suggesting "symbolic politics," or the use of policy to placate the public and/or constituencies.[48] Overlaying all this is the tokenism which women professionals face in male-dominated bureaucracies. This implies a deep and profound pattern of resistance, for which special and unique compliance strategies will be necessary. Unless equity policy is put into practice, it will have been but a fleeting, symbolic gesture and not part of government standard operating procedure and therefore impact on people.

Notes

1. Michael Lipsky, *Street-Level Bureaucracy* (New York: Russell Sage, 1980), p. xii; and Herbert Kaufman, *The Forest Ranger* (Baltimore: Johns Hopkins University Press, 1960), p. vi.

2. "The Earnings Gap Between Women and Men," Women's Bureau, U.S. Dept. of Labor, Employment Standards Administration, 1976; Joan Abramson, *Old Boys New Women: The Politics of Sex Discrimination* (New York: Praeger, 1979).

3. Elliot M. Zashin, "Affirmative Action and Federal Personnel Systems," *Public Policy 28,* 3 (Summer 1980): 351–80.

4. For example, see "Equal Opportunity Report: USDA Programs," Office of Equal Opportunity, U.S. Dept. of Agriculture, 1976; and Kathleen A. Staudt, "Tracing Sex Differentiation in Donor Agricultural Policy," Paper presented at the American Political Science Association Meeting, Washington, D.C. 1979. For an exception, see "Need to Ensure Nondiscrimination in CETA Programs," U.S. General Accounting Office, June 17, 1980. GAO examined program impact and found sex and other discrimination; they recommended to the Department of Labor that reporting systems be improved, but DOL responded that it aims to "eliminate noncritical reporting." For an example of research addressed to examining distributive patterns in Kenya agricultural policy by sex, see Staudt, "Agricultural Productivity Gaps: Male Preference in Government Policy Implementation," *Development and Change* (July 1978), pp. 439–58.

5. Dale Rogers Marshall and Janell Anderson, "Implementation and the ERA," in California Commission on the Status of Women, *Impact ERA: Limitations and Possibilities* (Millbrae, Calif.: Les Femmes, 1976); and Ronnie Steinberg Ratner, ed., *Equal Employment Policy for Women: Strategies for Implementation in the U.S., Canada, and Western Europe* (Philadelphia: Temple University Press, 1980).

6. Among the many studies on implementation, see Jeffrey Pressman and Aaron Wildavsky, *Implementation* (Berkeley: University of California Press, 1973); Eugene Bardach, *The Implementation Game* (Cambridge: MIT Press, 1977); Anthony Downs, *Inside Bureaucracy* (Boston: Little, Brown, 1966); and a special issue on implementa-

tion in *Public Policy 26* 2 (Spring 1978).

7. Staudt, *Breaking the Invisible Barrier: Bureaucratic Resistance to Women's Programs* (unpublished manuscript, 1981). Much of the material in this analysis is taken from Chapters 3 and 4 of this manuscript.

8. The author spent one year in the Women in Development office as social science analyst/program officer under the Intergovernmental Personnel Act.

9. United Nations, "Effective Mobilization of Women in Development," Report of the Secretary General, 1978.

10. Mayra Buvinic, Nadia Youssef, and Barbara Von Elm, "Women Headed Households: The Ignored Factor in Development Planning," Monograph submitted to the Office of Women in Development, AID, March, 1978.

11. Ester Boserup, *Woman's Role in Economic Development* (London: Allen and Unwin, 1970); and Irene Tinker and Michele Bo Bramsen, *Women and World Development* (Washington, D.C.: Overseas Development Council, 1976), especially Tinker's "The Adverse Impact of Development on Women."

12. Sidney Mintz, "Men, Women and Trade," *Comparative Studies in Society and History, 1971;* and selections in Rayna Reiter, *Toward an Anthropology of Women* (New York: Monthly Review Press, 1975).

13. Staudt, "Agricultural Productivity Gaps"; for a review of those cases, see Elsa Chaney, Emmy Simmons, and Kathleen Staudt, "Women in Development," in *Background Papers for the U.S. Delegation,* World Conference on Agrarian Reform and Rural Development, FAO, Rome, 1979 (Washington, D.C.: AID, 1979).

14. Elsa Chaney and Marianne Schmink, "Women and Modernization: Access to Tools," in *Sex and Class in Latin America,* ed. June Nash and Helen Safa (New York: Praeger, 1976); and Roslyn Dauber and Melinda Cain, eds., *Women and Technological Change in Developing Countries* (Bounder: Westview, 1980).

15. UNESCO, "Estimation and Projections of Illiteracy" (Paris: Unesco Office of Statistics on Education, 1978). A massive review of studies, existing data, and projections indicates that percentage of female enrollments is less than male enrollments, except in Latin America from age 6–11, for all years, regions, and ages in developing countries. By 1985, Africa and Asia will have approximately half of primary-age girls enrolled, compared to two-thirds to three-quarters of eligible boys; secondary-school projections are a third of girls and a half of boys (David Kahler and Janis Droegkamp, "Characteristics and Needs of Out-of-School Youth," Prepared for USAID/DS/ED April, 1980, p. 28).

16. Projects alone, however, do not operate in isolation from the broader social, economic, and political structure, in both national and international arenas. A comprehensive treatment of women in development must consider the functions of women producers and reproducers in prevailing national and international distribution patterns. (See Wingspread Workshop report on "Women and Development" convened by the Center for Research and Development, Wellesley and prepared by the editorial committee [Lourdes Casal, Suad Joseph, Achola Pala, and Ann Seidman], 1976.) This paper considers only a part of that process.

17. Section 113 of the Foreign Assistance Act of 1961 as amended. Senator Charles Percy (thus, the "Percy Amendment") introduced the measure on behalf of women activists, some of whom are in the WID Coalition (see pp. 273–4).

18. The best treatment of political appointees can be found in Hugh Heclo, "Issue Networks and the Executive Establishment," in *The New American Political System,* ed. Anthony King (Washington, D.C.: American Enterprise Institute for Public Policy Research, 1978).

19. Carmen Diana Deere, "The Agricultural Division of Labor by Sex: Myths, Facts and Contradictions in the Northern Peruvian Sierra," Latin American Studies Associa-

tion Annual Meeting, November 2-5, 1977, Houston; Ann Stoler, "Class Structure and Female Autonomy in Rural Java," *Signs 3,* 1 (Autumn 1977): 74–89.

20. Judith Tendler, *Inside Foreign Aid* (Baltimore: Johns Hopkins University Press, 1975).

21. Heclo, "Issue Networks," p. 91.

22. For a good discussion of this general problem, see Herbert Kaufman, *Red Tape: Its Origins, Uses and Abuses* (Washington, D.C.: Brookings Institute, 1973).

23. Tendler, *Inside Foreign Aid,* Chap. 4; Francis Rourke, *Bureaucracy, Politics and Public Policy* (Boston: Little, Brown, 1976), p. 87; Phyllis Piotrow, *World Population Crisis: The U.S. Response* (New York: Praeger, 1973), p. 63.

24. Tendler, *Inside Foreign Aid,* p. 42.

25. On contracting, see Harold Seidman, *Politics, Position and Power* (New York: Oxford University Press, 1970), p. 262; on reorganization, Rourke, *Bureaucracy, Politics and Public Policy,* p. 87; Downs is discussed in Tendler, *Inside Foreign Aid,* p. 43.

26. Material in this paragraph comes from internal agency documents. A more extensive discussion is found in Staudt, *Breaking the Invisible Barrier,* Chap. 1; and Staudt, "Tracing Sex Differentiation." AN&RD represents just over half the near $2 billion bilateral development assistance effort of AID; slightly surpassing that amount is the security supporting assistance category representing economic aid granted more on political than development grounds (*AID Congressional Presentation FY80,* 1979).

27. Graham Allison and Morton Halperin, "Bureaucratic Politics: A Paradigm and Some Policy Implications," *World Politics 24* (Spring 1972).

28. Bardach, *The Implementation Game,* pp. 109–24. See Beryl Radin, *Implementation, Change and the Federal Bureaucracy* (New York: Columbia University Teachers College Press, 1977), on the political vulnerability of threats to terminate funding.

29. "Report to Congress," Office of Women in Development, AID, 1978, pp. 20–1.

30. Some of these studies include Buvinic et al., "Women Headed Households"; Marilyn Hoskins, "Women in Forestry for Local Community Development"; and International Center for Research on Women, "Keeping Women Out: A Structural Analysis of Women's Employment in Development Countries," and "The Productivity of Women in Developing Countries: Measurement Issues and Recommendations," 1980.

31. Hanna Papanek, "The Differential Impact of Programs and Policies on Women in Development," in *Women and Development,* Workshop conducted by the AAAS in preparation for the U.N. Conference on Science and Technology for Development, March 26–27, 1979.

32. U.S. Congress, "International Women's Issues," Hearings and Briefings before the Subcommittee on International Organizations and on International Development of the Committee on International Relations, House of Representatives, 95th Congress, March 8 and 22, 1978, p. 85.

33. Jane Jaquette, "Review Essay: Political Science," *Signs 2,* 1 (Autumn 1976).

34. Elsa Chaney, "If Only We Could Find a Good Woman . . . : Women as Policy-makers in Development," presented at the American Political Science Association Annual Meeting, New York City, 1978, p. 22.

35. Rosabeth Kanter, *Men and Women of the Corporation* (New York: Basic, 1977), chap. 8.

36. Martin Rein and Francine Rabinovitz, "Implementation: A Theoretical Perspective," in *American Politics and Public Policy,* ed. Walter Burnham and Martha Weinberg (Cambridge: MIT Press, 1978), p. 323.

37. U.S. Congress, "International Women's Issues," p. 83.

38. Matthew Holden, "Imperialism in Bureaucracy," *American Political Science Review 60* (December 1966): 943–51. The internal agency memorandum is D. Bliss thru ExSec to Administrator, 7/12/74.

39. Chaney, Simmons, and Staudt, "Women in Development."

40. Elsa Chaney (former deputy coordinator), personal communication, 1979.

41. Graham Allison and Peter Szanton, *Remaking Foreign Policy: The Organizational Connection* (New York: Basic, 1976), p. 22.

42. This section is focused on the benefits of interaction for the WID office and AID. Substantial benefits also flow to the constituencies, but are not discussed here (see Staudt, *Breaking the Invisible Barriers,* Chap. 4).

43. See the special issue on leadership of *Quest: A Feminist Quarterly 2,* 4 (Spring 1976); and Jo Freeman, *The Politics of Women's Liberation* (New York: David McKay, 1975).

44. Radcliffe College, Radcliffe Club of Washington, D.C., "Women and Power: An Exploratory View," Symposium, Washington, D.C., March, 1979.

45. Jean Lipman-Blumen, "The Dialectic between Research and Social Policy," in *Sex Roles and Social Policy: A Complex Social Science Equation,* ed. Jean Lipman-Blumen and Jessie Bernard (Beverly Hills: Sage, 1979).

46. The term is Heclo's "Issue Networks," p. 96.

47. Douglas Yates, "Decentralization: Innovation and Implementation in New York City," in *Innovation and Implementation in Public Organizations,* ed. Richard Nelson and Douglas Yates (Lexington, Mass.: Lexington Books, 1978).

48. Murray Edelman, *The Symbolic Uses of Politics* (Urbana: University of Illinois Press, 1964).

Chapter 15

Women, Men, and Military Service: Is Protection Necessarily a Racket?

Judith Hicks Stiehm

The policy agenda asks: "Should women serve in combat?" "Should women be drafted?" More basic are the questions: "Should men monopolize legitimate violence?" and "Does protection necessarily become a racket?"

States do many things but the one thing that they all do is hold a monopoly on the exercise of legitimate force.[1] Debates over policy or lack of policy, over definitions of the public and the private, over participation and over representation sometimes arouse and sometimes pacify citizens. But however heated the debate, those who exercise the state's force are the persons who give final definition to the public's opinion. They set priorities and they determine what will in fact be required or forbidden. Those who exercise society's force are given great discretion and formidable instruments. They are often given honor and high position as well. They describe themselves as protectors—police are said to protect citizens from robbery, murder, rape, and riot; the military protect against invasion, rebellion, perceived threats to international order, and occasionally natural disasters.

In the United States, protective forces are said to be under civilian control. In most countries, though, the military is closely integrated with or even *is* the government. Thus, in some states military service is as normal a route to governmental office as is the law in the United States. Still, recruitment to the military and to the police is always selective. One criterion involves competency—education, vision, mental health. A second screens for loyalty and reliability—nationality, political views. Often a third requirement is being male. Here we must pause. Why is this so? Why are protectors mostly men and why has this fact been so accepted for so long? It is rarely argued that women as a group are incompetent, disloyal, and/or unreliable. But it is also rare to hear testimony proclaiming that women can and should assume protective roles. Even rarer is any inquiry into the implications of giving men a monopoly on the state's use of legitimate violence. Does it not matter that all women fall into the category of the protected and that nearly all protectors are men? Is it true that most aggressors are men as well? If so, if men are both the attackers and the protectors, and if women are only victims or protectees, can it be said that men are participating in an old-fashioned protection racket? When Charlotte Perkins Gilman's friend insisted on accompanying her on an evening walk because he was her "natural protector," and when she asked, "Against what?" both realized that what women most fear is, ironically, their natural protectors![2]

Today women are participating in the American military in greater proportion and in more roles than ever before. Still, their number and their use remain restricted. There was little debate about the use of women when they were few in number. It was their increase in number (from under 2 to 1981's 8 percent) which caused the army to declare a "pause" in its further recruitment of enlisted women and which moved the issue close to the top of the public policy agenda.

This chapter first examines how U.S. policy makers have used women in the military in the past. It then explores the reasons that men give for maintaining their monopoly on the use of legitimate force. It probes why most women accept the roles of victim and protectee, and finally, consideration is given to (1) the consequences of being excluded from service as a protector, (2) the meaning of a decision which prohibits the use of legitimate violence to a majority of the population, and (3) the implications of being considered a resource to be "used" rather than a participant in one's own defense.

WOMEN IN THE U.S. MILITARY

Reality and policy do not always coincide. The fact is that women have fought and died in every war. Policy proclaims usually that they should do neither. In exigency, though, authorities do use women. What is unusual about the use of American women today is that there is no exigency. Women are being recruited into a peacetime army. As of September 1979 they represented 6.9 percent of military officers and 7.4 percent of enlisted personnel.[3]

The change in the 15-year period from 1964 to 1979 is remarkable. Female active-duty officers almost doubled (from 10,600 to 18,900). Moreover, the increase was almost entirely in line officers; the number of medical officers was almost constant although they dropped from 84 percent to 59 percent of the total. Enlisted women also increased in number (19,200 to 131,000) and they shifted from having only 7 percent in "nontraditional" jobs to 46 percent there.

The increase in the numbers of women in the military is due to the all-volunteer force. Before the United States decided to maintain a standing army without a draft, women were less than 2 percent of the total and 90 percent of them were in traditional fields. The necessity created by the all-volunteer force was assisted by public commitment to the concept of equal employment opportunity, and by the public's understanding that much military activity is analagous to civilian work; that is, for most people, most of the time, being in the service is just having a job—thus it represents an opportunity. Before examining the various roles of women in the different services today let us consider their past participation.[4]

When the United States fought at home, some women fought too. They did so as irregulars or disguised as men. Before the twentieth century none had regular military status though many worked as civilians in such jobs as nurses, cooks, and laundresses.

Women first donned uniforms when the army established a nurse corps in 1901; the navy followed suit in 1908. During World War I women were enlisted with full rank and status in the naval and marine reserves; inevitably they became known as "yeomanettes" and "marinettes." The army's enlistment-authorizing legislation, however, referred to "male persons" (the navy's referred to "persons"). Since Congress did not change that legislation, the army could not and did not recruit women until World War II. The skills sought in both World Wars I and II were clerical and the standards high. For instance, in 1918 women marine privates had to submit three letters of recommendation and were expected to have a personal interview with the head of the office to which they would be assigned.[5]

Between the World Wars the only women in the military were nurses. Two army proposals to recruit women were developed and rejected. A 1926 plan called for a women's service corps under the command of women officers which would fulfill women's traditional military role of "releasing a man for the front." A later plan recommended the militarization (and integration) of women serving overseas or in danger zones.[6]

Cynthia Enloe correctly refers to women as "the reserve army of the army."[7] Women's military role has traditionally been minimized in peacetime. When war comes, however, women are accepted almost immediately. In fact, the bill authorizing the recruitment of an army auxiliary was approved by the Bureau of the Budget four days after Pearl Harbor.

The World War II women's military corps were "auxiliary" (army), "volunteer emergency" (navy), "reserve" (marine and Coast Guard), or "service" (Air Force pilots). They were separate and not regular. They were intended to fill medical, administrative, and communications slots. But the fact is that they were used as needed (except for direct combat). Women went overseas, became

POWs, and served as mechanics and gunnery instructors, and ferried combat aircraft. Some 260,000 women were serving at the end of the war. By 1948 only 14,000 remained.

Peace brought an end to the draft in 1947. The military's reponse was to propose regular status for women but to limit enlisted numbers to 2 percent of enlisted personnel and to limit officers (other than nurses) to 10 percent of the enlisted number. In addition, women had to be 18 (men 17) and have their parents' permission if under 21 (men if under 18); only one woman per service could hold the rank of colonel or commander and that only temporarily; finally, women's dependents had to demonstrate dependency. (The spouses and children of men were assumed to be dependent.)

The draft was reinstituted shortly after the Women's Armed Services Integration Act was passed in 1948. With the reinstitution the manpower needs of the Korean War were met and women were never even to reach the 2 percent quota.[8]

The Vietnam War increased pressure on recruiters and consequently increased the demand for women. New opportunities were opened. In a 1967 law, the 2 percent enlisted quota was abolished, colonel and captain became the top regular rank, and women could become flag officers (generals and admirals) temporarily; finally, women were awarded the same retirement rights as men.

The 1970s brought further change. The army appointed two women generals in 1970, the U.S. Supreme Court ruled (*Frontiero* v. *Richardson,* 411 U.S. 677, 1973) that women's dependency benefits should be like those of men, and Congress decided that women might enter the service academies. New policies also gave women in the military the right to command organizations composed of both men and women, to have children, and to fly. Only one major restriction remains. Women are not assigned to combat although many receive combat training.

The pattern has been that women are used when and as needed. Generally, the military determines need, although Congress may have to pass confirming legislation. Only once has Congress required the military to accept an equal role for women when the services opposed. This was the 1975 decision to permit women (who were already an important part of ROTC and OTS) to enter the military academies. The services argued that the academies' purpose was to train combat officers. Congress responded that their mission was to train career officers. Two classes including women have now graduated but resistance remains; for example, a bill has been introduced in the House of Representatives which would again close the academies to women.

Existing legislation forbids air force women to fly in combat. They may, however, fly and they may (and have in Vietnam) serve in combat zones on the ground. Existing legislation forbids navy women on combat ships although a federal court has said that this does *not* mean women can be excluded from all ships.[9] No legislation controls the use of army women. It is only policy which keeps army women from the front. Still, understanding the combat issue is fundamental to the understanding of women's military role.

Once many assignments were closed to women. Now only those directly related to combat are forbidden. As recently as 1971, 61 percent of army, 76 percent of navy, and 49 percent of air force occupations were closed. Today, 5 percent of army, 14 percent of navy, and 2 percent of air force occupations are closed. "Nontraditional" roles are no longer reserved. But opportunities remain limited because large numbers of personnel are in the combat specialities (especially in the army) and because personnel must be able to rotate to noncombat slots (especially in the navy which must provide regular shore duty). In fact, the highest percentage of women the Defense department has ever considered recruiting is on the order of 12 percent.[10]

Women's careers, then, are limited in two ways. First, their numbers are severely restricted. This means the military can set higher recruitment standards with the result that the women are generally older and better educated than their male peers. Second, because women cannot command or serve in combat, the principal route to promotion is closed to them. Women top out. There are few places for them to go after lieutenant colonel because top positions require certain kinds of experience and have specific duties, both of which are often forbidden women. The questions which require answers are therefore: why do men argue that women should be banned from combat? and why do women accept that ban?

WHY MEN OPPOSE WOMEN IN COMBAT POSITIONS

The arguments *for* women's being in combat revolve around opportunity and include denials of women's incapacity. The arguments *opposing* them tend to begin with women's incapacity but end in doubts about men's behavior in a sexually integrated military. Both sides assume that women *can be* excluded from combat. Unfortunately this is, perhaps, the greatest myth of all. Because the United States has fought its wars in other countries for more than a century, Americans seem to think that if we keep American women (including American service women) at home, they will be exempt from war's suffering. Citizens of other nations know that no exemptions are possible. Noncombatants suffer and die just as passengers die in auto accidents. To exclude women from combat is analogous to denying them driver's licenses to protect them from traffic accidents. It is to deny them control and responsibility without removing risk.

For some, opposition focuses on women's supposed frailty, especially their relative lack of upper-body strength. Since our ideal types probably portray men as larger than life and women as smaller, the actual size difference of about five inches and twenty-five pounds is probably exaggerated in our thinking. Moreover, it is absolute, not relative, strength that matters. What counts is whether or not one can (and will) do what is needed. After all, it was never said that the United States would win in Vietnam or in Korea because Americans were, on average, bigger and stronger than their opponents.

Current army fears about women relate to their "preparedness." In fact, the army has "paused" in its recruitment of enlisted women, stating that their high rate of pregnancy casts doubt on their readiness in time of emergency. The army reports a pregnancy rate of 10 percent, compared to the air force rate of 2 percent. (A retired air force general has suggested that the army's women suffer from "lack of leadership."[11]) Interestingly enough, Defense Department data on days lost from work, one indicator of preparedness, show similar amounts of time for women and men. Only the cause is different: for women it is pregnancy; for men, drugs, alcohol, or absence without leave.[12]

Men's particular fears and reservations about women are often not based on fact. Efforts to demythologize (as above), however, are often ineffective. Either information goes unabsorbed or new myths spring up to take the place of the old. This suggests that the fears and reservations are deeply rooted and must be treated seriously even if they seem trivial on the surface.

Men kill women and other civilians regularly in war. Susan Brownmiller's analysis of the treatment of women in war makes it clear that women serve as surrogate victims, that, as defenseless opponents they can be an attractive (easy) target which will result in suffering for the men to whom the women are related.[13] Apparently what men actually object to is not having women in combat per se, but having women on *their* side in combat, that is, to having "their" women in combat. Presumably, men are empathetic with their women. Of equal importance, though, must be their sense that it is their duty to protect women and that failure to do so is dishonorable.[14]

With honor at stake, men suffer twice when a woman peer is injured or dies; they feel loss and failure. But they fear something else as well. They fear that their judgment will suffer if their action involves a situation in which a woman is in jeopardy. In essence they doubt their own discipline. If only because they have not had occasion to test themselves, they fear that their chivalry may overcome their judgment.

Even if they themselves practice self-control, most men fear that *other* men might behave chivalrously rather than wisely. The point, then, is not that women are unreliable but that their presence may make men unreliable, imprudent, or impetuous. Even putting aside the possibility of sexual rivalry, the intrusion of a woman into a previously all-male group changes its dynamics. In a situation of jeopardy the unpredictable is discomfiting, the possibility of a call to increased risk taking intolerable.

Other arguments based on male performance are made. War and combat are to the death but they also involve the establishment of dominance. War does not require that all participants of one side die or become disabled before it ends. Conventions and rules for surrender exist. When women participate in a struggle of this kind men may fear that the possibilities for surrender are reduced. First, the enemy may find it difficult to surrender to forces which include women, and second, women may not know how to accept submission. Being unused to the measured rituals for the establishment of hierarchy women may believe that war ends only in total victory and they may urge their fellows on to complete destruction. Margaret Mead suggested that women should not be entrusted with the use of violence for just that reason—because they were not accustomed to the use of *limited* violence—to restrained destruction.[15] Finally, George Quester has suggested that the use of women in combat signals fierce commitment, a commitment rooted in a morality which exceeds the bounds of pure rationality.[16]

More fundamentally, it seems clear that having women participate in an activity changes the very meaning of that activity for some men. It is depreciated, it loses significance, its importance is diminished. When, and why? Probably when the activity is arduous enough that part of the motivation for men is to prove that they *are* men and probably because men generally devalue women. The result is that if women can do something, it becomes unworthy of doing.

Men's devaluation of women may stem from their asymmetrical roles in reproduction. Women have a biological definition which men lack. They give birth and nurture. Men's role in reproduction is more limited and the individual's role is not susceptible to proof. To compensate, to achieve equilibrium, men have staked out certain social rules to give them distinction. Their most unique role is that of warrior or policeman. Lacking biological definition they seek social definition. Thus, to copy or join them is to threaten their identity. To imitate is to degrade them in their own eyes. To meet or accept women on equal terms is to lower their self-esteem.

Let us reiterate this argument. Men do not petulantly say, "If women do it, I won't," if only because they have no other unique role on which to base their claim to a positive identity. A negative identity will not suffice; men do not wish to think of themselves merely as "women's other." Thus, women's presence and their successful performance can be severely demotivating to men if a primary attraction of a particular role or activity is women's absence.

The appeal to manhood is very much a part of military training. From the familiar, "This is my rifle, this is my gun; one is for killing, one is for fun," to "The Marines need a few good men," pride of manhood is a part of recruitment and training. When an institution tries to organize and control large numbers of unruly young men, when it tries to teach self-regard to young men who have little, it is helpful to be able to tell them that they are, by nature, better than half the population.

But many men have no wish to join the military. Most who do not must be drafted, exposed to rigorous training, and put in jeopardy before they will fight. Note that this is done mostly to 18-year-olds—men who are most vulnerable if doubts about their manhood are the issue. It may be that one reason men are not drafted at 30 when their physique remains strong but their judgment has matured, is that older men who are more likely to be secure in their manhood, simply would not go. Thus, the drafting of young men and the sending of them to war is a fully patriarchal act. The control of young men by old differs from that of women by men only in that the young who complete the test successfully will eventually become patriarchs themselves.

In sum, men resist the idea of having women join them in combat. The reasons given are numerous but at bottom they reflect men's doubt about their own performance and identity. To the degree that women's presence impairs men's performance it might be argued that women are not "useful." But, for men to warn that they (the men) will not perform if women are present and then not perform when they are approaches blackmail.

WHY WOMEN ACCEPT EXEMPTION FROM COMBAT

Why do women accept their legal exemption from combat? Their definition as protectee? First, of course, because combat is an unpleasant and dangerous place to be. Second, because convention and law prescribe their absence. Third, since our wars have been foreign wars, there has been no way to get to the combat. In fact, most women accept the restriction, including many military women!

What are the reasons (some) women give for removing the restriction? Some follow the Defense department in arguing the classic liberal position: to end restriction is to give freedom to individual talent and to increase social utility. Others argue for equal opportunity and for career progression. They note that when women are "needed" they will certainly be used. To hold women in reserve is to keep them out of the military when it is safest, and to keep them out of combat slots is to limit women's careers. Thus, limiting the number of women in the military and keeping them from combat both inhibit any chance women might have to hold top positions or to enjoy the sustained 20-year career which is needed to bring an individual to a policy-making position.

Still, most women have probably not even considered the implications of being excluded from combat and restricted in service. Even though women are the victims of violence and even though women use violence, and prepare in increasing numbers to use violence in their personal defense, they seem reluctant to use society's legitimate violence. They often respond to questions about legal force by saying that they are opposed to force. It might be said that they are adopting a position of pseudopacifism.

A truly pacifist position commands respect. It does not flinch from reality; it challenges and risks; it accepts suffering too. In contrast, pseudopacifists choose safety; they refuse to hurt others but they permit others to hurt for them. Women accept, even expect, the police and military to provide protection. They only superficially accept Camus' charge to be neither victims nor executioners; they do not accept the responsibility he assigns the moral human being.[17] Pacifism is not the issue for women, as most are satisfied to be protectees.

IMPLICATIONS OF EXEMPTING WOMEN FROM COMBAT

"Protectee" would seem to be a relatively simple concept. It is not, however, a status which is explored by political theorists though most of them must be (and have been) protectees. What would a conscious and conscientious analysis of that status reveal? What is the protectee's self-concept? How is she or he regarded by her or his protector? To what degree is it false consciousness to think a protector's actions are either altruistic or directed by the protectee?

What images does one have of a protectee? Standing on a pedestal and out of touch? Crouched, dependent, behind a warrior? Secure within a stockade and without freedom? Perhaps the status of protectee is desirable when it is considered in relation to the attacker. Survival comes first after all. But the relationship vis-à-vis one's protector may, in fact, not be desirable, may be of long duration, of broad scope, and may involve competition for resources.

By accepting a categorical prohibition against women's exercise of society's force, all women become protectees and all men potential protectors. Not having direct access to force makes women appear as potential victims, while men who are accustomed to acting with force become potential attackers— even if only to demonstrate their capacity as protectors! Does this gender bifurcation lead women to be (or be perceived as) disabled, and men to be (or be perceived as) enabled? Does the bifurcation reduce information about each other, especially about men's weaknesses and women's strengths? Does it lead women to ignorance about the police and the military—an ignorance profound enough to be likened to burying one's head in the sand?

The most visible rewards given protectors are veteran's preference points which have made public employment the special preserve of the ex-military man (and occasionally woman).[18] Less obvious is the link between military service (or at least liability for it) and full citizenship. The pattern seems to be military performance first, citizenship, second. Political democracy seems to follow military democracy.[19] Thus, black men won the vote in this country after participating in the Civil War, and women's suffrage followed *their* first use as military personnel. This should not be surprising. If Weber's definition of the state is accepted, then participation in the state's defining function should be the mark of citizenship. Citizens, after all, are not defined solely as being subject to the state, they also give definition *to* the state. They do so by ratifying policies, selecting and serving as policymakers, and by being available for policy implementation.

While one does not want to fall into the trap of demanding something simply because it is denied, shared risk and responsibility would seem to be the sine qua non of citizenship. To be spared military service, then, is simply to be treated as a child. Because the standing army is new to us, and because our military activity has been invisible (at least before the first television war—Vietnam), that understanding may have been buried in the nation's subconscious. Now it must be addressed. Just as policymakers reflect upon the consequences of a military which is unrepresentative whether for reasons of class or ethnicity, so must we consider the consequences of having a military which is overwhelmingly male.[20] If the elite is worried about arming too many minorities and too many members of the lower class for fear of disloyalty, do the same reasons apply to arming women? If a volunteer military is supposed to be a loyal and disciplined military because it is voluntary, why worry about disproportion at all?

Women in this country have never been compelled to military service. How can they justify compulsion for some (men) and voluntarism for themselves? Men regularly experience institutional coercion. Women seem to experience coercion primarily as personal (familial). They have not been so subject to the rewards and punishments of institutions as men and seem inclined to think they have the luxury of choosing only the personal coercion of the domestic arena.

CONCLUSION

Policy makers believe that the issue on their agenda is women and the draft. Discussions are often framed as though the issue were one of discrimination against women. In a case, *Rostker* v. *Goldberg,* heard by the Supreme Court on June 25, 1981, however, it was argued that the issue is discrimination against men. In deciding that it was not, the Court held 1) that the Constitution requires the Court's deference to Congress in matters of national defense and military affairs and 2) that Congress has indicated that registration and the draft exist for the purpose of raising combat troops. Since Congress has restricted women from combat, the Court concluded that women need not be registered.

This decision shows that the root question, indeed, concerns combat. Present policy excludes/exempts women. The reasons usually offered are utilitarian. They focus on the primary distinction between women and men—physiology. But in assessing the arguments it becomes apparent that much of our thinking about the military is not "scientific" but conventional, and occasionally as irrational as war itself. When evidence can so easily dispel a policy justification, one begins to understand that one is not really engaged in disproving but in demythologizing. And demythologizing can be futile activity if the underlying need for a myth continues.

If women's physiology does not support a ban on their exemption from combat, is it men's psychology and women's compliance with this psychology that does so? Most arguments suggest this is the case. Thoughts and behavior are admittedly more susceptible to policy directives than physiology, but, even so, the policy debate flounders on the belief that national security is so important that no risks can be taken, no experiments undertaken, no change instituted. Moreover, even if they do not hold full citizenship so long as they accept legal exemption from combat, most women seem not to mind. Indeed, they seem to think little of it.

The ultimate question we must ask is how defense differs from protection. Are defenders, like citizens, persons who participate? Are they persons who share, as opposed to accept? Can protectors and the protected share? Or do their antithetical positions lead to exploitation and debilitation? And is the issue a general one applying to different men as well as to differences between women and men? Can equality be sustained between those citizens who volunteer and those who do not? Is any pattern which requires military service for some and not others acceptable? 's a random selection acceptable?

The United States has been accustomed to raising armies on an emergency basis and to winning its wars. We are now committed to a standing, peacetime army which must have a wholly different meaning for its participants and for the state than our armies have had in the past. Further, policy makers who have never experienced the unambiguousness of a war like World War II will eventually move into federal policy-making positions as some have already done in the states and in the legislature. Perhaps it will then be easier to ask whether or not our exalted commitment to protect other nations has cast us into conflicts we would never have entered if we had seen ourselves only as defenders. Perhaps then we will ask if a nation can continue to exist half protectors, half protectected. Perhaps then we can discern when protection becomes a racket—when "protectors" align themselves to their mutual advantage while offering false protection to persons forbidden to participate in their own defense.

Notes

1. According to Max Weber; see "Politics as a Vocation," in *From Max Weber* (New York: Oxford University Press, 1958), p. 77f.

2. Charlotte Perkins Gilman, *The Living of Charlotte Perkins Gilman* (New York: Harper Colophon Books, 1975), p. 72.

3. Pentagon briefing to the Defense Advisory Committee on Women in the Services, April 22, 1980.

4. The basic source for U.S. Women's military history is Mattie Treadwell, *The Women's Army Corps* (Washington, D.C.: Department of the Army, 1954).

5. Linda L. Hewitt, *Women Marines in World War I* (Washington, D.C.: Headquarters, U.S. Marine Corps, 1974), p. 6.

6. Martin Binkin and Shirley J. Bach, *Women and the Military* (Washington, D.C.: The Brookings Institute, 1977), p. 6.

7. Cynthia Enloe, "Women—The Reserve Army of Army Labor," *The Review of Radical Political Economics, 12,* 2 (Summer 1980): 42–52.

8. Binkin and Bach, *Women and the Military,* p. 12.

9. *Owens* v. *Brown,* 455 F. Supp. 291 (D.D.C. 1978).

10. Ellen C. Collier, *Women in the Armed Forces,* Issue Brief Number IB 79045. (Washington, D.C.: The Library of Congress, Congressional Research Service, 1979), appendix.

11. Tom Philpott, "Services Want to Enlist Fewer Women Until Impact on Readiness is Known" *Navy Times,* January 19, 1981, p. 28.

12. Army women show more lost time, navy less, air force almost the same. Office of the Assistant Secretary of Defense (Manpower, Reserve Affairs, and Logistics), *Background Study: Use of Women in the Military,* 2nd ed. September 1978, F 32.

13. Susan Brownmiller, *Against Our Will* (New York: Bantam Books, 1976).

14. For a discussion of honor, see Peter Dodd, "Family Honor and the Forces of Change in Arab Society," *International Journal of Middle East Studies 4* (1973): 40–54.

15. Margaret Mead, "National Service as a Solution to National Problems," in *The Draft,* ed. Sol Tax (Chicago: University of Chicago Press, 1967), pp. 107–8.

16. George Quester, "Women in Combat," *International Security 1* (Spring 1977), 80–91.

17. Albert Camus, "Neither Victims Nor Executioners," reprinted in *Liberation* (February, 1960).

18. In June 1979 the U.S. Supreme Court upheld a Massachusetts law giving absolute preference to any veteran over any nonveteran. More commonly, veterans have points added to their examination scores.

19. See Judith Stiehm, "Women and the Combat Exclusion," *Parameters 10,* 2 (June 1980): 56; Sebastian de Grazia, "Political Equality and Military Participation" *Armed Forces and Society 7,* 2 (Winter 1981): 181–6; and David R. Segal, Nora Scott Kinzer, and John C. Woeful, "The Concept of Citizenship and Attitudes Toward Women in Combat," *Sex Roles 3,* 5 (1977).

20. Cynthia H. Enloe discusses the consequences of selective recruitment in *Police, Military, and Ethnicity: Foundations of State Power* (New Brunswick, N.J.: Transaction Books, 1979).

Part VII
Conclusions

Chapter 16
Strategies for the Eighties
Ellen Boneparth

In January 1981, when President Reagan proposed in his inaugural address to use government revenues only "for legitimate government purposes," adding that the taxing power of government "must not be used to regulate the economy or bring about social change," he left no doubt in the minds of feminists that he was speaking to them, among others. The president's message contains two important, and related, ideas. First, it makes clear that he sees the claims of certain interests as legitimate and the claims of other interests as illegitimate. Then, the message reveals Reagan's view that social change processes, if only unencumbered by government interference, will bring about societal well-being.

Activists who are committed to changing the status of women may well be disturbed by this view. Underlying Reagan's philosophy is the traditional public/private distinction in which "male" concerns such as the military and the economy are public and therefore legitimate, while "female" concerns such as women's roles, motherhood, families, sexuality, sexual oppression, and violence against women, are private and therefore illegitimate. If the president has his way, social change processes which are currently weakening women's positions in society—an increasing wage gap between men and women, increasing occupational segregation based on sex, the movement of ever-increasing numbers of women into the ranks of the poor as a result of divorce, death, and economic displacement, and increasing violence against women—will continue to disrupt the lives of women and their families without any counterbalancing efforts by government.

Women's groups cannot allow President Reagan's views to take hold. The struggle to promote policy change for women must proceed based on a careful analysis of the effects of different variables on the policy-making process in the 1980s. Here, we return to the analytical framework proposed in the introduction of this volume. While women's concerns today are clearly threatened, the analysis suggests that there may be ways to maintain the status quo, and even to effect some new policy change, if women's groups successfully oppose, artfully utilize, and even occasionally adapt to the changing political times. Once we have examined environmental, systemic, and political variables, and policy characteristics in the contemporary context, we will propose new strategic directions for the women's movement of the 1980s.

ENVIRONMENTAL VARIABLES

At the beginning of the 1980s, the social environment does not appear promising for feminists who seek to change the status of women. An increasingly vocal movement on the right—the new conservatives, supported by numerous political, religious, and special interest groups—is calling for a return to traditional values. What this means for women is a return to traditional family patterns with women confined to roles of wife, mother, and homemaker, insulated from the rigors of work, political involvement, and changing life-styles. In the view of Reverend Jerry Falwell, leader of the Moral Majority, "many women have never accepted their God-given roles."[1]

The new conservatives have taken their cause beyond political discourse, turning it into a moral crusade. In their view immorality underlies many women's issues such as the ERA, abortion, divorce, and lesbian rights; they perceive government intervention in family matters such as child care or domestic violence as destructive of the American social fabric. Again, in the Reverend Falwell's words, "ERA is not merely a political issue but a moral issue as well."[2]

The new conservatives are combining with the old conservatives on the economic issues of cutting government spending and balancing the budget. The goal is to move away from government support of social programs in favor of greater spending on defense and decreased taxation of business and wealthy individuals. Women are the least likely beneficiaries of conservative economics. For the most part they neither earn sufficient incomes nor own sufficient wealth to benefit from tax cuts. They do depend on the public sector for programs to enforce antidiscrimination, enhance economic opportunity, address social needs, and promote role change—all purposes which President Reagan views as illegitimate. As Congresswoman Patricia Schroeder commented in a speech on Reagan's proposed budget cuts, "a disproportionate share of the budget reductions are directed at programs in which women have a heavy investment."[3]

The political climate at the beginning of the 1980s mirrors the changing social and economic climates. Women's concerns and women leaders are conspicuous by their absence from the national scene. A conservative presidential administration is bolstered by a Republican Senate with leading conservatives in key positions of power. Despite lobbying efforts by women's groups for the appointment of women, the Reagan administration lags far behind the previous three administrations in the recruitment of women to senior executive posts. Gains for women in the 1980 elections were concentrated at the state and local levels of government and were made primarily by moderate and conservative Republican women who are unlikely to provide legislative leadership for the women's movement. Finally, the policy-making arena has changed in the 1980s such that women's groups are not only facing organized opposition to items on *their* policy agenda, but are also facing the need to oppose conservative efforts to terminate existing programs and to reestablish policies circumscribing women's rights.

Environmental variables clearly constitute serious obstacles for women seeking to effect public policy change in the 1980s. Strategies are needed to challenge conservative ideology. At the same time, the bleak climate must not blind women to the possibility of using this ideology, whenever possible, to advantage.

The revolutionary changes in women's family and work lives which occurred throughout the 1960s and 1970s will continue throughout the 1980s, creating a serious tension between rhetoric and reality. It was in just such a tense climate in the 1950s that the seeds for the rebirth of the women's movement were sown. When prevailing ideology becomes highly discordant with reality, momentum builds to challenge the ideology. As has been shown throughout this volume, the social realities of women's lives today belie traditional concepts of family and mother-at-home. The women's movement must therefore dramatize the gap between rhetoric and reality by exposing the harsh facts of women's lives and the compelling motivations for the choices women are making. A sustained educational effort in this vein would not only work to render neoconservative dogma irrelevant but would also rally new supporters among women caught in a netherworld of traditional ideology and changing roles.

Women's groups must use a three-pronged strategy to sustain their programs in the prevailing economic climate. First, they must battle to conserve already existing programs by functioning as veto groups in the budgetary process. The politics of persuasion must become the politics of obstruction as women and their political allies work to maintain the policy initiatives gained in the 1970s. The bipartisan congressional support given to the Reagan administration in its first budget-cutting efforts reveals how difficult a task this will be. Therefore, women's groups must also explore ways to use already existing funding sources for their own objectives. If support for new programs cannot be generated, administrative guidelines for programs in place must be modified to allow women to compete with other interests. As seen in Wexler's chapter on domestic violence, women's concerns breach a variety of bureaucracies and can qualify for support in many different guises. Finally, women must turn the emphasis on economic growth to their own advantage. If, for example, incentives are to be provided to the private sector to increase productivity, the needs of women workers for child care and alternative employment patterns can be promoted on these grounds. While women may prefer to argue for their needs on grounds of social justice, they must, when possible, exploit conservative themes to further their ends.

In some respects, the political climate presents the greatest obstacle for women. With few political allies holding elective or appointive office, women's concerns are likely to lose visibility. On the one hand, women's lobbies cannot simply abandon insider strategies; they will have to initiate communications as best they can with public officials not previously identified with their issues. On the other hand, such a political environment lends itself to a revival of protest politics. The potential to mobilize exists—as evidenced by the fact that the National Organization for Women gained 12,000 new members in the months immediately following Reagan's election. The revival of protest politics has the double advantage of directly engaging grass-roots women in movement political activities, while making women working on the inside appear more legitimate in the eyes of officeholders. Thus, women's groups which labored hard to establish themselves as insiders on the political scene in the 1970s must place renewed attention in the 1980s on protest.

Because protests fail to engage popular attention with constant use, the outsider strategy cannot be effective over an extended period. The women's movement must therefore extend its involvement in electoral politics in order to put more allies into office. The loss of several longstanding, powerful male supporters in the 1980 elections brings home the message that electing women cannot be the only goal. Especially in a conservative administration, women need political spokespersons of both sexes to keep their concerns visible—electoral campaigns are a critical way of doing so. The election and reelection of political allies must remain a top priority despite the inimical political climate. And, the creation of new legislative districts in the reapportionment following the 1980 census presents an opportunity for women to run in open races and must be used to advantage.

SYSTEMIC VARIABLES

Conservative political ideology expounds the virtue of decentralized government with particular emphasis on states' rights. The Reagan administration clearly intends to shift much authority over social programs from the federal government to the states. Coupled with this trend is a growing effort by groups on the right to use the constitutional amending process to achieve policy goals such as banning abortion or affirmative action. Thus, in the 1980s, state politics will have greater significance for feminists.

Although decentralized government has provided a stumbling block for women in recent years, the turn to the states has potential benefits for women's concerns. First, women in 1981 constituted 12 percent of state legislators making for better representation in state legislatures than in Congress. While female legislators are far from unanimous regarding women's issues, attitudinal surveys have revealed a high degree of support among these legislators for women's rights.[4] Women are also increasing their representation at the local level where they are in a position to influence funding priorities in city and county government.

A second advantage of state government lies in the progressive tradition of some states which have often pioneered public policy change on behalf of women. The reform of abortion and rape laws, the establishment of battered women's shelters and centers for displaced homemakers, and experiments with alternative work patterns all originated in state government before becoming policy proposals at the federal level. The potential for policy change in progressive states is clearly mitigated by the obstacles women face in less progressive states. Women's concerns have only been addressed in these states as a result of federal initiatives and are likely to receive even less attention under decentralized policy making.

While women's groups have been actively involved in state politics over the last decade, the 1980s will require an even greater involvement both to maintain support for women's issues and to defeat attempts by opposition groups to use the states to reverse federal commitments. How might women strengthen their presence in state and local government? Although women are more numerous in state legislatures than in other elected positions, they are still a small minority. To have an impact, they must combine their resources. In some states women office holders, together with leaders of women's groups, have formed organizations to research and develop policy on the status of women. Another base of support for women's issues has been women's commissions which could play an even more central role in policy making with greater support from the grass roots. Most importantly, women's lobbies at the state level need to participate in coalitions with other interest groups. In the past there has been a tendency for women's groups to go it alone in lobbying state legislatures; the expanding role for the states in social programs, however, necessitates that women's groups work, rather than compete, with unions, minority groups, and special interest groups in health, education, and criminal justice to achieve recognition of their special policy needs.

If policy innovation is most likely to occur in the progressive states in the 1980s, policy change can still be tackled at the federal level through incremental policy making. Building on existing policy models, women's groups in the 1980s must work to eliminate sex discrimination in social security, pensions, and insurance—areas where economic equity has yet to be achieved. Similarly, tax credits which have been used in the past for child care might be extended to other areas such as household work and volunteer activities.

While new policies may yet be achieved through incremental policy making, there are two major drawbacks in this approach. The first is that these policies tend to have a middle-class bias. They benefit homemakers and working women but do little to address the needs of poor women (most of whom are heads of households) for employment, child care, health and nutrition programs, or housing. Policy needs for women who are struggling for survival simply cannot be met through incremental policy making.

A second major drawback is that the focus on economic equity fails to address the issue of role change. As has been seen, policies dealing with sex stereotyping are much harder to achieve than antidiscrimination measures. The precedent established in the 1970s to eliminate sex stereotyping in education could be significantly extended to various fields of employment, military service, and the portrayal of women in the media. Since, however, the whole thrust of role change runs counter to the conservative ethic of preserving traditional sex roles, it is unlikely, even with some policy precedents, that policies involving role change can be achieved incrementally in the immediate future.

POLITICAL VARIABLES

The first part of this book traced the evolution of the women's movement from a grass-roots movement to a national lobby. Many of the chapters have described lobbying efforts by women's groups individually or in coalitions to achieve a variety of policy goals. Lobbying efforts by women have grown in sophistication, expertise, and effectiveness; yet, women's groups continue to be plagued by limited resources and a dearth of political allies.

How might these deficiencies be overcome? One strategy which has not been effectively used is to organize women *within* other major interest groups. There are several reasons for this. In the first place, the movement of women in significant numbers into professions such as law and medicine has been fairly recent. In those occupations where women have constituted a large proportion of the work force, their jobs have held so little status that they have been neither powerful enough to organize themselves nor secure enough to press their demands with male organizers. A contributing factor is that women who have been mobilized by the feminist movement have preferred to create their own groups than endure the frustration of working through male-dominated organizations which have little or no interest in women's concerns. Thus, women's voices in labor unions, business groups, and professional organizations have rarely been heard.

The time has come for women activists to take advantage of their memberships in other organized groups. The increasing numbers of working women and their increasing commitment to lifelong work patterns obviate the rationales used by organized labor in the past to ignore women's concerns. While it can be argued that women were once such a minority in the professions that organizing them was futile, that is no longer the case.[5] Thus, the potential exists for women to penetrate the decision-making structures of organized interests and to move them toward support of women's issues. How much more effective would the pressure for domestic violence legislation have been if the American Bar Association and American Medical Association had been lobbying for it? How much more successful would the fight for pay equity be if women's groups were supported by the AFL-CIO? How much greater will the chance for legislation dealing with rental discrimination be with women realtors organized to fight from within the real-estate lobbies? While it will not be easy to work through male-dominated interest groups, the benefits for the women's movement in terms of gaining new lobbying resources and powerful allies necessitate the effort.

The effectiveness of women's lobbies can be enhanced further by joining in coalition with other groups. In the 1970s women's groups joined with minority groups, senior citizen groups, and children's lobbies on such issues as social security reform, displaced homemaker programs, and child care. The budget-cutting plans of the Reagan administration led to the formation of a coalition of 157 groups, including several women's groups, to fight for the retention of a wide range of social programs. The conservative politics of the 1980s promise to provide a continuing basis for moderate and liberal groups to coalesce. It is critical that women's groups play a leadership role in these coalitions, educating other interests regarding the needs of women.

Women's lobbies must also adapt to the new leadership of the federal policy-making establishment. While women's groups have declared themselves bipartisan, in reality they have tended to focus on liberal Democratic legislators in pressing their policy demands. In the process they have occasionally overlooked liberal Republicans, some of whom now hold key leadership positions in the Senate. Women's groups need to develop ongoing working relationships with these senators and their staffs both to influence efforts by these senators to address women's issues and to reward them for their commitment to women's concerns.[6] In particular, women's groups must recognize that these policy makers may oppose them on key issues such as abortion and yet prove valuable allies on other issues such as employment and violence against women. Simply put, women's groups cannot afford to be, or appear to be, single-issue lobbies; while the fight for reproductive freedom is critical, victories are needed on other issues as well.

A second adaptation women's lobbies must make is to focus more of their attention on the federal executive. This was not as crucial in past administrations when women had allies in federal agencies who provided them with information on policy developments. The appointment of many conservatives to high level executive jobs in the Reagan administration, however, portends the undoing of existing policy by administrative fiat.[7] Given that allies will be difficult to find in the present administration, women's groups must closely monitor bureaucratic politics to expose moves to undermine existing policy through budget cuts, executive reorganization, or failure to implement or enforce regulations. Without friends in the executive, the only way to counter administrative sabotage is to expose the bureaucracy to congressional oversight and the glare of publicity.

POLICY CHARACTERISTICS

In the 1980s policy characteristics, including the ways in which women's policies are presented and perceived, will affect the prospects for policy change more than ever. While it is difficult to predict the precise manner in which policies will evolve, it is possible based on an understanding of the characteristics of different policies to anticipate some of the problems the women's movement will face.

Economic Issues

The best prospect for new policy is in the area of economic issues. At the beginning of the 1981 congressional session, a bipartisan group of senators and members of Congress introduced the Economic Equity Act which contains many important provisions for women: reform of civil service, military and private pensions; tax reforms with respect to the marriage tax, individual retirement accounts, and estate taxes on farms; tax credits for the hiring of displaced homemakers and for a larger share of the costs of day care; and the prohibition of sex discrimination in insurance.[8] In addition, the act makes new equity demands of the federal government, namely, the elimination of all federal regulations involving unequal treatment of the sexes and the removal of all gender-based distinctions in military promotions and retirement.

The Economic Equity Act has many promising features. It is incremental policy making at its best, building on earlier legislation designed to eliminate sex discrimination in employment and credit. The act holds President Reagan to his word that despite his opposition to the ERA, he is committed to eliminating legal inequalities based on sex. The legislation is sponsored by members of both parties, including two senior Republican senators who chair the subcommittees that will review the bill's main provisions. Most importantly, it promotes role equity for which there are many policy precedents and which is far less controversial than role change. With all these advantages, the fate of the act is nevertheless uncertain; many of its provisions will be opposed by business lobbies and fiscal conservatives who are opposed to tax credits and reforms. The Economic Equity Act will be a bellwether for progress on other economic issues: if it passes, there is hope for progress on other economic policies; if it fails, economic policy change benefiting women in the 1980s seems doubtful.

Assuming that strides can be made toward economic equity, what are the more controversial items on the economic agenda? Pay equity is certain to continue to arouse major opposition both because policy implementation would be very costly for the public and private sectors and because it would explicitly raise the occupational status of women vis-à-vis men. While seemingly a regulatory policy, pay equity would have eventual redistributive effects. It could effect role change by making the role of worker attractive to even larger numbers of women. Pay equity, although opposed by many, is an issue that most women's groups—traditional and feminist—can agree on; it has few of the divisive qualities of reproductive or family issues. The challenge for the women's movement will be to develop widespread grass-roots support for pay equity and to build national, state, and local lobbying coalitions which incorporate the support of the labor movement. Without such a base, progress on pay equity is unlikely; even with such a base, policy is likely to evolve incrementally, through litigation and local or statewide efforts, before becoming national policy.

Alternative patterns of employment present a somewhat less threatening policy innovation than pay equity. Successful experiments with alternative employment patterns have made management interested in, although not excessively enthusiastic about, these policies. Resistance has been strong among labor unions but can be countered by making unions parties to agreements on alternative work arrangements as Congresswoman Patricia Schroeder has done in her proposed legislation on work sharing.[9] The appeal of this policy is that it could benefit all workers and is not perceived exclusively as a women's issue. Perhaps that is why many women's groups have been slow to identify themselves with it and to link up with existing coalitions in this field. Progress on alternative patterns of employment will depend in large part on the ability of women's groups to embrace issues of general concern for which women are primary beneficiaries.

Perhaps the thorniest economic issue for women in the 1980s will be reform of social security. Two out of every three older persons living in poverty are women, many of whose only source of income is social security. While some inequities in the social-security system have been eliminated, women (most of whom receive dependent's benefits) continue to fare poorly, either because their labor has been restricted to the home or because their earning power has been limited compared with that of their husbands'. Studies of the social security system, focusing on the elimination of dependent's benefits, have yielded two approaches to reform. One approach, earnings sharing, would divide earnings of a married couple equally whether or not a spouse had paid employment. A second approach, the two-tiered plan, would provide a basic benefit to all people regardless of earnings and an additional benefit based on work history.[10] The first approach would do more to benefit the homemaker; the second would do more to benefit the working spouse.

No consensus has yet emerged within the women's movement or among concerned policy makers regarding the appropriate direction for social security reform. The issue is complex, enormous in scope, and potentially divisive, pitting homemakers against working women. Even with consensus on the issue, the costs of reforming social security, either through increased governmental expenditures or decreased payments to men, are likely to engender fierce opposition. Nevertheless, debate on this issue is vital to highlight women's economic contributions to society and to address the economic needs of older women.

Motherhood Issues

In contrast to economic issues, motherhood issues will be more difficult for feminists to move on in the 1980s because they explicitly challenge traditional notions of women's roles. Policy battles over motherhood issues will involve preserving the status quo rather than pressing for new programs. There is now little hope, for example, of achieving a national child-care program. A realistic goal is to modify the present system of tax credits by increasing child-care allowances, establishing a sliding scale of credits to provide more assistance for low-income families, and providing monthly refunds of child-care payments for the poor so that child-care expenses may be met on a continuing basis. Several bills introduced in 1981 would do just that.

One innovation to the child-care field, included in the Economic Equity Act, has potential. Senator Robert Packwood (R-Oregon) has proposed an amendment to the Internal Revenue Code to allow employees to provide child-care assistance, either in the form of direct payments or child-care services, as a tax-free fringe benefit to employees. Such a proposal, while failing to provide a governmental solution, at least makes it more feasible for employees to press for child-care in their unions or directly with management. This opportunity can only be effectively utilized if women workers are better organized than they are today; making child care a bargainable right can, however, be used as an organizing tool among women workers, as well as producing a limited amount of additional child care. But whatever progress is made on the issue is unlikely to alter the overall picture of a widespread demand for child care and a limited supply. Until women can persuade policy makers that child care is a right rather than a fringe benefit, women will continue to labor under the burden of dual roles as workers and mothers.

The most serious threat to the women's movement today is the continuing assault by the "pro-life" movement on the right to abortion. Reproductive freedom remains a critical concern for the women's movement for without reproductive choices, role change is impossible. The political gains made by abortion opponents in the 1980 elections, including the election of President Reagan and additional antiabortion legislators, the movement of abortion foes into leadership positions in the Senate, and the appointment of antiabortionists to high-level positions in the executive, make a total ban on abortion a fearsome possibility.

The attack on abortion is being waged on three fronts. First, abortion opponents are pushing in Congress for a "human life" constitutional amendment which would define human life as beginning at the moment of fertilization, thereby making abortion at any stage of pregnancy equivalent to murder. The antiabortion forces, uncertain that they have the votes to pass a constitutional amendment, are simultaneously pursuing a second strategy: the passage of a "human life" bill which would define life in the same way as the proposed amendment, but would move the initiative to ban abortion to the states by prohibiting federal intervention on the issue. This strategy has evolved both because a human life bill only requires simple majorities for passage and because many members of Congress, weary of abortion battles, would like to move the issue entirely out of the congressional arena. In the event that a congressional approach fails, the "pro-life" movement is continuing to press state legislatures for resolutions to call a constitutional convention on abortion, as has been done in 19 states.

Like most movements, the "pro-life" movement has internal divisions. There is disagreement over whether a ban on abortion should include exceptions for rape, incest, or endangerment of the mother's life, and over the effectiveness of legislation versus a constitutional amendment. Moreover, some of the more extreme groups in the movement are seeking to extend the abortion ban to certain methods of contraception. The intrauterine device and some forms of the pill are seen by these groups as murder because they prevent pregnancy by keeping a fertilized egg, defined as a human life, from implantation.

The pro-choice coalition of population groups, civil liberties organizations, proabortion groups, and women's groups has little choice but to counter the "pro-life" movement on all fronts. The coalition must communicate the immediacy of the threat of a total abortion ban and expand grass-roots involvement on the issue. The fact that membership in the National Abortion Rights Action League rose dramatically after the 1980 elections suggests that many of the silent majority who support the right to abortion are mobilizable.[11] As the antiabortion movement broadens its cause to include certain forms of contraception, new allies for the pro-choice coalition can be found among the health lobbies and pharmaceutical industries. Legal challenges to the constitutionality of human life legislation must expose the extent to which the state will invade women's lives by enforcing involuntary motherhood. Lastly, the divisions within the "pro-life" movement must be exploited by publicizing the extreme positions being taken by some of the antiabortion groups.

There are signs that the women's movement is faltering on abortion. While organizational commitments remain strong, some feminists, frustrated by the erosion of abortion rights and troubled by the divisive character of the issue, are moving away from the battle in the hope that somehow the abortion controversy will lose steam. Opponents of abortion, however, will not stop until they have achieved a total ban. Feminists who believe that progress can be made on other issues while losing on abortion miss the crucial point that the "pro-life" movement and other right-wing groups, while starting with abortion, have geared up to attack women's rights in all areas.[12]

Sexuality and Crime

The attack on abortion signals an equally difficult battle for programs to aid victims of sexual oppression. Under the banner of morality, the new conservatives put the blame for violence against women back on women as evidenced by Phyllis Schlafly's testimony before Congress that "virtuous" women are not subject to sexual harassment.[13] Logically, in this view, virtuous women are not subject to rape or battering either, and virtuous girls are not subject to incest.

The "pro-family" positions of the New Right add to the difficulties of passing programs to assist women victims. Legislation was blocked by conservatives in 1980 on the grounds that domestic-violence programs are a governmental invasion into family life. Likewise, there is little empathy on the right for the displaced homemaker whose appropriate role is seen as maintaining the home and family, despite pressing economic needs, rather than moving out into the work force. Lack of empathy for female victims is paralleled by a lack of concern for female offenders. The right's war on crime extends to women despite the fact that most female crime is nonviolent and related to economic need. Thus, the call for equal treatment under the criminal justice system and for meaningful alternatives to incarceration is also likely to fall on the deaf ears of many policy makers.

How can the women's movement make gains on issues of sexuality, violence, and criminal justice in the face of these attitudes? Again, the movement must undertake an educational effort; until larger segments of the population are aware of the extent of women's economic and sexual victimization, the slogans of the right regarding morality and family preservation will continue to have appeal. Beyond education, women must organize around these issues at the state and local levels since it is there that criminal law reform is effected and sources of funding for community-based programs may be found. At the federal level, programs for women victims must be pressed under the aegis of programs in the health and justice fields in order to take advantage of existing resources and to reduce opposition to these programs by including them as part of a broader effort. Policy progress on issues of sexual oppression will be difficult to achieve because these issues involve role change—the assertion by women of control over their sexual roles. For women offenders, policy change will be equally if not more difficult to achieve, because an improvement in their lot requires the use of political power by and for the most marginal women in society.

Foreign and Military Issues

The new conservatism is, ironically, providing an incentive for feminists to increase their involvement in foreign and military affairs. The aggressive foreign policy stances of the Reagan administration have impelled women to join with other groups in speaking out against American military involvement in Central America and the Middle East. The Reagan administration's plans for the military have mobilized women's groups to oppose increases in defense spending, while at the same time supporting a greater role for women in the military. As with so many of the issues mentioned above, much effort will also have to be directed at maintaining the status quo. Particularly in the international development field, women's groups have made some progress in raising women's issues and will need to fight to maintain a presence in international agencies.

The task of building support for less aggressive foreign and military policies is a major one. While women at the grass roots are generally more pacifist in their attitudes than men, they also reveal themselves in public opinion polls to be less interested than men in international affairs. Even at the leadership level, as shown in this volume, women differ little from men on most foreign policy beliefs except that women are far less likely than their male counterparts to support an interventionist role for the United States.

Women's groups will face many obstacles as they attempt to influence foreign and military policy: developing a consensus on issues, generating interest among their members and women generally on these issues, influencing the thinking of women leaders whose attitudes have already been formed. The Reagan administration's position, however, favoring increased defense spending and balanced budgets over social programs is so antithetical to the goals of women's groups that women can no longer limit their voices to issues of domestic policy.

PROMOTING WOMEN'S POLICIES:
A GENERAL STRATEGY

We have seen that how policies are perceived strongly affects their chances for success. Policies on the status of women have been negatively perceived for several reasons. First, women's policies have been perceived as prescriptions for *all* women, thus threatening women who wish to maintain traditional roles.

Some, although certainly not all, of the opposition to abortion and child care is based on the notion promoted by the right that all women will be compelled to have abortions or to put their children in child-care centers. Similarly, opponents of the ERA have successfully persuaded many people that the amendment would require all women to go to work or serve in the military and would deny all divorced women alimony or child support.

Why has this occurred? In pressing for policy change, the women's movement has often failed to make clear its concern with expanding *options* for women. On occasion, there has been a tendency to portray the homemaker as a relic of the past. This is understandable, given the movement's fundamental concern for women who are trapped by traditional role expectations or who may prefer traditional roles of wife and mother but are compelled by economic necessity to move into roles as workers. Nevertheless, in order to neutralize some of its opposition, the movement must stress that its policies are aimed at providing *choices* and that women who *choose* traditional roles also make valuable social contributions as mothers, homemakers, and community volunteers.

A second failure in the promotion of women's policies has involved the implication that these policy benefits to women will be proffered at the expense of men. Feminists must emphasize that policies which have *direct* benefits for women have *indirect* benefits for men. Expanding economic opportunity for women yields greater total family income. Policies which assist in integrating family and work roles not only help mothers, but also fathers, with the responsibilities of child rearing. Policies aimed at reducing violence against women provide men with needed protection for their mothers, wives, friends, and daughters.

Men are not unaware of the benefits of women's policies. As public opinion polls have shown, men support changes in the status of women at roughly the same levels as women. Promoting the policy benefits of women's issues to men, however, would generate a larger and stronger base of male support. While it has been useful to label policies "women's issues" in order to give them visibility among women's groups and policy makers, broader labels would emphasize the benefits of these policies to men and women, and make it easier for policy makers who are negative or lukewarm about the women's movement to endorse these policies.[14]

Certain policies such as affirmative action, Title IX regulations involving athletics, and women in combat have generated intense opposition from men on the grounds that women are seeking to enter into activities which are men's rightful preserve. It seems clear that policies which attack sex stereotyping and promote role change will be resisted no matter what the labels. Support for these policies can only be gained through a continuing educational effort which emphasizes that women have both the right to choose and the capacity to fulfill roles as executives, athletes, or military officers. Opposition to these policies is deeply embedded in the ideology of sexism; the fear is that these policies would be redistributive, taking from men their near monopoly of high-level positions in management and the military, for example, and redistributing them to women. While feminists are aware that in the long run these policies might indeed redefine sex roles, these policies must be promoted simply as regulating institutional behavior to open up access to women in certain fields.

A third important approach for the promotion of policy in the 1980s involves challenging the right at the symbolic and substantive levels over its claim to speak for that most basic of American institutions, the family. The right seems intent on taking women back to the nineteenth century as evidenced by the provisions of the proposed Family Protection Act which, among other things, prohibits funding for domestic violence programs, repeals most provisions of Title IX, and requires parental notification when a minor receives contraceptives or treatment for venereal disease. While feminists certainly agree on the need to protect families, policy must reflect the realities of changing family patterns—families with both parents working, families headed by female heads of households, and families in transition as a result of divorce, death, and economic dislocation. A true "Family Protection Act" would include measures for displaced homemakers, child care, fair and affordable housing, domestic violence, and social security reform.

Equally vexing is the claim of the New Right to be the guardian of "human life." The reform of abortion laws had its origin in the guarding of human life, the life of the mother, when illegal abortions were responsible for the injury and deaths of countless numbers of women. Concern for human life meant, as well, concern for the lives of women, including many preteen and teenage girls whose unwanted children were conceived either as a result of rape or incest or out of ignorance of, or failure to use contraception.

The women's movement must make clear that it is not possible to stabilize the American family through policies which only recognize the nuclear family or which compel motherhood. At the same time, the movement must do a better job of promoting its own policies as family protection, in essence, stealing the thunder of the right. If programs such as child nutrition, family planning, prenatal health care, and child care are promoted as providing for family welfare, the burden of proof will be on the right to show that families headed by women, poor families, or families in transition are any less "families" and any less worthy of government assistance than the traditional nuclear family.

Finally, an important strategic consideration for the women's movement is to change the perception that women's groups are losing ground in the battle for public policy. Assessments of how interest groups are faring sway undecided policy makers to one side of an issue or another. The recent successes of the antiabortion forces have, in part, been due to the perception that opposition to abortion is increasing in momentum. In reality, opposition to abortion has become more vocal but not necessarily more widespread. What has helped abortion opponents create the impression of a groundswell on the issue has been their steady chipping away at abortion rights as the result of unified support of a long-term strategy.

The women's movement today needs victories in order to change perceptions of its ability to influence policy making. Women's groups need, more than ever, to coalesce around the same issues and to work in terms of a long-range plan. While individual women's groups are developing lobbying expertise, there is still a need to work in concert on an agreed-upon policy agenda. In order to get a realistic sense of what policies are obtainable in the short run, women's groups must work more closely with contacts in the policy-making process—the Congressswomen's Caucus, male legislative supporters in both parties, feminist staff in Congress and the agencies, and office holders in state and local government. And even the first small victories necessary to establish the climate for more significant policy change must be achieved with the support of other interest groups.

Strategies for the women's movement in the 1980s must go beyond simply meeting the conservative challenge. It is true that the conservative program has more negative consequences for women than any other group in society. But it is also true that even without the new conservatism, it will be more and more difficult for the United States to provide for social needs in the future. The era of ever-expanding economic growth is over, if it ever existed at all. The women's movement must therefore find creative approaches to achieve role equity and role change—approaches which involve both the public and private sectors and bridge the gap between them. Some new approaches to women's concerns have been suggested in this volume; it is hoped that others will emerge. If the 1980s are to be a time when the liberal philosophies and institutions of an earlier era are discarded, there is a vital need for the women's movement, speaking not only for women but for everyone, to analyze past policy failures and to take the lead in setting new directions.

Notes

1. Jerry Falwell, *Listen, America!* (Garden City, N.Y.: Doubleday & Co., 1980), p. 150.

2. Ibid., p. 151.

3. *Congressional Record,* April 2, 1981, pp. E1539–40 and E1565–68.

4. "Profile of Women Holding Office II" in *Women in Public Office: A Biographical Directory and Statistical Analysis,* 2nd edition, compiled by Center for the American Woman and Politics (Metuchen, N.J.: The Scarecrow Press, 1978).

5. According to government estimates, women will constitute 16 percent of the physicians in the United States by 1990. Currently, one-third of the students entering law school are women.

6. In interviews with the author on Capitol Hill, April 1981, women staff working for

Republican senators reported that women's groups rarely contacted Republican office-holders and "have a hard time adapting to the idea that Republicans are okay."

7. A Senate staff member confided in an interview with the author in April 1981 that conservative senators were not too concerned about passing a constitutional amendment banning affirmative action because new conservative appointees in the Reagan administration were unlikely to enforce affirmative action policies anyway.

8. The Economic Equity Act of 1981 was introduced in the Senate by Senators Robert Packwood, Dave Durenberger, and Mark Hatfield. In the House of Representatives, it was introduced by Congresswomen Patricia Schroeder, Margaret Heckler, Pat Ferraro, Shirley Chisholm, Lindy Boggs, Barbara Mikulski, and Rosemary Oakar.

9. On April 2, 1981, Congresswoman Patricia Schroeder introduced the Short Time Compensation Act of 1981 which would establish a three-year experimental program to encourage the states to make partial payments of unemployment compensation benefits to employees working under an employer-designed, union-approved, work-sharing plan.

10. An excellent study of proposed social security reforms may be found in *Social Security and the Changing Roles of Men and Women* (Washington, D.C.: U.S. Department of Health, Education and Welfare, 1979).

11. A staff member of the National Abortion Rights Action League reported in an interview in April 1981 that the organization had gained over 10,000 new members in the six months after President Reagan's election and had a total membership of over 100,000 members.

12. The head of the Moral Majority, the Rev. Jerry Falwell opposes the ERA, homosexual rights, domestic violence programs, sex education, Title IX of the Education Amendments Act of 1972, and women in combat in his book, *Listen, America!*

13. *Spokeswoman 11,* 5 (May 1981): 3.

14. As an example, the Economic Equity Act was originally entitled the Women's Economic Equity Act. Proponents of the legislation and women's groups wisely agreed to drop the word "women" from the title in order to make the legislation less controversial.

Index

About the Contributors

SUE BESSMER teaches Interdisciplinary Social Science, Criminal Justice and Women's Studies at San Francisco State University.

ELLEN BONEPARTH is Associate Dean, School of Social Sciences and Associate Professor of Political Science, San Jose State University. She is the founder and Director of the Aegean Women's Studies Institute.

ANNE COSTAIN is an Associate Professor of Political Science at the University of Colorado, Boulder. She is currently compiling a book on women's movements and political change in the U.S.

IRENE DIAMOND is Chair of Women's Studies and Assistant Professor of Political Science at Purdue University. She is the author of *Sex Roles in the State House* (Yale University Press, 1977) and has published articles on women and public policy issues in *Signs* and the *American Political Science Review* among other publications.

JO FREEMAN is the author of *The Politics of Women's Liberation* (Longman, 1975) and editor of *Women: A Feminist Perspective* (Mayfield, 1975, 1979, 1984) and *Social Movements of the Sixties and Seventies* (Longman, 1972). Dr. Freeman has worked as a political organizer, university professor, writer, lecturer, attorney, photographer, landlady and button-seller.

JO ANN GRUNE is a founding member of the National Committee on Pay Equity and editor of the *Manual on Pay Equity*. She works at the Labor Institute for Human Enrichment in Washington D.C., has been an organizer with Service Employees International Union and Working Women, and taught Women's Studies and Sociology at the University of Pittsburgh.

OLE R. HOLSTI is the George V. Allen Professor and Chair of the Political Science Department at Duke University. He is author of *Crisis, Escalation, War: Content Analysis for the Social Sciences and Humanities* and several other books and articles.

PATRICIA HUCKLE is Associate Professor and Chair of Women's Studies at San Diego State University. Her research interests include employment policy, intercollegiate athletics and feminist futures planning.

WENDY KAHN is a partner in the law firm of Zwerdling, Schlossberg, Leibig and Kahn specializing in employment and labor law. She is a member of the Board of Directors of the Women's Legal Defense Fund, a member of the National Committee on Pay Equity and an adjunct professor at Georgetown School of Law where she teaches Labor Relations in State and Local Government.

ELIZABETH F. MOULDS teaches in the Department of Government at California State University, Sacramento. She teaches courses on California politics, judicial politics, and women and politics. She also directs a California legislative internship program, the Sacramento Semester, serving the 19 campuses of the California State Universities and Colleges.

JILL NORGREN is an Associate Professor of Government at John Jay College of Criminal Justice, and City University of New York. She specializes in public policy research.

JAMES N. ROSENAU is Director of the Institute for Transnational Studies at the University of Southern California. His recent publications include *The Dramas of Political Life* (1980); *The Scientific Study of Foreign Policy* (revised ed., 1980); *The Study of Global Interdependence* (1980); and *The Study of Political Adaptation* (1981).

RINA ROSENBERG, the Executive Director of the Santa Clara County Commission on the Status of Women in California, has a law degree from University of Cape Town. She has taught courses on women's liberation and sex discrimination at Stanford University and has had numerous articles published in the news media.

KATHLEEN STAUDT is an Assistant Professor of Political Science and Liberal Arts Honors Program Director at the University of Texas at El Paso. She has published articles on women, agriculture, and women's organizations in *Development & Change, Journal of Developing Areas, Western Political Quarterly, Journal of Politics,* and *Rural Africana.*

JUDITH STIEHM is an Associate Professor of Political Science and past Chair of the Program for the Study of Women and Men in Society at the University of Southern California. She is the author of *Bring Me Men and Women: Mandated Change at the U.S. Air Force Academy* (University of

California Press, 1981) and also of *Non-Violent Power: Active and Passive Resistance in America* (D.C. Heath, 1972).

EMILY STOPER is Professor of Political Science and Coordinator of the Women's Studies Program at California State University, Hayward. As a member of the staff of Congressman Stephen J. Solarz, she helped secure passage of the Flexible Hours Act of 1978.

SANDRA WEXLER has been involved in several studies analyzing the effects of social policy decisions on women and children. Since coming to the URSA Institute in 1979, Ms. Wexler has worked primarily on the National LEAA Family Violence Program Evaluation. Ms. Wexler received an MA in Political Science from San Francisco State University.